Second Workshop on Arabic Natural Language Processing

(ANLP 2015)

Co-located with ACL-IJCNLP 2015

Beijing, China
30 July 2015

ISBN: 978-1-5108-0948-2

Printed from e-media with permission by:

Curran Associates, Inc.
57 Morehouse Lane
Red Hook, NY 12571

Printed by Curran Associates, Inc. (2015)

Association for Computational Linguistics
209 N. Eighth Street
Stroudsburg, Pennsylvania 18360

Phone: 1-570-476-8006
Fax: 1-570-476-0860

acl@aclweb.org

Additional copies of this publication are available from:

Curran Associates, Inc.
57 Morehouse Lane
Red Hook, NY 12571 USA
Phone: 845-758-0400
Fax: 845-758-2634
Email: curran@proceedings.com
Web: www.proceedings.com

ANLP Workshop 2015

The Second Workshop on Arabic Natural Language Processing

Proceedings of the Workshop

July 30, 2015
Beijing, China

Foreword

Assalamu 3alaykum wa nín hăo! Welcome to the Second Arabic Natural Language Processing Workshop held at ACL 2015 in Beijing, China.

A number of Arabic NLP (or Arabic NLP-related) workshops and conferences have taken place, both in the Arab World and in association with international conferences. The Arabic NLP workshop at ACL 2015 follows in the footsteps of these previous efforts to provide a forum for researchers to share and discuss their ongoing work. As in the first Arabic NLP workshop held at EMNLP 2014 in Doha, Qatar, this workshop includes a shared task on Automatic Arabic Error Correction, which was designed in the tradition of high profile NLP shared tasks such as CONLL's grammar/error detection and numerous machine translation campaigns by NIST/WMT/MEDAR, among others.

We received 23 main workshop submissions and selected 15 (65%) for presentation in the workshop. Nine papers will be presented orally and six as part of a poster session. The presentation mode is independent of of the ranking of the papers. The papers cover a diverse set of topics from designing orthography conventions and annotation tools to speech recognition and deep learning for sentiment analysis.

The shared task was a success with eight teams from six countries participating. The shared task system descriptions (short) papers are included in the proceedings to document the shared task systems, but were not reviewed with the rest of the papers of the main workshop. These papers will be presented as posters. A long paper describing the shared task will be presented orally.

The quantity and quality of the contributions to the main workshop, as well as the shared task, are strong indicators that there is a continued need for this kind of dedicated Arabic NLP workshop.

We would like to acknowledge all the hard work of the submitting authors and thank the reviewers for their diligent work and for the valuable feedback they provided. We are also thankful to the work of the shared task committee, website committee and the publication co-chairs. It has been an honor to serve as program co-chairs. We hope that the reader of these proceedings will find them stimulating and beneficial.

Nizar Habash, Stephan Vogel and Kareem Darwish

Organizers:

Program Co-chairs:

Nizar Habash, New York University Abu Dhabi
Stephan Vogel, Qatar Computing Research Institute
Kareem Darwish, Qatar Computing Research Institute

Publication Co-chairs:

Nadi Tomeh, Paris 13 University, Sorbonne Paris Cité
Houda Bouamor, Carnegie Mellon University Qatar

Publicity chair:

Wajdi Zaghouani, Carnegie Mellon University Qatar

Shared Task Committee:

Alla Rozovskaya (co-chair), Columbia University
Houda Bouamor (co-chair), Carnegie Mellon University Qatar
Behrang Mohit, Ask.com
Wajdi Zaghouani, Carnegie Mellon University Qatar
Ossama Obeid, Carnegie Mellon University Qatar
Nizar Habash (advisor), New York University Abu Dhabi

Program Committee:

Abdelmajid Ben-Hamadou, University of Sfax, Tunisia
Abdelsalam Nwesri, University of Tripoli, Libya
Achraf Chalabi , Microsoft Research, Egypt
Ahmed Ali, Qatar Computing Research Institute, Qatar
Ahmed El Kholy, Columbia University, USA
Ahmed Rafea, The American University in Cairo, Egypt
Alberto Barrón Cedeño, Qatar Computing Research Institute, Qatar
Alexis Nasr, University of Marseille, France
Ali Farghaly, Monterey Peninsula College, USA
Almoataz B. Al-Said, Cairo University, Egypt
Aly Fahmy, Cairo University, Egypt
Azzeddine Mazroui, University Mohamed I, Morocco
Bassam Haddad, University of Petra, Jordan
Emad Mohamed, Suez Canal University, Egypt
Fransisco Guzman, Qatar Computing Research Institute, Qatar
Ghassan Mourad, Université Libanaise, Lebanon
Hamdy Mubarak, Qatar Computing Research Institute, Qatar
Hazem Hajj, American University of Beirut, Lebanon
Hend Alkhalifa, King Saud University, Saudi Arabia
Houda Bouamor, Carnegie Mellon University Qatar, Qatar
Imed Zitouni, Microsoft Research, USA
Joseph Dichy, Université Lyon 2, France

Kareem Darwish, Qatar Computing Research Institute, Qatar
Karim Bouzoubaa , Mohammad V University, Morocco
Kemal Oflazer, Carnegie Mellon University Qatar, Qatar
Khaled Shaalan, The British University in Dubai, UAE
Khaled Shaban, Qatar University, Qatar
Khalid Choukri, ELDA, European Language Resource Association, France
Lamia Hadrich Belguith, University of Sfax, Tunisia
Mohamed Elmahdy, Qatar University, Qatar
Mohamed Maamouri, Linguistic Data Consortium, USA
Mona Diab, George Washington University, USA
Mustafa Jarrar, Bir Zeit University, Palestine
Nada Ghneim, Higher Institute for Applied Sciences and Technology, Syria
Nadi Tomeh, University Paris 13, Sorbonne Paris Cité, France
Nizar Habash, New York University Abu Dhabi, UAE
Otakar Smrž, Džám-e Džam Language Institute, Czech Republic
Owen Rambow, Columbia University, USA
Preslav Nakov, Qatar Computing Research Institute, Qatar
Ramy Eskander, Columbia University, USA
Salwa Hamada, Cairo University, Egypt
Samantha Wray, Qatar Computing Research Institute, Qatar
Shahram Khadivi, Tehran Polytechnic, Iran
Sherri Condon , The MITRE Corporation, USA
Stephan Vogel, Qatar Computing Research Institute, Qatar
Taha Zerrouki, University of Bouira, Algeria
Wael Salloum, Columbia University, USA
Walid Magdy, Qatar Computing Research Institute, Qatar

Table of Contents

Workshop Program

July 30, 2015

09:00–10:00 Main Workshop Papers - Oral Presentations - Session 1

09:00–09:20 *Classifying Arab Names Geographically*
Hamdy Mubarak and Kareem Darwish

09:20–09:40 *Deep Learning Models for Sentiment Analysis in Arabic*
Ahmad Al Sallab, Hazem Hajj, Gilbert Badaro, Ramy Baly, Wassim El Hajj and Khaled Bashir Shaban

09:40–10:00 *A Light Lexicon-based Mobile Application for Sentiment Mining of Arabic Tweets*
Gilbert Badaro, Ramy Baly, Rana Akel, Linda Fayad, Jeffrey Khairallah, Hazem Hajj, Khaled Shaban and Wassim El-Hajj

10:00–10:30 Shared Task Talk

10:00–10:30 *The Second QALB Shared Task on Automatic Text Correction for Arabic*
Alla Rozovskaya, Houda Bouamor, Nizar Habash, Wajdi Zaghouani, Ossama Obeid and Behrang Mohit

10:30–11:00 *Break*

11:00–12:00 Main Workshop Papers - Oral Presentations - Session 2

11:00–11:20 *Natural Language Processing for Dialectical Arabic: A Survey*
Abdulhadi Shoufan and Sumaya Alameri

11:20–11:40 *DIWAN: A Dialectal Word Annotation Tool for Arabic*
Faisal Al-Shargi and Owen Rambow

11:40–12:00 *POS-tagging of Tunisian Dialect Using Standard Arabic Resources and Tools*
Ahmed Hamdi, Alexis Nasr, Nizar Habash and Nuria Gala

12:00–14:00 *Lunch + Poster Setup*

July 30, 2015 (continued)

14:00–15:30 Poster Session

\+ ***Posters: Main Workshop Papers***

A Conventional Orthography for Algerian Arabic
Houda Saadane and Nizar Habash

A Pilot Study on Arabic Multi-Genre Corpus Diacritization
Houda Bouamor, Wajdi Zaghouani, Mona Diab, Ossama Obeid, Kemal Oflazer, Mahmoud Ghoneim and Abdelati Hawwari

Annotating Targets of Opinions in Arabic using Crowdsourcing
Noura Farra, Kathy McKeown and Nizar Habash

Best Practices for Crowdsourcing Dialectal Arabic Speech Transcription
Samantha Wray, Hamdy Mubarak and Ahmed Ali

Joint Arabic Segmentation and Part-Of-Speech Tagging
Shabib AlGahtani and John McNaught

Multi-Reference Evaluation for Dialectal Speech Recognition System: A Study for Egyptian ASR
Ahmed Ali, Walid Magdy and Steve Renals

\+ ***Posters: Shared Task Papers***

Arib@QALB-2015 Shared Task: A Hybrid Cascade Model for Arabic Spelling Error Detection and Correction
Nouf AlShenaifi, Rehab AlNefie, Maha Al-Yahya and Hend Al-Khalifa

CUFE@QALB-2015 Shared Task: Arabic Error Correction System
Michael Nawar

GWU-HASP-2015@QALB-2015 Shared Task: Priming Spelling Candidates with Probability
Mohammed Attia, Mohamed Al-Badrashiny and Mona Diab

QCMUQ@QALB-2015 Shared Task: Combining Character level MT and Error-tolerant Finite-State Recognition for Arabic Spelling Correction
Houda Bouamor, Hassan Sajjad, Nadir Durrani and Kemal Oflazer

July 30, 2015 (continued)

QCRI@QALB-2015 Shared Task: Correction of Arabic Text for Native and Non-Native Speakers' Errors
Hamdy Mubarak, Kareem Darwish and Ahmed Abdelali

SAHSOH@QALB-2015 Shared Task: A Rule-Based Correction Method of Common Arabic Native and Non-Native Speakers' Errors
Wajdi Zaghouani, Taha Zerrouki and Amar Balla

TECHLIMED@QALB-Shared Task 2015: a hybrid Arabic Error Correction System
Djamel MOSTEFA, Jaber ABUALASAL, Omar ASBAYOU, Mahmoud GZAWI and Ramzi Abbès

UMMU@QALB-2015 Shared Task: Character and Word level SMT pipeline for Automatic Error Correction of Arabic Text
Fethi Bougares and Houda Bouamor

15:30–16:00 ***Break***

16:00–17:00 **Main Workshop Papers - Oral Presentations - Session 3**

16:00–16:20 *Robust Part-of-speech Tagging of Arabic Text*
Hanan Aldarmaki and Mona Diab

16:20–16:40 *Answer Selection in Arabic Community Question Answering: A Feature-Rich Approach*
Yonatan Belinkov, Alberto Barrón-Cedeño and Hamdy Mubarak

16:40–17:00 *EDRAK: Entity-Centric Data Resource for Arabic Knowledge*
Mohamed H. Gad-elrab, Mohamed Amir Yosef and Gerhard Weikum

17:00–18:00 ***Workshop Group Discussion***

Classifying Arab Names Geographically

Hamdy Mubarak, Kareem Darwish
Qatar Computing Research Institute
Hamad Bin Khalifa University
Doha, Qatar
{hmubarak, kdarwish}@qf.org.qa

Abstract

Different names may be popular in different countries. Hence, person names may give a clue to a person's country of origin. Along with other features, mapping names to countries can be helpful in a variety of applications such as country tagging twitter users. This paper describes the collection of Arabic Twitter user names that are either written in Arabic or transliterated into Latin characters along with their stated geographical locations. To classify previously unseen names, we trained naive Bayes and Support Vector Machine (SVM) multi-class classifiers using primarily bag-of-words features. We are able to map Arabic user names to specific Arab countries with 79% accuracy and to specific regions (Gulf, Egypt, Levant, Maghreb, and others) with 94% accuracy. As for transliterated Arabic names, the accuracy per country and per region was 67% and 83% respectively. The approach is generic and language independent, and can be used to collect and classify names to other countries or regions, and considering language-dependent name features (like the compound names, and person titles) yields to better results.

1 Introduction

Geo-locating tweets and tweeps (Twitter users) has captured significant attention in recent years. Geographical information is important for many applications such as transliteration, social studies, directed advertisement, dialect identification, and Automatic Speech Recognition (ASR) among others. In social studies, researchers may be interested in studying the views and opinions of tweeps for specific geographical locations. Similarly, tweets can offer a tool for linguists to study different linguistic phenomena. For ASR, training language models using dialectal Arabic tweets that are associated with different regions of the Arab world was shown to reduce recognition error rate for dialectal Egyptian Arabic by 25% (Ali, et. al, 2014).

Previous work has looked at a variety of features that may geo-locate tweets and tweeps such as the dialect of tweet(s), words appearing in tweets, a tweep's social network, etc. In this work we examine the predictive power of tweep names in predicting a tweep's location or region of origin. We define geographic units at two different levels, namely: country level and region level. The country level geographic units are defined based on political boundaries regardless of the size and proximity of different geographic entities. Thus, Qatar and Bahrain as well as Lebanon and Syria are considered as different units. At the region level, we conflate nearby countries into regions. Conflation was guided by previous work on dialects, where dialects were categorized into five regional language groups, namely: Egyptian (EGY), Maghrebi (MGR), Gulf (Arabian Peninsula) (GLF), Iraqi (IRQ), and Levantine (LEV) (Zbib et al., 2012; Cotterell et al., 2014). Sometimes, the Iraqi dialect is considered to be one of the Gulf dialects (Cotterell et al., 2014). In this paper we consider Iraq as a part of the Gulf region.

Thus the goal of this work is to build a classifier that can predict a tweep's country/region of residence/origin. To build the classifier we obtained tweep names and their self-declared locations from Twitter. Many tweeps use pseudonyms, such as "white knight", and fake or irregular, such as "in phantasmagoria" or "Eastern Province". Hence, identifying fake tweep names may be necessary, and

Proceedings of the Second Workshop on Arabic Natural Language Processing, pages 1–8,
Beijing, China, July 26-31, 2015.

locations need to be mapped to countries. We built multiple classifiers using either a naive Bayes or a Support Vector Machine (SVM) classifier using bag-of-words features, namely word unigrams. We also considered improvements that entailed using character n-gram features and word position weighting. For our work, we tried to collect tweets for all 22 Arab countries, but we did not find Arabic tweets from Mauritania, Somalia, Djibouti and Comoros. The contributions of this paper are:

1. We show that we can use Twitter as a source for collecting person names for different Arab countries by mapping user location to one of the Arab countries.
2. We show that we can build a classifier of Arabic names at the county level or region level with reasonable accuracy.
3. we show the characteristics of Arabic names and how they differ among different countries or regions.

The paper is organized as follows: Section 2 surveys previous work on person name classification; Section 3 describes some features of Arabic names including dialectal variation in transliteration; section 4 describes how names are collected from Twitter, cleaned and classified; section 5 shows results of name classification experiments; and Section 6 contains conclusion and future work.

2 Previous Work

The problem of classifying names at country level is not well explored. As far as we know, there are no studies for Arabic person name classification. Some work has been done on clustering and classifying person names by origin like (Fei et al., 2005), where they used the LDC bilingual person name lists to build a name clustering and classification framework. They considered that several origins may share the same pattern of transliteration and applied their technique to a name transliteration task by building letter n-gram language models for source and target languages. They clustered names into typical origin clusters (English, Chinese, German, Arabic., etc.).

Balakrishnan (Balakrishnan, 2006) extracted a list of person names from the employee database of a multinational organization covering 9 countries: US, UK, France, Germany, Canada, Japan, Italy, India, and China. Equal number of names is chosen from each country (1,000 names for each). He used pattern search for first and second names and used k-nearest neighbor and Levenshtein edit distance to measure the distance between two names. He reported a classification accuracy = 0.67 for supervised training set and 0.63 for unsupervised training set.

Fu et al. (Fu et al., 2010) mentioned that humans often identify correctly the origins of person names, and there seem to be distinctive patterns in names to distinguish origins. They constructed an ontology containing all linguistic knowledge that can directly contribute to language origin identification, and this was employed for the analysis of name structure. They reported an average performance of 87.54% using ME-based language identifier for 8 languages (Arabic, Chinese, English, French, German, Japanese, Russian, and Spanish-Portuguese).

Rao et al. (Rao et al., 2010) classified the latent user attributes including gender, age, regional origin, etc., using features like n-grams models and number of followers/followees (in a social graph information) among others.

Mahmud et al. (Mahmud et al., 2012) collected tweets using the geo-tag filter option on Twitter until they received tweets from 100 unique users from the top 100 cities in US. They used this corpus for inferring home locations of users at the level of their cities. They reported a recall of 0.7 for 100 cities.

Huang et al. (Huang et al., 2014) discussed the challenges of detecting the nationality of Twitter users using profile features and they studied the effectiveness of different features for inferring nationalities. They reported an accuracy of 83.8% for these nationality groups: Qatari, Arabs, Western, Southeast Asia, Indian, and Others. They mentioned that due to the unbalanced data distribution, the performance of less populated groups is not very high. We observe similar results in this paper.

3 Person Names in Arabic

3.1 Compound Names

Single Arabic names typically are made up of single words, but sometimes they may be composed of 2 or 3 words. We refer here to single names with more than one word as 'compound names'. There are some words such as الله (Allh[1] – meaning "God") and الدين (Aldyn – meaning "religion") that trail other words as in عبد الله (Ebd Allh – meaning "slave of Allah") constructing the name "Abdullah" and as in صلاح الدين (SlAH Aldyn – meaning "perfection of religion") constructing the name "Salahudin" (Saladin). In some countries, father and family names are often preceded by words meaning "son of" such as بن (bn), ابن (Abn) or ولد (wld) or the word آل (|l – meaning family of). An example that combines the aforementioned variations of compound names is the name of the former king of Saudi Arabia عبد الله بن عبد العزيز آل سعود (Ebd Allh bn Ebd AlEzyz |l sEwd – "Abdullah ibn Abdelaziz Aal Saud"). A list of common words used in compound names are listed in table 1. When processing the names in our collection, we heuristically split the full names into single Arabic names, whether compound or not. As in the previous example, عبد الله بن عبد العزيز آل سعود (Ebd Allh bn Ebd AlEzyz |l sEwd), it was split into: عبد الله (Ebd Allh), بن عبد العزيز (bn Ebd AlEzyz), and آل سعود (|l sEwd). The heuristic involved always attaching the words marked in Table 1 as *pre* to the trailing words and ones that are marked as post to preceding words.

Type	Word	Example
Pre	الله، الدين، الإسلام، الرسول Allh, Aldyn, Al<slAm, Alrswl	سيف الإسلام syf Al<slAm
Post	بو،أبي،أبا،أبو،أم،بنت،ابن،بن،عبد، ولد Ebd, bn, Abn, bnt, >m, >bw, >bA, >by, bw, wld	بنت ناصر ولد محمد bnt nASr, wld mHmd

Table 1: Words that are parts of a name.

3.2 Dialectal Variations of Names

Names in Arabic are normally written without diacritics, and when they are transliterated, these hidden diacritics are shown in addition to dialectal differences in pronunciation among countries as shown in table 2. Since we are classifying names that are written in both Arabic and Latin scripts, spelling variations can perhaps be helpful in ascertaining the country/region of origin.

[1]Buckwalter transliteration is used exclusively in the paper

3.3 Religion and Gender

Names can also be indicative of other attributes such as religion and gender. For example, the names شنودة ($nwdp – "Shnouda"), عبد الحسين (Ebd AlHsyn – "Abdul Hussein"), and عمر (Emr – "Omar") are typically Coptic, Shia, and Sunni respectively. And for gender, feminine names frequently end with ة ، اء ، ى ، ا (p, A', Y, A), such as فاطمة (FaTmp – "Fatima") and هناء (hnA' – "Hannah"). Second names, either father or family names, are mostly masculine. Though guessing a tweep's religion and gender are interesting, such is beyond the scope of this paper.

Name Variations	Phonetic Mapping
ماجد (mAjd) Maged (EGY), Ma**j**ed (GLF)	g/j
عثمان (EvmAn) Osman (EGY), O**th**man (GLF)	s/th
أشرف (A$rf) A**sh**arf (EGY), A**ch**raf (MGR)	sh/ch
فهد (fhd) Fahd (EGY), Fah**a**d (GLF)	diacritics
الوكيل (Alwkyl) **El** Wakil (EGY), **Al** Wakil (GLF)	Determiner

Table 2: Dialectal effects on Transliteration.

4 Data Collection

Twitter user profiles contain user-declared information like: Twitter account name, screen name **(user name)**, user location, description, etc. User names are normally written in Arabic or Latin characters, and user locations are written in full or abbreviated, formal or informal, etc. as shown in Figure 1.

We used the Twitter4J[2] interface to the Twitter API to collect Arabic tweets during the whole of

[2]http://twitter4j.org

Figure 1: User Profile Information

March 2014. We searched using the query "lang:ar", which indicates any Arabic tweet. In all we collected 175 million tweets that were authored by 5.5 million unique tweeps. We used the users self-declared locations to map them to countries. We mapped the locations using the GeoNames[3] geographical database, which contains 8M place names and a database of of the most commonly used 10,000 user locations on Twitter (Mubarak et al., 2014). If the location referred to two or more different countries, as in "UK and Kuwait", it was removed. User location was successfully mapped to one of the Arab countries for 1M unique user names. After name cleaning (described later in this section), we have 170 thousand Names$_{arb}$ and 182K Names$_{trans}$ that are considered as valid names and mapped to only one country.

Per-country distributions are shown in Figure 2 and Figure 3. One of the interesting observations from these figures is that people from Saudi Arabia (SA[4]) are the majority in both cases, and they tend to write their names in Arabic, while people from Egypt (EG) tend to write their names as transliterated. We opted not to limit our collection to tweeps who have geo-tagged tweets (tweets with latitude and longitude), because geo-tagged tweets represent less than 1% of the total number of tweets[5]. We found that 0.3% of the collected tweets are geo-tagged.

Table 3 shows some examples of the collected names. We took samples of 200 random names from each set and found that 70% of the names are real and the rest are unreal person names (fake). We plan to identify fake names from real names in future.

Name cleaning included ignoring words that are composed of single letters, special characters outside the Arabic or the Latin alphabets, entries that are single words only, and entries having stopwords. Names were normalized in the manner described by Darwish et al. (2012), which involved removing diacritics, kashidas, normalizing different forms of alef, ya and alef maqsoura, and ha and ta marbouta, and mapping letters from other languages such as Farsi that use the Arabic script to Arabic letters. Further, titles, such as Dr., and numbers were removed. We also identified compound names as described earlier. For example, the user name "Dr. Abdullah Bin Fahad AL MUTAIRI1973" will be normalized to "abdullah bin_fahad al_mutairi".

User name	Real/Unreal
طلال القحطاني (TlAl AlqHTany), Bassam Jawad	Real names
أنيقة وكفى (Anyqa wKfY), Sweet Boy	Unreal names

Table 3: Examples of user names

5 Name Classification Experiments

Given the 170K Names$_{arb}$ and 182K Names$_{trans}$ that we collected, we randomly split the set into 80/20 training and testing splits. We used word unigrams as features. We also examined giving first and last names different weights and character trigrams as a back-off for unseen words. Further, we trained two classifiers namely a Naive Bayes classifier and an SVM classifier. When using a Naive Bayes classifier and a name was not observed during training in general or for a class, we used KenLM language modeling toolkit to compute the smoothing probability of it (Heafield, 2011).

Our baseline involved tagging all test items with the tag of the majority class, which means that every tweep would assigned to SA at country level and the Gulf at region level. Table 4 shows the baseline re-

[3]http://www.geonames.org

[4]We use "ISO 3166-1 alpha-2" for country codes

[5]http://thenextweb.com/2010/01/15/twitter-geofail-023-tweets-geotagged/

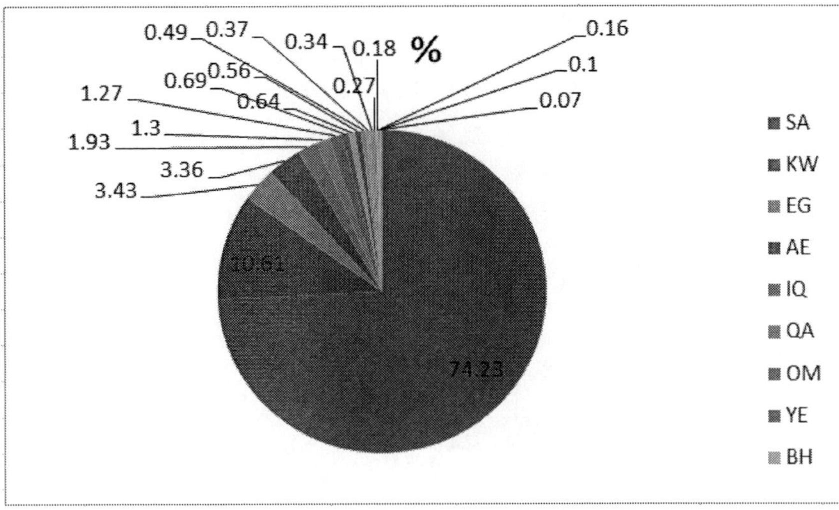

Figure 2: Country Distribution for Names$_{arb}$

sults in term of accuracy. Precision for the majority class would be identical to the overall accuracy and recall would be one. Precision and recall would be zero for all the other classes.

Name type	**Accuracy**
Names$_{arb}$ Country	74.2%
Names$_{arb}$ Region	91.4%
Names$_{trans}$ Country	44.3%
Names$_{trans}$ Region	67.4%

Table 4: Baseline Results

Table 5 and Table 6 show the results for Names$_{arb}$ per country and per region respectively using word unigrams only. Similarly, Table 7 and Table 8 show the results for Names$_{trans}$ per country and per region respectively using word unigrams only. Micro and Macro averages refer to computing metrics per test example or taking the average of per country results respectively. As can be seen, the naive Bayes classifier performed better than SVM classifier for the vast majority of countries and in overall accuracy and F-measure. Mostly the SVM classifier had higher precision with less recall.

In further experiments, we exclusively used the naive Bayes classifier. We tried two modifications of the classifier. The first involved giving different weights to different single names in the full name, such that a person's last name would get a higher weight than his/her first name. The intuition is that different countries may have different common family names that may indicate their place of origin, family, or tribe. The weight of the word based on its position is determined using the following formula:
$weight_i = \frac{1}{no\_of\_single\_names - i + 1}$
Where i ranged between 1 and number of single names in the full name. Thus the last single name would get a weight of 1 and all previous single names would get a weight of 1/2, 1/3, etc. (from end to beginning).

The second entailed using a character trigram model as a back-off for out of vocabulary words, which were not seen during training. We used KenLM to train a trigram character model using all the names in the training set (Heafield, 2011).

Table 9 and Table 10 compare the plain Bayesian classifier with using the classifier with single name weighting and character trigram back-off for Names$_{arb}$ at country and region level respectively. Table 11 and Table 12 compare the same for Names$_{trans}$. As the results show, both methods improved overall accuracy with consistent improvements in precision and improvements in recall most of the time. Using single name weighting had a greater effect on precision.

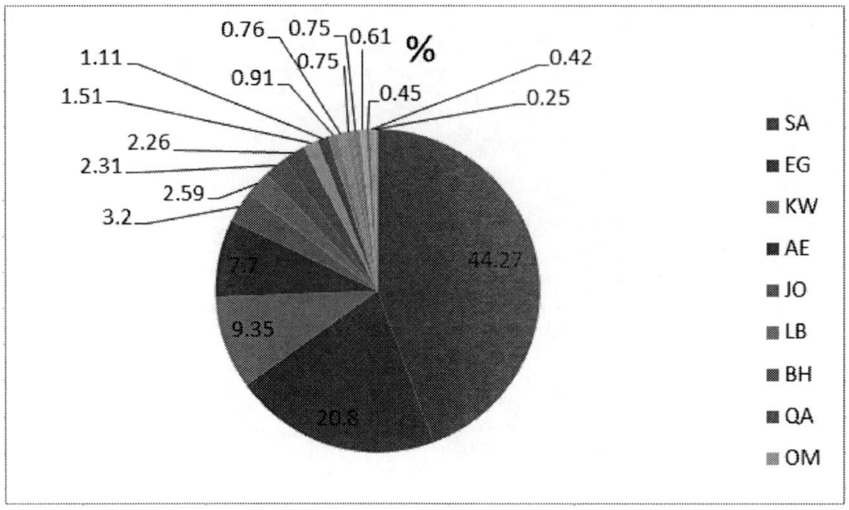

Figure 3: Country Distribution for Names_{trans}

6 Conclusion and Future Work

In this paper, we presented our work on classifying person names based on their country or region. To construct training data, we collected Twitter user names that authored Arabic tweets with their associated self-declared locations, which we mapped to Arab countries and regions. We experimented with Bayesian and SVM classifiers and the Bayesian classifier outperformed the SVM classifier most of the time. Adding position information and back-off to a character trigram model for names not observed during training generally improved results. Classifying user names at region level generally yielded better results than at country level.

Because majority of user names written in Arabic are from the Gulf region (93%), the classification improvement above the majority baseline was not that big, but when we applied the same approach for classifying transliterated user names, we achieved an increase of the accuracy by 52% and 20% at the country level and group level in order, and an increase in the F-measure by 135% and 46% at the country level and region level in order.

In future, we want to incorporate the user name feature in conjunction with other features in the context of geo-locating Twitter users. We need to test our engine for classifying names collected for each country from outside Twitter, think in other ways to collect user names from regions like the Maghreb, and detect more information from user profile like the gender and religion.

References

Ahmed Ali, Hamdy Mubarak, Stephan Vogel. 2014. Advances in Dialectal Arabic Speech Recognition: A Study Using Twitter to Improve Egyptian ASR. International Workshop on Spoken Language Translation (IWSLT 2014).

Balakrishnan, Raju. 2006. Country wise classification of human names. Proceedings of the 5th WSEAS Int. Conf. on Artificiall Intelligence, Knowledge Engineering and Data Bases, Madrid, 2006.

Ryan Cotterell and Chris Callison-Burch. 2014. A Multi-Dialect, Multi-Genre Corpus of Informal Written Arabic. LREC-2014, pages 241–245.

Kareem Darwish, Walid Magdy, and Ahmed Mourad. 2012. Language processing for arabic microblog retrieval. Proceedings of the 21st ACM international conference on Information and knowledge management. ACM, 2012.

Huang, Fei, Stephan Vogel, and Alex Waibel. 2005. Clustering and classifying person names by origin. Proceedings of the National Conference on Artificial Intelligence. Vol. 20. No. 3. Menlo Park, CA; Cambridge, MA; London; AAAI Press; MIT Press; 1999, 2005.

Fu, Yu, Feiyu Xu, and Hans Uszkoreit. 2010. Determin-

	NB			SVM		
Country	P	R	F	P	R	F
EG	0.40	0.50	0.45	0.48	0.14	0.22
DZ	0.18	0.16	0.17	0.71	0.07	0.13
SD	0.13	0.07	0.09	0.50	0.03	0.06
IQ	0.51	0.33	0.40	0.69	0.12	0.20
MA	0.20	0.07	0.10	0.00	0.00	0.00
SA	0.84	0.91	0.88	0.77	0.99	0.87
YE	0.35	0.17	0.22	0.50	0.02	0.03
SY	0.21	0.11	0.14	0.62	0.07	0.12
TN	0.04	0.03	0.04	0.50	0.03	0.06
AE	0.52	0.38	0.44	0.71	0.11	0.19
JO	0.21	0.11	0.14	0.62	0.03	0.06
LY	0.28	0.11	0.16	0.90	0.06	0.11
PL	0.18	0.10	0.13	0.83	0.03	0.06
LB	0.03	0.09	0.05	0.71	0.08	0.14
OM	0.50	0.29	0.37	0.85	0.07	0.14
KW	0.49	0.34	0.40	0.58	0.10	0.17
QA	0.50	0.23	0.32	0.63	0.06	0.12
BH	0.28	0.15	0.20	0.70	0.08	0.15
Macro Avg	0.33	0.23	0.26	0.63	0.12	0.16
Micro Avg	0.74	0.77	0.75	0.73	0.76	0.69
Accuracy	0.77			0.76		

Table 5: Names_{arb} Results per country

	NB			SVM		
Country	P	R	F	P	R	F
EGY	0.40	0.50	0.45	0.48	0.14	0.22
GLF	0.96	0.96	0.96	0.94	0.99	0.97
LEV	0.19	0.14	0.16	0.70	0.05	0.09
MGR	0.24	0.13	0.17	0.65	0.05	0.09
OTHER	0.29	0.14	0.19	0.50	0.02	0.04
Macro Avg	0.42	0.38	0.39	0.66	0.25	0.28
Micro Avg	0.92	0.92	0.92	0.92	0.94	0.91
Accuracy	0.92			0.94		

Table 6: Names_{arb} Results per region

ing the Origin and Structure of Person Names. LREC. 2010.

Heafield, Kenneth. 2011. KenLM: Faster and Smaller Language Model Queries. Proceedings of the EMNLP 2011 Sixth Workshop on Statistical Machine Translation. pp 187–197

Huang, Wenyi, Ingmar Weber, and Sarah Vieweg. 2014. Inferring nationalities of Twitter users and studying inter-national linking. Proceedings of the 25th ACM conference on Hypertext and social media. ACM, 2014.

Mahmud, Jalal, Jeffrey Nichols, and Clemens Drews. 2012. Where Is This Tweet From? Inferring Home Locations of Twitter Users. ICWSM. 2012.

Hamdy Mubarak, Kareem Darwish. 2014. Using Twitter to collect a multi-dialectal corpus of Arabic. ANLP 2014.

Rao, Delip, David Yarowsky, Abhishek Shreevats, Manaswi Gupta. 2010. Classifying latent user attributes in twitter. Proceedings of the 2nd international workshop on Search and mining user-generated contents. ACM, 2010.

Rabih Zbib, Erika Malchiodi, Jacob Devlin, David Stallard, Spyros Matsoukas, Richard Schwartz, John Makhoul, Omar F. Zaidan, Chris Callison-Burch. 2012. Machine translation of Arabic dialects. NAACL-2012, pages 49–59.

	NB			SVM		
EG	0.68	0.78	0.73	0.68	0.43	0.53
DZ	0.18	0.19	0.18	0.33	0.08	0.14
SD	0.22	0.14	0.17	0.26	0.05	0.08
IQ	0.15	0.12	0.14	0.25	0.04	0.08
MA	0.38	0.27	0.32	0.50	0.23	0.32
SA	0.71	0.80	0.75	0.54	0.94	0.68
YE	0.00	0.00	0.00	0.50	0.01	0.02
SY	0.22	0.10	0.14	0.18	0.02	0.03
TN	0.29	0.32	0.30	0.46	0.16	0.24
AE	0.43	0.33	0.37	0.50	0.16	0.24
JO	0.38	0.24	0.29	0.39	0.07	0.13
LY	0.03	0.10	0.05	0.33	0.01	0.03
PL	0.13	0.08	0.10	0.22	0.01	0.02
LB	0.48	0.42	0.45	0.54	0.31	0.39
OM	0.61	0.40	0.48	0.69	0.13	0.22
KW	0.54	0.40	0.46	0.52	0.18	0.27
QA	0.44	0.23	0.31	0.75	0.06	0.11
BH	0.45	0.28	0.34	0.46	0.09	0.15
Macro Avg	0.35	0.29	0.31	0.45	0.17	0.20
Micro Avg	0.60	0.62	0.61	0.55	0.55	0.49
Accuracy	0.62			0.55		

Table 7: Names$_{trans}$ Results per country

	NB			SVM		
EGY	0.68	0.78	0.73	0.68	0.43	0.53
GLF	0.88	0.86	0.87	0.77	0.94	0.85
LEV	0.51	0.35	0.42	0.59	0.17	0.27
MGR	0.25	0.38	0.30	0.57	0.22	0.31
OTHER	0.22	0.10	0.14	0.15	0.04	0.06
Macro Avg	0.51	0.50	0.49	0.55	0.36	0.40
Micro Avg	0.79	0.79	0.79	0.73	0.75	0.72
Accuracy	0.79			0.75		

Table 8: Names$_{arb}$ Results per region

		P	R	F	Acc
NB	Macro	0.33	0.23	0.26	0.77
	Micro	0.74	0.77	0.75	
Pos weight	Macro	0.51	0.20	0.26	0.79
	Micro	0.75	0.79	0.75	
Char n-gram	Macro	0.37	0.26	0.30	0.79
	Micro	0.76	0.79	0.77	

Table 9: Names$_{arb}$ Results by country for plain Naive Bayes, position weighting, and char n-gram back-off

		P	R	F	Acc
NB	Macro	0.42	0.38	0.39	0.92
	Micro	0.92	0.92	0.92	
Pos weight	Macro	0.59	0.34	0.39	0.94
	Micro	0.93	0.94	0.93	
Char n-gram	Macro	0.47	0.38	0.41	0.93
	Micro	0.93	0.93	0.93	

Table 10: Names$_{arb}$ Results by country for plain Naive Bayes, position weighting, and char n-gram back-off

		P	R	F	Acc
NB	Macro	0.35	0.29	0.31	0.62
	Micro	0.60	0.62	0.61	
Pos weight	Macro	0.48	0.27	0.32	0.65
	Micro	0.62	0.65	0.61	
Char n-gram	Macro	0.45	0.30	0.35	0.66
	Micro	0.63	0.66	0.63	

Table 11: Names$_{trans}$ Results by country for plain Naive Bayes, position weighting, and char n-gram back-off

		P	R	F	Acc
NB	Macro	0.51	0.50	0.49	0.79
	Micro	0.79	0.79	0.79	
Pos weight	Macro	0.64	0.46	0.50	0.81
	Micro	0.80	0.81	0.80	
Char n-gram	Macro	0.61	0.50	0.53	0.82
	Micro	0.81	0.82	0.81	

Table 12: Names$_{trans}$ Results by country for plain Naive Bayes, position weighting, and char n-gram back-off

Deep Learning Models for Sentiment Analysis in Arabic

Ahmad A. Al Sallab
Electrical and Communication Department,
Faculty of Engineering, Cairo University, Egypt
ahmad.elsallab@gmail.com

Ramy Baly, Gilbert Badaro, Hazem Hajj
Electrical and Computer Engineering Department,
American University of Beirut, Lebanon
{rgb15, ggb05 hh63}@aub.edu.lb

Wassim El Hajj
Computer Science Department,
American University of Beirut, Lebanon
we07@aub.edu.lb

Khaled B. Shaban
Computer Science and Engineering Department,College of Engineering,
Qatar University
khaled.shaban@qu.edu.qa

Abstract

In this paper, deep learning framework is proposed for text sentiment classification in Arabic. Four different architectures are explored. Three are based on Deep Belief Networks and Deep Auto Encoders, where the input data model is based on the ordinary Bag-of-Words, with features based on the recently developed Arabic Sentiment Lexicon in combination with other standard lexicon features. The fourth model, based on the Recursive Auto Encoder, is proposed to tackle the lack of context handling in the first three models. The evaluation is carried out using Linguistic Data Consortium Arabic Tree Bank dataset, with benchmarking against the state of the art systems in sentiment classification with reported results on the same dataset. The results show high improvement of the fourth model over the state of the art, with the advantage of using no lexicon resources that are scarce and costly in terms of their development.

1 Introduction

With the revolution of web 2.0 and the amount of opinionated data generated by online users, personal views and opinions are no longer constrained to authors in newspapers or custom opinion surveys. Instead, almost anyone can express opinions through social media. The abundance of these opinions and their availability and accessibility gave birth to automated applications that use sentiment analysis (opinion mining) as a key factor in predicting stock market, evaluating products, surveying the public, etc. However, automated sentiment analysis is still far from producing output with quality comparable to humans due to the complexity of the semantics. Furthermore, the Arabic language adds another dimension of difficulty to automated sentiment analysis due to its morphological richness, ambiguity, and the large number of dialectal variants. These challenges add to the complexity of the required natural language processing (NLP).

Many methods have been suggested in literature to address automated sentiment analysis. One of the prominent approaches is the use of machine learning (ML) techniques, where sentiment analysis is formalized as a classification task. The predicted classes are typically chosen to be positive or negative sentiment. The classification tasks range from classifying the sentiment of words, phrases, sentences, or sometimes documents. Deep learning has been recently considered for sentiment analysis (Socher et al. 2013). Socher et al. 2013 worked on phrase level sentiment classification using the Recursive Neural Tensor Network (RNTN) over a fine grained phrase level annotated corpus (Stanford Sentiment Tree Bank). Other deep learning models that can potentially be used in sentiment analysis include deep neural networks (DNN), convolutional neural networks (CNN) (LeCun et al. 1995), Deep Belief Networks (DBN) with fast inferencing of the model parameters (Hinton et al. 2006), and recurrent neutral network (RNN) (Socher et al. 2013).

Proceedings of the Second Workshop on Arabic Natural Language Processing, pages 9–17,
Beijing, China, July 26-31, 2015.

We aim in this work to investigate the merit of using deep models for sentiment analysis in Arabic, focusing on the sentence level sentiment classification. To the best of our knowledge, this is the first attempt to explore deep learning models for sentiment classification in Arabic. For the vector space representation of text, we utilize ArSenL (Badaro et al. 2014), a recently published sentiment lexicon. Each word in the lexicon is associated with three sentiment scores indicating levels of positivity, negativity, and neutrality. ArSenL includes 28,780 Arabic lemmas with the corresponding number of 157,969 synsets. We explore four deep learning models: DNN, DBN, Deep Auto Encoder (DAE), and combined DAE with DBN. DNN applies back propagation to a conventional neural network, but with several layers. DBN applies generative pre-training phase before feeding a discriminative fine tuning step. DAE provides a generative model representation for the original but with reduced dimensionality. Finally, the RAE aims at parsing the raw sentence words in the best order that minimizes the reconstruction error of re-generating the same sentence words in the same order; in other words, it aims at discovering the best parse tree that maximizes the probability of the input data.

Both DAE and RAE models aim at providing a compact representation of the input sentence. Both models are based on unsupervised learning, where their objective is the minimization of reconstruction error of the input, so no manual annotation is needed. The main difference is that; RAE considers the context and order of parsing of the sentence. This recursion enables parsing variable length sentences. While the DAE is parsing the whole sentence words at once in the first layer, with no consideration of the order of parsing of words, and keep feeding the representation forward in the deep architecture on the hope that useful features are extracted at each layer of depth. This property makes it mandatory to have fixed length features vector, which promotes the Bag-of-Words (BoW) model.

Both DAE and RAE models require a classifier on top of their obtained representation. In case of DAE, the classifier is the DBN, while in case of RAE, the classifier is a softmax layer.

The Linguistic Data Consortium Arabic Tree Bank (LDC ATB) dataset is used to evaluate the proposed models. The input data to the first three models depend on the BoW model, with the utilization of lexicon scores. In our case it is ArSenL, as special sentiment features.

The rest of the paper is organized as follows: Section 2 overviews the work related to sentiment classification in Arabic. Section 3 describes the features employed from ArSenL. Section 4 includes a description of the proposed deep learning models. Section 5 presents the results of the evaluation on LDC ATB, and section 6 concludes the paper.

2 Related Work

This section presents an overview of different approaches proposed to perform opinion mining in Arabic focusing on practices pertaining to preprocessing, feature engineering, modeling, and evaluation methods.

Word n-grams are considered the most common features that have been used, with different preprocessing and representation settings, to train classification models. In general, using higher-order n-grams (bigrams and trigrams) – represented with term-frequency inverse-document-frequency (TFiDF) weights achieved better results compared to unigrams (Rushdi et al. 2011, Mountassir et al. 2012). These features were used to train different classification models with support vector machines (SVM) achieving better performances (Rushdi et al. 2011, Aly and Attiya 2013, Al-Kabi et al. 2013, Shoukry et al. 2013) with a few exceptions where Naïve Bayes was found superior (Mountassir et al. 2012, Elawady et al. 2014). Ensemble techniques were also utilized for additional performance improvement (Omar et al. 2013). The impact of stylistic features was introduced in (Abbasi et al. 2008). These features were found beneficial when used along with syntactic features.

Arabic sentiment lexicons are also used to engineer features. Examples are ArSenL (Badaro et al. 2014), SIFAAT (Abdul-Mageed et al. 2011) and ArSeLEX (Ibrahim et al. 2015). Deep learning models have recently gained popularity, and can potentially be used in sentiment analysis. These models include DNN, CNN (LeCun et al. 1995), DBN, DBN with fast inference of the model parameters (Hinton et al. 2006), and RNN (Socher et al. 2013). Recently, Socher et al. (Socher et al. 2013) worked on phrase level sentiment classification in English using Recursive Neural Tensor Networks over a fine grained phrase level annotated corpus (Stanford Sentiment Tree Bank).

Raw sentence	فالمهم هو التوصل الى اتفاق جيد					
	جيد	اتفاق	الى	التوصل	هو	فالمهم
Binarized input (variable length)	1398	1045	24	256	43	103
Semantic word embedding representation	$Lb_{\text{جيد}} \in \Re^N$	$Lb_{\text{اتفاق}} \in \Re^N$	$Lb_{\text{الى}} \in \Re^N$	$Lb_{\text{التوصل}} \in \Re^N$	$Lb_{\text{هو}} \in \Re^N$	$Lb_{\text{فالمهم}} \in \Re^N$
RAE representation	$\hat{x} \in \Re^N$					

Table 1 Example of parsing a sentence from its raw words into their embedding representation

Lastly, a variety of corpora have been used for evaluation such as OCA (Opinion Corpus for Arabic) (Rushdi-Saleh 2011), LABR (Large-scale Arabic Book Reviews) (Mountassir et al. 2012), sentences from the Penn Arabic Treebank (PATB) part 1, version 3.0 (Abdul-Mageed et al. 2011) and many other self-created corpora.

3 Data Feeding Deep Learning

In the first three deep learning models (DNN, DBN and DAE), we employ features based on ArSenL where the words in each sentence are represented in a vector of length equal to the number of entries in the lexicon. Instead, of using TFIDF scores or binary representations of the words, we focus the evaluation on the impact of sentiment lexicon features due to their demonstrated relevance in past literature. In ArSenL, there are 3 scores for each lemma (denoting positive, negative and neutral polarity). The sum of the 3 scores adds up to 1. As a result, the feature vector will be three times the size of the selected text in the corpus. For the LDC ATB dataset, 3795 entries are matched to in ArSenL, resulting in a feature vector of length 11385. It is worth noting that this vector representation is sparse, and we refer to it as *arsenl_lemma*. We also use aggregated sentiment score for the whole sentence, thus obtaining three scores per sentence for positive, negative and neutral polarities. In this case, the feature vector is of length three and we refer to it as *arsenl_sentence*.

For the forth and last model (RAE), the input is the raw words indices that constitute each sentence, hence, the length of input is variable per sentence. The words' indices are drawn from a known vocabulary obtained from a separate and independent training set. Test set words that are not encountered in training are considered "UNKNOWN" and are given a special index. Stop words are not removed.

For the RAE, the main preprocessing steps are:

1) Vocabulary vector build: parse the whole dataset to obtain the encountered vocabulary words. No stop words removal or stemming is done.
2) Each sentence is represented as list of word indices $b_{word} \in \Re^{|V|}$, where $|V|$ is the size of the vocabulary, in our case for the LDC ATB dataset, it is 31850 words. Each word in a sentence is looked up in the table $L \in \Re^{Nx|V|}$ where N is the size of the resulting embedding representation vector (in our experiments it is set to 50)
3) The resulting sequence of representations is fed forward in the parse tree of the RAE to obtain one representation $\hat{x} \in \Re^N$ for the whole sentence.

An example of a parsed sentence is described in Table 1

4 Deep Learning Models for Sentiment Analysis in Arabic

Three models are proposed under deep learning framework: DNN, DBN, and a combined Auto Encoder with DBN. The network architecture in terms of depth, breadth, and hyper parameters settings are set based on the recommendations in (Bengio et al. 2009) and (Bengio et al. 2012).

For the DNN architecture, the number of neurons in each layer is selected to yield the best accuracy for a selected development data set. For the considered data, the number of neurons came out at, 40 per layer. The depth of the DNN network is selected by iteratively incrementing the number of layers one at a time while evaluating the accuracy at every increment. The depth of 3 layers was found to yield the best accuracy with the selected data set. A decision softmax layer composed of two neurons was then added on top of the three network layers. For training the model, we used supervised back propagation. The objective of the model is to minimize the error of the network output versus the true sentiment class label for each training case. The remaining settings for DNN model are: (1) conjugate gradient algorithm is used for gradient updates with three line searches; (2) weights are randomly initialized from Gaussian distribution of 0 mean and standard deviation of 1; and (3) the activation function of each neuron is taken as hyperbolic tangent activation. Training is conducted in batches of size 100 cases for 50 epochs. The resulting architecture of the DNN model is shown in Figure 1.

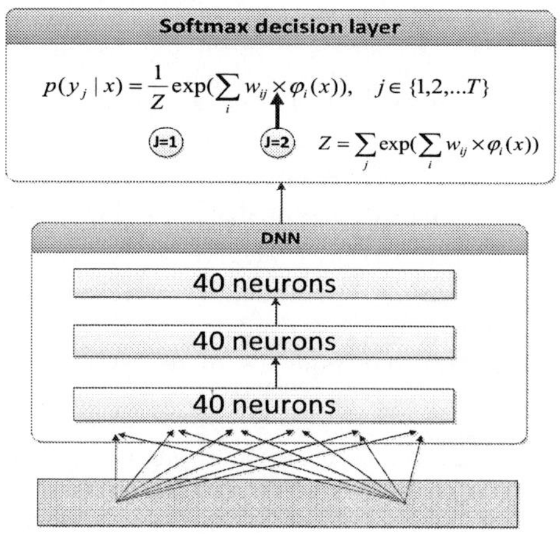

Figure 1. DNN Architecture

The second model is based on the DBN model described in (Hinton et al. 2006). The learning process is performed in two phases. First, a generative unsupervised pre-training phase is developed based on stacked Restricted Boltzmann Machine wake-sleep algorithm at each layer (Hinton et al. 2006). In the second phase, the weights of the network are used to initialize a discriminative supervised model similar to DNN. The difference with the conventional DNN is the addition of the pre-training phase, which was found to avoid model over fitting (Bengio et al. 2012). The same network architecture of DNN is used for both, pre-training and fine-tuning phases. Both phases undergo 50 epochs of weights updates. The resulting DBN model architecture is depicted in Figure 2.

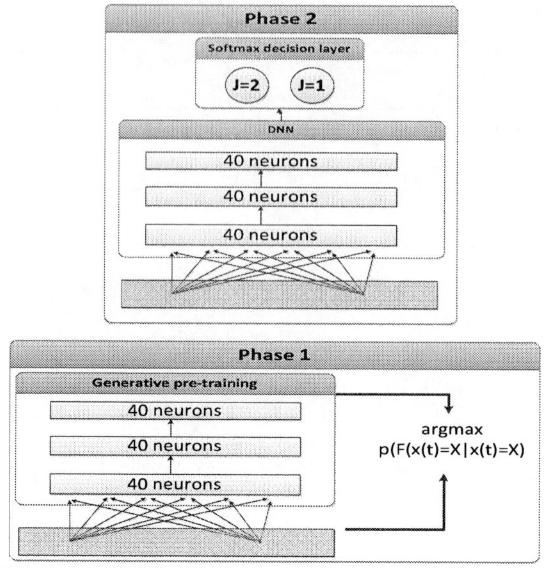

Figure 2. DBN Architecture

For the third model, a generative deep auto encoder model is first trained with the objective of minimizing the error between the applied and the reconstructed vectors. The result of the autoencoder is then followed by a model similar to the DBN model, with pre-training and fine tuning phases. The error function is taken as the difference between the applied features vector and the reconstructed vector in the reverse order of the deep auto encoder. The auto encoder architecture is taken as 100-50-20 in three respective layers. The idea is to obtain a reduced dense dimension vector with accurate representation of the input data. Since the input vector is sparse, we cannot directly consider its dimension as the real dimension representing the input data, as it contains many zeros. Hence, we consider the 40 neurons, which were taken in the first two models as the hidden layers dimensions, and we target 50% reduction in the deep auto encoder. To achieve this reduction ratio, we start at 100 neurons and reduce the number of neurons by 50% as we go deeper in the model. The resulting architecture is shown in Figure 3. The figure shows the unfolded architecture of the employed encoder. The encoded data representing the input is taken from the third activation layer. The reconstructed output is then taken from the 6th layer, which is equivalent to the 1st layer by symmetry of the proposed architecture.

After the deep auto encoder is derived, the training data is fed to the encoder to obtain the representative 20 dimension codes for each entry of the dataset. The new obtained codes are then used as training data for another DBN. This time, no pre-training is run in the DBN model since pre-training already happened during the deep auto encoder training. The obtained 20 dimension vectors are dense, unlike the original feature vectors of the training set. Hence different architecture needs to be employed in the DBN to account for different combinations of the dense data inside the code vectors. The best architecture of the layers for the DBN in this case was found to be three layers with 400 neurons in each layer

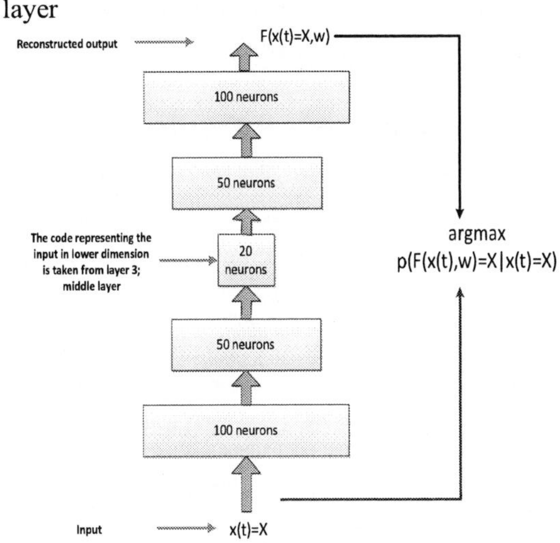

Figure 3 DAE Architecture.

So far, the input data to the first three models depend on the BoW, with the utilization of lexicon scores, in our case it is ArSenL, as special sentiment features. The BoW suffers two main issues: 1) Poor representation of features, which generates sparse vectors of words, where most of its encoded information and features are not relevant to the classification of the current case at hand. This sparseness hurts the reconstruction of the DAE and causes high errors resulting in poor representations of the input. 2) No consideration of context, where the words are encoded irrespective to their order in the original sentence. The BoW model renders the lexicon scores useless, and sometimes misleading, because it draws them out of context. In other words, a word cannot be absolutely positive or absolutely negative. However, the sentiment of a word is usually context dependent. For example, the word "beat" is usually a negative word. However, in the context of "We have beaten the other team", it becomes a positive one. Also, positivity and negativity of a word is perspective dependent. For example: "team A has beaten team B" is a positive context for team A, but negative for team B. This renders the absolute lexicon scores useless or even misleading in some cases if taken without the consideration of the context.

The fourth and last model is the Recursive Auto Encoder (RAE). The RAE is a member of the recursive family of deep learning models (Socher 2011, 2013). The main advantage of the RAE is that; it is unsupervised, so it does not require parse tree annotation like other members of this family, like Recurrent Neural Networks (RNN). The basic block of the RAE is the normal auto encoder described earlier, where the objective is to minimize the error between the original raw input vector and the reconstructed one, called the reconstruction error. They have been used for dimensionality reduction and hash space search.

In NLP, the input is usually the BoW vector, with 1's at the positions where a word of the vocabulary is encountered in the current sentence at hand, leaving many irrelevant zeros at the rest of the vector positions. This hurts badly the reconstruction capability of the AE and makes its convergence harder. Also, no context is captured in this model. To address this, the second component of the RAE model is the recursion parse tree, where the sentence words are parsed/visited in a certain order that captures their semantic meaning, and how they influence and sometimes inflect the meanings of each other. For example, the meaning of "good" is the opposite of "not good".

The basic block of recursion is the AE, which is a binary encoder in our case. The goal of auto encoders is to learn a representation of their inputs. The algorithm in Socher et al. 2013 is described in brief here. At each step of parsing, the weights of the basic AE are updated so as to minimize the reconstruction error (see Figure 5). However, this procedure assumes that the parse tree order is known, which is not. A prior step is required to discover the best parse tree first. This is done through a greedy breadth first algorithm. At each recursion step, all the possible remaining words of the sentence are attempted; generating a representation and associated reconstruction error. The next node to be included in the tree is the one that generated the minimum reconstruction error. This algorithm is greedy because it considers the best solution at the current step without considering the global situation, which simplifies calculations and reduces the processing time.

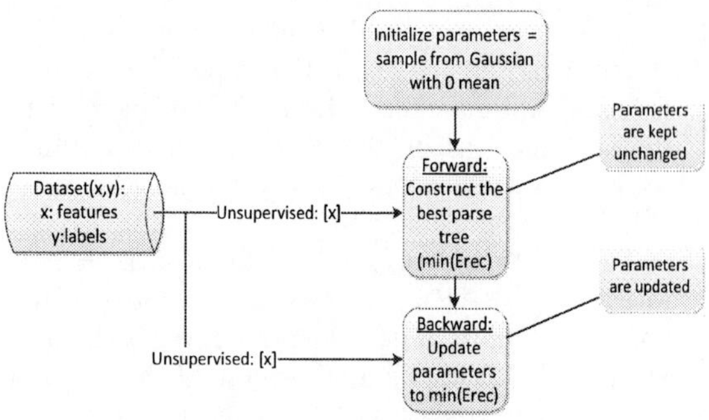

Figure 4 Training procedure of RAE with greedy discovery of the best parse tree

So the RAE learning process with tree structure discovery shall go as follows (shown in Figure 4):

1) Initialize the RAE weights and word embeddings L with zero mean Gaussian samples
2) Forward path:
    a. Initialize the parents node list to null
    b. At each step, try all possible extension leaves to the tree from the list of all candidate leaves
    c. For each extension, evaluate the reconstruction error
    d. Choose the leaf that minimizes the error and add it to the parents list
3) Backward path:
    a. Once the tree is constructed, the weights of RAE can be adjusted same as done in the normal training of the AE described
4) Repeat 2 and 3 for each training case

At this step, we have obtained a RAE that is able to provide a sentence wide representation by recursively parsing its words in the best order. However, to build a sentiment classifier using this learnt network two components are missing. The first one is concerned with handling the raw input words, and obtaining a good representation out of it that encodes the context of the word. This is often referred to as the word embedding. In our approach, this block is implemented as a lookup table $L \in \Re^{Nx|V|}$ where N is the size of the resulting embedding representation. In our setting, this block is initialized by sampling it from a zero mean Gaussian distribution. During the learning process described, the weights of this block are learnt from the unsupervised data.

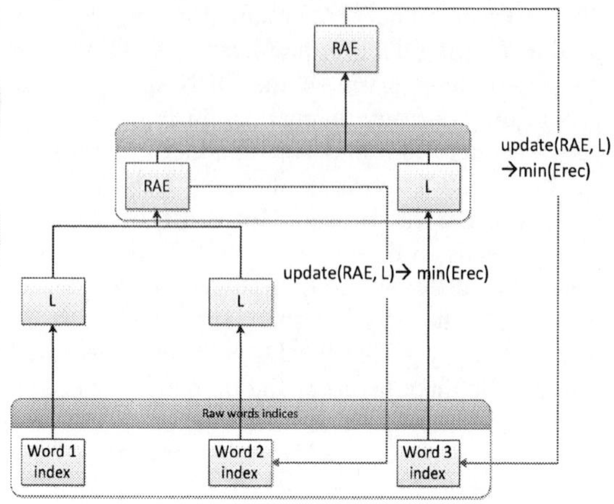

Figure 5 Word embedding matrix update in the training process of RAE.

The other missing block, is the classifier on top of the RAE representation. This is the supervised part of the system, where it is trained based on the sentiment annotations given to each training case. It could be any supervised machine learning classifier. In our case, it was a simple softmax layer.

The full architecture of the system is shown in Figure 6. The main steps are as follows:

1) Build the word embedding matrix L.
    a. The input are the raw sentences represented as sequence of its constituting words indices.
    b. The output is the semantic representation, i.e. the result of look up of each word index in the matrix L.
2) Construct the RAE parse tree and update its weights for best reconstruction.
    a. The input is the sequence of semantic representations obtained from the word embedding block.
    b. The output is the top level compact representation of the parsed sentence.
3) Train a classifier on top of the RAE representations. In our case this is just a softmax (MaxEnt) layer.
    a. The input is the representation obtained from the RAE
    b. The output is the classification decision. In our case; positive or negative.

The RAE model has the following advantages: 1) The phase of RAE construction and parse tree discovery is completely unsupervised, while the only supervised part is the fine tuning phase. This property enables the adaptation and enhancement of the system on any un-annotated dataset. 2) The input is completely raw words indices, with no lexicon required, which are a hard to build language resource in terms of effort and cost.

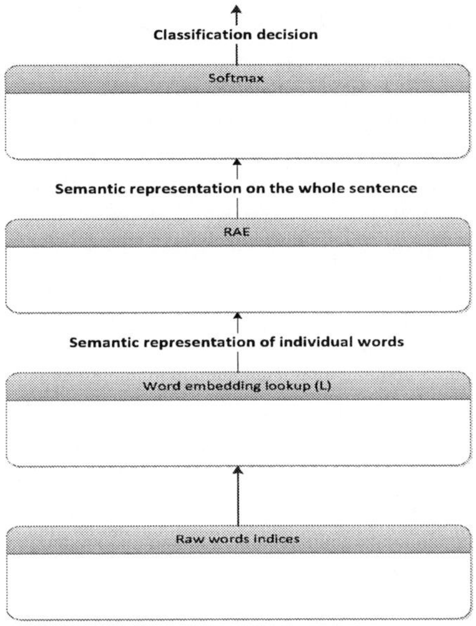

Figure 6 Sentiment classification using RAE

The problem of context handling is partially solved by the RAE model, where the order of parsing is variable with each new sentence, and hence a different representation is obtained for each sentence according to its semantics. However, as far as the task of sentiment classification is concerned, the sentimental context is not captured, but the semantic context is depicted. In other words, the parse tree is discovered according to which n-grams sequence are valid or form a meaningful constituent, and hence the parse tree is formed. However, the sentiment context of such n-grams is not considered. To tackle this issue, a different parse tree is needed; a sentiment parse tree. An example of which, is the Stanford sentiment Tree Bank (Socher et al. 2013), which requires a huge and specialized annotation effort for the whole parse tree of the sentence not the overall sentence sentiment. The classification is then based on RNN. This is considered as a future work due to the unavailability of such sentiment tree bank as a required language resource for this type of networks.

5 Evaluation

To evaluate the models, LDC ATB dataset is used for training and testing. The dataset is split into 944 training sentences and 236 test sentences. Only positive and negative classes are considered for the data represented by *Arsenl_lemma*, and *Arsenl_sentence* features separately.

The results in Table 2 show that both, DBN and Auto Encoder (models 2 and 3) do not suffer over fitting while model 1 does. This is in line with the observation in (Bengio et al. 2012) which indicates that pre-training provides kind of regularization on the learned weights of the network. This is expected because deep auto encoder output provides good generalization of the input data, and has even less tendency to over-fit training data. With selected architectures, and in most cases, the F1 measures were close to SVM, and sometimes superior. The accuracy measures were not superior.

The input representation in the first three models is based on the BoW encoding of the ArSenL scores, which makes the features vector very sparse with too many zeros. This hurts badly the reconstruction capability of the network, because slight errors around zeros add up. This effect is reduced when the features vectors are first fed to a DAE to obtain a compact representation rather than a sparse one.

A better representation would be to select only the vocabulary words that are encountered in the sentence under focus. However, this will make the features vector length variable. A recursive model addresses this problem by parsing the sentence words recursively to obtain sentence wide representation considering only the vocabulary words that exist in the sentence. This is one of the reasons why the RAE is superior to the other three models.

The RAE model outperforms all the other models by a large margin of around 9%. As pointed out earlier, in this model, semantic context and the parsing order of words are considered. In the same time, no lexicon is used, and no special features are used, but only raw words as input. Table 3 shows the result of benchmarking the deep learning models proposed against other systems in literature, like linear SVM applied to ArSenL scores (Badaro el al. 2013) and SIFAAT (Abdul-Mageed et al. 2011), which represent the state of the art results on the LDC ATB dataset in Arabic sentiment classification. RAE outperformed SIFAAT by around 14%, while it outperformed linear SVM on ArSenL scores by around 9%.

	RAE		*Linear SVM*		*DNN (model 1)*		*DBN (model 2)*		*Deep auto – DBN (model 3)*	
Feature	*Accuracy (%)*	*F1 score (%)*	*Accuracy (%)*	*F1 score (%)*	*Accuracy (%)*	*F1 score (%)*	*Accuracy (%)*	*F1 score (%)*	*Accuracy (%)*	*F1 score (%)*
Arsenl_lemma	-	-	66.1	59.2	55.5	44.5	57.5	46.8	60.4	60.5
Ar-senl_sentence	-	-	61.4	62.8	53.4	44.3	53.4	40.1	56.1	43.5
Raw words	**74.3**	**73.5**	45.2	44.1	39.5	39.1	41.3	40.5	43.5	43.7

Table 2. Evaluation results on LDC ATB

	RAE	*SIFAAT*	*Linear SVM - ArsenL*	*DNN (model 1)*	*DBN (model 2)*	*DAE – DBN (model 3)*
Average F1 score (%) (Pos/Neg)	**73.5**	59.2	64.5	44.5	46.8	60.5

Table 3. Benchmark results on LDC ATB

In our experiments on RAE we focus on the idea of obtaining a representation that takes into consideration the context of the word. At the same time, we want to take advantage of the unsupervised nature of RAE that avoids the use of sentiment lexicon. Another future direction will be to consider using ArSenL lexicon to create better representation of word embeddings. This can be done by creating special word embedding blocks with the objective of generating the ArSenL sentiment scores, and then use this representation as input to the RAE. This is considered as a pre-training step to the embedding block rather than random initialization or n-gram validity task. Also, the pre-training using ArSenL enables the consideration of the individual words sentiment in addition to the semantic words context.

6 Conclusion

In this paper, a deep learning approach is proposed for the sentiment classification problem on Arabic text. Three architectures were proposed and derived for: DNN, DBN and Deep Auto Encoders. The features vector used the sentiment scores from ArSenL lexicon. LDC ATB dataset was used to evaluate the models, comparing their accuracy and F1 scores. It was found that, Deep Auto encoder model gives better representation of the input sparse vector. We also proposed a forth model, RAE, which was the best deep learning model according to our results, although it requires no sentiment lexicon. The results show around 9% improvement in average F1 score over the best reported results in literature on the same LDC ATB dataset in the sentiment classification task for Arabic.

Future work includes: 1) the enhancement of the word embedding block by employing large unsupervised corpus, and 2) enhancing the way the parse tree is constructed by improving the search method and its objective, so that it could be more directed towards semantic and syntactic correctness of the resulting parse tree, rather than depending on the reconstruction error alone.

Acknowledgement

This work was made possible by NPRP 6-716-1-138 grant from the Qatar National Research Fund (a member of Qatar Foundation). The statements made herein are solely the responsibility of the authors.

References

Gilbert Badaro, Ramy Baly, Hazem Hajj, Nizar Habash, and Wassim El-Hajj. "A Large Scale Arabic Sentiment Lexicon for Arabic Opinion Mining." ANLP 2014 (2014): 165.

Socher, Richard, Alex Perelygin, Jean Y. Wu, Jason Chuang, Christopher D. Manning, Andrew Y. Ng, and Christopher Potts. "Recursive deep models for semantic compositionality over a sentiment treebank." In Proceedings of the Conference on Empirical Methods in Natural Language Processing (EMNLP), pp. 1631-1642. 2013.

Socher, Richard, et al. "Semi-supervised recursive autoencoders for predicting sentiment distributions." Proceedings of the Conference on Empirical Methods in Natural Language Processing. Association for Computational Linguistics, 2011.

R. Collobert and J. Weston. 2008. A unified architecture for natural language processing: deep neural networks with multitask learning. In Proceedings of ICML, pages 160–167.

Abdul-Mageed, M., Diab, M. and Korayem, M. (2011). Subjectivity and sentiment analysis of modern standard Arabic. *In Proceedings of the 49th Annual Meeting of the Association for Com-putational Lin-guistics: Human Language Technol-ogies: short pa-pers*-Volume 2. Association for Computational Lin-guistics.

Abdul-Mageed, M., & Diab, M. (2012). Toward building a large-scale Arabic sentiment lexicon. In *Proceedings of the 6th International Global WordNet Conference* (pp. 18-22).

G. E. Hinton; S. Osindero; Y. Teh, "A fast learning algorithm for deep belief nets" Neural Computation, vol. 18, pp. 1527–1554, 2006.

Ruslan Salakhutdinov. 2009."Learning Deep Generative Models" PhD thesis, Graduate Department of Computer Science, University of Toronto.

Larochelle, Hugo, Yoshua Bengio, Jérôme Louradour, and Pascal Lamblin. "Exploring strategies for training deep neural networks." The Journal of Machine Learning Research 10 (2009): 1-40.

Bengio, Yoshua. "Practical recommendations for gradient-based training of deep architectures." In Neural Networks: Tricks of the Trade, pp. 437-478. Springer Berlin Heidelberg, 2012.

LeCun, Yann, and Yoshua Bengio. "Convolutional networks for images, speech, and time series." The handbook of brain theory and neural networks3361 (1995): 310.

Rushdi-Saleh, M., Martín-Valdivia, M. T., Ureña-López, L. A., & Perea-Ortega, J. M. "OCA: Opinion Corpus for Arabic." Journal of the American Society for Information Science and Technology 62.10, 2045-2054, 2011

Rushdi-Saleh, M., Martín-Valdivia, M. T., Ureña-López, L. A., & Perea-Ortega, J. M. "Bilingual Experiments with an Arabic-English Corpus for Opinion Mining." Proceedings of Recent Advances in Natural Language Processing, 2011

Mountassir, Asmaa, Houda Benbrahim, and Ilham Berrada. "A Cross-study of Sentiment Classification on Arabic Corpora." Research and Development in Intelligent Systems XXIX, Springer London, 2012

Aly, M. A., & Atiya, A. F. "LABR: A Large Scale Arabic Book Reviews Dataset." Proceedings of the 51st Annual Meeting of the Association for Computational Linguistics, 2013

Elawady, Rasheed M., Sherif Barakat, and Nora M. Elrashidy "Sentiment Analyzer for Arabic Comments", International Journal of Information Science and Intelligent System, 3(4): 73-86, 2014

Al-Kabi, Mohammed N., Nawaf A. Abdulla, and Mahmoud Al-Ayyoub "An Analytical Study of Arabic Sentiments: Maktoob Case Study." Proceedings of the 8th International Conference for Internet Technology and Secured Transactions (ICITST), IEEE, 2013

Shoukry, A., & Rafea, A. "Sentence-level Arabic Sentiment Analysis." Proceedings of International Conference on Collaboration Technologies and Systems (CTS), IEEE, 2012

Omar, N., Albared, M., Al-Shabi, A., & Al-Moslmi, T. "Ensemble of Classification Algorithms for Subjectivity and Sentiment Analysis of Arabic Customers' Reviews." International Journal of Advancements in Computing Technology, 14(5), 2013

Abbasi, Ahmed, Hsinchun Chen, and Arab Salem. "Sentiment Analysis in Multiple Languages: Feature Selection for Opinion Classification in Web forums." ACM Transactions on Information Systems (TOIS) 26.3, 2008

Ibrahim, Hossam S., Sherif M. Abdou, and Mervat Gheith. "Sentiment Analysis for Modern Standard Arabic and Colloquial." International Journal on Natural Language Computing (IJNLC) Vol. 4, No.2, April 2015

Abdul-Mageed, M., & Diab, M. T. " Subjectivity and Sentiment Analysis of Modern Standard Arabic." Proceedings of the 5th Linguistic Annotation Workshop, Association for Computational Linguistics, 2011

Nabil, Mahmoud, Mohamed Aly, and Amir Atiya. "LABR: A Large Scale Arabic Sentiment Analysis Benchmark", 2015

ElSahar, H., and El-Beltagy S.R. "Building Large Arabic Multi-domain Resources for Sentiment Analysis." Computational Linguistics and Intelligent Text Processing. Springer International Publishing, 2015

Arabic Tree Bank Part 3, http://www.ldc.upenn.edu/Catalog/catalogEntry.jsp?catalogId=2005T20

A Light Lexicon-based Mobile Application for Sentiment Mining of Arabic Tweets

Gilbert Badaro, Ramy Baly, Rana Akel, Linda Fayad, Jeffrey Khairallah, Hazem Hajj, Wassim El-Hajj, Khaled Bashir Shaban*
American University of Beirut, Lebanon
{ggb05;rgb15;rba09;laf05;jbk07;hh63;we07}@aub.edu.lb
*Qatar University, Qatar
khaled.shaban@qu.edu.qa

Abstract

Most advanced mobile applications require server-based and communication. This often causes additional energy consumption on the already energy-limited mobile devices. In this work, we provide to address these limitations on the mobile for Opinion Mining in Arabic. Instead of relying on compute-intensive NLP processing, the method uses an Arabic lexical resource stored on the device. Text is stemmed, and the words are then matched to our own developed ArSenL. ArSenL is the first publicly available large scale Standard Arabic sentiment lexicon (ArSenL) developed using a combination of English SentiWordnet (ESWN), Arabic WordNet, and the Arabic Morphological Analyzer (AraMorph). The scores from the matched stems are then processed through a classifier for determining the polarity. The method was tested on a published set of Arabic tweets, and an average accuracy of 67% was achieved. The developed mobile application is also made publicly available. The application takes as input a topic of interest and retrieves the latest Arabic tweets related to this topic. It then displays the tweets superimposed with colors representing sentiment labels as positive, negative or neutral. The application also provides visual summaries of searched topics and a history showing how the sentiments for a certain topic have been evolving.

1 Introduction

With the growth of social media and online blogs, people express their opinion and sentiment freely by providing product reviews, as well as comments about celebrities, and political and global events. These texts reflecting opinions are of great interest to companies and individuals who base their decisions and actions upon them (Feldman, 2013; Taboada et al., 2011). In particular, there is an increased interest in easy access to Arabic opinion from mobiles. In fact, around "10.8 million tweets come from the Arab region every day. 73.6% of all the tweets from the region are now in Arabic" (Radcliffe, 2013).

There have been many attempts to build sentiment analysis engines and several applications for performing opinion mining for English texts. Most opinion mining approaches in English are based on SentiWordNet (ESWN) (Esuli and Sebastiani, 2006; Baccianella & al., 2010) for extracting word-level sentiment polarity. Some researchers used the stored positive or negative connotation of the words to combine them and derive the polarity of the text (Esuli and Sebastiani, 2005).

Recently, special interest has been given to opinion mining from Arabic texts, and as a result, there has also been interest in developing Arabic lexicons for word-level sentiment evaluation. The availability of a large scale Arabic based SWN is still limited (AlHazmi et al., 2013; Abdul-Mageed and Diab, 2012; Elarnaoty et al., 2012; Elarnaoty et al., 2012). In fact, there is no publicly available large scale Arabic sentiment lexicon similar to ESWN. Additionally, there are limitations with existing Arabic lexicons including deficiency in covering the correct num-

Proceedings of the Second Workshop on Arabic Natural Language Processing, pages 18–25,
Beijing, China, July 26-31, 2015.

ber and type of lemmas. Moreover, few applications exist for performing opinion mining in Arabic.

Sophisticated opinion mining models requires highly computational natural language processing tools. As an example for the Arabic language, MADAMIRA (Pasha et al., 2014) is a tool that performs tokenization, POS tagging and sense disambiguation by lemmatizing a given sentence in Arabic. However, the tool cannot be integrated in a mobile application without using a server.

Hence, in this work, we propose a method for opinion mining of Arabic tweets on mobile devices without the need for reliance on compute-intensive NLP tools. We propose a computationally light method that uses a lexicon-based approach for Arabic tweets. Our newly developed large-scale sentiment lexicon, ArSenL, is leveraged for the method. ArSenL was created by matching Arabic WordNet (AWN) (Black et al., 2006) and lemmas in AraMorph lexicon to ESWN. Each lemma entry in the lexicon has three scores derived from the mapping with ESWN: positive, negative, and objective. The sum of the three scores is 1. Ideally, one should use NLP tools to process text and produce lemmas that can be matched to ArsenL. However, to keep processing light on the mobile, we produce a stemmed version of ArSenL, and then use word stems for matching. This design reduces the energy and performance costs caused by input/output and transmission operations on the mobile. A mobile application is designed and implemented to automatically analyze Arabic tweets, extract sentiments related to the tweets, and provide a visualization summary of the results. The user inputs a keyword of interests to him/her and the output displays a summary of the tweets' sentiments. The method is deigned to use limited computational and storage resources while achieving acceptable accuracy.

The rest of the paper is organized as follows. A literature review is presented in section 2 covering work that involved developing opinion mining methods based on lexical resources. In section 3, we detail the method, with descriptions of ArsenL and the developed application. Section 4 includes an evaluation of the sentiment model and a description of the developed mobile application. In section 5, we conclude our work and outline possible extensions.

2 Literature Review

There have been numerous efforts for creating sentiment lexicons in English and Arabic to perform sentiment mining. The primary target for these resources is to aid in automated analysis of sentiment content in text.

In fact, the Arabic language in social media presents several challenges for sentiment mining as detailed by El-Beltagy & Ali (2013). First, the unavailability of colloquial Arabic parsers makes the morphological analysis task harder. Moreover, there is no publicly available sentiment lexicon for Arabic. Entity name recognition and handling idiomatic Arabic expressions in different dialects are also additional challenges for Arabic sentiment mining. For more information on Arabic morphological complexity and dialectal variations, see Habash (2010).

Denecke (2008) and Ohana and Tierney (2009) developed a lexicon sentiment model based on the success of the work of Esuli and Sebastiani, in 2006 who introduced ESWN as a resource that assigns for each synset in the English WordNet (EWN) scores for objectivity, positivity, and negativity. The model of Denecke (2008) is proposed to work with multilingual applications where the document is first translated from a foreign language into English and the three sentiment scores are then extracted based on ESWN. The scores are then used as features for the sentiment model. The processing of the document includes stemming and part of speech tagging.

While Denecke (2008) and Ohana and Tierney (2009) relied on ESWN to develop their sentiment mining model, Abdul-Mageed et al. (2011) used manually annotated adjective lexicon (SIFAAT (Abdul-Mageed and Diab, 2012) to develop an opinion mining model for Arabic. The model uses morphological features and polarity labels of the adjectives matched to SIFAAT. As an extension to their work on lexicon based opinion mining models, Abdul-Mageed and Diab (2014) extended the lexicon to create SANA, a subjectivity and sentiment lexicon for Arabic. SANA has a mix of lemmas and inflected forms, many of which are not diacritized. However, SANA was not tested in the context of an opinion mining model.

As another attempt to create a lexicon-based approach for sentiment mining, Alhazmi et al. (2013) linked the Arabic WordNet to ESWN through the provided synset offset information.

The efficiency of the lexicon for sentiment mining was not evaluated.

While the previous approaches were mainly based on the availability of sentiment lexical resources, El-Halees (2011) developed a three steps opinion-mining model for Arabic documents. First, the documents are passed through a classification model that is based on lexical resources. This part classifies the majority of the document. The resultant classified documents are used as training set for maximum entropy method which then classifies some other documents. Finally, a K-nearest method is employed to classify the remaining documents using the output of the previous two classification models.

Using ESWN, Mukherjee et al. (2012) developed TwiSent which collects tweets and classifies them as positive, negative or objective. Besides detecting the sentiment of the tweet, TwiSent addresses four known problems for tweets: spams, structural anomalies, entity specifications and pragmatics. Addressing these inputs improved sentiment classification by 10 % compared to other sentiment mining applications that were trained on the same tweets' set. Moreover, this work is only limited to the English language.

Davidov et al. (2010) describe a technique that transforms hashtags and smileys in tweets into sentiments. The described process is divided into two parts: identifying sentiment expressions, and determining the polarity of the identified expressions. Each tweet is divided into 4 different groups: words, punctuation, n-grams, and patterns. Then for each group a separate technique is applied to detect a positive or a negative sentiment. Although this approach analyzes hashtags and smileys which are multilingual, it is still mainly designed for the English language.

Last but not least, Aly & Atia (2013) presents a LABR: Large Arabic Book Reviews dataset consisting of 63K book reviews with rating from 1 to 5. The authors present baseline approaches for performing sentiment mining and set benchmarks for future research and approaches in sentiment mining.

In summary, while previous methods exist for English sentiment mining, none exist for real-time sentiment mining on mobile for Arabic. Additionally, those methods that do exist, and only for English, often rely on extensive computations making them infeasible for extensive use on a mobile. In this work, we provide a method that uses a recently developed Arabic sentiment lexicon, and requires minimal computations for the mobile.

3 Proposed Approach

In this section we describe the method, the Arabic sentiment lexicon, and the developed mobile application.

3.1 Method Overview

The processing steps of the model are shown in Figure 1. The pre-processing steps include: Tweet tokenization, hashtag removal, stemming, sentiment scores inference for the stemmed words, and then sentiment classification. The scores are then used to derive three aggregate features containing the sum of positive scores, the sum of negative scores, and the sum of objective or neutral scores. In this paper, we use objective and neutral interchangeably. These pre-processing steps are further detailed here.

Removing Hashtags: This step is essential to clean the data from hashtags and keep their corresponding words for sentiment analysis given their importance in the sentiment of the tweet.

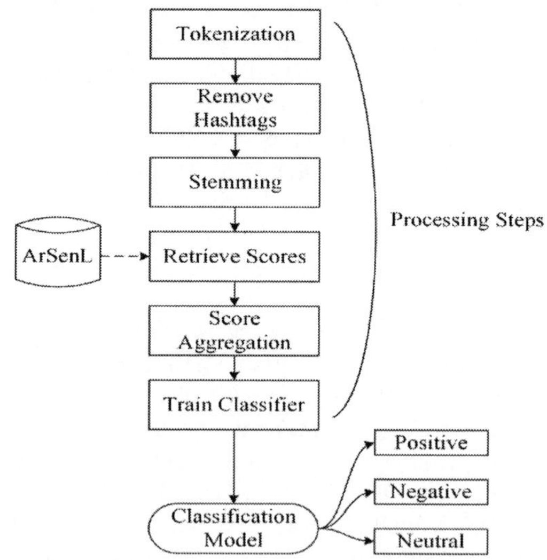

Figure 1. Efficient sentiment mining model in Arabic for mobile use.

Stemming: Each tokenized tweet is stemmed to match it to a stemmed version of ArSenL. Lemmatization would have produced higher accuracy, however it would have required more computations. As a result, we used stemming to keep the processing light. Khoja's stemmer (1999) was utilized in the implementation.

Getting the Score of Tweets: Each stemmed word is matched to the stemmed version of ArSenL in order to retrieve the corresponding sentiment scores. If a word in the tweet did not have any match in ArSenL, a zero score is assigned for each of the positive, the negative and the objective scores of the word. The sentiment scores are then summed for each tweet. It is worth noting that we tried using an average score per tweet instead of the sum but the sum gave better accuracy results.

3.2 Arabic Sentiment Lexicon

For the Arabic Sentiment lexicon, we generate a stemmed version of ArSenL (Badaro et al., 2014). ArSenL was developed based on extending other existing resources in Arabic and English: English WordNet (EWN) (Miller et al., 1990), Arabic WordNet (AWN), English SentiWordNet (ESWN) and AraMorph were used. The lemma entries in the Arabic resources were linked to the English synsets. The validated version was demonstrated to outperform the other version as well as state-of-the-art lexicons for Arabic sentiment.

A public interface to browsing ArSenL is available at http://www.oma-project.com. ArSenL can also be downloaded for research use. The interface allows the user to search for an Arabic word. The output shows the different scores for the Arabic word along with the corresponding sentiment scores. A snapshot of the homepage is shown in Figure 2. The scores are the sentiment scores that were extracted from ESWN after establishing the linking across different resources as detailed in Badaro et al work. Further details can be found in Badaro et al. paper.

3.3 Features and Mining Model

3.3.1 Training Data

A corpus of 2300 manually annotated Arabic Tweets (~30k words) is utilized (Mourad and Darwish, 2013). The dataset was randomly sampled from Twitter out of 65 million unique tweets in Arabic. It was annotated by two native Arabic speakers. In case of disagreement, the two annotators discussed the issue of the tweet to resolve it. In case the disagreement remains, the tweet was dropped.

3.3.2 Features

The features used to build the classification model were only restricted to the sum of sentiment scores per tweet as retrieved from ArSenL. We made the features simple in order to reduce the processing and computation efforts given that our aim is to design an energy efficient sentiment model for mobile.

3.3.3 Classification Model

To predict the sentiment of a tweet, we decided to use decision trees as a classification model for ease of results' interpretation. The design is an ensemble classifier consisting of three binary classifiers: positive/not positive, negative/not negative and objective/not objective as shown in Figure 3. In order to train each classifier, an equal number of tweets is used for each class. The results of the three classifiers are then evaluated against custom developed rules that combine the results of the three classifiers in order to assign the correct sentiment label for a given tweet: positive, negative or neutral sentiment.

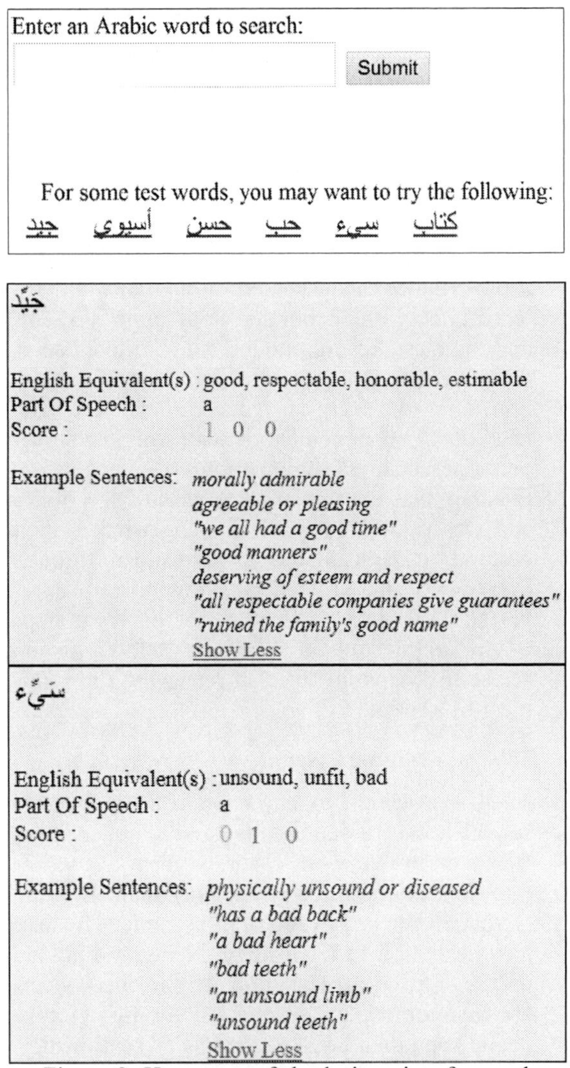

Figure 2. Homepage of the lexicon interface and snapshots of examples searched through the interface. Positive, negative and objective scores are represented in green, red and gray respectively.

For example, a tweet classified as positive, not negative and objective by the three binary classifiers respectively will be labeled as a positive tweet. These rules were chosen to achieve higher accuracy, and are shown in Figure 3 and the input to the rules are the results of the three binary classifiers. The classification model is shown in Figure 3.

3.4 Mobile Application Development

3.4.1 Application Architecture

A 3-tier architecture shown in Figure 4 is used for the design of the application. The design is divided into three main components. The user interface is the component where the model takes as input the topic of interest and where the tweets are displayed after being classified as positive, negative or objective. The logic part consists of the processing performed in order to match the stemmed tweets to the stemmed lemmas in ArSenL and extract sentiment scores. The sentiment scores are fed to the classification model described above. The Data component represents all the sources of data that the application makes use of: the tweets accessed through an API, filtered tweets based on the input topic, ArSenL and the classification model. No additional servers are required to perform sentiment classification. Thus, the energy is reduced since there is no need for I/O communication with a remote server or for server-level computations. The mobile application was developed for Android OS mobiles and was titled "شو رأين؟" meaning what is their opinion. It is available for download through http://www.oma-project.com. An example reported in Table 1 to illustrate the different steps of the architecture in Figure 4. Below, we describe the steps involved in retrieving the sentiment of a tweet.

3.4.2 Fetching Tweets

There is a search box at the top of the main page in which the user enters the keyword of interest. Based on the keyword entered, recent tweets are fetched using Twitter API with Arabic filtering so that all fetched tweets are in Arabic. The user has the option to fetch more tweets by clicking on the "Show More" button. The fetched tweets are then stored in an array list for further processing and then deriving the related sentiment.

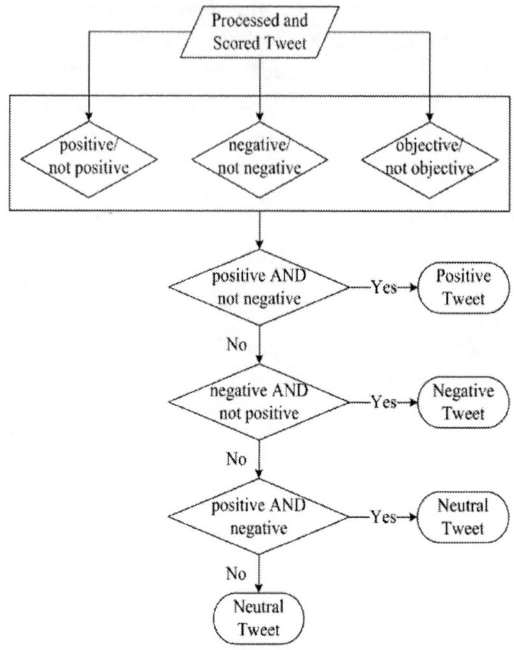

Figure 3. Three-way ensemble decision trees sentiment classifier.

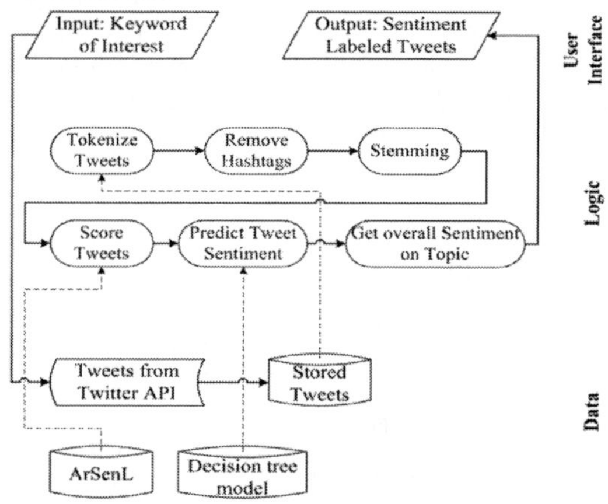

Figure 4. A 3-tier architecture of the mobile application.

3.4.3 User Interface Displaying Results

3.4.3.1 Detailed Tweets View

The fetched tweets are processed and labeled as positive, negative or objective as described. The tweets are displayed to the user and colored according to their sentiment label: green color for positive sentiments, red color for negative opinions and gray color for objective tweets. A snapshot of the interface is shown in Figure 5, showing classified tweets for the topic "لبنان" (Lebanon). These tweets reflect the latest tweets available on Twitter.

3.4.3.2 Summary Charts

Instead of looking at each tweet separately, a summary overview on the sentiments towards a specific topic can be accessed through the visual summaries available in the application. A pie chart is used to visualize the summary of the recently analyzed tweets, showing the distribution of the sentiment labels with the three colors green, red and gray. A sample snapshot of the visualization is shown in Figure 6.

Tweet	لبنان بلد جميل(Lebanon is a beautiful country)		
Tokens	جميل	بلد	لبنان
Stems	جمل	بلد	لبن
Scores (Positive, Negative, Objective)	0.75,0,0.25	0,0,1	0,0,1
Positive/Not Positive	Positive		
Negative/Not Negative	Not Negative		
Objective/Not Objective	Objective		
Final Classification	Positive		

Table 1. Example of a processed and classified tweet.

3.4.3.3 Most Hashtag Used

Since hashtags are essential features in tweets and are usually highly correlated with the topic of the tweet, the design of the application allows the user to see the most used hashtags corresponding to the searched topic. A snapshot of this view in the application is shown in Figure 7.

3.4.3.4 History Fragments

Another important feature in the application is the availability of the history track. This option allows the user to keep track of the evolution of sentiment distributions regarding a specific topic through time. A snapshot reflecting the history fragment is shown in Figure 8.

4 Evaluation

In this section we evaluate three items: the sentiment model developed for identifying the sentiments of Arabic tweets, and the mobile application performance.

4.1 Accuracy of Sentiment Model

As described in section 3, an ensemble model is used to assess the sentiment of the tweet using three decision trees. The model was developed using WEKA data mining tool. The features of the model were the sums of the three sentiment scores per tweet. The dataset which consists of 2300 manually annotated Arabic Tweets (~30k words) is utilized (Mourad and Darwish, 2013) to train the model and construct the trees. The model was optimized with custom rules to achieve a high accuracy in prediction. A 5-fold cross validation was used to evaluate the developed sentiment model. Accuracy measure is used to evaluate the system. Each classifier is evaluated separately and trained using the same number of tweets per class to avoid any bias or over fit in the model. The results are shown in Table 2.

Figure 5. Snapshot of analyzed tweet on "لبنان" Lebanon topic.

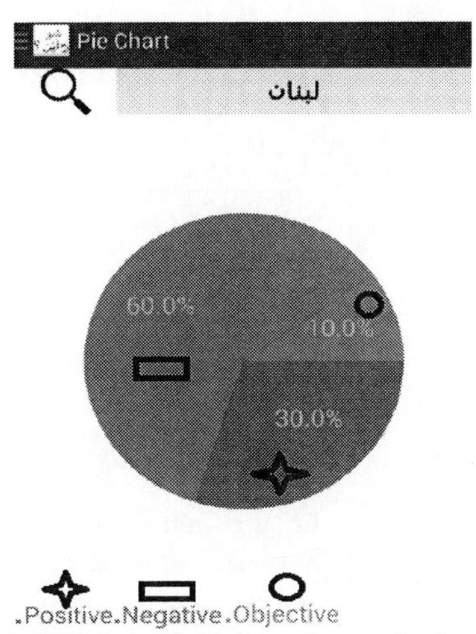

Figure 6. Snapshot of quick summary pie chart of sentiment distributions for the topic "لبنان" Lebanon.

Figure 7. Most occurring hashtags for the topic "لبنان" Lebanon.

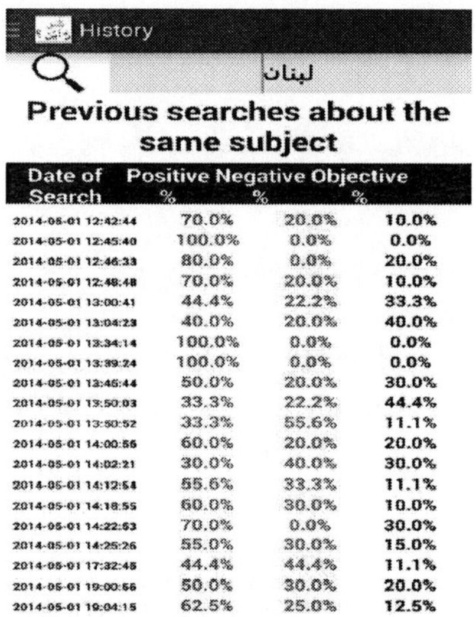

Figure 8. History scores displayed by date of search for the topic "لبنان" Lebanon.

Model	Accuracy (%)
Positive/Not Positive	61.2
Negative/Not Negative	72.9
Objective/Not Objective	67.8
Full System	67.3

Table 2. Accuracy percentages for each classifier and for the full system.

An average accuracy of 67.33% was achieved for the full system.

4.2 Mobile Application Performance

The performance of the application was also evaluated. At first 20 tweets were being retrieved and processed but the response time was relatively long. Hence, we made the application fetch 10 tweets at a time. More tweets can be retrieved by pressing on the "Show More" button as seen in Figure 5. All other processing and computations were done using mobile resources. In this way, we achieved our target of creating a sentiment mining application fully runnable on mobile. Moreover, the user interface of the application has been updated several times to optimize performance and user-friendliness based on users' feedback.

5 Conclusion

We presented in this paper a light lexicon-based mobile application for sentiment mining of Arabic Tweets. A 3-tier architecture was designed to classify tweets as positive, negative or objective. The mobile application was designed to minimize energy consumption of the mobile by having an algorithm with minimal computational needs and no remote communication for computation. As an essential resource for the development of the mobile application, a stemmed version of ArSenL was generated. Different visualizations options are presented to the user. An ensemble classifier was developed based on manually annotated corpus of Arabic tweets and an average accuracy of 67.3% was achieved for sentiment classification through the mobile application. As future work, we consider enhancing the processing by integrating further intelligence in the classification model to retrieve negations. We are also considering developing the application for other mobile platforms.

6 Acknowledgments

This work was made possible by NPRP 6-716-1-138 grant from the Qatar National Research Fund (a member of Qatar Foundation). The statements made herein are solely the responsibility of the authors.

Reference

Abdul-Mageed, M., Diab, M. and Korayem, M. (2011). Subjectivity and sentiment analysis of modern standard Arabic. In *Proceedings of the 49th Annual Meeting of the Association for Computation Linguistics: Human Language Technologies: short papers*- Volume2. Association for Computational Linguistics.

Abdul-Mageed, M., & Diab, M. (2012). Toward building a large-scale Arabic sentiment lexicon. In *Proceedings of the 6th International Global WordNet Conference* (pp. 18-22).

Abdul-Mageed, M., & Diab, M. (2014). SANA: A Large Scale Multi-Genre, Multi-Dialect Lexicon for Arabic Subjectivity and Sentiment Analysis. *In Proceedings of the Language Resources and Evaluation Conference (LREC)*. Reykjavik, Iceland.

Alhazmi, S., Black, W., & McNaught, J. (2013). Arabic SentiWordNet in Relation to SentiWordNet 3.0. *2180-1266*, 4(1), 1-11.

Aly, M. A., & Atiya, A. F. (2013, August). LABR: A Large Scale Arabic Book Reviews Dataset. *In ACL* (2) (pp. 494-498).

AraMorph. (n.d.). Retrieved May 19, 2015, from http://sourceforge.net/projects/aramorph/

Baccianella, S., Esuli, A., & Sebastiani, F. (2010, May). SentiWordNet 3.0: An Enhanced Lexical Resource for Sentiment Analysis and Opinion Mining. In *LREC* (Vol. 10, pp. 2200-2204).

Badaro, G., Baly, R., Hajj, H., Habash, N., & El-Hajj, W. (2014). A Large Scale Arabic Sentiment Lexicon for Arabic Opinion Mining. *ANLP 2014*, 165.

Black, W., Elkateb, S., & Vossen, P. (2006). Introducing the Arabic wordnet project. In *Proceedings of the third International WordNet Conference (GWC-06)*.

Davidov, D., Tsur, O., & Rappoport, A. (2010, August). Enhanced sentiment learning using twitter hashtags and smileys. In *Proceedings of the 23rd International Conference on Computational Linguistics: Posters* (pp. 241-249). Association for Computational Linguistics.

Denecke, K. (2008, April). Using sentiwordnet for multilingual sentiment analysis. In *Data Engineering Workshop, 2008. ICDEW 2008. IEEE 24th International Conference* on (pp. 507-512). IEEE

Elarnaoty, M., AbdelRahman, S., & Fahmy, A. (2012). A Machine Learning Approach for Opinion Holder Extraction in Arabic Language. *International Journal of Artificial Intelligence & Applications*, 3(2).

El-Beltagy, S. R., & Ali, A. (2013, March). Open issues in the sentiment analysis of Arabic social media: A case study. *In Innovations in Information Technology (IIT), 2013 9th International Conference* on (pp. 215-220). IEEE.

El-Halees, A. (2011). Arabic opinion mining using combined classification approach.

Esuli, A., & Sebastiani, F. (2005). Determining the semantic orientation of terms through gloss classification. In *Proceedings of the 14th ACM international conference on Information and knowledge management* (pp. 617-624). ACM.

Esuli, A., & Sebastiani, F. (2006). Sentiwordnet: A publicly available lexical resource for opinion mining. In *Proceedings of LREC* (Vol. 6. pp. 417-422).

Feldman, R. (2013). Techniques and applications for sentiment analysis. *Communications of the ACM*, 56(4), 82-89.

Graff, D., Maamouri, M., Bouziri, B., Krouna, S., Kulick, S., & Buckwalter, T. (2009). Standard Arabic Morphological Analyzer (SAMA) Version 3.1, 2009. Linguistic Data Consortium LDC2009E73.

Habash, Nizar. Introduction to Arabic Natural Language Processing, Synthesis Lectures on Human Language Technologies, Graeme Hirst, editor. Morgan & Claypool Publishers., 2010.

Khoja, S., & Garside, R. (1999). Stemming arabic text. Lancaster, UK, Computing Department, Lancaster University.

Mourad, A., & Darwish, K. (2013, June). Subjectivity and sentiment analysis of modern standard Arabic and Arabic microblogs. In Proceedings of the 4th Workshop on Computational Approaches to Subjectivity, Sentiment and Social Media Analysis (pp. 55-64).

Mukherjee, S., Malu, A., AR, B., & Bhattacharyya, P. (2012, October). TwiSent: a multistage system for analyzing sentiment in twitter. *In Proceedings of the 21st ACM international conference on Information and knowledge management* (pp. 2531-2534). ACM.

Ohana, B., & Tierney, B. (2009, October). Sentiment Classification of reviews using SentiWordNet. In *9th. IT & T Conference* (p.13).

Pasha, Arfath, Mohamed Al-Badrashiny, Mona Diab, Ahmed El Kholy, Ramy Eskander, Nizar Habash, Manoj Pooleery, Owen Rambow and Ryan M. Roth. MADAMIRA: A Fast, Comprehensive Tool for Morphological Analysis and Disambiguation of Arabic. In Proceedings of the Language Resources and Evaluation Conference (LREC), Reykjavik, Iceland, 2014.

Radcliffe, D. (2013). Twitter takes off in Saudi – and other news of social media in the Arab world. *British Broadcasting Corporation*.

Taboada, M., Brooke, J., Tofiloski, M., Voll, K., & Stede, M. (2011). Lexicon-based methods for sentiment analysis. *Computational linguistics*, 37(2), 267-307.

The Second QALB Shared Task on Automatic Text Correction for Arabic

Alla Rozovskaya[1], Houda Bouamor[2], Nizar Habash[3], Wajdi Zaghouani[2], Ossama Obeid[2] and Behrang Mohit[4]

[1]Center for Computational Learning Systems, Columbia University
[2]Carnegie Mellon University in Qatar
[3]New York University Abu Dhabi
[4]Ask.com

alla@ccls.columbia.edu, hbouamor@qatar.cmu.edu, nizar.habash@nyu.edu
wajdiz@qatar.cmu.edu, owo@qatar.cmu.edu, behrang@cmu.edu

Abstract

We present a summary of QALB-2015, the second shared task on automatic text correction of Arabic texts. The shared task extends QALB-2014, which focused on correcting errors in Arabic texts produced by native speakers of Arabic. The competition this year, in addition to native data, includes texts produced by learners of Arabic as a foreign language. The report includes an overview of the QALB corpus, which is the dataset used for training and evaluation, an overview of participating systems, results of the competition and an analysis of the results and systems.

1 Introduction

The task of text correction has recently been attracting a lot of attention in the Natural Language Processing (NLP) community, but most of the effort in this area concentrated on English, especially on errors made by learners of English as a Second Language. Four competitions devoted to error correction for non-native English writers took place recently: HOO (Dale and Kilgarriff, 2011; Dale et al., 2012) and CoNLL (Ng et al., 2013; Ng et al., 2014). Shared tasks of this kind are extremely important, as they bring together researchers and promote the development of relevant techniques and dissemination of key resources, such as benchmark data sets.

In the area of Arabic text correction, there has been a significant body of work, as well (Shaalan et al., 2003; Hassan et al., 2008). However, due to the lack of a common benchmark data set, making progress on this task has been difficult. The QALB shared task on automatic text correction of Arabic, organized within the framework of the Qatar Arabic Language Bank (QALB) project,[1] is the first effort aimed at constructing a benchmark data set, which will allow for development and evaluation of automatic correction systems for Arabic.

In this paper, we present a summary of the second edition of the QALB competition. The first one – QALB-2014 (Mohit et al., 2014) – took place in conjunction with the Arabic NLP workshop at EMNLP-2014 and focused on errors found in online commentaries produced by native speakers of Arabic. QALB-2014 attracted a lot of attention and resulted in nine systems being submitted with a variety of approaches that included rule-based frameworks, machine-learning classifiers, and statistical machine translation methods. This year's competition extends the first edition by adding another track that focuses on errors found in essays written by learners of Arabic.

Eight teams participated in the competition this year, including several participants from last year who submitted improved systems for the native track. The non-native (L2) track also allowed the participants to determine to what extent their approaches need to be modified to adapt to a new set of errors. Overall, QALB-2015 generated a diverse set of approaches for automatic text correction of Arabic.

The rest of the paper is organized as follows. In Section 2, we present the shared task framework. This is followed by an overview of the QALB corpus (Section 3). Section 4 describes the shared task data, and Section 5 presents the approaches adopted by the participating teams. Section 6 discusses the results of the competition. Section 7 concludes the paper.

[1] http://nlp.qatar.cmu.edu/qalb/

Proceedings of the Second Workshop on Arabic Natural Language Processing, pages 26–35,
Beijing, China, July 26-31, 2015.

2 Task Description

The QALB-2015 shared task extends QALB-2014, the first shared task on Arabic text correction that was created as a forum for competition and collaboration on automatic error correction in Modern Standard Arabic and took place in conjunction with the Arabic NLP workshop at EMNLP-2014 (Mohit et al., 2014).

QALB-2014 addressed errors in online user comments written to Aljazeera articles by native Arabic speakers. This year's competition includes two tracks – native and non-native. In addition to the Aljazeera commentaries written by native speakers, it also includes texts produced by learners of Arabic as a foreign language (L2).

Both the native and the non-native data is written in Modern Standard Arabic and is part of the *QALB corpus* (see Section 3), a manually-corrected collection of Arabic texts. The Aljazeera section of the corpus is presented in Zaghouani et al. (2014). The L2 data is extracted from two learner corpora of Arabic – the Arabic Learners Written Corpus (ALWC) (Farwaneh and Tamimi, 2012) and the Arabic Learner Corpus (ALC) (Alfaifi and Atwell, 2012). For details about the L2 data, we refer the reader to Zaghouani et al. (2015a).

The shared task participants were provided with training and development data to build their systems, but were also free to make use of additional resources, including corpora, linguistic resources, and software, as long as these were publicly available.

For evaluation, a standard framework developed for similar error correction competitions in English and that we also used last year has been adopted: system outputs are compared against gold annotations using *Precision*, *Recall* and F_1. Systems are ranked based on the F_1 scores obtained on the test sets.

3 The QALB Corpus

The QALB corpus was created as part of the QALB project. One of the goals of the QALB project is to develop a large manually corrected corpus for a variety of Arabic texts, including texts produced by native and non-native writers, as well as machine translation output. Within the framework of this project, comprehensive annotation guidelines and a specialized web-based annotation interface have been developed (Zaghouani et al., 2014; Obeid et al., 2013; Zaghouani et al., 2015a).

The texts are manually annotated for errors by native Arabic speakers. The annotation begins with an initial automatic pre-processing step. Next, the files are processed with the morphological analysis and disambiguation system MADAMIRA (Pasha et al., 2014) that corrects a common class of spelling errors. The files are then assigned to a team of trained human annotators who were instructed to correct all errors in the input.

The errors include spelling, punctuation, word choice, morphology, syntax, and dialectal usage. However, it should be stressed that the error classification was only used for guiding the annotation process; the annotators were not instructed to mark the type of error but only needed to specify an appropriate correction.

Once the annotation was complete, the corrections were automatically grouped into the following seven *action categories* based on the *action* required to correct the error: {*Edit, Add, Merge, Split, Delete, Move, Other*}.[2]

Table 1 presents a sample Arabic news comment along with its manually corrected form, its romanized transliteration,[3] and the English translation. The errors in the original and the corrected forms are underlined and co-indexed. Table 2 presents a subset of the errors for the example shown in Table 1 along with the error types and annotation actions. The Appendix at the end of the paper lists **all** annotation actions for that example.[4]

Essays written by L2 speakers differ from the native texts both because of the genre and the types of mistakes. For this reason, the general QALB L1 annotation guidelines were extended by adding new rules describing the error correction procedure in texts produced by L2 speakers (Zaghouani et al., 2015a). Because the genres are different, the writing styles exhibit different distributions of words, phrases, and structures. Further, while native texts mostly contain orthographic and punctuation mistakes, non-native writings also reveal lexical choice errors, missing and extraneous words (e.g. articles, prepositions), and mistakes in word

[2] In the shared task, we specified two *Add* categories: *add_before* and *add_after*. Most of the add errors fall into the first category, and we combine these here into a single *Add* category.

[3] Arabic transliteration is presented in the Habash-Soudi-Buckwalter scheme (Habash et al., 2007): (in alphabetical order) *AbtθjHxdðrzsšSDTĎςγfqklmnhwy* and the additional symbols: ’ ء, Â أ, Ǎ إ, Ā آ, ŵ ؤ, ŷ ئ, ħ ة, ý ى.

[4] Tables 1 and 2, and the appendix are reproduced from Mohit et al. (2014) to help explain the format of the files used in QALB-2014 and QALB-2015 shared task evaluations.

Original	Corrected
لا تتصوروا مدي سعادتي عند قرائة هذة التحليلات الرائعة و المحترمة لأاني شاب و كنت بتمني من الله ان أؤدي العمرة مرورا بالمسجد الاقصي و كان يبدوا ان هذا بعيد المنال فكل ما في حد يسمع الامنية كان بيقول انك ممكن تتمني ان أحفاد أحفادك يحققوهالأن امنيتك مستحيلة.	لا تتصوروا مدى سعادتي عند قراءة هذه التحليلات الرائعة والمحترمة. لأنني شاب وكنت أتمنى من الله أن أؤدي العمرة مرورا بالمسجد الأقصى، وكان يبدو أن هذا بعيد المنال، فكل واحد يسمع الأمنية كان يقول أنك ممكن أن تتمنى أن أحفاد أحفادك يحققوها لأن أمنيتك مستحيلة.
lA ttSwrwA mdy[1] sςAdty ςnd qrAŷħ[2] hðħ[3] AltHlylAt AlrAŷςħ w AlmHtrmħ[4] lÂAny[6] šAb w knt[7] btmny[8] mn Allh An[9] Âŵdy Alςmrħ mrwrA bAlmsjd AlAqSy[10] w kAn[12] ybdwA[13] An[14] hðA bςyd AlmnAl fkl mA[16] fy[17] Hd[18] ysmς AlAmnyħ[19] kAn byqwl[20] Ank[21] mmkn ttmny[23] An[24] ÂHfAd ÂHfAdk yHqqwhAlÂn[25] Amnytk[26] mstHylħ.	lA ttSwrwA mdý[1] sςAdty ςnd qrA'ħ[2] hðh[3] AltHlylAt AlrAŷςħ wAlmHtrmħ[4].[5] lÂnny[6] šAb wknt[7] Âtmný[8] mn Allh Ân[9] Âŵdy Alςmrħ mrwrA bAlmsjd AlÂqSý[10],[11] wkAn[12] ybdw[13] Ân[14] hðA bςyd AlmnAl,[15] fkl wAHd[18] ysmς AlÂmnyħ[19] kAn yqwl[20] Ânk[21] mmkn Ân[22] ttmný[23] Ân[24] ÂHfAd ÂHfAdk yHqqwhA lÂn[25] Âmnytk[26] mstHylħ.

Translation

You cannot imagine the extent of my happiness when I read these wonderful and respectful analyses because I am a young man and I wish from God to perform Umrah passing through the Al-Aqsa Mosque; and it seemed that this was elusive that when anyone heard the wish, he would say that you can wish that your great grandchildren may achieve it because your wish is impossible.

Table 1: A sample of an original (erroneous) text along with its manual correction and English translation. The indices in the table are linked with those in Table 2 and the Appendix.

#	Error	Correction	Error Type	Correction Action
#1	مدي mdy	مدى mdý	Spelling	Edit
#6	لأاني lÂAny	لأنني lÂnny	Spelling	Edit
#8	بتمني btmny	أتمنى Âtmný	Dialectal	Edit
#11	*Missing Comma*	،	Punctuation	Add_before
#12	و كان w kAn	وكان wkAn	Spelling	Merge
#13	يبدوا ybdwA	يبدو ybdw	Morphology	Edit
#25	يحققوهالأن yHqqwhAlÂn	يحققوها لأن yHqqwhA lÂn	Spelling	Split

Table 2: Error type and correction action for seven examples extracted from the sentence pair in Table 1. The indices are linked to those in Table 1 and the Appendix.

order, as shown in Table 3. Finally, even when a sentence written by a non-native writer does not contain obvious mistakes, it often still does not sound fluent to a native speaker.

4 Shared Task Data

To develop their systems, participants were provided with training and development data three months prior to the release of the blind test sets. For the native (*Aljazeera*) track, the participants used the data sets from QALB-2014. We refer to these data sets as *Alj-train-2014*, *Alj-dev-2014*, and *Alj-test-2014*. The L2 track includes *L2-train-2015* and *L2-dev-2015*. The systems were evaluated on blind test sets *Alj-test-2015* and *L2-test-2015*.

Both for the native and L2 data, we ensured that sentences from the same comment or essay belonged to the same set, i.e. training, development, or test. Furthermore, Aljazeera comments belonging to the same article were included only in one of the shared task subsets (i.e., training, development or test). The commentaries were also split by the annotation time.

Similar to QALB-2014, the data was made available to the participants in three versions:

Error	الدينة الدينة منوره جميل جدا جوه *Almdynħ* ***Almdynħ mnwrh*** *jmyl jdA* ***jwh***
Edit	الدينة المنورة جميل جدا جوها *Almdynħ* ***Almnwrħ*** *jmyl jdA* ***jwhA***
English	The Madinah Munawwarah's atmosphere is very beautiful

Table 3: Example of three errors shown in bold and described in order. The word الدينة *Almdynħ* is repeated and should be removed. The word منوره *mnwrh* is missing the definite article ال *Al* at the beginning of the word and the Ta-Marbuta ة *ħ* is confused with the letter Ha ه *h*. The correct word should be المنورة *Almnwrħ*. Finally, there is a possessive pronoun agreement error in the word جوه *jwh* and it should be spelled جوها *jwhA* instead.

Data	**Error type (%)**						
	Edit	**Add**	**Merge**	**Split**	**Delete**	**Move**	**Other**
Alj-train-2014	55.3	32.4	5.9	3.5	2.2	0.1	0.5
Alj-dev-2014	53.5	34.2	5.0	3.7	2.0	0.1	0.5
Alj-test-2014	51.9	34.7	5.9	3.5	3.3	0.2	0.5
Alj-test-2015	51.9	34.7	5.9	3.5	3.3	0.2	0.5
L2-train-2015	60.7	27.2	5.0	1.9	4.4	<1	-
L2-dev-2015	60.8	26.9	5.2	1.5	4.4	1.4	-
L2-test-2015	60.3	27.5	5.2	1.5	4.6	1.1	-

Table 5: Distribution of annotations by type in the shared task data. Error types denotes the action required in order to correct the error.

Data set	**# of words**	**# of corrections**
Alj-train-2014	1M	306K
Alj-dev-2014	54K	16K
Alj-test-2014	51K	16K
Alj-test-2015	49K	13K
L2-train-2015	43K	13.2K
L2-dev-2015	25K	7.3K
L2-test-2015	23K	6.6K

Table 4: Statistics on the shared task data.

(1) plain text, one document per line; (2) text with annotations specifying errors and the corresponding corrections; (3) feature files specifying morphological information obtained by running MADAMIRA, a tool for morphological analysis and disambiguation of Modern Standard Arabic (Pasha et al., 2014). MADAMIRA performs morphological analysis and contextual disambiguation. Using the output of MADAMIRA, we generated for each word thirty-three features. The features specify various properties: the part-of-speech (POS), lemma, aspect, person, gender, number, and so on.

Among its features, MADAMIRA generates normalization forms and as a result corrects a large subset of a special class of spelling mistakes in words containing the letters *Alif* and final *Ya*. These letters are a source of the most common spelling types of spelling errors in Arabic and involve *Hamzated Alifs* and *Alif-Maqsura/Ya* confusion (Habash, 2010; El Kholy and Habash, 2012). We refer to these errors as *Alif/Ya* errors (see also Section 6). Several participants this year and in QALB-2014 (e.g. Rozovskaya et al. (2014)) used MADAMIRA predictions as part of their systems. We show the performance of the MADAMIRA baseline in Sec. 6.

Table 4 presents statistics on the shared task data for native and non-native tracks separately. Table 5 shows the distribution of annotations by the action type. The majority of corrections (over 50%) belong to the type *Edit*. This is followed by mistakes that require an insertion of missing word or punctuation (about a third of all errors). With respect to the differences between Aljazeera and L2 data, note that the L2 data has a higher percentage of corrections of type *Edit* but fewer additions of missing words. This could be explained by the fact that a large percentage of Aljazeera errors (over 40%) involve missing punctuation. In addition to this difference, there are almost twice as many deletions and five time more moves in the L2 data, which could be due to grammatical errors that are not typical for native speakers.

Team Name		Affiliation
ARIB	(AlShenaifi et al., 2015)	King Saud University (Saudi Arabia)
CUFE	(Nawar, 2015)	Cairo University (Egypt)
GWU	(Attia et al., 2015)	George Washington University (USA)
QCMUQ	(Bouamor et al., 2015)	Carnegie Mellon University in Qatar (Qatar) and Qatar Computing Research Institute (Qatar)
QCRI	(Mubarak et al., 2015)	Qatar Computing Research Institute (Qatar)
SAHSOH	(Zaghouani et al., 2015b)	Bouira University (Algeria) and Carnegie Mellon University in Qatar (Qatar)
TECH	(Mostefa et al., 2015)	Techlimed.com (France)
UMMU	(Bougares and Bouamor, 2015)	Laboratoire d'Informatique de l'Université du Maine (France) and Carnegie Mellon University in Qatar (Qatar)

Table 6: List of teams that participated in the shared task.

Team	Approach	External Resources
ARIB	Corrections proposed by MADAMIRA; rules; levenshtein distance for spelling correction; Probabilistic-Based Spelling Correction; autocorrect Ghaltawi; Punctuation module	KSU corpus of classical Arabic; Open Source Arabic Corpora; Al Sulaiti Corpus; KACST Arabic Corpus; KHAWAS tool; autocorrect Ghaltawi
CUFE	Rules extracted from the Buckwalter morphological analyser; their probabilities are learned using the training data	Buckwalter morphological analyzer Version 2.0 (Buckwalter, 2004)
GWU	A CRF model for punctuation errors; a dictionary, probabilistic candidate generation, and a language model for spelling and grammar errors; regular expressions and normalization rules	AraComLex Extended dictionary (Attia et al., 2012); Arabic Gigaword Fourth Edition (Parker et al., 2009)
QCMUQ	Rule-based techniques; MADAMIRA corrections; SMT; language models; finite-state automata	AraComLex dictionary (Attia et al., 2012);Arabic Gigaword Fourth Edition (Parker et al., 2009); news commentary corpus
QCRI	Case-specific correction module; language model	Aljazeera articles
TECH	(1) Rule-based system using Hunspell (2) Hybrid system: Statistical MT with Madamira and rules	Newspaper articles from Open Source Arabic Corpora; other corpora collected online; Hunspell
SAHSOH	Rules, regular expressions, Ghaltawi	Arabic word list; JRC-Names; Alfaifi L1 and L2 corpus; Hunspell; Ayaspell dictionary; Ghalatawi; AkhtaBot script
UMMU	MADAMIRA corrections; word-level SMT and character-level SMT systems	Native Arabic data

Table 7: Approaches adopted by the participating teams.

5 Participants and Approaches

Eight teams participated in the shared task. Table 6 presents the list of participating institutions and their names in the shared task. Each team was allowed to submit up to three outputs. Overall, we received 12 outputs for the native track and 10 outputs for the non-native track (one of the teams – TECH – did not participate in the non-native track).

The submitted systems included a diverse set of approaches that incorporated rule-based frameworks, statistical machine translation and machine-learning models, as well as hybrid systems. The teams that scored at the top employed hybrid methods by combining a variety of techniques. For example, the CUFE system extracted rules from the morphological analyzer and learned their probabilities using the training data, while the UMMU system combined statistical machine-translation with MADAMIRA corrections. Table 7 summarizes the approaches adopted by each team.

6 Results

In this section, we present the results of the competition. As was done in QALB-2014, we adopted the standard Precision (P), Recall (R), and F_1 metric. This metric was also used in recent shared tasks on grammatical error correction in English: HOO competitions (Dale and Kilgarriff, 2011; Dale et al., 2012) and CoNLL (Ng et al., 2013). The results are computed using the M2 scorer (Dahlmeier and Ng, 2012) that was also used in the CoNLL shared tasks.

Tables 8 and 9 present the official results of the evaluation on the test sets for the Aljazeera data and the L2 data, respectively. The results are sorted according to the F_1 scores obtained by the

Rank	Team	P	R	F_1
1	CUFE	88.85	61.76	**72.87**
2	UMMU-1	70.28	71.93	71.10
3	GWU	74.69	67.51	70.92
4	UMMU-2	72.69	67.52	70.01
5	QCRI	84.74	58.10	68.94
6	QCMUQ	71.39	65.13	68.12
7	TECH-2	71.20	64.94	67.93
8	TECH-1	71.08	64.74	67.76
9	TECH-3	69.99	60.41	64.85
10	ARIB-1	64.50	56.50	60.23
11	ARIB-2	67.56	51.61	58.52
12	SAHSOH	81.88	40.24	53.97
	MADAMIRA	80.32	39.98	53.39

Table 8: Official results on the test set (Alj-test-2015). Column 1 shows the system rank according to the F_1 score. MADAMIRA refers to the *baseline* of applying corrections proposed by MADAMIRA.

Rank	Team	P	R	F_1
1	UMMU-1	54.12	33.26	**41.20**
2	QCMUQ	50.37	31.68	38.90
3	UMMU-2	55.83	29.47	38.58
4	CUFE	70.92	23.85	35.69
5	GWU	55.66	23.32	32.87
6	ARIB-3	48.79	24.57	32.68
7	ARIB-2	50.08	22.30	30.86
8	QCRI-1	45.86	20.16	28.01
9	QCRI-2	54.87	17.63	26.69
10	SAHSOH	59.75	15.90	25.12
	MADAMIRA	45.24	13.09	20.30

Table 9: Official results on the test set (L2-test-2015). Column 1 shows the system rank according to the F_1 score. Column 1 shows the system rank according to the F_1 score. MADAMIRA refers to the *baseline* of applying corrections proposed by MADAMIRA.

systems. The range of the scores is quite wide – from 53 to 72 F_1 on the native data and from 25 to 41 on non-native. Observe that the performance on the non-native data is substantially lower for all of the teams. This is to be expected as non-native writers exhibit a variety of errors – spelling, grammar, word choice. In contrast, the native data contains many punctuation and spelling mistakes that can be handled by MADAMIRA and are much easier to address (see also analysis below). In fact, we used MADAMIRA as a baseline system (last row in the tables). As the results show, MADAMIRA provides quite a competitive baseline, especially on the native data. But all of the teams managed to beat this baseline, in many cases by a large margin. This suggests that even though MADAMIRA is a sophisticated system, it cannot handle all of the errors, and the participating teams developed approaches that are complementary to it.

It is interesting to compare the obtained results to those obtained on similar shared tasks on English as a Second Language (ESL) writings. While the performance on native MSA data in Table 8is better than on ESL, performance on L2 writings is quite similar. For instance, the highest score in the HOO-2011 shared task (Dale and Kilgarriff, 2011) that addressed all errors was 21.1 (Rozovskaya et al., 2011); the highest performance in the CoNLL-2013 shared task that also used the same evaluation metric was 31.20 (Rozovskaya et al., 2013).[5]

In addition to providing the official rankings, we also analyze system performance for different types of mistakes by automatically assigning errors to one of the following categories: punctuation errors; errors involving *Alif* and *Ya*; and all other errors. Punctuation errors account for 39% of all errors in the Aljazeera data.[6] Tables 6 and 6 show the performance of the teams in three settings: with punctuation errors removed; with *Alif/Ya* errors removed; and when both punctuation and *Alif/Ya* errors are removed. In general, both for the native and the non-native data, performance drops when the *Alif/Ya* errors are removed, which indicates that these errors may be easier. When the punctuation errors are removed, the performance on the native data improves slightly, but goes down a little on the non-native data. Overall, it can be concluded that the punctuation mistakes do not significantly affect the performance and are of the same difficulty level as the remaining of the errors.

Finally, the majority of the teams participated last year and relied on the findings from the previous round. Overall, it can be said that the participants were able to make progress and to im-

[5]This is not a fair comparison, though, since the CoNLL-2013 shared task only evaluated on 5 types of errors and ignored about 50% of all mistakes in the data. In CoNLL-2014 that evaluated on all errors the top teams scored 35-37 points but the evaluation favored precision twice as much as recall.

[6]For example, there many sentences with missing final periods; we speculate that this may be due to the fact that the data was collected online.

Team	No punc. errors			No Alif/Ya errors			No punc. No Alif/Ya errors		
	P	R	F_1	P	R	F_1	P	R	F_1
ARIB-1	73.57	59.86	66.01	49.87	44.87	47.24	54.53	38.47	45.11
CUFE	85.80	77.98	81.70	84.25	43.29	57.19	80.12	58.24	**67.45**
GWU	81.12	76.60	78.79	61.15	52.32	56.39	67.80	54.86	60.65
QCMUQ	75.89	76.29	76.09	56.45	48.73	52.31	59.05	54.77	56.83
QCRI	81.28	75.62	78.35	75.90	36.52	49.31	69.78	51.68	59.38
SAHSOH	83.85	55.65	66.90	71.44	24.78	36.79	79.86	41.45	54.57
TECH-2	81.90	70.74	75.91	54.82	46.40	50.26	65.77	39.53	49.38
UMMU-1	82.98	80.98	**81.97**	56.46	58.09	**57.26**	73.09	61.44	66.76

Table 10: **Alj-test-2015**: Results on the test set in different settings: with punctuation errors removed from evaluation; normalization errors removed; and when both punctuation and normalization errors are removed. Only the best output from each team is shown.

Team	No punc. errors			No Alif/Ya errors			No punc. No Alif/Ya errors		
	P	R	F_1	P	R	F_1	P	R	F_1
ARIB-3	50.13	20.28	28.88	41.38	18.46	25.53	36.80	10.11	15.86
CUFE	65.05	28.43	39.57	65.68	16.46	26.32	58.28	17.83	27.31
GWU	54.39	22.60	31.93	45.27	15.63	23.24	38.28	10.76	16.79
QCMUQ	55.17	27.60	36.79	43.25	24.53	31.31	44.74	15.85	23.40
QCRI-1	42.71	25.82	32.18	32.88	11.46	17.00	28.51	13.51	18.34
SAHSOH	58.95	21.70	31.72	48.82	09.37	15.73	49.23	12.69	20.18
UMMU-1	57.32	30.49	**39.81**	47.45	26.15	**33.72**	48.79	18.98	**27.32**

Table 11: **L2-test-2015**: Results on the test set in different settings: with punctuation errors removed from evaluation; normalization errors removed; and when both punctuation and normalization errors are removed. Only the best output from each team is shown.

prove their systems since last year. Although direct comparison is not possible since the test sets are not the same and the test data from last year was used for development, we observe that four teams scored more than 70 F_1 points on the native data this year, while last year the best result that was obtained by the CLMB system (Rozovskaya et al., 2014) was 67.91 points. We refer the reader to the system description papers for more detail on how the respective systems have been improved.

7 Conclusion

This paper presented a report on QALB-2015, the second shared task on text correction of Arabic. QALB-2015 extended QALB-2014 that took place last year and focused on correcting texts written by native Arabic speakers. This year, we added a second track, on non-native data. We received 12 system submissions from eight teams. We are pleased with the extent of participation, the quality of results and the diversity of approaches. Many participants continued from last year and improved and extended their systems. We feel motivated to conduct new research competitions in the near future.

8 Acknowledgments

We would like to thank the organizing committee of ACL 2015 and its Arabic NLP workshop and also the shared task participants for their ideas and support. We thank Al Jazeera News (and especially, Khalid Judia) for providing the user comments portion of the QALB corpus. We also thank the QALB project annotators: Hoda Fathy, Dhoha Abid, Mariem Fekih, Anissa Jrad, Hoda Ibrahim, Noor Alzeer, Samah Lakhal, Jihene Wefi, Elsherif Mahmoud and Hossam El-Husseini. This publication was made possible by grant NPRP-4-1058-1-168 from the Qatar National Research Fund (a member of the Qatar Foundation). The statements made herein are solely the responsibility of the authors.

Appendix A: Sample annotation file

The sequence of manual corrections for the example in Table 1 is shown below.

<table>
<tr><td>#1</td><td>مدي</td><td>A 2 3|||Edit|||مدى|||REQUIRED|||-NONE-|||0</td></tr>
<tr><td>#2</td><td>قرائة</td><td>A 5 6|||Edit|||قراءة|||REQUIRED|||-NONE-|||0</td></tr>
<tr><td>#3</td><td>هذة</td><td>A 6 7|||Edit|||هذه|||REQUIRED|||-NONE-|||0</td></tr>
<tr><td>#4</td><td>و المحترمة</td><td>A 9 11|||Merge|||والمحترمة|||REQUIRED|||-NONE-|||0</td></tr>
<tr><td>#5</td><td></td><td>A 11 11|||Add_before|||.|||REQUIRED|||-NONE-|||0</td></tr>
<tr><td>#6</td><td>لأاني</td><td>A 11 12|||Edit|||لأنني|||REQUIRED|||-NONE-|||0</td></tr>
<tr><td>#7</td><td>و كنت</td><td>A 13 15|||Merge|||وكنت|||REQUIRED|||-NONE-|||0</td></tr>
<tr><td>#8</td><td>بتمني</td><td>A 15 16|||Edit|||أتمنى|||REQUIRED|||-NONE-|||0</td></tr>
<tr><td>#9</td><td>ان</td><td>A 18 19|||Edit|||أن|||REQUIRED|||-NONE-|||0</td></tr>
<tr><td>#10</td><td>الاقصي</td><td>A 23 24|||Edit|||الأقصى|||REQUIRED|||-NONE-|||0</td></tr>
<tr><td>#11</td><td></td><td>A 24 24|||Add_before|||،|||REQUIRED|||-NONE-|||0</td></tr>
<tr><td>#12</td><td>و كان</td><td>A 24 26|||Merge|||وكان|||REQUIRED|||-NONE-|||0</td></tr>
<tr><td>#13</td><td>يبدوا</td><td>A 26 27|||Edit|||يبدو|||REQUIRED|||-NONE-|||0</td></tr>
<tr><td>#14</td><td>ان</td><td>A 27 28|||Edit|||أن|||REQUIRED|||-NONE-|||0</td></tr>
<tr><td>#15</td><td></td><td>A 31 31|||Add_before|||،|||REQUIRED|||-NONE-|||0</td></tr>
<tr><td>#16</td><td>ما</td><td>A 32 33|||Delete|||||REQUIRED|||-NONE-|||0</td></tr>
<tr><td>#17</td><td>في</td><td>A 33 34|||Delete|||||REQUIRED|||-NONE-|||0</td></tr>
<tr><td>#18</td><td>حد</td><td>A 34 35|||Edit|||واحد|||REQUIRED|||-NONE-|||0</td></tr>
<tr><td>#19</td><td>الامنية</td><td>A 36 37|||Edit|||الأمنية|||REQUIRED|||-NONE-|||0</td></tr>
<tr><td>#20</td><td>بيقول</td><td>A 38 39|||Edit|||يقول|||REQUIRED|||-NONE-|||0</td></tr>
<tr><td>#21</td><td>انك</td><td>A 39 40|||Edit|||أنك|||REQUIRED|||-NONE-|||0</td></tr>
<tr><td>#22</td><td></td><td>A 41 41|||Add_before|||أن|||REQUIRED|||-NONE-|||0</td></tr>
<tr><td>#23</td><td>تتمني</td><td>A 41 42|||Edit|||تتمنى|||REQUIRED|||-NONE-|||0</td></tr>
<tr><td>#24</td><td>ان</td><td>A 42 43|||Edit|||أن|||REQUIRED|||-NONE-|||0</td></tr>
<tr><td>#25</td><td>يحققوهالأن</td><td>A 45 46|||Split|||يحققوها لأن|||REQUIRED|||-NONE-|||0</td></tr>
<tr><td>#26</td><td>امنيتك</td><td>A 46 47|||Edit|||أمنيتك|||REQUIRED|||-NONE-|||0</td></tr>
</table>

References

A. Alfaifi and E. Atwell. 2012. Arabic Learner Corpora (ALC): A Taxonomy of Coding Errors. In *The 8th International Computing Conference in Arabic*.

N. AlShenaifi, R. AlNefie, M. Al-Yahya, and H. Al-Khalifa. 2015. ARIB@QALB-2015 Shared Task: A Hybrid Cascade Model for Arabic Spelling Error Detection and Correction . In *Proceedings of ACL Workshop on Arabic Natural Language Processing*, Beijing, China, July.

M. Attia, P. Pecina, Y. Samih, K. Shaalan, and J. van Genabith. 2012. Improved Spelling Error Detection and Correction for Arabic. In *Proceedings of COLING*.

M. Attia, M. Al-Badrashiny, and M. Diab. 2015. GWU-HASP-2015: Priming Spelling Candidates with Probability . In *Proceedings of ACL Workshop on Arabic Natural Language Processing*, Beijing, China, July.

H. Bouamor, H. Sajjad, N. Durrani, and K. Oflazer. 2015. QCMUQ@QALB-2015 Shared Task: Combining Character level MT and Error-tolerant Finite-State Recognition for Arabic Spelling Correction. In *Proceedings of ACL Workshop on Arabic Natural Language Processing*, Beijing, China, July.

F. Bougares and H. Bouamor. 2015. UMMU@QALB-2015 Shared Task: Character and Word level SMT pipeline for Automatic Error Correction of Arabic Text. In *Proceedings of ACL Workshop on Arabic Natural Language Processing*, Beijing, China, July.

T. Buckwalter. 2004. Buckwalter Arabic Morphological Analyzer Version 2.0.

D. Dahlmeier and H. T. Ng. 2012. Better Evaluation for Grammatical Error Correction. In *Proceedings of NAACL*.

R. Dale and A. Kilgarriff. 2011. Helping Our Own: The HOO 2011 Pilot Shared Task. In *Proceedings of the 13th European Workshop on Natural Language Generation*.

R. Dale, I. Anisimoff, and G. Narroway. 2012. A Report on the Preposition and Determiner Error Correction Shared Task. In *Proceedings of the NAACL Workshop on Innovative Use of NLP for Building Educational Applications*.

A. El Kholy and N. Habash. 2012. Orthographic and morphological processing for English–Arabic statistical machine translation. *Machine Translation*, 26(1-2).

S. Farwaneh and M. Tamimi. 2012. Arabic Learners Written Corpus: A Resource for Research and Learning. *The Center for Educational Resources in Culture, Language and Literacy*.

N. Habash, A. Soudi, and T. Buckwalter. 2007. On Arabic Transliteration. In A. van den Bosch and A. Soudi, editors, *Arabic Computational Morphology: Knowledge-based and Empirical Methods*. Springer.

N. Habash. 2010. *Introduction to Arabic Natural Language Processing*. Morgan & Claypool Publishers.

A. Hassan, S. Noeman, and H. Hassan. 2008. Language Independent Text Correction using Finite State Automata. In *Proceedings of the Third International Joint Conference on Natural Language Processing (IJCNLP 2008)*, pages 913–918, Hyderabad, India.

B. Mohit, A. Rozovskaya, N. Habash, W. Zaghouani, and O. Obeid. 2014. The First QALB Shared Task on Automatic Text Correction for Arabic. In *Proceedings of EMNLP Workshop on Arabic Natural Language Processing*, Doha, Qatar, October.

D. Mostefa, J. Abualasal, O. Asbayou, M. Gzawi, and R. Abbès. 2015. TECHLIMED@QALB-Shared Task 2015: a hybrid Arabic Error Correction System. In *Proceedings of ACL Workshop on Arabic Natural Language Processing*, Beijing, China, July.

H. Mubarak, K. Darwish, and A. Abdelali. 2015. QCRI@QALB-2015 Shared Task: Correction of Arabic Text for Native and Non-Native Speakers' Errors . In *Proceedings of ACL Workshop on Arabic Natural Language Processing*, Beijing, China, July.

M. Nawar. 2015. QALB 2015 Shared Task: CUFE Arabic Error Correction System. In *Proceedings of ACL Workshop on Arabic Natural Language Processing*, Beijing, China, July.

H. T. Ng, S. M. Wu, Y. Wu, Ch. Hadiwinoto, and J. Tetreault. 2013. The CoNLL-2013 Shared Task on Grammatical Error Correction. In *Proceedings of CoNLL: Shared Task*.

H. T. Ng, S. M. Wu, T. Briscoe, C. Hadiwinoto, R. H. Susanto, and C. Bryant. 2014. The CoNLL-2014 Shared Task on Grammatical Error Correction. In *Proceedings of CoNLL: Shared Task*.

O. Obeid, W. Zaghouani, B. Mohit, N. Habash, K. Oflazer, and N. Tomeh. 2013. A Web-based Annotation Framework For Large-Scale Text Correction. In *The Companion Volume of the Proceedings of IJCNLP 2013: System Demonstrations*. Asian Federation of Natural Language Processing.

R. Parker, D. Graff, K. Chen, J. Kong, and K. Maeda. 2009. Arabic Gigaword Fourth Edition. LDC Catalog No.: LDC2009T30, ISBN: 1-58563-532-4.

A. Pasha, M. Al-Badrashiny, M. Diab, A. El Kholy, R. Eskander, N. Habash, M. Pooleery, O. Rambow, and R. Roth. 2014. MADAMIRA: A Fast, Comprehensive Tool for Morphological Analysis and Disambiguation of Arabic. In *Proceedings of the Ninth International Conference on Language Resources and Evaluation (LREC)*.

A. Rozovskaya, M. Sammons, J. Gioja, and D. Roth. 2011. University of Illinois System in HOO Text Correction Shared Task. In *Proceedings of the European Workshop on Natural Language Generation (ENLG)*.

A. Rozovskaya, K.-W. Chang, M. Sammons, and D. Roth. 2013. The University of Illinois System in the CoNLL-2013 Shared Task. In *Proceedings of CoNLL Shared Task*.

A. Rozovskaya, N. Habash, R. Eskander, N. Farra, and W. Salloum. 2014. The Columbia System in the QALB-2014 Shared Task on Arabic Error Correction. In *Proceedings of EMNLP Workshop on Arabic Natural Language Processing: QALB Shared Task*.

K. Shaalan, A. Allam, and A. Gomah. 2003. Towards Automatic Spell Checking for Arabic. In *Proceedings of the 4th Conference on Language Engineering, Egyptian Society of Language Engineering (ELSE)*, Cairo, Egypt.

W. Zaghouani, B. Mohit, N. Habash, O. Obeid, N. Tomeh, A. Rozovskaya, N. Farra, S. Alkuhlani, and K. Oflazer. 2014. Large Scale Arabic Error Annotation: Guidelines and Framework. In *Proceedings of the Ninth International Conference on Language Resources and Evaluation (LREC'14)*, Reykjavik, Iceland.

W. Zaghouani, N. Habash, H. Bouamor, A. Rozovskaya, Behrang B. Mohit, A. Heider, and K. Oflazer. 2015a. Correction annotation for non-native arabic texts: Guidelines and corpus. In *Proceedings of The 9th Linguistic Annotation Workshop*, pages 129–139, Denver, Colorado, USA, June. Association for Computational Linguistics.

W. Zaghouani, T. Zerrouki, and A. Balla. 2015b. SAHSOH@QALB-2015 Shared Task: A Rule-Based Correction Method of Common Arabic Native and Non-Native Speakers' Errors. In *Proceedings of ACL Workshop on Arabic Natural Language Processing*, Beijing, China, July.

Natural Language Processing for Dialectical Arabic: A Survey

Abdulhadi Shoufan
Khalifa University
Abu Dhabi, U.A.E.
abdulhadi.shoufan@kustar.ac.ae

Sumaya Al-Ameri
Khalifa University
Abu Dhabi, U.A.E.
sumaya.alameri@kustar.ac.ae

Abstract

This paper presents a wide literature review of natural language processing for dialectical Arabic. Four main research areas were identified and the dialect coverage in research work was outlined. The paper can be used as a quick reference to identify relevant contributions that address a specific NLP aspect for a specific dialect.

1 Introduction

The last ten years have experienced a growing interest in natural language processing for dialectical Arabic. This growth can be attributed to several factors including the wide usage of Arabic dialects in social media. The topics treated by computational linguists for Arabic dialects range from fundamental language aspects including morphology up to sophisticated solutions such as machine translation.

To have an overview of the research that has been done in this area we went through as many papers as possible and tried to specify the main contributions of each paper. We could identify four main categories, whereas each category has some subcategories. The main categories are basic language analyses, building language resources, semantic-level analysis and synthesis, and identifying Arabic dialects. Then, we mapped each paper to categories and subcategories as well as to the addressed dialect or dialects in a matrix form as given in Table 1. By this means, it can be easily identified what has been done in the Arabic NLP, by whom, and for what dialects.

The following four sections describe the related work in the four main categories. For space reasons, however, we limited the description to main aspects. The final section provides a brief discussion of the findings of this survey.

2 Basic Language Analyses

Several solutions have been proposed for the morphological analysis, syntactical analysis, and orthographic analysis and generation. The following three sections describe these solutions, respectively.

2.1 Morphological Analysis and POS Tagging

The morphology of dialectal Arabic had gained early attention by computational linguists. In (Habash & Rambow, 2006), a morphological analyzer and generator, denoted MAGED, was presented. This tool is able to analyze the Levantine dialect and to convert MSA to Levantine. In a later publication the authors detailed the morphophonemic and the orthographic rules encoded in MAGEAD (Habash & Rambow, 2007).

In (Habash, Eskander, & Hawwari, 2012), a morphological analyzer for Egyptian Arabic is proposed with further development in (Salloum & Habash, 2014).

In (Almeman & Lee, 2012), two morphological analyzers for Gulf, Levantine, Egyptian, North African, Sudani, and Iraqi dialects were presented. The first one relies on a MSA morphological analyzer. The second one applies word segmentation and uses web data as a corpus to produce statistical information about the frequency of different segment combinations. In (Zribi, Khemakhem, & Belguith, 2013), a morphological analyzer for the Tunisian dialect based on a MSA analyzer was proposed. Furthermore, a lexicon for the Tunisian dialect is built as an expansion of a MSA lexicon. An unsupervised approach for morphological segmentation was applied to improve machine translation from the Qatari dialect to English (Al-Mannai et al., 2014).

In (Duh & Kirchhoff, 2005), a part-of-speech tagger for Egyptian Arabic was proposed based on a morphological analyzer for MSA and a min-

Proceedings of the Second Workshop on Arabic Natural Language Processing, pages 36–48,
Beijing, China, July 26-31, 2015.

imally supervised approach that requires raw text data from several Arabic varieties.

In (Al-Sabbagh & Girju, 2012a), a function-based POS tagger is proposed that was trained on a manually-annotated Egyptian Arabic corpus.

In (Habash et al., 2013) a MSA morphological tagger is retargeted to Egyptian Arabic. The solution performs part-of-speech tagging, diacritization, lemmatization, and tokenization.

A rule-based stemmer for Arabic Gulf dialect was proposed in (Abuata & Al-Omari, 2015), and a fine-grained POS tagger for Tunisian dialect was presented in (Boujelbane et al., 2014).

2.2 Syntax and Parsing

The syntax of Arabic dialects was purely addressed in the context of computational linguistics. In (Brustad, 2000), the author presented a comparative study of Moroccan, Egyptian, Syrian, and Kuwaiti dialects with respect to syntax however without computational aspects.

In (Chiang et al., 2006) a parser for the Levantine Arabic is proposed. The parser doesn't rely on annotated Levantine corpus or a parallel Levantine-MSA corpus. Rather, the Levantine word is translated into a bag of MSA words that are scored and decoded relying on MSA corpus. The resulting text is then parsed using an MSA parser. Finally, the terminal nodes in the resulting parse structure are replaced with the original Levantine words.

Levantine was also the dialect treated in (Maamouri et al., 2006). In this work a pilot Levantine Arabic Treebank is developed by a morphological and syntactic annotation of 26,000 words of Levantine Arabic conversational telephone speech. The Treebank was used to develop and evaluate parsers for Levantine texts. Grammatical mapping rules were defined to provide language resources for machine translation from Tunisian dialect to MSA and other target languages in (Sadat, Mallek, et al., 2014).

2.3 Orthographic Analysis

In contrast to MSA, dialectical Arabic has no orthographic standard. The same word can be written in different forms. This poses difficulties to NLP tools. In (Dasigi & Diab, 2011), first steps towards normalizing Arabic dialects orthography for Levantine and Egyptian were made. For that, different similarity measures were employed that exploit string similarity and contextual semantic similarity.

In (Habash, Diab, & Rambow, 2012), a conventional orthography is proposed to help building computational models for Arabic dialects in general and Egyptian in particular. The rules and guidelines produced were named CODA.

Recently, a conventional orthography for Tunisian Arabic was proposed in (Zribi et al., 2014). Also, Several papers on the transliteration from Arabizi into Arabic orthography appeared (Bies et al., 2014), (Darwish, 2013), (Masmoudi et al., 2015). Arabizi is Arabic text written in Latin characters.

In (Zribi, Graja, et al., 2013), orthography guidelines for Tunisian dialect were presented for the purpose of transcribing a Tunisian speech corpora. The rules presented are based on the standard Arabic transcription conventions. This work was later used in (Zribi, Khemakhem, & Belguith, 2013) for morphological analysis presented in the Morphological Analysis and POS Tagging section.

3 Building Resources for Dialectal Arabic

The problem of the lack of language resources in dialectical Arabic is well known. Many researchers addressed this problem by creating lexicons, wordnets, corpora, and treebanks.

In (Zaghouani, 2014), a useful survey of freely available Arabic corpora including lexicons was presented. The author highlighted the huge lack of freely available dialectal corpora because only two resources could be identified (Graja et al., 2010), (Almeman & Lee, 2013)

In (Sansò, 2004), the MED-TYP project was presented which aimed at building a typological database for Mediterranean languages including MSA and Arabic dialects. While the researchers found out that the Mediterranean could not be identified as a linguistic area in the traditional sense, a number of significant contact phenomena were discovered.

3.1 Building Lexicons and Lexical Analysis

In (Graff et al., 2006), a lexicon for the Iraqi dialect was presented. The lexicon comprises words from recorded speech tagged with pronunciation data, morphology information, and part-of-speech. The annotation was performed manually with the aid of a user interface and supporting tools.

In (Al-Sabbagh & Girju, 2010) a lexicon for Egyptian Cairene Arabic is described. Each Cairene entry was mapped to its MSA synonym and tagged with its part-of-speech. Additionally, the entry is tagged with its top-ranked meaning according to web queries.

A spelling corrector for the Iraqi dialect was presented in (Rytting et al., 2011). An orthographic density metric is used to motivate the need for a fine-grained ranking method for candidate words.

In (Graff & Maamouri, 2012), the update of three bilingual dictionaries for English-speaking learners of Moroccan, Syrian and Iraqi Arabic was presented. The original editions of the dictionaries were developed by the Linguistic Data Consortium and Georgetown University Press in the 1960's. In the updated dictionaries, both Arabic script and International Phonetic Alphabet orthographies are used. A web interface enables searching, editing, reviewing and managing the lexicon efficiently.

In (Boujelbane et al., 2013), a Tunisian dialect text corpus as well as a method for building a bilingual dictionary are described. The target is to create a language model for a speech recognition system for the Tunisian Broadcast News.

In (Duh & Kirchhoff, 2006), a Levantine lexicon was built using transductive learning through partially annotated text. For the purpose of sentiment analysis of social networks data, a dedicated lexicon for slang sentimental words and idioms was developed in (Hedar & Doss, 2013).

In (Cavalli-Sforza et al., 2013) an Iraqi WordNet is presented based on the MSA WordNet, the English WordNet, and an English-Iraqi dictionary. A Tunisian dialect WordNet was built in (Bouchlaghem & Elkhlifi, 2014) starting from a Tunisian corpus.

3.2 Building Corpora and Treebanks

In (Al-Sabbagh & Girju, 2012b), a primary work on building a multi-genre corpus for Egyptian Arabic was described. The corpus data is compiled from Twitter, blogs, forums, and online knowledge market services. The paper addresses different aspects related to building dialectal Arabic corpora such as function-based web harvesting, dialect identification, vowel-based spelling variation, linguistic hypercorrection, unsupervised part-of-speech tagging and base phrase chunking for dialectal Arabic.

Using the web as a source was also described in (Almeman & Lee, 2013), where multi-dialect Arabic corpora were built for Gulf, Levantine, Egyptian and North African dialects. The work by Boujelbaneon et al. on building a lexicon for Tunisian dialect can be recited here due to building a corpus from Tunisian broadcast news (Boujelbane et al., 2013).

In (Cotterell & Callison-Burch, 2014), a multi-dialect, multi-genre corpus for Egyptian, Gulf, Levantine, Maghrebi, and Iraqi dialects was presented. Another multi-dialecti corpus based on twitter data was built in (Mubarak & Darwish, 2014) for seven different dialects. A preliminary work on a corpus for Palestinian dialect with 43K words was presented in (Jarrar et al., 2014). A parallel corpus for Algerian dialect and MSA was proposed in (Harrat et al., 2014) for the purpose of machine translation.

In (Maamouri et al., 2006), which was cited in Section 2.2, a pilot Levantine Arabic Treebank was presented. A conversational telephone speech with about 26,000 words was annotated with morphological and syntactic data. Recently, Maamouri et al. presented a treebank for the Egyptian Dialect (Maamouri et al., 2014).

As the quality of the annotation process is essential for building accurate language resources, some researchers payed special attention to this process. In (Diab et al., 2010), multiple systems to develop NLP resources for Arabic dialects including Levantine, Egyptian, Moroccan, and Iraqi were presented. The systems utilized MAGEAD (Habash & Rambow, 2006) as well as Buckwalter morphological analyzer and generator (BAMA) (Buckwalter, 2004). The COLABA ability to process Arabic dialects was evaluated through the COLABA information retrieval system.

A web application for annotating Egyptian, Iraqi, Levantine, and Moroccan dialects was proposed in (Benajiba & Diab, 2010). The authors follow non-functional objectives including optimizing speed, accuracy, and efficiency while maintaining the security and integrity of the data. In (Zaidan & Callison-Burch, 2011), the building of a 52M-word Arabic online commentary dataset rich in dialectal content was presented. The long-term annotation effort to identify the dialect level in each sentence was also discussed. The authors of (Elfardy & Diab, 2012b) presented a set of guidelines for detecting code switching in Arabic on the word and token levels. These guidelines were used to annotate a corpus that is rich in Egyptian, Levantine, and Iraqi dialects with frequent code switching to MSA. In (Habash et al., 2008a), guidelines for identifying the level of dialectalness of a certain text were presented. Three levels for dialectalness were proposed: MSA with non-standard orthography, MSA words with dialect morphology, and a Dialectal lexeme.

In (Hawwari et al., 2014), a framework for classifying and annotating Egyptian multi-word expressions in a specialized computational lexicon was proposed. A graphical tool for annotating Moroccan tweets was presented in (Tratz et al., 2013).

In (Zaghouani et al., 2014), comprehensive guidelines for annotating an Arabic corpus including Qatar dialect was proposed. The corpus is denoted Qatar Arabic Language Bank (QALB). A special attention in this work is paid to the manual correction which should provide training data for learning-based Arabic error correction tools.

4 Semantic-Level Analysis and Synthesis

Most work in this area relates to machine translation from or to Arabic dialects. Some papers treat other tasks such as information retrieval and sentiment analysis.

4.1 Machine Translation

In (Bakr et al., 2008), the authors proposed a hybrid approach to convert an Egyptian sentence into its corresponding diacritized MSA. The approach is generic, i.e., it can be extended to other Arabic dialects. Some techniques for lexical acquisition of colloquial words are developed.

In (Sawaf, 2010), a hybrid machine translation system was extended to handle Arabic dialects from 15 regions including Northern Iraq, Baghdad, Southern Iraq, Saudi-Arabia, Southern Arabic Peninsula, Egypt, Sudan, Libya, Morocco, Tunisia, Lebanon, North Syria, Damascus, Palestine and Jordan. A decoding algorithm was developed to normalize non-standard, spontaneous and dialectal Arabic into Modern Standard Arabic.

In (Salloum & Habash, 2011), the quality of Arabic-English statistical machine translation was improved to deal with Levantine and Egyptian dialects using morphological knowledge. A simple rule-based approach was used to generate MSA paraphrases for dialectal Arabic out-of-vocabulary words and low frequency words.

In (Zbib et al., 2012), crowdsourcing was applied to build Levantine-English and Egyptian-English parallel corpora, consisting of 1.1M words and 380k words, respectively. The dialectal sentences were selected from a large corpus of Arabic web text, and translated using Amazon's Mechanical Turk. The data was used to build dialectal machine translation systems.

In (Jehl et al., 2012), the authors collected bilingual sentence pairs for training statistical machine translation systems to translate microblog messages. The paper addressed the Gulf, Levantine, and Egyptian dialects as well as MSA. The technique presented was found to perform better than other methods such as techniques based on extracting phrases from similar text.

In (Al-Gaphari & Al-Yadoumi, 2012) an algorithm was proposed that normalizes Sanaáni dialect to MSA based on morphological rules. Input text was tokenized and each token was analyzed into stem and affixes. The stem and the affixes can be either dialect-specific, MSA-specific, or both. For each morphological rule the algorithm checks the possibility of applying such a rule.

In (Salloum & Habash, 2012), a rule-based approach for machine translation from Arabic dialects to MSA was presented. The approach relies on morphological analysis, morphological transfer rules and dictionaries in addition to language models to produce MSA paraphrases of dialectal sentences. The treated dialects are Levantine, Egyptian, Iraqi, and Gulf Arabic.

In (Mohamed et al., 2012), a translator from MSA to the Egyptian dialect was presented. Among others, this process helps in the annotation of the Egyptian dialect and in the translation from this dialect to English.

In (Soltau et al., 2011), a corpus-based translator from MSA to Levantine was described. The translator is trained on corpora with a mixture of Levantine dialect and MSA.

The Iraqi dialect was studied with respect to MT in two papers by Condon et al. In (Condon et al., 2010), a two-way evaluation of English-Iraqi dialog translation was performed. Four MT systems were evaluated and error types were specified. The English-Iraqi speech translation systems were evaluated using automated metrics. The study described Iraqi speech data features and the difficulties it presents on machine translation quality evaluation.

In (Jeblee et al., 2014), domain and dialect adaptation was suggested to produce a statistical machine translation system from English to the Egyptian dialect with MSA as a pivot. A machine translation system of the Moroccan dialect into MSA based on statistical models and a rule-based approach was proposed in (Tachicart & Bouzoubaa, 2014).

4.2 Other Semantic Tasks

Sentiment and subjectivity analysis (SSA) was treated in several papers. In (Abdul-Mageed et al., 2014), the authors investigated how to treat Arabic dialects and whether genre-specific features have a measurable impact on performance of a sentiment analyzer.

In (Hedar & Doss, 2013), a classifier for Arabic slang that applies sentiment analysis to classify news and comments on Facebook was presented.

In (Mourad & Darwish, 2013), the issue of limited Arabic SSA lexicons was addressed by providing baselines that employ Arabic specific processing including stemming, POS tagging, and tweets normalization. Also, a random graph walking algorithm was employed to expand SSA lexicons. Open issues in sentiment analysis were discussed in (El-Beltagy & Ali, 2013) and a sentiment lexicon for Egyptian dialect was presented.

Recently, other sentiment analysis systems for social media data were proposed in (Duwairi et al., 2014) and (Ibrahim et al., 2015) for the Jordanian and Egyptian dialects, respectively.

In (El-Fishawy et al., 2014), a microblog summarization technique based on machine learning for Egyptian dialect was presented. The results achieved were compared to several well-known algorithms such as SumBasic, TF-IDF, PageRank, MEAD, and human summaries.

(Pasha et al., 2013) addressed the challenges of retrieving information in Arabic dialects, which have significant linguistic differences from Standard Arabic. The presented tool automatically generates dialect search terms with relevant morphological variations from English or Standard Arabic query terms.

In (Zirikly & Diab, 2014) and (Zirikly & Diab, 2015) different approaches for Named Entity Recognition in the Egyptian dialect were proposed. Named entity recognition in microblogs was also treated by Darwish and Gao, however, for MSA mainly (Darwish & Gao, 2014).

In (Darwish & Magdy, 2014), a general study of Arabic information retrieval was presented. The survey includes different domains and applications of Arabic IR systems as well as the specific challenges in this NLP area.

5 Dialect Identification and Recognition

The recognition of dialectal content in an Arabic text or speech gained a special interest in the literature.

5.1 Dialect Identification in Text

Some of the previously cited work on text annotation, e.g. (Diab et al., 2010) and (Zaidan & Callison-Burch, 2011), or machine translation, e.g., (Soltau et al., 2011), implicitly include components for dialect identification.

In (Habash et al., 2008b), standard annotation guidelines to identify a switching between MSA and an Egyptian or a Levantine dialect in written text were presented. The guidelines can be used to annotate large collections of data used for training and testing NLP tools.

In (Elfardy & Diab, 2013), a supervised approach on the sentence level is proposed to differentiate between MSA and the Egyptian dialect. Token level labels are used to derive sentence-level features that are employed with other core and meta features to train a generative classifier that predicts the correct label for each sentence in the given input text. This work was extended to the Iraqi, Levantine and Moroccan dialects by the same authors in (Elfardy & Diab, 2012a).

In (Zaidan & Callison-Burch, 2012), the authors used a large annotated dataset to train and evaluate automatic classifiers for the sake of Arabic dialect identification. Given an Arabic sentence, the task consists in determining the variety of Arabic in which it is written. The variety can be MSA, Maghrebi, Egyptian, Levantine, Iraqi, or Gulf.

Recently, a native Bayes classifier based on character bi-gram model was proposed to identify 18 different Arabic dialects (Sadat, Kazemi, & Farzindar, 2014). In (Darwish et al., 2014), the authors based their identification approach of the Egyptian dialect on lexical, morphological, as well as phonological information.

In (Zaidan & Callison-Burch, 2014), the authors created a large monolingual dataset with dialect

Table 1. Dialectical Arabic NLP- Literature Overview

	Basic Language Analyses			Building Language Resources		Dialect Identification and Recognition		Semantic Analysis	
	Morph.	Syntax	Orthog.	Lexica	Corpora	From Text	From Speech	M. Translation	Others
Gulf	(Almeman & Lee, 2012), (Abuata & Al-Omari, 2015)		(Darwish, 2013), (Masmoudi et al., 2015)		(Zaidan & Callison-Burch, 2011), (Almeman et al., 2013), (Cotterell& Callison-Burch, 2014)	(Zaidan & Callison-Burch, 2011), (Sadat, Kazemi, & Farzindar, 2014), (Zaidan & Callison-Burch, 2014)	(Belgacem et al., 2010), (Zaidan&Callison-Burch, 2012), (Zhang et al., 2013), (Biadsy et al., 2009), (Akbacak et al.,2011)	(Jehl et al., 2012), (Salloum & Habash, 2012), (Sawaf, 2010)	(Mourad & Darwish, 2013)
Kuwaiti					(Mubarak & Darwish, 2014)	(Sadat, Kazemi, & Farzindar, 2014)	(Iskra et al., 2004)		
Saudis					(Mubarak & Darwish, 2014)	(Sadat, Kazemi, & Farzindar, 2014)	(Alghamdi et al., 2008), (Iskra et al., 2004)	(Sawaf, 2010)	
UAE					(Mubarak & Darwish, 2014)		(Lei & Hansen, 2009), (Iskra et al., 2004)	(Khamis, 2007)	
Qatari					(Mubarak & Darwish, 2014), (Zaghouani et al., 2014)	(Sadat, Kazemi, & Farzindar, 2014)	(Iskra et al., 2004)	(Al- Mannai et al., 2014)	
Bahraini						(Sadat, Kazemi, & Farzindar, 2014)	(Iskra et al., 2004)		
Omani						(Sadat, Kazemi, & Farzindar, 2014)	(Iskra et al., 2004)		
S. A. Peninsula								(Sawaf, 2010)	
Yemeni					(Belgacem et al., 2010)				
Sana´ani								(Al- Gaphari & Al Yadoumi, 2012)	
North Africa	(Almeman & Lee, 2012), (Habash et al., 2013)		(Masmoudi et al., 2015), (Darwish, 2013)		(Almeman & Lee, 2013)				
Egyptian	(Duh & Kirchhoff 2005), (Habash et al., 2012), (Almeman & Lee, 2012), (Al-Sabbagh & Girju, 2012a), (Salloum &Habash, 2014)		(Dasigi & Diab, 2011), (Habash, Diab, & Rambow, 2012), (Bies et al., 2014)	(Hedar & Doss, 2013)	(Habash et al.,2008), (Diab et al., 2010), (Benajiba & Diab, 2010), (Zaidan & Callison-Burch, 2011), (Al-Sabbagh & Girju, 2012), (Elfardy& Diab, 2012b), (Elfardy& Diab,2012c), (Almeman& Lee,2013), (Mubarak& Darwish, 2014), (Cotterell& Callison-Burch,2014), (Maamouri et al., 2014), (Hawwari et al., 2014), (Maamouri et al.,2014)	(Diab et al., 2010), (Zaidan & Callison-Burch, 2011), (Elfardy & Diab, 2012), (Elfardy & Diab, 2013), (Zaidan & Callison-Burch, 2012), (Habash et al., 2008b), (Zaidan & Callison-Burch, 2014), (Darwish et al., 2014)	(Belgacem et al., 2010), (Zhang et al., 2013), (Lei & Hansen, 2009), (Biadsy et al., 2009), (Akbacak et al., 2011), (Kirchhoff & Vergyri, 2005), (Iskra et al., 2004)	(Zbib et al.,2012), (Salloum & Habash, 2011), (Jehl et al., 2012), (Bakr et al.,2008), (Salloum & Habash, 2012), (Sawaf, 2010), (Mohamed et al., 2012), (Jeblee et al., 2014)	(Pasha et al., 2013), (Hedar & Doss, 2013), (El- Fishawy et al., 2014), (Ibrahim et al., 2015), (Mourad & Darwish, 2013), (Zirikly & Diab, 2014/2015), (El-Beltagy & Ali, 2013), (Darwish & Gao, 2014)
Cairene				(Al-Sabbagh & Girju, 2010)					
Morrocan				(Graff & Maamouri , 2012)	(Benajiba & Diab, 2010), (Diab et al., 2010), (Tratz et al., 2013) , (Mubarak & Darwish,	(Sadat, Kazemi,& Farzindar, 2014)	(Elfardy & Diab, 2012a), (Belgacem et al., 2010), (Iskra et al., 2004)	(Sawaf, 2010), (Tachicart & Bouzoubaa,	

	Basic Language Analyses			Building Language Resources		Dialect Identification and Recognition		Semantic Analysis	
	Morph.	Syntax	Orthog.	Lexica	Corpora	From Text	From Speech	M. Translation	Others
					2014)			2014)	
Tunisian	(Zribi, Khemakhem, & Belguith, 2013), (Boujelbane et al., 2014)		(Zribi et al., 2013), (Zribi et al., 2014)	(Boujelbane et al., 2013)	(Boujelbane et al., 2013), (Zribi, Graja, et al., 2013)	(Sadat, Kazemi, & Farzindar, 2014)	(Belgacem et al., 2010), (Boujelbane et al., 2013), (Iskra et al., 2004)	(Sawaf,2010), (Sadat, Mallek, et al., 2014)	
Libyan				(Graja et al., 2010)		(Sadat, Kazemi, & Farzindar, 2014)	(Iskra et al., 2004)	(Sawaf, 2010)	
Sudani	(Almeman & Lee, 2012)				(Mubarak & Darwish, 2014)	(Sadat, Kazemi, & Farzindar, 2014)		(Sawaf, 2010)	
Algerian					(Harrat et al., 2014)	(Harrat et al., 2015), (Sadat, Kazemi, & Farzindar, 2014)	(Iskra et al., 2004)		
Maghrebi*					(Cotterell & Callison-Burch, 2014)	Zaidan & Callison-Burch, 2012), (Zaidan & Callison-Burch, 2014)			
Levantine	(Habash &Rambow, 2006), (Habash &Rambow,2007) (Almeman & Lee, 2012),	(Chiang et al., 2006), (Maamouri et al., 2006)	(Habash &Rambow, 2007), (Dasigi & Diab, 2011), (Darwish, 2013), (Masmoudi et al., 2015)	(Duh & Kirchhoff 2006)	(Maamouri et al., 2006), (Diab et al., 2010), (Benajiba & Diab, 2010), (Soltau et al., 2011), (Zaidan & Callison-Burch, 2011), (Elfardy& Diab, 2012b), (Almeman& Lee,2013), (Almeman et al., 2013), (Cotterell & Callison-Burch, 2014)	(Habash et al., 2008), (Habash et al., 2008b), (Diab et al., 2010), (Zaidan & Callison-Burch, 2011), (Zaidan & Callison-Burch, 2012), (Elfardy & Diab, 2012c), (Zaidan & Callison- Burch, 2014)	(Elfardy & Diab, 2012a), (Zhang et al., 2013), (Biadsy et al., 2009), (Akbacak et al., 2011), (Iskra et al., 2004)	(Zbib et al., 2012), (Salloum & Habash, 2011), (Jehl et al., 2012), (Salloum & Habash, 2012), (Soltau et al., 2011)	(Mourad & Darwish, 2013)
Syrian				(Graff & Maamouri , 2012)		(Harrat et al., 2015), (Sadat, Kazemi, & Farzindar, 2014)	(Belgacem et al., 2010), (Lei & Hansen, 2009), (Iskra et al., 2004)		
North Syrian								(Sawaf, 2010)	
Damascus								(Sawaf, 2010)	
Lebanese						(Sadat, Kazemi, & Farzindar, 2014)	(Iskra et al., 2004)	(Sawaf, 2010)	
Jordanian	(Salloum &Habash, 2014)					(Sadat, Kazemi, & Farzindar, 2014)	(Iskra et al., 2004)	(Sawaf, 2010)	(Duwairi et al., 2014)
Palestinian					(Jarrar et al., 2014)	(Harrat et al., 2015), (Sadat, Kazemi, & Farzindar, 2014)	(Lei & Hansen, 2009), (Iskra et al., 2004)	(Sawaf, 2010)	
Iraqi	(Almeman & Lee, 2012)		(Masmoudi et al., 2015), (Darwish, 2013)	(Graff et al., 2006), (Rytting et al., 2011), (Graff & Maamouri 2012), (Cavalli-Sforza et al., 2013)	(Diab et al., 2010), (Habash et al., 2008a), (Benajiba & Diab, 2010), (Elfardy & Diab, 2012b), (Cotterell& Callison-Burch, 2014)	(Zaidan & Callison-Burch, 2012), (Zaidan & Callison-Burch, 2014), (Sadat, Kazemi, & Farzindar, 2014)	(Elfardy & Diab, 2012), (Belgacem et al., 2010), (Zhang et al., 2013), (Lei & Hansen, 2009), (Biadsy et al., 2009), (Akbacak et al., 2011)	(Condon et al., 2010), (Salloum & Habash, 2012)	
South Iraqi								(Sawaf, 2010)	
North Iraqi								(Sawaf, 2010)	
Baghdadi								(Sawaf, 2010)	

* The Maghrebi overlaps with other listed dialects such as Moroccan. But we kept it because authors of related work were not specific.

annotations to identify Levantine, Gulf, Egyptian, Iraqi, and Maghrebi dialects. The identification of several Maghrebi dialects in addition to Syrian and Palestinian Arabic was an aspect in the cross-dialectical study proposed in (Harrat et al., 2015).

5.2 Dialect Recognition in Speech

In (Lei & Hansen, 2009), a factor analysis-based modeling technique was proposed to describe the composition of the supervector defined by the Gauss Mixture Model for dialect identification. The method utilizes knowledge types of information contained in the transcript file of the data. The addressed dialects in this work are the Emirati, the Egyptian, the Iraqi, the Palestinian, and the Syrian dialects.

In (Biadsy et al., 2009), the authors described a system that automatically identifies the Arabic dialect (Gulf, Iraqi, Levantine, Egyptian and MSA) of a speaker given a sample of his/her speech.

In (Akbacak et al., 2011), the authors studied the effectiveness of recently developed language recognition techniques based on speech recognition models for the discrimination of Arabic dialects.

In (Belgacem et al., 2010), an automatic recognition system for Arabic dialects was proposed. The analyzed dialects are Tunisian, Moroccan, Algerian, Egyptian, Syrian, Lebanese, Yemeni, Iraqi, and Gulf. The proportion of vocalic intervals and the standard deviation of consonantal intervals are analyzed using the platform Alize and Gaussian Mixture Models.

In (Zhang et al., 2013), the authors investigated variations to supervector pre-processing for dialect identification based on phone recognition-support vector machines. They studied the normalization of supervector dimensions in the pre-squashing stage, the impact of alternative squashing functions, and the N-gram selection for supervector dimensionality reduction. Addressed dialects include Iraqi, Gulf, Egyptian, and Levantine.

Speech recognition for Arabic dialects was addressed in (Kirchhoff & Vergyri, 2005), (Boujelbane et al., 2013), and (Alghamdi et al., 2008) for the Egyptian, Tunisian and Saudi dialects, respectively. In (Kirchhoff & Vergyri, 2005), the authors described the use of MSA acoustic data to improve the recognition of Egyptian conversational dialect. To simplify this task, the MSA data is vowelized automatically before combining it with the Egyptian conversational dialect data. The corpus building in (Boujelbane et al., 2013) was motivated by the need to create language models towards a speech recognition system for the Tunisian Broadcast News.

Recently, Ali et al. presented a system for Egyptian speech recognition that reduces word error rate using micro blog data(Ali, 2014).

In (Alghamdi et al., 2008), the authors aimed to present a speech database by native speakers across Saudi Arabia. The paper shows an approach that enables researchers to select samples from a population to produce a speech database where a dialect map is unobtainable. The resulted corpus was used to train a speech recognition system.

In (Iskra et al., 2004), the results of the OrienTel project were presented. This European project dealt with building telephony databases across Northern Africa and the Middle East.

6 Discussion

Table 1 summarizes the discussed research work on Arabic NLP. The columns represent the different research areas and the rows show the different covered dialects. Based on this table and on the discussions in the previous sections the following comments can be made.

1. By counting all published works, it can be seen that the research on computational linguistics for dialectal Arabic, as an alternative to Modern Standard Arabic, is emerging. Given that the different Arabic dialects are spoken by more than 390 million people in total, the total amount of research conducted in this area is still very limited.

2. The most treated dialect in Arabic NLP is the Egyptian Arabic. This may be attributed to the fact that Egypt is the country with the largest population in the Arabic world. However, such a population argument fails to explain why the Levantine Arabic has been paid relatively high attention, while the dialects of some population-rich countries such as Sudan, Morocco, and Algeria have been treated very poorly. The relatively high concentration on Levantine Arabic may be associated with geopolitical issues and the Middle-East conflict.

3. Most research work has been spent on building and annotating dialectical corpora due to the fact that dialectical Arabic is still a resource-poor language. Dialect identification and speech recognition were also researched intensively. Recall that these two tasks are frequently performed towards building language resources. While the morphology of dialectical Arabic was addressed in some papers, the syntactical analysis is almost ignored in research.

4. The selection of the geographic granularity level on which Arabic dialects are treated is not clear. The majority of related work that addresses Levantine, for instance, treats this variety as one dialect. Levantine, however, is spoken in Syria, Jordan, Lebanon, and Palestine. In each of these countries, furthermore, a lot of varieties can be identified.

From this discussion it is obvious that the research on Arabic dialects should be enhanced both on the dialect as well as on the topic level. A hierarchical scheme should be introduced to define the granularity of Arabic dialects so that researchers can be more specific in assigning their work to some dialect or dialects. The built language resources especially annotated corpora should be made available to accelerate the research in this area. More research on the syntactical analysis of Arabic dialects is required to improve the quality of related tools.

Acknowledgments

This work was partially funded by Lockheed Martin Company.

References

Abdul-Mageed, M., Diab, M., & Kübler, S. (2014, January). Samar: Subjectivity and sentiment analysis for arabic social media. *Comput. Speech Lang.*, *28*(1), 20–37. Retrieved from `http://dx.doi.org/10.1016/j.csl.2013.03.001` doi: 10.1016/j.csl.2013.03.001

Abuata, B., & Al-Omari, A. (2015). A rule-based stemmer for arabic gulf dialect. *Journal of King Saud University-Computer and Information Sciences*.

Akbacak, M., Vergyri, D., Stolcke, A., Scheffer, N., & Mandal, A. (2011). Effective arabic dialect classification using diverse phonotactic models. In *Interspeech* (Vol. 11, pp. 737–740).

Al-Gaphari, G., & Al-Yadoumi, M. (2012). A method to convert sanaani accent to modern standard arabic. *International Journal of Information Science and Management (IJISM)*, *8*(1), 39–49.

Alghamdi, M., Alhargan, F., Alkanhal, M., Alkhairy, A., Eldesouki, M., & Alenazi, A. (2008). Saudi accented arabic voice bank. *Journal of King Saud University-Computer and Information Sciences*, *20*, 45–64.

Ali, A. (2014). Advances in dialectal arabic speech recognition: A study using twitter to improve egyptian asr. In *Proceedings of the international workshop on spoken language translation (iwslt).*

Al-Mannai, K., Sajjad, H., Khader, A., Al Obaidli, F., Nakov, P., & Vogel, S. (2014). Unsupervised word segmentation improves dialectal arabic to english machine translation. *ANLP 2014*, 207.

Almeman, K., & Lee, M. (2012). Towards developing a multi-dialect morphological analyzer for arabic. In *4th international conference on arabic language processing, rabat, morocco.*

Almeman, K., & Lee, M. (2013). Automatic building of arabic multi dialect text corpora by bootstrapping dialect words. In *Communications, signal processing, and their applications (iccspa), 2013 1st international conference on* (pp. 1–6).

Al-Sabbagh, R., & Girju, R. (2010). Mining the web for the induction of a dialectical arabic lexicon. In *Lrec.*

Al-Sabbagh, R., & Girju, R. (2012a). A supervised pos tagger for written arabic social networking corpora. In *Proceedings of konvens* (pp. 39–52).

Al-Sabbagh, R., & Girju, R. (2012b). Yadac: Yet another dialectal arabic corpus. In *Lrec* (pp. 2882–2889).

Bakr, H. A., Shaalan, K., & Ziedan, I. (2008). A hybrid approach for converting written egyptian colloquial dialect into diacritized arabic. In *The 6th international conference on informatics and systems, infos2008. cairo university.*

Belgacem, M., Antoniadis, G., & Besacier, L.

(2010). Automatic identification of arabic dialects. In *Lrec*.

Benajiba, Y., & Diab, M. (2010). A web application for dialectal arabic text annotation. In *Proceedings of the lrec workshop for language resources (lrs) and human language technologies (hlt) for semitic languages: Status, updates, and prospects.*

Biadsy, F., Hirschberg, J., & Habash, N. (2009). Spoken arabic dialect identification using phonotactic modeling. In *Proceedings of the eacl 2009 workshop on computational approaches to semitic languages* (pp. 53–61).

Bies, A., Song, Z., Maamouri, M., Grimes, S., Lee, H., Wright, J., ... Rambow, O. (2014). Transliteration of arabizi into arabic orthography: Developing a parallel annotated arabizi-arabic script sms/chat corpus. *ANLP 2014*, 93.

Bouchlaghem, R., & Elkhlifi, A. (2014). Tunisian dialect wordnet creation and enrichment using web resources and other wordnets. *ANLP 2014*, 104.

Boujelbane, R., BenAyed, S., & Belguith, L. H. (2013). Building bilingual lexicon to create dialect tunisian corpora and adapt language model. *ACL 2013*, 88.

Boujelbane, R., Mallek, M., Ellouze, M., & Belguith, L. H. (2014). Fine-grained pos tagging of spoken tunisian dialect corpora. In *Natural language processing and information systems* (pp. 59–62). Springer.

Brustad, K. (2000). *The syntax of spoken arabic: A comparative study of moroccan, egyptian, syrian, and kuwaiti dialects.* Georgetown University Press.

Buckwalter, T. (2004). *Buckwalter arabic morphological analyzer version 2.0. ldc catalog number ldc2004l02* (Tech. Rep.). ISBN 1-58563-3-0.

Cavalli-Sforza, V., Saddiki, H., Bouzoubaa, K., Abouenour, L., Maamouri, M., & Goshey, E. (2013). Bootstrapping a wordnet for an arabic dialect from other wordnets and dictionary resources. In *Computer systems and applications (aiccsa), 2013 acs international conference on* (pp. 1–8).

Chiang, D., Diab, M. T., Habash, N., Rambow, O., & Shareef, S. (2006). Parsing arabic dialects. In *Eacl*.

Condon, S., Parvaz, D., Aberdeen, J. S., Doran, C., Freeman, A., & Awad, M. (2010). Evaluation of machine translation errors in english and iraqi arabic. In *Lrec*.

Cotterell, R., & Callison-Burch, C. (2014). A multi-dialect, multi-genre corpus of informal written arabic. In *Proceedings of the language resources and evaluation conference (lrec)*.

Darwish, K. (2013). Arabizi detection and conversion to arabic. *arXiv preprint arXiv:1306.6755*.

Darwish, K., & Gao, W. (2014). Simple effective microblog named entity recognition: Arabic as an example. *Proc. of LREC, Reykjavik, Iceland*.

Darwish, K., & Magdy, W. (2014). *Arabic information retrieval.* Now Publishers.

Darwish, K., Sajjad, H., & Mubarak, H. (2014). Verifiably effective arabic dialect identification. *EMNLP-2014*.

Dasigi, P., & Diab, M. T. (2011). Codact: Towards identifying orthographic variants in dialectal arabic. In *Ijcnlp* (pp. 318–326).

Diab, M., Habash, N., Rambow, O., Altantawy, M., & Benajiba, Y. (2010). Colaba: Arabic dialect annotation and processing. In *Lrec workshop on semitic language processing* (pp. 66–74).

Duh, K., & Kirchhoff, K. (2005). Pos tagging of dialectal arabic: a minimally supervised approach. In *Proceedings of the acl workshop on computational approaches to semitic languages* (pp. 55–62).

Duh, K., & Kirchhoff, K. (2006). Lexicon acquisition for dialectal arabic using transductive learning. In *Proceedings of the 2006 conference on empirical methods in natural language processing* (pp. 399–407).

Duwairi, R., Marji, R., Sha'ban, N., & Rushaidat, S. (2014). Sentiment analysis in arabic tweets. In *Information and communication systems (icics), 2014 5th international conference on* (pp. 1–6).

El-Beltagy, S. R., & Ali, A. (2013). Open issues in the sentiment analysis of arabic social media: A case study. In *Innovations in information technology (iit), 2013 9th international conference on* (pp. 215–220).

Elfardy, H., & Diab, M. (2012a). Aida: Automatic identification and glossing of dialectal arabic. In *Proceedings of the 16th eamt conference (project papers)* (pp. 83–83).

Elfardy, H., & Diab, M. T. (2012b). Simplified guidelines for the creation of large scale dialectal arabic annotations. In *Lrec* (pp. 371–378).

Elfardy, H., & Diab, M. T. (2013). Sentence level dialect identification in arabic. In *Acl (2)* (pp. 456–461).

El-Fishawy, N., Hamouda, A., Attiya, G. M., & Atef, M. (2014). Arabic summarization in twitter social network. *Ain Shams Engineering Journal*, *5*(2), 411–420.

Graff, D., Buckwalter, T., Jin, H., & Maamouri, M. (2006). Lexicon development for varieties of spoken colloquial arabic. In *Proceedings of the fifth international conference on language resources and evaluation (lrec)* (pp. 999–1004).

Graff, D., & Maamouri, M. (2012). Developing lmf-xml bilingual dictionaries for colloquial arabic dialects. In *Lrec* (pp. 269–274).

Graja, M., Jaoua, M., & Hadrich Belguith, L. (2010). Lexical study of a spoken dialogue corpus in tunisian dialect. In *The international arab conference on information technology (acit), benghazi–libya.*

Habash, N., Diab, M. T., & Rambow, O. (2012). Conventional orthography for dialectal arabic. In *Lrec* (pp. 711–718).

Habash, N., Eskander, R., & Hawwari, A. (2012). A morphological analyzer for egyptian arabic. In *Proceedings of the twelfth meeting of the special interest group on computational morphology and phonology* (pp. 1–9).

Habash, N., & Rambow, O. (2006). Magead: a morphological analyzer and generator for the arabic dialects. In *Proceedings of the 21st international conference on computational linguistics and the 44th annual meeting of the association for computational linguistics.*

Habash, N., & Rambow, O. (2007). Morphophonemic and orthographic rules in a multi-dialectal morphological analyzer and generator for arabic verbs. In *International symposium on computer and arabic language (iscal), riyadh, saudi arabia.*

Habash, N., Rambow, O., Diab, M., & Kanjawi-Faraj, R. (2008a). Guidelines for annotation of arabic dialectness. In *Proceedings of the lrec workshop on hlt & nlp within the arabic world* (pp. 49–53).

Habash, N., Rambow, O., Diab, M., & Kanjawi-Faraj, R. (2008b). Guidelines for annotation of arabic dialectness. In *Proceedings of the lrec workshop on hlt & nlp within the arabic world* (pp. 49–53).

Habash, N., Roth, R., Rambow, O., Eskander, R., & Tomeh, N. (2013). Morphological analysis and disambiguation for dialectal arabic. In *Proceedings of naacl-hlt* (pp. 426–432).

Harrat, S., Meftouh, K., Abbas, M., Jamoussi, S., Saad, M., & Smaili, K. (2015). Cross-dialectal arabic processing. In *Computational linguistics and intelligent text processing* (pp. 620–632). Springer.

Harrat, S., Meftouh, K., Abbas, M., & Smaili, K. (2014). Building resources for algerian arabic dialects. *Corpus (sentences)*, *4000*(6415), 2415.

Hawwari, A., Attia, M., & Diab, M. (2014). A framework for the classification and annotation of multiword expressions in dialectal arabic. *ANLP 2014*, 48.

Hedar, A. R., & Doss, M. (2013). Mining social networks arabic slang comments. *IEEE Symposium on Computational Intelligence and Data Mining (CIDM).*

Ibrahim, H. S., Abdou, S. M., & Gheith, M. (2015). Sentiment analysis for modern standard arabic and colloquial. *arXiv preprint arXiv:1505.03105.*

Iskra, D. J., Siemund, R., Borno, J., Moreno, A., Emam, O., Choukri, K., ... others (2004). Orientel-telephony databases across northern africa and the middle east. In *Lrec.*

Jarrar, M., Habash, N., Akra, D., & Zalmout, N. (2014). Building a corpus for palestinian arabic: a preliminary study. *ANLP 2014*, 18.

Jeblee, S., Feely, W., Bouamor, H., Lavie, A., Habash, N., & Oflazer, K. (2014). Domain and dialect adaptation for machine translation into egyptian arabic. *ANLP 2014*, 196.

Jehl, L., Hieber, F., & Riezler, S. (2012). Twitter translation using translation-based cross-lingual retrieval. In *Proceedings of the seventh workshop on statistical machine translation* (pp. 410–421). Stroudsburg, PA, USA: Association for Computational Linguistics. Retrieved from `http://dl.acm.org/citation`

.cfm?id=2393015.2393074

Kirchhoff, K., & Vergyri, D. (2005). Cross-dialectal data sharing for acoustic modeling in arabic speech recognition. *Speech Communication*, *46*(1), 37–51.

Lei, Y., & Hansen, J. H. (2009). Factor analysis-based information integration for arabic dialect identification. In *Acoustics, speech and signal processing, 2009. icassp 2009. ieee international conference on* (pp. 4337–4340).

Maamouri, M., Bies, A., Buckwalter, T., Diab, M., Habash, N., Rambow, O., & Tabessi, D. (2006). Developing and using a pilot dialectal arabic treebank. In *Proceedings of the fifth international conference on language resources and evaluation, lrec06*.

Maamouri, M., Bies, A., Kulick, S., Ciul, M., Habash, N., & Eskander, R. (2014). Developing an egyptian arabic treebank: Impact of dialectal morphology on annotation and tool development. *Proc. of LREC, Reykjavik, Iceland*.

Masmoudi, A., Habash, N., Ellouze, M., Estève, Y., & Belguith, L. H. (2015). Arabic transliteration of romanized tunisian dialect text: A preliminary investigation. In *Computational linguistics and intelligent text processing* (pp. 608–619). Springer.

Mohamed, E., Mohit, B., & Oflazer, K. (2012). Transforming standard arabic to colloquial arabic. In *Proceedings of the 50th annual meeting of the association for computational linguistics: Short papers-volume 2* (pp. 176–180).

Mourad, A., & Darwish, K. (2013). Subjectivity and sentiment analysis of modern standard arabic and arabic microblogs. In *Proceedings of the 4th workshop on computational approaches to subjectivity, sentiment and social media analysis* (pp. 55–64).

Mubarak, H., & Darwish, K. (2014). Using twitter to collect a multi-dialectal corpus of arabic. *ANLP 2014*, 1.

Pasha, A., Al-Badrashiny, M., Altantawy, M., Habash, N., Pooleery, M., Rambow, O., ... Diab, M. (2013). Dira: Dialectal arabic information retrieval assistant. In *The companion volume of the proceedings of international joint conference on natural language processing (ijcnlp)* (pp. 13–16).

Rytting, C. A., Zajic, D. M., Rodrigues, P., Wayland, S. C., Hettick, C., Buckwalter, T., & Blake, C. C. (2011). Spelling correction for dialectal arabic dictionary lookup. *ACM Transactions on Asian Language Information Processing (TALIP)*, *10*(1), 3.

Sadat, F., Kazemi, F., & Farzindar, A. (2014). Automatic identification of arabic language varieties and dialects in social media. *SocialNLP 2014*, 22.

Sadat, F., Mallek, F., Sellami, R., Boudabous, M. M., & Farzindar, A. (2014). Collaboratively constructed linguistic resources for language vari-ants and their exploitation in nlp applications–the case of tunisian arabic and the social media. In *Workshop on lexical and grammatical resources for language processing* (p. 102).

Salloum, W., & Habash, N. (2011). Dialectal to standard arabic paraphrasing to improve arabic-english statistical machine translation. In *Proceedings of the first workshop on algorithms and resources for modelling of dialects and language varieties* (pp. 10–21).

Salloum, W., & Habash, N. (2012). Elissa: A dialectal to standard arabic machine translation system. In *Coling (demos)* (pp. 385–392).

Salloum, W., & Habash, N. (2014). Adam: Analyzer for dialectal arabic morphology. *Journal of King Saud University-Computer and Information Sciences*, *26*(4), 372–378.

Sansò, A. (2004). Med-typ: A typological database for mediterranean languages. In *Lrec*.

Sawaf, H. (2010). Arabic dialect handling in hybrid machine translation. In *Proceedings of the conference of the association for machine translation in the americas (amta), denver, colorado*.

Soltau, H., Mangu, L., & Biadsy, F. (2011). From modern standard arabic to levantine asr: Leveraging gale for dialects. In *Automatic speech recognition and understanding (asru), 2011 ieee workshop on* (pp. 266–271).

Tachicart, R., & Bouzoubaa, K. (2014). A hybrid approach to translate moroccan arabic dialect. In *Intelligent systems: Theories and applications (sita-14), 2014 9th inter-*

national conference on (pp. 1–5).

Tratz, S., Briesch, D., Laoudi, J., & Voss, C. (2013). Tweet conversation annotation tool with a focus on an arabic dialect, moroccan darija. *LAW VII & ID*, 135.

Zaghouani, W. (2014). Critical survey of the freely available arabic corpora. In *Proceedings of the workshop on free/open-source arabic corpora and corpora processing tools workshop programme* (p. 1).

Zaghouani, W., Habash, N., & Mohit, B. (2014). The qatar arabic language bank guidelines.

Zaidan, O., & Callison-Burch, C. (2011). The arabic online commentary dataset: an annotated dataset of informal arabic with high dialectal content. In *Acl (short papers)* (pp. 37–41).

Zaidan, O., & Callison-Burch, C. (2012). Arabic dialect identification. *Computational Linguistics (submitted)*.

Zaidan, O., & Callison-Burch, C. (2014). Arabic dialect identification. *Computational Linguistics*, *40*(1), 171–202.

Zbib, R., Malchiodi, E., Devlin, J., Stallard, D., Matsoukas, S., Schwartz, R., ... Callison-Burch, C. (2012). Machine translation of arabic dialects. In *Proceedings of the 2012 conference of the north american chapter of the association for computational linguistics: Human language technologies* (pp. 49–59).

Zhang, Q., Boril, H., & Hansen, J. H. (2013). Supervector pre-processing for prsvm-based chinese and arabic dialect identification. *IEEE ICASSP 2013*.

Zirikly, A., & Diab, M. (2014). Named entity recognition for dialectal arabic. *ANLP 2014*, 78.

Zirikly, A., & Diab, M. (2015). Named entity recognition for arabic social media. In *Proceedings of naacl-hlt* (pp. 176–185).

Zribi, I., Boujelbane, R., Masmoudi, A., Ellouze, M., Belguith, L., & Habash, N. (2014). A conventional orthography for tunisian arabic. In *Proceedings of the language resources and evaluation conference (lrec), reykjavik, iceland.*

Zribi, I., Graja, M., Khmekhem, M. E., Jaoua, M., & Belguith, L. H. (2013). Orthographic transcription for spoken tunisian arabic. In *Computational linguistics and intelligent text processing* (pp. 153–163). Springer.

Zribi, I., Khemakhem, M. E., & Belguith, L. H. (2013). Morphological analysis of tunisian dialect. In *International joint conference on natural language processing* (pp. 992–996).

DIWAN: A Dialectal Word Annotation Tool for Arabic

Faisal Al-Shargi
Universität Leipzig
Leipzig
Germany
alshargi@informatik.uni-leipzig.de

Owen Rambow
CCLS, Columbia University
New York, NY
USA
rambow@ccls.columbia.edu

Abstract

This paper presents DIWAN, an annotation interface for Arabic dialectal texts. While the Arabic dialects differ in many respects from each other and from Modern Standard Arabic, they also have much in common. To facilitate annotation and to make it as efficient as possible, it is therefore not advisable to treat each Arabic dialect as a separate language, unrelated to the other variants of Arabic. Instead, we make analyses from other variants available to the annotator, who then can choose to use them or not.

1. Introduction

Arabic is a Central Semitic language, closely related to Aramaic, Hebrew, Ugaritic and Phoenician. It is spoken by 420 million speakers (native and non-native) in the Arab World. Arabic also is a liturgical language of 1.6 billion Muslims around the world.

Modern Standard Arabic (MSA) is the official *Arabic* language. It is the educational language and official language used in news and official communication across the Arabic-speaking world. When Arabs communicate spontaneously in informal settings, they use dialectal Arabic (DA). There are divisions of many dialects of the Arabic language that occur between the spoken languages of different regions. Some varieties of Arabic in North Africa, for example, are incomprehensible to an Arabic speaker from the Levant or the Arabian Peninsula.[1]

Within these broad regions, further and considerable geographic distinctions exist – within countries, across country borders, and between cities and villages. Some examples include Gulf Arabic, Bahraini Arabic, Najdi Arabic, Hijazi Arabic, Yemeni Arabic, Yemeni Hadhrami Arabic, Yemeni Sanaani Arabic, Yemeni Ta'izzi-Adeni Arabic, Dhofari Arabic, Omani Arabic, Shihhi Arabic, and the Peninsular Arabic dialects.

Despite this diversity, all Arabic dialects share certain properties: much of their phonology, templatic morphology augmented by affixes and a large set of clitics, large parts of their syntax, and important (though unpredictable) parts of the lexicon.

Current natural language processing (NLP) tools work well with MSA because they were designed specifically for the processing of MSA, and because of the abundance of MSA resources. Applying the NLP tools designed for MSA directly to DA yields significantly lower performance (Chiang et al., 2006; Habash and Rambow, 2006; Benajiba et al., 2010; Habash et al., 2012). This makes it imperative to direct research to building resources and tools for DA processing.

[1] When Arabic speakers of different dialects meet, they tend to navigate towards a *middle* Arabic that encapsulates the shared aspects they are aware of in order to maximize communication. A better and harder test of comprehension is to eavesdrop on a conversation in another dialect.

Proceedings of the Second Workshop on Arabic Natural Language Processing, pages 49–58,
Beijing, China, July 26-31, 2015.

ID	ara word	bw word	S_ID	w position	Sentence
☐ 6	هو	hw	2	2	ما هو حال الت عندكن
☐ 17	هو	hw	3	4	للازكياء فقط ما هو الجواب
☐ 1555	هو	hw	232	8	قال : أنني لي وكل ما أملك هو لك
☐ 1772	هو	hw	277	4	نهاية العالم في 2012 ? قال : كله كلام فاضي عندي علية نونة بنتهي في 2015

Figure 1: An example of MSA and DA code switching

Arabic dialects lack large amounts of consistent data due to two main factors: the lack of orthographic standards for the dialects, and the lack of overall Arabic content on the web (Benajiba et al., 2010). While the rise of the internet has increased the amount of DA being written, sometimes Arabic dialects come mixed with the MSA in various forms of text (see Figure 1, which shows the code switching in our DIWAN tool). Furthermore, language used in social media poses a challenge for NLP tools in general in any language due to the difference in genre. Therefore, in order to create tools for dialectal Arabic, annotated DA corpora are needed in a variety of dialects.

The goal of our **Di**alectal **W**ord **An**notation tool (DIWAN) is to address these gaps on the resource creation level. In designing DIWAN, we have determined several important design goals:

1. We want to exploit the similarity between dialects as much as possible to facilitate annotation, which in general is costly and slow.
2. We want to use a convention for orthography (which the input text does not necessarily follow).
3. We want to create data which can be used both for creating morphological analyzers (which produce all morphological analyses for a word outside of any context) and morphological taggers (which determine the correct morphological analysis -- including the POS tag -- for a word in context).

This paper explains the design decisions we have made in order to meet these goals. DIWAN is fully implemented for use on Microsoft Windows and is currently in use for the annotation of Palestinian, Yemeni, and Moroccan Arabic.

This paper is structured as follows. In Section 2, we review the NLP components we use in DIWAN. In Section 3, we describe the workflow when using DIWAN. In Section 4, we describe the specific annotation tasks the annotator performs. Section 5 gives some technical detail about the implementation. Section 6 discusses related work. We conclude in Section 7 with a discussion of future work.

2. NLP Resources used in DIWAN

In order to make the annotation task easier, DIWAN uses three main existing NLP resources: the MSA morphological analyzer SAMA, the Egyptian morphological analyzer CALIMA-EGY, and the morphological tagger MADAMIRA which works for both MSA and Egyptian. We describe them in turn.

The first resource is the Standard Arabic Morphological Analyzer, SAMA 3.1 (Graff et al. 2009), which is based on the BAMA analyzer (Buckwalter 2004). This system uses lexical databases, divided into prefixes, stems, and suffixes, to assign words all possible MSA analyses. A sample output is shown in Figure 2 (in Buckwalter transliteration), for the input word ماشي *mA$i*, which is ambiguous between various inflected forms of a verb meaning `walk'.

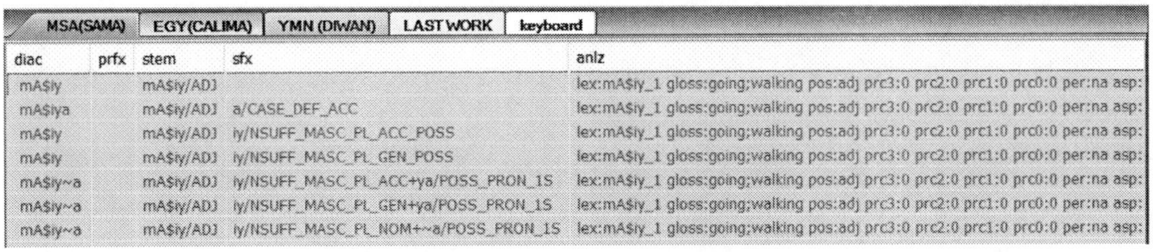

MSA(SAMA) | EGY(CALIMA) | YMN (DIWAN) | LAST WORK | keyboard

diac	prfx	stem	sfx	anlz
mA$iy		mA$iy/ADJ		lex:mA$iy_1 gloss:going;walking pos:adj prc3:0 prc2:0 prc1:0 prc0:0 per:na asp:
mA$iya		mA$iy/ADJ	a/CASE_DEF_ACC	lex:mA$iy_1 gloss:going;walking pos:adj prc3:0 prc2:0 prc1:0 prc0:0 per:na asp:
mA$iy		mA$iy/ADJ	iy/NSUFF_MASC_PL_ACC_POSS	lex:mA$iy_1 gloss:going;walking pos:adj prc3:0 prc2:0 prc1:0 prc0:0 per:na asp:
mA$iy		mA$iy/ADJ	iy/NSUFF_MASC_PL_GEN_POSS	lex:mA$iy_1 gloss:going;walking pos:adj prc3:0 prc2:0 prc1:0 prc0:0 per:na asp:
mA$iy~a		mA$iy/ADJ	iy/NSUFF_MASC_PL_ACC+ya/POSS_PRON_1S	lex:mA$iy_1 gloss:going;walking pos:adj prc3:0 prc2:0 prc1:0 prc0:0 per:na asp:
mA$iy~a		mA$iy/ADJ	iy/NSUFF_MASC_PL_GEN+ya/POSS_PRON_1S	lex:mA$iy_1 gloss:going;walking pos:adj prc3:0 prc2:0 prc1:0 prc0:0 per:na asp:
mA$iy~a		mA$iy/ADJ	iy/NSUFF_MASC_PL_NOM+~a/POSS_PRON_1S	lex:mA$iy_1 gloss:going;walking pos:adj prc3:0 prc2:0 prc1:0 prc0:0 per:na asp:

Figure 2: SAMA result for search on word ماشي *mA$y*

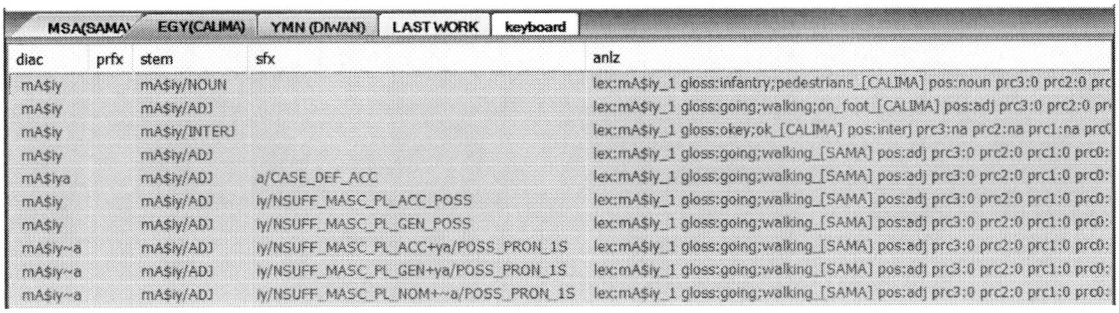

MSA(SAMA) | EGY(CALIMA) | YMN (DIWAN) | LAST WORK | keyboard

diac	prfx	stem	sfx	anlz
mA$iy		mA$iy/NOUN		lex:mA$iy_1 gloss:infantry;pedestrians_[CALIMA] pos:noun prc3:0 prc2:0 prc
mA$iy		mA$iy/ADJ		lex:mA$iy_1 gloss:going;walking;on_foot_[CALIMA] pos:adj prc3:0 prc2:0 pr
mA$iy		mA$iy/INTERJ		lex:mA$iy_1 gloss:okey;ok_[CALIMA] pos:interj prc3:na prc2:na prc1:na prc
mA$iy		mA$iy/ADJ		lex:mA$iy_1 gloss:going;walking_[SAMA] pos:adj prc3:0 prc2:0 prc1:0 prc0:
mA$iya		mA$iy/ADJ	a/CASE_DEF_ACC	lex:mA$iy_1 gloss:going;walking_[SAMA] pos:adj prc3:0 prc2:0 prc1:0 prc0:
mA$iy		mA$iy/ADJ	iy/NSUFF_MASC_PL_ACC_POSS	lex:mA$iy_1 gloss:going;walking_[SAMA] pos:adj prc3:0 prc2:0 prc1:0 prc0:
mA$iy		mA$iy/ADJ	iy/NSUFF_MASC_PL_GEN_POSS	lex:mA$iy_1 gloss:going;walking_[SAMA] pos:adj prc3:0 prc2:0 prc1:0 prc0:
mA$iy~a		mA$iy/ADJ	iy/NSUFF_MASC_PL_ACC+ya/POSS_PRON_1S	lex:mA$iy_1 gloss:going;walking_[SAMA] pos:adj prc3:0 prc2:0 prc1:0 prc0:
mA$iy~a		mA$iy/ADJ	iy/NSUFF_MASC_PL_GEN+ya/POSS_PRON_1S	lex:mA$iy_1 gloss:going;walking_[SAMA] pos:adj prc3:0 prc2:0 prc1:0 prc0:
mA$iy~a		mA$iy/ADJ	iy/NSUFF_MASC_PL_NOM+~a/POSS_PRON_1S	lex:mA$iy_1 gloss:going;walking_[SAMA] pos:adj prc3:0 prc2:0 prc1:0 prc0:

Figure 3: CALIMA-Egyptian result for search on word ماشي *mA$y*

The second resource is the Columbia Arabic Language and dialect Morphological Analyzer for Egyptian (CALIMA-EGY) (Habash et al. 2012b). It is an analyzer for Egyptian. A sample output is shown in Figure 3 for the input word ماشي *mA$y*. CALIMA returns the MSA readings shown in Figure 2, and in addition has Egyptian readings, in particular the interjection `OK'.

The third resource is MADAMIRA (Pasha et al. 2014). MADAMIRA is a system for morphological analysis and disambiguation of Arabic that combines some of the best aspects of two previously commonly used systems for Arabic processing, MADA (Habash and Rambow, 2005; Habash et al., 2009; Habash et al., 2013) and AMIRA (Diab et al., 2007). MADAMIRA improves upon the two systems with a more streamlined Java implementation that is more robust, portable, extensible, and is faster than its ancestors by more than an order of magnitude. Contrary to SAMA and CALIMA-EGY, which provide all morphological analyses for a word regardless of context, MADAMIRA chooses a single analysis given the context of the word in a sentence. For example, in the sentence ماشي كده ؟ *mA$i kdh?* `Is that OK?', the interjection meaning will be chosen.

3. DIWAN Workflow

We designed and built DIWAN as a desktop application which can work locally (offline) or online. As an annotation tool, we have designed DIWAN with two types of users: administrators and annotators. The administrator's responsibility is to create the DIWAN database, specify its settings, and track the annotator's work.

The administrator has several roles:

1. She can create, edit and delete tables in the database.
2. She can create, edit and delete annotator accounts.
3. She can check the status of the annotation tasks for each annotator.
4. She can trace the annotator progress, work time, errors, etc.
5. She can generate reports and statistics on the underlying database (created by the annotators).
6. She can of course also annotate the data.

The annotators can only annotate data. The administrator assigns tasks to each annotator, and the annotations are added to the DIWAN database. As the annotator creates annotations, he can reuse the resulting lexical entries in the DIWAN tool as a new resource for himself or for other annotators.

To work with DIWAN, the administrator first prepares the data. We assume that the data is DA written in Arabic script. There are two ways of preparing the data:

1. The administrator can either simply use DIWAN itself to identify sentences and words in the corpus. DIWAN extracts sentences and words from the prepared file and builds a DIWAN database.
2. Or the administrator can send the corpus to MADAMIRA. MADAMIRA not only identifies sentences and words, it also performs morphological analysis (using MSA and Egyptian resources) and tagging, making a single analysis available for each input word in context. After getting the resulting data from MADAMIRA, DIWAN will present the analysis for each word to the annotator as a default annotation option. As in the previous case, DIWAN extracts sentences and words from the prepared file and builds a DIWAN database (which now includes the MADAMIRA analysis).

These two options are shown in Figure 4.

The annotator makes the dialect annotations by using the DIWAN GUI. We describe this process in detail in Section 4.

4. Annotation Tasks

We describe the workflow of the annotator.

4.1. Initialization of the Annotation GUI

The annotator starts out by choosing if he wants to work locally, i.e., offline, or connected to the database. The offline option is useful when an internet connection is not reliable. In that case, the work is uploaded in batch at the end of the session.

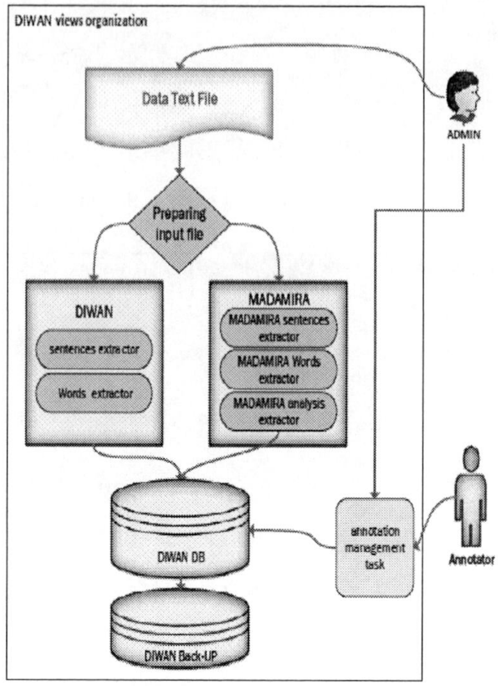

Figure 4: DIWAN setup workflow

When online, several annotators can work at once, sharing their work immediately through the centralized database.

4.2. Choice of Word to Annotate and Using the Resources

The annotator has three options of how to order the words he wants to annotate: by frequency, by text order, or by coverage. The frequency-based approach has the advantage that a large number of tokens can be annotated at once, while the text order provides a natural right-to-left annotation order through the text. Ordering by coverage moves those words to the top of the list which the MADAMIRA system cannot analyze as MSA or Egyptian. This typically (but not always, of course) means that the word is specific to the dialect in question (for example, كتب *ktb* 'wrote (3ms)' is common to all dialects, while مشبوجة *m$bwjp* 'puffy (fs)' is specific to Yemeni). Therefore, ordering by coverage will move words specific to the dialect to the top. Of course, ordering by coverage also misses dialectal words which look like a word in MSA or Egyptian, but mean something else than the MSA or Egyptian counterpart ("faux amis").

In our experience, the frequency-based ordering is useful at the beginning, when the annotator can quickly annotate high-frequency words which typically don't change in form or meaning. Often, these words are dialect-specific. However, once a sufficient number of high-frequency words have been annotated, the annotator can choose to switch to the text-order view. He then continues to annotate lower-frequency words in their textual order. The color coding shows him which words are already annotated. The annotator can also hide the annotated words by clicking on a button. If an annotation effort is interested in creating a dialect-specific lexicon quickly, the ordering-by-coverage approach may be the most appropriate.

Whatever ordering criterion the annotator chooses, he sees an ordered list of words, with the already annotated words in green and the words to be annotated in red. The annotator then clicks on a word in the word panel on the left, and sees in a panel at the top of the GUI a scrollable list of all occurrences of this word in the corpus (one per line), shown in context. The annotator chooses which instances of the word he wants to annotate (i.e., which instances have the same analysis) by clicking a checkbox corresponding to that instance. Typically, he would survey all occurrences and judge which ones have the same analysis. He then chooses a representative example, clicks on it, and proceeds to the main annotation panel. When the annotator clicks on the word's checkbox, by default he will get the MADAMIRA result in the annotation panel (assuming the administrator has chosen to include the MADMIRA analyses).

The annotator performs the annotation tasks in the main annotation panel. There are several input boxes which the annotator needs to fill in as part of the annotation; we will explain them in Section 4.3. As mentioned, DIWAN retrieves an proposed analysis in context for the chosen word token from MADAMIRA and populates all text input boxes and checkboxes automatically with the analysis MADAMIRA finds, which may be based on an MSA analysis or an Egyptian analysis. In some cases, MADAMIRA does not find an analysis, in which case this is clearly shown. The annotator now has several choices as to how to enter the annotation.

1. He can accept the MADAMIRA analysis as correct in this dialect as well.
2. He can modify the MADAMIRA analysis and save the changes.
3. He can look at the list of SAMA analyses for the word (interpreting the word as MSA), and choose one. This analysis then populates all input boxes. He can then choose to accept this analysis, or modify and save it.
4. He can look at the list of CALIMA analyses for the word (interpreting the word as Egyptian), and choose one. This analysis then populates all input boxes. He can then choose to accept this analysis, or modify and save it.
5. He can do word substitution: if the word does not produce the correct (or any) analysis in SAMA or CALIMA, but he knows a word that does and that has the same morphological analysis, then he can enter that word, search in SAMA or (more likely) CALIMA, and then edit the analysis, but only to modify the word itself. For example, assume the annotator is working on Yemeni and the input word is يقطب *yqTb `speeds up (3ms)'*. This does not produce an analysis in SAMA or CALIMA. So instead, the annotator searches for يكتب yktb `writes (3ms)', which has exactly the same morphological analysis, and then edits the stem by replacing كتب with قطب , and updates the gloss to `hasten, speed up'.
6. Finally, he can create an analysis from scratch. This would normally be the most time consuming option.

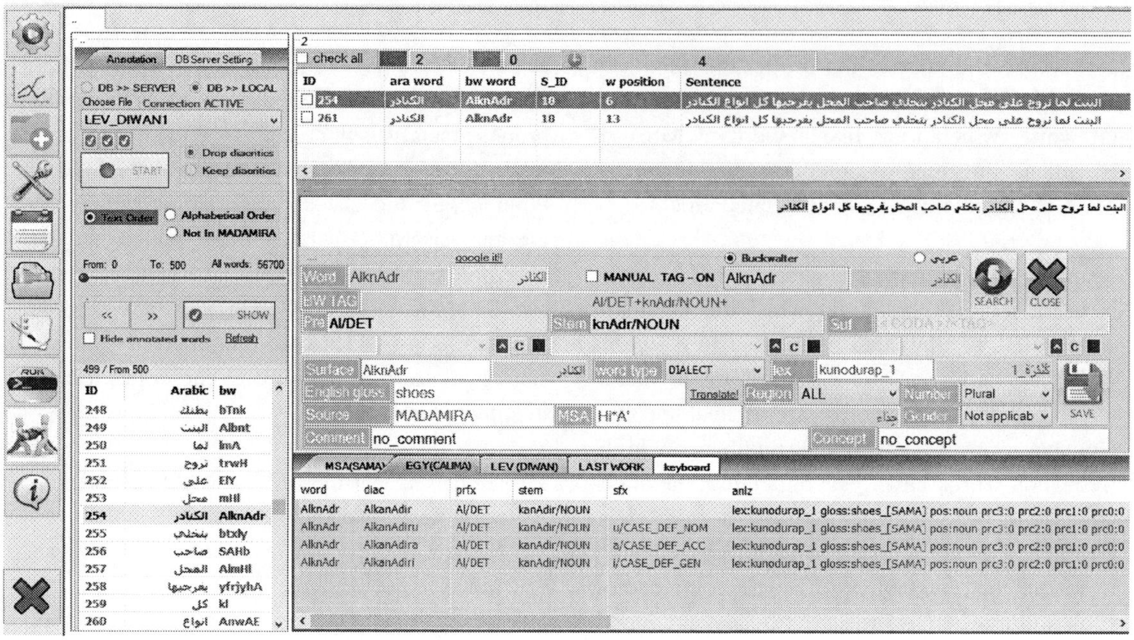

Figure 5: The main DIWAN annotation interface

4.3. Specific Annotation Tasks

Each annotation task corresponds to a specific input device. The interface is shown in Figure 5. Note that here we describe the annotation task as if it is performed from scratch (option 6 in Section 4.2 above).

1. Rewriting the word in the conventionalized orthography (CODA) defined for that dialect (Habash et al. 2012a). Note that CODA may include diacritics or not; in the examples we show in this paper, it does not.
2. Breaking into prefix, stem and suffix. These two tasks are performed jointly in three text input boxes.
3. Adding morph-specific features (in the style of the Linguistic Data Consortium Arabic resources). This task is performed using drop-down menus separately for the prefix, stem, and suffix.
4. Adding the English gloss and MSA equivalent. This task is performed in two dedicated text input boxes.
5. Adding functional morphology. The morpheme-based annotation performed using drop-down menus adds morphological information to morphs. For example, Egyptian باصات `busses' is annotated at the morph level as bAS/NOUN+At/NSUFF_FEM_PL, since ات+ is the suffix for regular feminine plural nouns. However, the form is in fact a masculine plural form (and thus a type of broken plural), so that the annotator would mark باصات as functionally masculine and plural. This task is performed using two drop-down menu boxes (one for number, one for gender). Note that none of the existing resources (MADAMIRA, SAMA, or CALIMA) mark functional number and gender, so that this task needs to be performed manually for each word in any case.
6. Marking Arabic variant. The annotator can choose to mark whether a word is in fact MSA rather than dialect (the default assumption). This is useful when code switching occurs, and the annotator does not want to add an MSA word to the dialectal vocabulary. Furthermore, the annotator can choose a specific region within the dialect. This is useful when a dialectal form is not typical for the region that the text is from. For example a Lebanese word may occur in a Palestinian Arabic text, such as بيي وعيلتي كلها بالضفه *byy wEylty*

klhA bAlDfh `my father and all my family in West Bank', where all words are Palestinian, except بيي byy 'my father', which is more used in Lebanese Arabic.[2]

When everything is correct, the annotator can save his annotation directly to the database; as a result, the color of the analyzed word token or tokens will change from red to green.

In addition, we have added some functionalities in order to help the annotators in their annotation, like Google search on a word (which the annotator can use to verify the meaning; often image search is useful for this purpose), and Google translation for finding the English gloss.

5. The Database and Output Files

In this section, we briefly summarize the databases and file formats used by DIWAN. Only the administrator has the ability to directly access these databases, the annotators can only access it through the DIWAN interface. This ensures the integrity of the DIWAN data. The database has three main tables, the D_sentences table, the D_madamira table, and the D_result table. The D_sentences table includes all the words organized into sentences from the input. The D_madamira table contains the result of the MADAMIRA analysis on the input text. The D_result table is the table that contains all work by the annotators.

The administrator can at any time produce a file output from DIWAN which reflects the annotation. The file includes the results of MADAMIRA if no manual annotation has been done on it. A sample output is shown in Figure 6. We briefly summarize this format:

[2] Palestinian Arabic is particularly challenging due the common dialect mixing in different sub-varieties of it resulting from the particular situation of Palestinian refugees in different countries.

```
ثلاثه زعران قاعدين بمزرعه - vlAvh zErAn qAEdyn bmzrEh

924 ثلاثة vlAvp diac:vlAvp lex:valAv_1 bw:+vlAv/NOUN_NUM+p/NSUFF_FEM_SG msa:valAv_1 gloss:three pos:noun_num gen:f num:s region:ALL diwan_source:MADAMIRA source_mod:no source_search:vlAvp anno:diwan_approved

925 زعران zErAn diac:zErAn lex:>azoEar_2 bw:+zErAn/NOUN+ msa:>azoEar_2 gloss:brigands;scoundrels pos:noun gen:m num:p region:ALL diwan_source:MADAMIRA source_mod:yes source_search:zErAn anno:diwan_approved

926 قاعدين qAEdyn diac:qAEdyn lex:qAEid_1 bw:+qAEd/ADJ+yn/NSUFF_MASC_PL msa:jAls_1 gloss:sitting;seated;lazy;inactive;evaders_(draft_dodgers) pos:adj gen:m num:p region:ALL diwan_source:MADAMIRA source_mod:no source_search:qAEdyn anno:diwan_approved

927 بمزرعه bmzrEh diac:bmzrEp lex:mazoraE_1 bw:b/PART+mzrE/NOUN+p/NSUFF_FEM_SG msa:mazoraE_1 gloss:farm;plantation pos:noun gen:f num:s region:ALL diwan_source:EGY source_mod:no source_search:bmzrEp anno:diwan_approved
```

Figure 6: Extract of an output file generated by DIWAN of an annotated text in context

924: the word number in the text

ثلاثة, vlAvp: the word in Arabic script and Buckwalter transliteration

diac:vlAvp: The CODA spelling (which, recall, may or may not be diacritized)

lex:valAv_1: the lexeme

bw:+vlAv/NOUN_NUM+p/NSUFF_FEM_SG The Buckwalter part-of-speech and morpheme split; this is a the morpheme-based morphological annotation; the plusses indicate the boundaries between prefix, stem, and suffix.

msa:valAv_1: MSA equivalent

gloss:three: English gloss

pos:noun_num: The core part-of-speech tag

gen:f: functional gender

num:s: functional number
region:ALL: applicable dialectal subregion
diwan_source:MADAMIRA: which resource did the annotator use in DIWAN
source_mod:no: did the annotator modify the source?
source_search:vlAvp: what keyword did the annotator use to search the resource? (In this case, since the resource is MADAMIRA, the search keyword is necessarily the word itself.)
anno:diwan_approved: did an annotator work on this word?

6. Related Work

There are two related interfaces that have been used for annotating dialectal Arabic that we are familiar with.

The annotation tool used at the Linguistic Data Consortium for annotating the Egyptian Treebank (Maamouri et al. 2014) is based on previous interfaces used at the LDC for treebanking, notably for MSA. The approach towards morphological annotation used at the LDC is a bootstrapping approach, which aims at developing an annotated corpus in conjunction with a morphological analyzer. The morphological analyzer developed in conjunction with the Egyptian Arabic Treebank is in fact, the same CALIMA-Egyptian system we use. In contrast to DIWAN, there is no attempt at incorporating resources from other dialects, which is also due to the fact that the Egyptian Treebank was a pioneer in the area of resources for dialectal Arabic. Furthermore, the LDC interface does not support annotation of functional number and gender, and concentrates on morpheme-based annotation (which DIWAN also supports, following the LDC approach).

The COLABA annotation tool (Diab et al. 2010a) is a web application, unlike DIWAN which is a desktop application. As a result, unlike DIWAN, the COLABA tool does not support offline work. The most important difference is that COLABA is oriented towards lexicon creation, not annotation in context. Thus, words in context are not assigned morphological features. For our work, it is crucial that we get an annotation of morphological features in context so that DIWAN can be used to create corpora to train taggers. Furthermore, COLABA does not use resources from other dialects, as does DIWAN.

7. Conclusion and Future Work

We have presented DIWAN, a tool designed for the morphological annotation of Arabic dialectal text. It incorporates resources from other dialects (and new resources can be included as they become available) in order to lighten the annotator burden. It uses a conventionalized spelling for Arabic dialects which is maintained in parallel with the naturally occurring spontaneous orthography. And it generates a file format which preserves the linear order of the input text, so that it can be used both for deriving morphological analyzers, and for training morphological taggers.

DIWAN has been used to annotate Levantine (Palestinian) Arabic (Jarrar et al. 2014). The annotators for Levantine quickly became proficient with using the tool after annotating about 100 words. The Palestinian corpus includes 45,000 annotated words (tokens). We are currently using DIWAN to annotate Yemeni (Sana'ai) Arabic. The Yemeni corpus contains 32,325 words (tokens), and the annotator for Yemeni is the first author of the present paper. Finally, we have embarked on a small project for Moroccan Arabic. We have collected 64,171 words of Moroccan for annotation. In separate publications in the future, we will report on the Yemeni and Moroccan annotation efforts. We will also report on a general methodology about how to use such resources to create morphological analyzers and taggers.

One interesting question is how our tool compares to other annotation tools. We believe that the built-in access to morphological analyzers for other variants is unique, and provides a specific advantage in annotating Arabic dialects. However, we have not performed experiments to show this. While such experiments would be very useful, they would also be quite costly, since the same texts would need to be annotated twice by different annotators.

We will continue to improve the DIWAN tool. As more dialects are annotated, we intend to add the created resources to the interface to make them available to users working on new dialects (parallel to the SAMA and CALIMA-Egyptian resources).

Currently, DIWAN is available only for Microsoft Windows. We are investigating reimplementing it in a platform-independent manner. DIWAN is freely available; for information, please consult the following URL:

http://volta.ccls.columbia.edu/~rambow/diwan/home.html

Acknowledgments

This paper is based upon work supported by DARPA Contract No. HR0011-12-C-0014. Any opinions, findings and conclusions or recommendations expressed in this paper are those of the authors and do not necessarily reflect the views of DARPA. We thank Nizar Habash for many helpful suggestions, including the idea of providing the ability of searching using similar words. We thank three anonymous reviewers for helpful feedback which has improved the presentation of this paper. We thank Mustafa Jarrar for very useful discussions and feedback. We also thank the Levantine annotators, Faeq Alrimawi, Diyam Akra, and Linda Alamir, as well as Aidan Kaplan who is developing the Moroccan corpus, for their feedback which helped improve the tool.

References

Y. Benajiba and M. Diab. 2010. A web application for dialectal Arabic text annotation. In *Proceedings of the LREC Workshop for Language Resources (LRs) and Human Language Technologies (HLT) for Semitic Languages: Status, Updates, and Prospects.*

T. Buckwalter. 2004. Buckwalter Arabic Morphological Analyzer Version 2.0. Linguistic Data Consortium, University of Pennsylvania. LDC Catalog No.: LDC2004L02, ISBN 1-58563-324-0

D. Chiang, M. Diab, N. Habash, O. Rambow, and S. Shareef. 2006. Parsing Arabic Dialect. In Proceedings of the European chapter of the Association of Computational Linguistics (EACL).

M. Diab, N. Habash, O. Rambow, M. AlTantawy, and Y. Benajiba. 2010a. COLABA: Arabic Dialect Annotation and Processing. In Proceedings of the Language Resources (LRs) and Human Language Technologies (HLT) for Semitic Languages at LREC.

M. Diab, K. Hacioglu, and D. Jurafsky. 2007. Automated Methods for Processing Arabic Text: From Tokenization to Base Phrase Chunking. In van den Bosch, A. and Soudi, A., editors, Arabic Computational Morphology: Knowledge-based and Empirical Methods. Kluwer/Springer.

D. Graff, M. Maamouri, B. Bouziri, S. Krouna, S. Kulick, and T. Buckwalter. 2009. Standard Arabic Morphological Analyzer (SAMA) Version 3.1. Linguistic Data Consortium LDC2009E73.

N. Habash and O. Rambow. 2005. Arabic Tokenization, Part-of-Speech Tagging and Morphological Disambiguation in One Fell Swoop. In Proceedings of the 43rd Annual Meeting of the Association for Computational Linguistics (ACL'05), pages 573–580, Ann Arbor, Michigan.

N. Habash and O. Rambow. 2006. MAGEAD: A Morphological Analyzer and Generator for the Arabic Dialects. In Proceedings of ACL, Sydney, Australia.

N. Habash, M. Diab, and O. Rabmow. 2012a. Conventional Orthography for Dialectal Arabic. In *Proceedings of the Language Resources and Evaluation Conference (LREC)*, Istanbul.

N. Habash, R. Eskander, and A. Hawwari. 2012b. A Morphological Analyzer for Egyptian Arabic. In Proc. of the Special Interest Group on Computational Morphology and Phonology, Montréal, Canada.

N. Habash, O. Rambow, and R. Roth. 2009. MADA+TOKAN: A toolkit for Arabic tokenization, diacritization, morphological disambiguation, POS tagging, stemming and lemmatization. In Choukri, K. and Maegaard, B., editors, Proceedings of the Second International Conference on Arabic Language Resources and Tools. The MEDAR Consortium, April.

N. Habash, R. Roth, O. Rambow, R. Eskander, and N. Tomeh. 2013. Morphological Analysis and Disambiguation for Dialectal Arabic. In Proceedings of the 2013 Conference of the North American Chapter of the Association for Computational Linguistics: Human Language Technologies (NAACL-HLT), Atlanta, GA.

M. Jarrar, N. Habash, D. Akra, and N. Zalmout 2014. "Building a Corpus for Palestinian Arabic: a Preliminary Study." In *Proceedings of the Workshop on Arabic Natural Language Processing (ANLP 2014).*

M. Maamouri, A. Bies, S. Kulick, M. Ciul, N. Habash and R. Eskander. 2014. Developing a dialectal Egyptian Arabic Treebank: Impact of Morphology and Syntax on Annotation and Tool Development. In Proceedings of the Lan- guage Resources and Evaluation Conference (LREC), Reykjavik, Iceland.

A. Pasha, M. Al-Badrashiny, M. Diab, A. El Kholy, R. Eskander, N. Habash, M. Pooleery, O. Rambow and R. M. Roth. MADAMIRA: A Fast, Comprehensive Tool for Morphological Analysis and Disambiguation of Arabic. In Proc. of LREC, Reykjavik, Iceland, 2014.

POS-tagging of Tunisian Dialect Using Standard Arabic Resources and Tools

Ahmed Hamdi[1] **Alexis Nasr**[1] **Nizar Habash**[2] **Núria Gala**[1]
(1) Laboratoire d'Informatique Fondamentale de Marseille, Aix-Marseille University
(2) New York University University Abu Dhabi
{ahmed.hamdi,alexis.nasr,nuria.gala}@lif.univ-mrs.fr
nizar.habash@nyu.edu

Abstract

Developing natural language processing tools usually requires a large number of resources (lexica, annotated corpora, etc.), which often do not exist for less-resourced languages. One way to overcome the problem of lack of resources is to devote substantial efforts to build new ones from scratch. Another approach is to exploit existing resources of closely related languages. In this paper, we focus on developing a part-of-speech tagger for the Tunisian Arabic dialect (TUN), a low-resource language, by exploiting its closeness to Modern Standard Arabic (MSA), which has many state-of-the-art resources and tools. Our system achieved an accuracy of 89% (~20% absolute improvement over an MSA tagger baseline).

1 Introduction

The Arabic language is characterized by diglossia (Ferguson, 1959) : two linguistic variants live side by side: a standard written form and a large variety of spoken dialects. While dialects differ from one region to another, the written variety, called Modern Standard Arabic (MSA), is generally the same. MSA, the official language for Arabic countries, is used for written communication as well as in formal spoken communications. Spoken varieties, generally used in informal daily discussions, are increasingly being used for informal written communication on the web. Such unstandardized varieties differ from MSA with respect to phonology, morphology, syntax and the lexicon. Unlike MSA which has an important number of NLP resources and tools, Arabic dialects are less-resourced. In this paper, we focus on the Tunisian Arabic dialect (TUN). It is the spoken language of twelve million speakers living mainly in Tunisia. TUN is the result of interactions and influences of a number of languages including Arabic, Berber and French (Mejri et al., 2009).

In this paper, we focus on the development of a part-of-speech (POS) tagger for TUN. There are two main options when developing such a tool for TUN. The first one is to build a corpus of TUN, which involves recording, transcribing and manually POS tagging. In order to have a state-of-the-art POS tagger one also needs to develop a lexicon. The second option is to *convert* TUN into an approximate form of MSA, that we will call pseudo MSA, and use an existing MSA POS tagger. We intentionally do not use the verb *translate* to describe the process of transforming a TUN text into a pseudo MSA text. The reason being that we are not translating between two natural languages: pseudo MSA is not meant to be read by humans. Its only purpose is to be close enough to MSA so that running it through NLP tools would give good results. The annotation produced is then projected back on the TUN text. More technically, the conversion process focuses on morphological and lexical aspects; it is based on morphological analyzers and generators for TUN and MSA as well as a TUN-MSA dictionaries which are themselves partly automatically produced using the morphological analyzers and generators. Besides producing a POS tagger for TUN, we aim at proposing a general methodology for developing NLP tools for dialects of Arabic.

The rest of the paper is organized as follows: we present, in section 2, phonological, lexical and morphosyntactic variations between TUN and MSA. We then discuss related works and existing POS taggers of Arabic dialects in section 3. Section 4 reviews the tools and resources used

Proceedings of the Second Workshop on Arabic Natural Language Processing, pages 59–68,
Beijing, China, July 26-31, 2015. ©2014 Association for Computational Linguistics

in this work. In section 5, we describe in detail our approach to tag TUN texts. Finally, Section 6 presents results evaluating our approach under several conditions.

2 Linguistic variations between MSA and TUN

The TUN dialect differs from MSA on the phonological, lexical, morphological, and syntactic levels. In this work, we focus on the three first levels.

- **phonological and orthographic variations**: TUN has all phonemes that exist in MSA. However, TUN has three extra phonemes /p/, /v/ and /g/. To a lesser extent, variations appear in some common words, that consist in dropping some short vowels[1] on the TUN side. For instance, كتاب *ktAb*[2] "*book*" and كتب *ktb* "*to write*" which exist in both languages but are pronounced differently: /kitAb/, /katab/ in MSA and /ktAb/, /ktib/ in Tunisian dialect. Concerning orthography, unlike MSA, which already has a standard orthography, Tunisian dialect is unstandardized. Zribi et al. (2014) proposes orthographic standards for TUN, following the works of Habash et al. (2012), that aim to establish a common orthographic convention for all Arabic dialects.
- **lexical variations**: from a lexical point of view, the differences between MSA and TUN are significant. They are mainly due to the influence of other languages. Such TUN words still generally follow MSA morphology, sharing the same inflectional and derivational rules. Table 1 gives some examples of words of different origins.
- **morphological variations**: All morphological phenomena that exist in MSA exist also in TUN, but they are sometimes expressed differently. As cliticization is concerned, several MSA prepositions are attached to words on the TUN side. For example, the MSA prepositions على *ςalaý* "*on*" and من *mino* "*from*" become in TUN respectively +ع ς+ and +م m+ proclitics when the word following is definite (marked by the determinant marker +ال Al+). Furthermore, indirect object pronouns are realized as enclitics in TUN verbs and not in MSA. On the other hand, some MSA clitics are detached in TUN. The MSA future particle proclitic +س *sa+* is realized as the autonomous particle باش *bAš* with TUN verbs. As for inflectional morphology, MSA has a richer system than TUN. In fact, MSA nominal case and verbal mood do not exist in TUN. The three MSA number values (singular, dual and plural) are reduced to singular and plural. On TUN side, the masculine and the feminine plural are consolidated. Concerning derivational morphology, TUN words, except loanwords, keep the same principle of word's derivation from a root and a pattern as MSA. The TUN words حجّم *Haj∼im "cap"* and حجّام *Haj∼Am "hair dresser"* are both derived from the root ح ج م *H j m* and the patterns *1a22i3* and *1a22A3* respectively.

MSA	TUN	gloss	origin
تين tiyn	كرموس karmuws	fig	Berber
ولّاعة wal∼Aςaħ	بريكيّة briykiy∼aħ	lighter	French
مكتب بريد maktab bariyd	بوسطة buwSTaħ	post office	Italian
أسود Âaswad	أكحل ÂakHil	black	Arabic
باخرة bAxiraħ	بابور bAbuwr	boat	Turkish

Table 1: Examples of lexical variations between TUN and MSA

3 Related work

Processing Arabic dialects

Most studies concerning Arabic dialects focus on Egyptian, Levantine and Iraqi. Some efforts have been done to create dialectal resources such as Al-Sabbagh and Girju (2010) who built an Egyptian/MSA lexicon exploiting available data from the web. Other researchers focused on building parallel corpora between Arabic dialects, MSA and English (Zbib et al., 2012; Bouamor et al., 2014; Harrat et al., 2014). Habash et al. (2008) and Elfardy and Diab (2012) proposed some standard guidelines for the annotation of Arabic dialects. Other efforts focused in dialect identification (Habash et al., 2008; Elfardy and Diab, 2013; Zaidan and Callison-Burch, 2014) and

[1] In Arabic orthography, short vowels are represented with optional diacritics which makes the language ambiguous.

[2] Arabic orthographic transliteration is presented in the Habash-Soudi-Buckwalter HSB scheme (Habash et al., 2007).

machine translation (Sawaf, 2010; Salloum and Habash, 2011; Sajjad et al., 2013). Concerning morphosyntactic analysis, Al-Sabbagh and Girju (2012) implemented a POS tagger of Egyptian trained on data extracted from the web. Chiang et al. (2006) developed lexicons and morphological rules to build Levantine treebanks from MSA resources in order to parse Levantine dialect.

POS tagging of one language using another language

There have been several attempts to build POS taggers for one language using resources and tools of other languages. The idea consists in transforming the source language for which more resources are available into a target language (Yarowsky et al., 2001), using, for instance, parallel corpora. The source side is tagged using an available tagger, the annotations are then projected on the target. Subsequently, a new tagger is trained on the target side. In the same way, (Das and Petrov, 2011) used a graph-based projection algorithm to project tags across eight European languages. Following this work, (Duong et al., 2013) showed that focusing on selected informative training sentences from the parallel corpus and employing self-training achieve equivalent performance. All these studies concerned unrelated languages.

This approach is more effective when the source and the target languages are closely related. Many researchers exploit this fact to create resources and tools for under-resourced languages using other related well-resourced languages. Duong et al. (2013), for example used the approach based on parallel corpora to build a POS tagger for some European languages. Some efforts looked into dictionaries extracted from Wikitionary instead of parallel corpora (Li et al., 2012) and others combined both resources (Täckström et al., 2013). Other approaches propose to adapt existing taggers of a more-resourced close related languages for miss-resourced languages. Feldman et al. (2006) built taggers for Czech and Catalan starting from existing Russian and Spanish taggers respectively. They trained the taggers on the source language and then adapt its parameter files on the target language by means of a list of cognate word pairs. Similarly, Bernhard et al. (2013) adapted a German tagger to Alsatian. Vergez-Couret (2013) showed that building POS taggers for less-resourced language using annotated corpora for a more-resourced related language is possible by translating only the most frequent words from the source side to the target side. In their experiments, they built two bilingual Occitan/French and Occitan/Castillan lexica of about 300 entries. After translating the most frequent words, existing French and Castillan taggers have been run on Occitan texts.

POS tagging of Arabic dialects

Concerning POS tagging of Arabic dialects, few efforts focused on creating resources for such dialects. (Al-Sabbagh and Girju, 2012) built an Egyptian POS tagger trained on manually annotated corpus of $400K$ tokens extracted from written Arabic social networking. They report an accuracy of 94% in tokenization and 88% in POS tagging. Similarly, Mohamed et al. (2012) annotated a small corpus to train an Egyptian tokenizer. Their system's performance reaches 91%. Some other efforts used existing tools of related languages as starting material to build POS taggers for dialects. The first system proposed by Duh and Kirchhoff (2005), built a Levantine and Egyptian POS tagger using raw text corpora and an existing MSA analyzer. Their POS accuracy achieves 71%. Similarly, Habash et al. (2013) and Pasha et al. (2014) developed an Egyptian morphological analyzer using two systems for Arabic morphology processing: MADA (Habash and Rambow, 2005; Roth et al., 2008) and AMIRA (Diab et al., 2013), they report 92.4% of POS accuracy on Egyptian Arabic.

Tunisian morphology processing

Processing Tunisian morphology has not been the object of many studies. Zribi et al. (2013) adapted an existing MSA morphological analyzer to handle TUN. In order to build such a tool, they used a TUN-MSA lexicon to add specific TUN roots and patterns. Their system achieved an F-measure performance of 88% in morphological analysis. In a similar setting, Boujelbane et al. (2014) used the same lexicon to transform a MSA training corpus to create a large TUN corpus. This resource was used to train a POS tagger. POS tagging of TUN transcribed texts using this tagger and achieved an accuracy of 78.5%.

Our approach is close to Boujelbane et al. (2014): we built a POS tagger for a less-resourced variant of a language using a system trained on an annotated close related language. Our approach differs from their mostly on the morphological processing: we perform a deeper morphological analysis, which allows us to generate a lemmatized version of the MSA text. We will show that performing the POS tagging at this level yields better results.

4 Tools and resources

In this section, we describe the various resources and tools we used in our experiments. We first describe MAGEAD, a morphological analyzer/generator. Then, we detail three lexica that relate MSA and TUN lemmas.

4.1 Morphological analysis and generation of Arabic and its dialect

MAGEAD is a morphological analyzer and generator for the Arabic language family (MSA and Arabic dialects). It processes Arabic verbs (Habash and Rambow, 2006; Habash et al., 2005) and Arabic nouns (Altantawy et al., 2010).

MAGEAD relates a deep representation of a word with its surface form through a sequence of transformations. It can be used bidirectionally, to generate, as well as to analyze, surface forms. At a deep representation level, MAGEAD represents a word as a root, a pattern and a set of feature-value pairs. The features are translated to abstract morphemes which are then ordered, and expressed as concrete morphemes. Finally, morphological and phonological rewrite rules are applied. To describe the different processes made by MAGEAD, we use the surface form واضطرّوا *waAiDTar∼uwA "and they were obliged"* as our example. The MAGEAD lexeme and features representation of this word form is as follows:

(1) root:Drr mbc:verb-VIII cnj:w per:3 gen:m num:prl asp:p vox:a

The lexeme is defined as the root *Drr* and a morphological behavior class (MBC) *verb-VIII*. The MBC maps sets of linguistic feature-value pairs to sets of abstract morphemes (AMs). In our example, the MBC verb-III maps asp:p and vox:a to the AM [PAT_PV:VIII][VOC_PV:VIII-act]. The feature value cnj:w is simply mapped to the AM [CNJ:W] while the features values per:3 gen:m num:prl asp:p is mapped to the AM [SUBJ_SUFF:3MP]. AMs are then ordered. At this point our example is represented as:

(2) [CNJ:W] + [ROOT:Drr] [PAT_PV:VIII] [VOC_PV:VIII-act] + [SUBJ_SUFF:3MP]

Note that the root, pattern, and vocalism are not ordered with respect to each other, they are simply juxtaposed. The '+' sign indicates the ordering of affixational morphemes. AMs are then mapped to CMs, which are concatenated in the specified order. Our example becomes:

(3) wa + Drr,V1tV2V3,iaa + uwA

Simple interdigitation of root, pattern and vocalism then yields the form (4) wa+iDtarar+uwA. At this point MAGEAD applies (if they exist) rules of the following type:

- Morphophonemic/phonological rules map the morphemic representation to the phonological and orthographic representations. In our example, two rules are applied. First, the gemination[3] rule, which allows to delete the vowel between the second and the third radical if it is followed by a suffix starting with a vowel. Then, a phonological rule that transforms the /t/ of the pattern *i1ta2a3* to /T/.[4] We get, at this step: /wa+iDTar∼+uwA/.
- Orthographic rules rewrite the orthographic representation. Using standard MSA diacritized orthography, our example becomes واضطرّوا *waAiDTar∼uwA*.

MAGEAD follows (Kiraz, 2000) in using a multi-tape representation. It extends the analysis of Kiraz by introducing a fifth tier. The five tiers are the following :

- Tier 1: pattern and affixational morphemes
- Tier 2: root
- Tier 3: vocalism
- Tier 4: phonological representation
- Tier 5: orthographic representation

In the generation direction, tiers 1 through 3 are input tiers. Tier 4 is an output tier, and an input tier for the orthographic representation.

MAGEAD handles Arabic nouns in the same way. Specific CMs, AMs and morpheme order are defined for nouns. The MBC hierarchy specifies relevant morphosyntactic features such as rationality. The MBC class name indicates the vocalized patterns according to the number and the gender values. Many nominal rules are similar to those presented for verbs. Others are specific, reflecting

[3]A geminate root is a root in which the second and the third radical are identical.

[4]The /t/ of the pattern *i1ta2a3* is converted to /T/ when the first root radical corresponds to /D/, /T/ or /Ď/.

the differences between Arabic nominal and verbal morphology.

We adapted MAGEAD to process TUN. Changes concerned only the representation of linguistic knowledge, leaving the processing engine unchanged. We modified the MBC hierarchy, in order to process TUN patterns and vocalisms. The AM ordering has been modified and new AMs have been added. The mapping from AMs to CMs and the definition of rules, which are variant-specific, have been written by a linguistically trained native speaker.

We also modified a number of morphophonemic rules in the TUN implementation. We briefly describe three changes. First, in MSA, the gemination rule deletes the vowel between the second and the third radical if it is followed by a suffix starting with a vowel: e.g., compare مددت *madad+tu* *'I extended'* with مدّت *mad∼+at' she extended'* (NOT *madad+at*). In TUN, however, a long vowel is inserted before consonant-initial suffixes following geminate verbs: مدّيت *mad∼+iy+t "I extended"* and مدّت *mad∼+it "she extended"*. Second, unlike MSA, the first root radical in TUN becomes a long vowel in the imperfective aspect when it corresponds to ء *' (hamza/glottal stop)* (يأكل *yÂkl* becomes ياكل *yAkl 'he/it eats'*). Finally, TUN verbs whose root ends with ء ', behave the same way as verbs whose final root radical ي *y* in the perfective aspect. For example, roots of TUN verbs بدينا *bdiynA "we started"* and رمينا *rmiynA "we threw"* are respectively ب د ء *bd'* and ر م ي *rmy*. For more details, see (Hamdi et al., 2013).

4.2 Lexica

Due to the lexical differences between MSA and TUN, the conversion process cannot be limited to morphological transformations and requires some lexical transformations. We used three lexica to map from TUN to MSA: a lexicon of verbs, a lexicon of deverbal nouns and a lexicon of particles.

4.2.1 Lexicon of verbs

The verbal lexicon consists of pairs of the form (P_{MSA}, P_{TUN}) where P_{MSA} and P_{TUN} are themselves pairs made of a root and a pattern. Its development was based on the Penn Arabic Tree Bank (*PATB*) (Maamouri et al., 2004) which contains $29,911$ verb tokens. Each token was then analyzed to extract its root and its pattern. Each lemma was translated, in context, to TUN by a Tunisian native speaker. Since the lemma is the result of combining a root and a pattern, the TUN pair (root, pattern) can be deduced. This process allowed us to define about 100 new roots for TUN. The lexicon contains $1,638$ entries. The TUN side contains 920 distinct pairs and the MSA side $1,478$ distinct pairs. This difference shows that MSA is lexically richer than TUN. On average, a TUN lemma corresponds to almost two MSA lemmas. For instance, the TUN verb مشى *mšaý* matches with MSA verbs ذهب *ðahab 'to go'* and مشى *mašaý 'to walk'*. The maximum ambiguity is 16 in the TUN $\rightarrow$ MSA direction and 4 in the opposite direction.

4.2.2 Lexicon of deverbal nouns

This lexicon is automatically built using the lexicon of verbs. In fact, many deverbal nouns can be derived from verbs such as participles, infinitive forms, adjectives, nouns of time and place ... The deverbal noun is produced by combining a root and a deverbal pattern. The deverbal patterns are derived from verbal patterns. Each pair (root, pattern) of the verbal lexica generates many deverbal entries by combining the root with all deverbal patterns that share the same meaning on both sides. This method overgenerates and can produce wrong pairs. In order to face this problem, we filtered the MSA part using the MSA large-scale lexicon SAMA (Graff et al., 2009). At the end of the process, a lexicon made of $33,271$ entries is created (Hamdi et al., 2014).

4.2.3 Lexicon of particles

Arabic particles cover many categories: conjunctions, prepositions, clitics ... Our lexicon, made of about 200 pairs (MSA particle, TUN particle), includes all of them. The MSA particles are extracted from the PATB and then translated to TUN (Boujelbane et al., 2013). In its current version, the lexicon matches 262 Tunisian particles to 143 MSA particles.

5 Architecture and experiments

Our system consists of three step: conversion, disambiguation and POS tagging.

The TUN input sentence $t_1\, t_2\, t_3 \ldots t_n$, is converted to a MSA lattice. The lattice is then disambiguated to produce a pseudo MSA target sentence $m_1\, m_2\, m_3 \ldots m_n$. Next, a MSA tagger assign to each target word its POS tag. The disambiguation step is optional, the MSA lattice can be sent directly to the POS tagger which tags the lattice and produces the most likely tag sequence.

Taking as an example the TUN sentence تجبر باش يقعد *tijbar bAš yuqςud* '*he was obliged to stay*', which correspond to the sequence of POS tags *verb-pass*[5] - *part* - *verb*. This sentence translates into MSA as اضطرّ إلى البقاء *AiðTar∼a Ăilaý AlbaqA'*. Our system produces for this sentence, after conversion and disambiguation, the sentence اضطرّ سوف يجلس *AuðTur∼a sawfa yajlisu* '*he was obliged will sit-down*' which receives the correct POS tags sequence *verb-pass* - *part* - *verb*, although the MSA translation is suboptimal. In the remainder of this section, we describe in detail each step of the whole process.

5.1 Conversion

The process of converting a source TUN word form to a target MSA form proceeds in three main steps: morphological analysis using MAGEAD for the source language, lexical transfer and morphological generation of target MSA forms. Figure 1 describes the process that allows to switch from a TUN source input to a MSA target output.

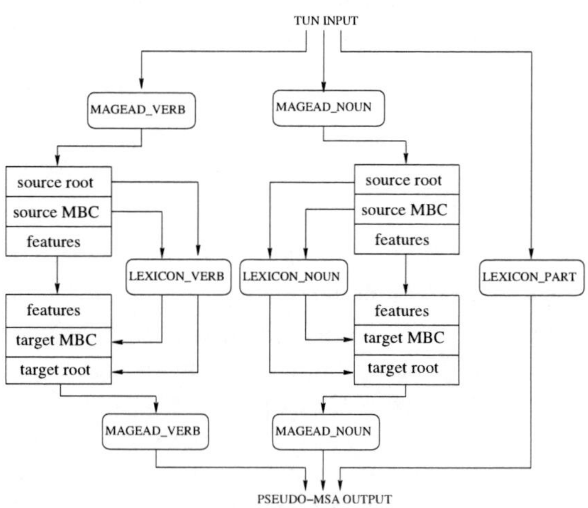

Figure 1: TUN-to-MSA conversion

Each TUN source word is processed by MAGEAD to produce several analyses; each of them is compound of a root, a pattern and a set of feature-value pairs. The root and the pattern are translated to a MSA root and pattern by a lexicon lookup. MAGEAD finally uses the target root and pattern and the feature-value pairs to generate a target MSA word.

This process was evaluated on 1,500 tokens of TUN verbal forms that were identified and translated in context to MSA by Tunisian native speakers. Table 2 gives the accuracy and the ambiguity resulting from the translation. The recall indicates the proportion of cases where the correct target form was produced while the ambiguity indicates the number of target forms produced on average for an input.

recall		ambiguity	
tokens	types	tokens	types
76.43%	74.52%	26.82	25.57

Table 2: Recall and ambiguity on translation of TUN verbs to MSA

In order to extend the coverage of the lexica, we introduced a back-off process. When a pair (root, MBC) is missing in the noun or the verb lexicon, the root and MBC are translated separately, using a root lexicon and an MBC correspondence table. The root lexicon is made of pairs (r_{MSA}, r_{TUN}), where r_{MSA} is a MSA root and r_{TUN} is a TUN root. The root lexicon contains 1,329 entries. The MBC correspondence tables indicates, for a TUN MBC, the most frequent corresponding MBCs on the MSA side. In cases of lexicon look-up failure, the MSA target word is produced by combining the target root lexicon and the target pattern. Table 3 gives the accuracy and the ambiguity resulting of the back-off process.

recall		ambiguity	
tokens	types	tokens	types
79.71%	78.94%	29.16	28.44

Table 3: Recall and ambiguity on translation of TUN verbs to MSA with back-off

Table 3 shows that this back-off mechanism reaches a reasonable recall but the price to pay is a high ambiguity. More details are given in (Hamdi et al., 2013).

5.2 Disambiguation

The conversion process contains two sources of ambiguity: the morphological analysis can create multiple outputs and the lexica may propose for a TUN input many MSA outputs. Each word in the TUN sentence is translated into a set of MSA words producing a lattice. The disambiguation can

[5]verb in the passive form

be performed by the POS tagger, as we will see below or it can be done independently, using a language model. We have trained a 1-gram and a 3-gram language models on a two million word MSA corpus. This corpus is itself made of two corpora. The first one is a written corpus, it is a collection of reports of the French press agency (AFP). The second one is a spoken corpus, it is a collection of political debates transcriptions. The trigram model is used to give the first best path while the unigram allowed to filter and score the lattice.

Three different inputs can be handled by the POS tagger: an unscored lattice derived from the conversion, a scored lattice produced by the disambiguation based on the unigram language model and the first best path generated by the 3-gram language model.

5.3 Pos-Tagging

The taggers used in this work are based on Hidden Markov Models (HMM). We have chosen this type of model mainly for their ability to take word lattices as input in a straightforward way. The tagger itself is a weighted finite state transducer and the tagging process is performed by a composition operation of the word lattice and the tagger, followed by a best path operation. When the tagger is fed with a lattice produced by the conversion step (containing potentially several MSA forms for a TUN form), the tagger actually does more than POS tagging, it also selects a sequence of words from the word lattice.

We built six taggers that differ in the order of the HMM they are based on (bigram or trigram) as well as in the nature of the observables of the HMM: forms, lemmas and *lmms*. The latter is the undiacritized form of a lemma. There are two main reasons for using lemmas and *lmms* based taggers: first, the translation task is more accurate and gives less ambiguity for lemmas and *lmms* than for forms. Second, the POS tagging achieves better results on lemmas and *lmms* than on forms, as shown in Table 4.

The taggers are trained on the Penn Arabic Treebank (PATB) Part 3 (Maamouri et al., 2004) in the representation of the Columbia Arabic Treebank (CATIB) (Habash and Roth, 2009). The corpus is made from $24K$ MSA sentences compound of $330K$ tokens and $30K$ types. The CATIB POS tagset consists of six tags only: nominal, proper noun, verb, verb-pass, particle and punctuation.

Table 4 gives the results of POS tagging of a MSA corpus using our different HMM taggers. These results are comparable to state-of-the-art MSA POS tagging systems: Habash and Roth (2009) report a higher result using the MADA system (Habash and Rambow, 2005). However, we cannot use the MADA system because it does not support POS tagging over a lattice, which we need for TUN POS tagging. It should be noted that the results in the table are for forms (real task), but also for gold lemmas and *lmms*. We present the lemma and *lmm* results only for comparative reasons as the starting point is artificial, and the performance numbers should be seen as upper bounds.

	forms	gold lemmas	gold *lmms*
bigram	94.52	97.61	96.84
trigram	94.72	97.63	96.94

Table 4: Accuracy of POS tagging of MSA corpus

The results in the table suggest that using the trigram HMM is slightly better than the bigram HMM models. For the rest of this paper, we will report only using the trigram model.

6 Evaluation

In order to evaluate our method, we used a transcribed and annotated corpus of 805 sentences containing $10,746$ tokens and $2,455$ types. These sentences were obtained from several sources: TV series and political debates, a transcribed theater play (Dhouib, 2007) and a transcribed corpus made of conversations between a customer and a railways officer. This selection aims to include different TUN spoken varieties. After transcribing, we have assigned to each token its lemma, *lmm* and POS tag using the same conventions as the corpus used to train the tagger.

Our baseline experiment consists of running the MSA POS tagger directly on TUN texts without any processing. This baseline will allow us to measure the contribution of converting TUN to pseudo MSA prior to POS tagging with the MSA tagger. The accuracy of tagging and the number of out-of-vocabulary words are given in Table 5. The lemmas and *lmms* used for the experiment are gold lemmas and *lmms*, presented again for comparative reasons. Our official baseline is with forms.

Table 5 shows that the baseline is very low, around 69%. The result on lemmas is even worse.

	forms	gold lemmas	gold *lmms*
accuracy	69.04%	67.41%	71.41%
OOVs	2891 26.90%	4766 44.35%	2705 25.17%

Table 5: Baseline Accuracy of POS tagging TUN using MSA POS tagger

This is not unexpected since the TUN lemma space is different from the MSA lemma space, which the tagger is trained on. Lemmas are completely diacritized and diacritics on lemmas are different on MSA and on TUN. For instance, the TUN undiacritized form يكتب *yktb "he writes"* exists in MSA side but its lemma *ktib "to write"* is different from the MSA one *katab*. Results are a bit higher on *lmms*, which do not contain diactritics. It is also interesting to note that the number of OOVs on *lmms* is still high, showing that lexica of MSA and TUN are quite different.

For our main experiment we convert TUN texts to pseudo MSA before POS tagging. The conversion step produces three lattices (forms, lemmas, *lmms*). The form lattice is disambiguated by the language models providing a scored lattice and the first best path. We ran the POS tagging of pseudo-MSA forms in three modes: on the best form path, on the scored lattice and the unscored lattice produced by the conversion. The final output is the sequence of POS tags for the words in the original sentence. Results are shown in Table 6.

	best path	scored lattice	unscored lattice
accuracy	77.2%	80.3%	82.5%
OOVs	16.9%	15.3%	13.5%

Table 6: Accuracy of POS tagging of pseudo MSA

Results show that the conversion decreases the number of OOVs and subsequently the POS-tagging accuracy of forms increases (comparing with Table 5). Disambiguation based on the POS tagger gives better accuracy (~82.5% on forms) than the language model (77.2%).

Our convertion process allows to produce, MSA lemmas and *lmms* rather then forms by leaving the morphological generation of MSA forms. The POS tagger was ran thus on the lattices of lemmas and *lmms*. In Table 7, we give results of POS tagging such inputs. We give again results on forms to compare these final results with the basline results (Table 5).

	forms	*predicted* lemmas	*predicted* *lmms*
accuracy	82.5%	86.9%	**89.1%**
OOVs	13.5%	6.2%	4.9%

Table 7: Accuracy of POS tagging of pseudo MSA lemmas and *lmms*

As shown in Table 7, POS tagging of lemmas and *lmms* outperforms POS tagging of forms. Our best accuracy, with *lmms*, jumps to 89.1%: a 20% absolute increase of the baseline of using the MSA POS tagger directly on the TUN sentences. An error analysis of the first 100 errors shows that 34 of them are due to bad conversion and 49 to bad disambiguation. Only, 17 of the errors came from POS tagging.

7 Conclusion

In this paper, we proposed, implemented and evaluated an approach to POS tagging of TUN using an MSA tagger. Prior to tagging, the TUN text is converted to pseudo MSA. The conversion process is composed of three steps: morphological analysis of the TUN words, followed by a lexical transfer and a morphological generation of MSA forms. The system achieved an accuracy of 89% (~20% absolute improvement over an MSA tagger baseline). Experiments showed that the best results were obtained by tagging at the level of lemmas, more precisely, lemmas from which diacritics were removed.

In future work, we aim to complete our processing chain by adding a TUN speech recognition system (since TUN is a primarily spoken language) at the beginning of the chain, and to evaluate our approach in some other NLP tasks such as syntactic parsing. We are also interested in applying these results to other dialects.

Acknowledgments

This paper is based upon work supported by the Defense Advanced Research Projects Agency (DARPA) under Contract Nos. HR0011-12-C-0014 and HR0011-12-C-0016. Any opinions, findings and conclusions or recommendations expressed in this paper are those of the authors and do not necessarily reflect the views of DARPA.

References

Rania Al-Sabbagh and Roxana Girju. 2010. Mining the web for the induction of a dialectical Arabic lexicon. In *LREC*.

Rania Al-Sabbagh and Roxana Girju. 2012. A supervised pos tagger for written Arabic social networking corpora. In *Proceedings of KONVENS*, pages 39–52.

Mohamed Altantawy, Nizar Habash, Owen Rambow, and Ibrahim Saleh. 2010. Morphological Analysis and Generation of Arabic Nouns: A Morphemic Functional Approach. In *Proceedings of the seventh International Conference on Language Resources and Evaluation (LREC)*, Valletta, Malta.

Delphine Bernhard, Anne-Laure Ligozat, et al. 2013. Hassle-free pos-tagging for the alsatian dialects. *Non-Standard Data Sources in Corpus Based-Research*.

Houda Bouamor, Nizar Habash, and Kemal Oflazer. 2014. A Multidialectal Parallel Corpus of Arabic.

Rahma Boujelbane, Siwar BenAyed, and Lamia Hadrich Belguith. 2013. Building bilingual lexicon to create dialect Tunisian corpora and adapt language model. *ACL 2013*, page 88.

Rahma Boujelbane, Mariem Mallek, Mariem Ellouze, and Lamia Hadrich Belguith. 2014. Fine-grained pos tagging of spoken Tunisian dialect corpora. In *Natural Language Processing and Information Systems*, pages 59–62. Springer.

David Chiang, Mona T Diab, Nizar Habash, Owen Rambow, and Safiullah Shareef. 2006. Parsing Arabic dialects. In *EACL*.

Dipanjan Das and Slav Petrov. 2011. Unsupervised part-of-speech tagging with bilingual graph-based projections. In *Proceedings of the 49th Annual Meeting of the Association for Computational Linguistics: Human Language Technologies-Volume 1*, pages 600–609. Association for Computational Linguistics.

E Dhouib. 2007. El makki w zakiyya. Maison d'Ãl'dition manshuwrat manara, Tunis.

Mona Diab, Nizar Habash, Owen Rambow, and Ryan Roth. 2013. Ldc Arabic treebanks and associated corpora: Data divisions manual. *arXiv preprint arXiv:1309.5652*.

Kevin Duh and Katrin Kirchhoff. 2005. Pos tagging of dialectal Arabic: a minimally supervised approach. In *Proceedings of the ACL Workshop on Computational Approaches to Semitic Languages*, pages 55–62. Association for Computational Linguistics.

Long Duong, Paul Cook, Steven Bird, and Pavel Pecina. 2013. Simpler unsupervised pos tagging with bilingual projections. In *ACL (2)*, pages 634–639.

Heba Elfardy and Mona T Diab. 2012. Simplified guidelines for the creation of large scale dialectal Arabic annotations. In *LREC*, pages 371–378.

Heba Elfardy and Mona T Diab. 2013. Sentence level dialect identification in Arabic. In *ACL (2)*, pages 456–461.

Anna Feldman, Jirka Hana, and Chris Brew. 2006. A cross-language approach to rapid creation of new morpho-syntactically annotated resources. In *Proceedings of LREC*, pages 549–554.

Charles Albert Ferguson. 1959. Diglossia. *WORD-JOURNAL OF THE INTERNATIONAL LINGUISTIC ASSOCIATION*, 15(2):325–340.

David Graff, Mohamed Maamouri, Basma Bouziri, Sondos Krouna, Seth Kulick, and Tim Buckwalter. 2009. Standard Arabic Morphological Analyzer (SAMA) Version 3.1. Linguistic Data Consortium LDC2009E73.

Nizar Habash and Owen Rambow. 2005. Arabic tokenization, part-of-speech tagging and morphological disambiguation in one fell swoop. In *Proceedings of the 43rd Annual Meeting on Association for Computational Linguistics*, pages 573–580. Association for Computational Linguistics.

Nizar Habash and Owen Rambow. 2006. Magead: a morphological analyzer and generator for the Arabic dialects. In *Proceedings of the 21st International Conference on Computational Linguistics and the 44th annual meeting of the Association for Computational Linguistics*, pages 681–688. Association for Computational Linguistics.

Nizar Habash and Ryan M Roth. 2009. Catib: The columbia Arabic treebank. In *Proceedings of the ACL-IJCNLP 2009 Conference Short Papers*, pages 221–224. Association for Computational Linguistics.

Nizar Habash, Owen Rambow, and George Kiraz. 2005. Morphological analysis and generation for Arabic dialects. In *Proceedings of the ACL Workshop on Computational Approaches to Semitic Languages*, pages 17–24. Association for Computational Linguistics.

Nizar Habash, Abdelhadi Soudi, and Tim Buckwalter. 2007. On Arabic Transliteration. In A. van den Bosch and A. Soudi, editors, *Arabic Computational Morphology: Knowledge-based and Empirical Methods*. Springer.

Nizar Habash, Owen Rambow, Mona Diab, and Reem Kanjawi-Faraj. 2008. Guidelines for annotation of Arabic dialectness. In *Proceedings of the LREC Workshop on HLT & NLP within the Arabic world*, pages 49–53.

Nizar Habash, Mona T Diab, and Owen Rambow. 2012. Conventional orthography for dialectal Arabic. In *LREC*, pages 711–718.

Nizar Habash, Ryan Roth, Owen Rambow, Ramy Eskander, and Nadi Tomeh. 2013. Morphological analysis and disambiguation for dialectal Arabic. In *HLT-NAACL*, pages 426–432. Citeseer.

Ahmed Hamdi, Rahma Boujelbane, Nizar Habash, and Alexis Nasr. 2013. The effects of factorizing root and pattern mapping in bidirectional Tunisian - standard Arabic machine translation. In *MT Summit, Nice*.

Ahmed Hamdi, Núria Gala, and Alexis Nasr. 2014. Automatically building a Tunisian lexicon for deverbal nouns. *COLING 2014*, page 95.

S Harrat, K Meftouh, M Abbas, and K Smaili. 2014. Building resources for algerian Arabic dialects. *Corpus (sentences)*, 4000(6415):2415.

George Anton Kiraz. 2000. Multitiered nonlinear morphology using multitape finite automata: a case study on Syriac and Arabic. *Computational Linguistics*, 26(1):77–105, March.

Shen Li, Joao V Graça, and Ben Taskar. 2012. Wiki-ly supervised part-of-speech tagging. In *Proceedings of the 2012 Joint Conference on Empirical Methods in Natural Language Processing and Computational Natural Language Learning*, pages 1389–1398. Association for Computational Linguistics.

Mohamed Maamouri, Ann Bies, Tim Buckwalter, and Wigdan Mekki. 2004. The penn Arabic treebank: Building a large-scale annotated Arabic corpus. In *NEMLAR conference on Arabic language resources and tools*, pages 102–109.

S. Mejri, S. Mosbah, and I. Sfar. 2009. Pluringuisme et diglossie en tunisie. *Synergies Tunisie n 1*, pages 53–74.

Emad Mohamed, Behrang Mohit, and Kemal Oflazer. 2012. Annotating and learning morphological segmentation of egyptian colloquial Arabic. In *LREC*, pages 873–877.

Arfath Pasha, Mohamed Al-Badrashiny, Ahmed El Kholy, Ramy Eskander, Mona Diab, Nizar Habash, Manoj Pooleery, Owen Rambow, and Ryan Roth. 2014. Madamira: A fast, comprehensive tool for morphological analysis and disambiguation of Arabic. In *In Proceedings of the 9th International Conference on Language Resources and Evaluation, Reykjavik, Iceland*.

Ryan Roth, Owen Rambow, Nizar Habash, Mona Diab, and Cynthia Rudin. 2008. Arabic morphological tagging, diacritization, and lemmatization using lexeme models and feature ranking. In *Proceedings of the 46th Annual Meeting of the Association for Computational Linguistics on Human Language Technologies: Short Papers*, pages 117–120. Association for Computational Linguistics.

Hassan Sajjad, Kareem Darwish, and Yonatan Belinkov. 2013. Translating dialectal Arabic to english. In *ACL (2)*, pages 1–6.

Wael Salloum and Nizar Habash. 2011. Dialectal to standard Arabic paraphrasing to improve Arabic-english statistical machine translation. In *Proceedings of the First Workshop on Algorithms and Resources for Modelling of Dialects and Language Varieties*, pages 10–21. Association for Computational Linguistics.

Hassan Sawaf. 2010. Arabic dialect handling in hybrid machine translation. In *Proceedings of the 9th Conference of the Association for Machine Translation in the Americas*.

Oscar Täckström, Dipanjan Das, Slav Petrov, Ryan McDonald, and Joakim Nivre. 2013. Token and type constraints for cross-lingual part-of-speech tagging. *Transactions of the Association for Computational Linguistics*, 1:1–12.

Marianne Vergez-Couret. 2013. Tagging occitan using french and castillan tree tagger. In *Proceedings of 6th Language & Technology Conference*.

David Yarowsky, Grace Ngai, and Richard Wicentowski. 2001. Inducing multilingual text analysis tools via robust projection across aligned corpora. In *Proceedings of the first international conference on Human language technology research*, pages 1–8. Association for Computational Linguistics.

Omar F Zaidan and Chris Callison-Burch. 2014. Arabic dialect identification. *Computational Linguistics*, 40(1):171–202.

Rabih Zbib, Erika Malchiodi, Jacob Devlin, David Stallard, Spyros Matsoukas, Richard Schwartz, John Makhoul, Omar F Zaidan, and Chris Callison-Burch. 2012. Machine translation of Arabic dialects. In *Proceedings of the 2012 Conference of the North American Chapter of the Association for Computational Linguistics: Human Language Technologies*, pages 49–59. Association for Computational Linguistics.

Inès Zribi, Mariem Ellouze Khemakhem, and Lamia Hadrich Belguith. 2013. Morphological analysis of Tunisian dialect. In *Proceeding of International Joint Conference on Natural Language Processing (IJCNLP 2013), Nagoya, Japan*.

Inès Zribi, Rahma Boujelbane, Abir Masmoudi, Mariem Ellouze, Lamia Belguith, and Nizar Habash. 2014. A conventional orthography for Tunisian Arabic. In *Proceedings of the Language Resources and Evaluation Conference (LREC)*.

A Conventional Orthography for Algerian Arabic

Houda Saadane[1] and **Nizar Habash**[2]

(1) Univ. Grenoble Alpes, LIDILEM, Grenoble, France
GEOLSemantics & Consulting, Paris, France
houda.saadane@e.u-grenoble3.fr

(2) New York University Abu Dhabi, United Arab Emirates
nizar.habash@nyu.edu

Abstract

Algerian Arabic is an Arabic dialect spoken in Algeria characterized by the absence of writing resources and standardization, hence it is considered as an under-resourced language. It differs from Modern Standard Arabic on all levels of linguistic representation, from phonology and morphology to lexicon and syntax. In this paper, we present a conventional orthography for Algerian Arabic, following a previous effort on developing a conventional orthography for Dialectal Arabic (or CODA), demonstrated for Egyptian and Tunisian Arabic. We explain the design principles of Algerian CODA and provide a detailed description of its guidelines.

1 Introduction

The Arabic language today is characterized by a complex state of polyglossia. Modern Standard Arabic (MSA) is the official variety of Arabic used primarily in written literal contexts. There is also a large number of dialects whose dominant features are noticeable to Arab-speaking people. The Arabic dialects differ from Modern Standard Arabic (MSA) on all levels of linguistic representation, from phonology and morphology to lexicon and syntax. MSA is classified as a high variety as is contains lot of normalization and standardization. It is generally considered as a prestigious, valued and official language; hence it is used for training (media and education). Arabic Dialects (DA) are considered a low variety which includes languages with less normalization and standardization. These languages are used in daily life, interviews and for informal conversations. Algerian Arabic (henceforth, ALG) is one of the Western group of Arabic dialects spoken in Algeria. ALG differs from other Arabic dialects, neighboring or far ones by having some specific features. In addition to MSA and DA, foreign languages, particularly French and English have been increasingly part of the Arabic spoken in daily basis.

With the emergence of Internet and social media, ALG (and other DAs) have become the language of informal online communication, for instance emails, blogs, discussion forums, SMS, etc. Most Arabic natural language processing (NLP) tools and resources were developed specially to treat MSA. Corresponding tools processing ALG are not as mature and sophisticated as those for MSA. This is due to the recent involvement of works on ALG dialect and the limit quantity of results and resources generated till today. To address this problem, some solutions propose to apply NLP tools designed for MSA directly to ALG. This proposition is interesting but yields to significantly low performance. This is why it is necessary to develop solutions and build resources for ALG treatment.

In this paper, we present a basic layout of ALG processing which is necessary to build efficient NLP tools and applications. This layout is a design of standard common convention orthography dedicated to ALG dialect. The proposed standard is an extension of that proposed in the work of Habash et al, (2012a) who proposed a Conventional Orthography for Dialectal Arabic (CODA). CODA is designed in order to develop computational models of Arabic dialects and provided a detailed description of its guidelines as applied to Egyptian Arabic (EGY).

In this paper, we present a conventional orthography for Algerian Arabic. The paper is organized as follows. Section 2, discusses related works. In Section 3, we present an historical overview of ALG. In Section 4, we highlight the

Proceedings of the Second Workshop on Arabic Natural Language Processing, pages 69–79,
Beijing, China, July 26-31, 2015.

linguistic differences between ALG and the languages MSA, EGY and TUN in order to motivate some of our ALG CODA decisions. In Section 5, we present ALG CODA guidelines.

2 Related works

Studying and processing dialects is an interesting recent research area which took progressively a big attention, especially with the explosion of internet public communications. Hence, there is actually a big interest to develop new tools to process an exploit the huge quantities of resources established using dialects (oral communications, web, social networks, etc.). However, Arabic dialects are languages without standardization or normalization, these why much efforts are necessary to modernize Arabic orthography and develop orthographies for Arabic dialects.

Maamouri et al. (2004) have developed a set of rules for Levantine dialects. These rules define the conversational Levantine Arabic transcription guidelines and annotation conventions. Habsh et al.(2012a) have proposed a conventional orthography for Egyptian dialectal (CODA). This work is inspired by the Linguistic Data Consortium (LDC) guidelines for transcribing. However, CODA is intended for general purpose writing allowing many abstracts from these variations, whereas the LDC guideline are dedicated for transcription, and thus focus more on phonological variations in sub-dialects. A proposition for transcription Algerain dialect are developed in (Harrat et., 2014) where a set of rules for transcription Algerain dialect are defined and a grapheme-to-phoneme converter for this dialect was presented. Grapheme-to-Phoneme (G2P) conversion or phonetic transcription is the process which converts a written form of a word to its pronunciation form; hence this technique focuses only on phonological variations.

To remedy the lack of building resources and tools dedicated to the treatment of ALG issue, (Harrat et al., 2014) built parallel corpora for Algerian dialects, because their ultimate purpose is to achieve a Machine Translation (MT) for Modern Standard Arabic (MSA) and Algerian dialects (AD), in both directions. They also propose language tools to process these dialects. First, they developed a morphological analysis model of dialects by adapting BAMA, a well-known MSA analyzer. Then they propose a diacritization system, based on a MT process which allows restoring the vowels to dialects corpora. And finally, they propose results on machine translation between MSA and Algerian dialects.

In the same way, (Harrat et al., 2015) present an Arabic multi-dialect study including dialects from both the Maghreb and the Middle-east that they compare to the Modern Standard Arabic (MSA). Three dialects from Maghreb are concerned by this study: two from Algeria : Annaba's dialect (ANB), the language spoken in the east of Algeria, on Algiers's dialect (ALG), the language used in the capital of Algeria, and one from Tunisia, on Sfax's dialect (TUN) spoken in the south of Tunisia and two dialects from Middle-east (Syria and Palestine). The resources which have been built from scratch have lead to a collection of a multi-dialect parallel resource.

Furthermore, (Zribi, et al., 2014) extend the CODA guidelines to take into account to Tunisian dialect and (Jarrar, et al., 2014) have adapted it to the Palestinian dialect. In addition, authors of Egyptian and Tunisian CODA encourage the adaptation of CODA to other Arabic dialects in order to create linguistic resources. Following this council, we extend in this paper CODA guidelines to ALG.

3 Algerian Arabic: Historical Overview

Arabic speakers have Arabic dialects or vernacular as their mother tongues. These dialects can be stratified in two big families of dialects: the Western group (the Maghreb) or North African group and the Eastern group (the Mashriq). Algerian dialect, noted ALG, is one of the Western group which is spoken in Algeria. This dialect is also called دارجة *daArjaħ*[1] or جزايري *jazaAyriy* or دزيري *dziyriy* simply meaning "Algerian". These variations do not create generally barriers to understand the dialect. In addition to ALG, the Algerian's population speaks also Berber but with different ratios: ALG is used by 70 to 80% of the population however; the Berber language is the mother tongue of 25% to 30% of population. Berber is used mainly in center of Algeria (Algiers and Kabylie), East of Algeria (Béjaia and Sétif), in Aures (chaoui), the Mzab (north of the

[1] Arabic transliteration is presented in the Habash-Soudi-Buckwalter (HSB) scheme (Habash et al., 2007). Phonological transcriptions will be presented between /.../ but we will use the HSB consonant forms when possible to minimize confusion from different symbol sets.

Sahara) and it is used by the Twaregue based in south of the Sahara (Hoggar mountains). Even if ALG is spoken by Algeria's population, estimated to 40 million of persons, it is characterized by variation of this same dialect according to geographic location of ALG's speakers.

This dialect cannot be presented as homogeneous linguistic system but it has many varieties. According to (Derradji et al., 2002) we distinguish four varieties for ALG as follow: I) the Oranais: is the variety spoken in the Western of Algeria, precisely from Moroccan frontiers to the limit of Ténès, ii) Algérois: this variety covers the central zones of Algeria to Béjaia and it is widely spread, iii) Rural: the speakers of this variety are located in the East of Algeria like Constantine, Annaba or Sétif, and iv) Sahara: is the dialect of the south of Algeria population. ALG is also the language used in press, television, social communication, internet exchanges, SMS, etc. Only in official communications, both reading and writing ones, where ALG is not used.

Furthermore, we note that ALG is enriched by the languages of the groups colonized or managed the Algerian population during the history of the country. Among these group's languages we can cite: Turkish, Spanish, Italian and more recently French. This enrichment, materialized by the presence of foreign words in the dialect, has contributed to create many varieties of ALG from one region to another one, with a quite complex linguistic situation resulting from this language mixture. Indeed, this language mixture has been studied by many socio-linguistic like (Morsly, 1986; Ibrahimi, 1997; Benrabah, 1999; Arezki, 2008). They described the linguistic landscape of Algeria as '*multilingualism*' or "poly-glossic" where multiple languages and language varieties coexist. In other words, the ALG is a suitable example of a complex socio-linguistic situation (Morsly, 1986).

Historically, Berber was the native language of the population of the Maghreb in general and Algeria in particular before the Islamic conquest, which introduced Arabic in all aspects of life. Centuries of various foreign powers introduced vocabulary from Turkish, Spanish and finally (and most dominantly today) French. French colonization tried to impose the French language as the only way of communication during its 132 year control of Algeria. This situation caused a significant decline in the Arabic language, characterized by increased French influence and the introduction of some other languages like Italian and Spanish due to migratory flow from Europe (Ibrahimi, 2006). The influence of these languages on ALG realizes in frequent code-switching without any phonology adaptation in daily conversations, particularly from French, e.g., "*lycée*", "salon", "*quartier*", "*normal*", etc.

4 Comparison among Algerian, Egyptian, Tunisian and Standard Arabic

There are many differences among ALG, EGY, TUN and MSA regarding many levels: phonological, morphological and orthographic. In this section we present some of these differences that are important and determinant of the distinction between these Arabic flavors. We refer the reader to (Habash, 2010) for further elements and discussions.

4.1 Phonological Variations

We give in the following list the major phonological differences between ALG and both MSA and EGY:
The consonant equivalent the MSA (ق) /q/ is one of the sounds that deserve special attention. This sound has many varieties of pronunciation in Algerian Arabic dialects that we can find in the different regions, cities and localities of Algeria. Hence, the pronunciation of "q" can be realized as *q*, *g*, *ʔ*, or *k*.

- *uvular stop* "ق" [q]: like Moroccan and Tunisian dialects, this pronunciation is present in ALG in different localities as in some urban cities like Algiers or Constantine.
- *palatal sound* "ڨ" [g]: this sound is also used in both Moroccan and Tunisian dialects in addition to the ALG one. In Algeria, this sound is used in some cities like Annaba and Sétif, in addition to the Bedouin dialects where this sound is widely employed.
- *glottal stop* [ʔ]: this sound is used in Tlemcen city in the same manner we find it in the Egyptian dialect.
- *k postpalatal:* this sound is a particularity of the ALG dialect that we do not find it in the other north African dialects. This sound is used in the rural localities and some cities like Kabylia, Jijel, Msirda and Trara.

We note that in the case of dialects not using glottal stop consonant, there are some exceptions where the pronunciation is the same way regardless of the dialect. This is the case of the word

بقرة *bagraħ*‘ cow’ which is pronounced in the same way using the palatal sound *bagra.*

The pronunciation of the consonant (ج) /j/ has also different from specific for a location or a group of speakers in the north of Africa. It is pronounced [dj] in Algiers and most of central Algeria as in the word نجاح *ndjaH* ‘success’, but when the consonant (ج) /j/ precedes a (د) /d/ consonant it will be pronounced with the allophone [j] like in the word جديد *jdid* ‘new’. In Egypt this consonant is pronounced as /g/. For Tunisian, Tlemcenian and east Algerian speakers, 'ج' is realized as /j/ or /z/ when the word contains the consonant (س) /s/ or (ز) /z/ like in the words جبس *ğibs* or *djibs* ‘plaster’ become زبس *zebs*; and عجوز *ςadjuwz* ‘old women’ become عزوز ςzuwz.

The MSA consonant (غ) /γ/ is assimilated in different manner according to some categories of speakers. In the eastern Algerian Sahara, like M'sila and BouSaâda, /γ/ is assimilated to (ق) /*q*/, for instance, the words غالي*γaAliy* ‘expensive’ and صغيرة *sγayraħ* ‘small’, are pronounced respectively /*qaAliy*/, and /*sqayra*/. Sometimes, it is assimilated to (خ) /*x*/, like Tunisian and eastern Algeria speakers, e.g., the word غسل‘washed’ is pronounced /xssel/ or /γssel/.

The interdental MSA consonant (ث) /θ/ can be pronounced as (ت) /t/, in both ALG and EGY dialects like for the word ' *uwmθ* ثوم‘garlic’ is pronounced as توم /tuwm/. But it is also pronounced /θ/ in some urban Algerian dialects as in the word ثوم *uwmθ*, (ف) /f/ like in nomadic dialects of Mostaganem where for instance the word ثاني *θaAniy* ‘also’ is pronounced فاني *faAniy*; or (س) /s/ in some cases in EGY dialect, for example, the word ثابت *θaAbit ‘fixe’* is pronounced سابت *saabit.* Another MSA interdental consonant has also special pronunciations; it is the consonant (ذ) /ð/. In the EGY dialect, it can be pronounced (د) /*d*/, like the word ذهب *ðhab* ‘gold’ pronounced دهب *dhab*, or (ز) /*z*/ for instance the word ذكي ‘clever’ is realized *zakiy*. However, in the ALG dialect, the consonant (ذ) /ð/ has one of the following pronunciations: (ذ) /ð/ or (د) /d/. For instance the word ذراع ‘arm’ can be pronounced *ðraAς* or *draAς*. Moreover, in some regions in Algeria, like Mostaganem, this consonant is realized as (ڥ) /*v*/, like for the word ذهب *ðhab*' gold’ pronounced ڥهب *vhab*.

The pronunciation of the glottal stop phoneme that appears in many MSA words in ALG dialect has different forms:

- *The glottal stop becomes longue:* this pronunciation is also present in TUN and EGY dialects. We can give as example the words : فأس *faÂs* /fa’s/ → /fa:s/ فاس *faAs* ‘pickaxe', ذئب *Diŷb* /Di’b/ → /Di:b/ ذيب *diyb* ‘wolf’, and مؤمن *muŵmin* /mu’men/ → /mumin/ مومن *muwmin* ‘beliver’.
- *The glottal stop disappears:* it consists on simply removing the glottal when pronouncing the word. This form is also used in TUN and EGY dialects. For instance, let us take the following word: زرقاء *zarqaA’* /zarqa:’/ → /zarqa:/ زرقا *zarqA* ‘blue’.
- *The glottal stop is replaced by a semi-vowel /w/ or /y/:* this pronunciation is found in ALG and TUN dialects and not in EGY one. It is used for instance in the case of the wordsأكّل /*Âak~al* /‘to give eating’ → وكّل *wuk~al*, أمس /*Âa*ms/ ‘yesterday’ → يامس *yaAmas*
- *The glottal stop is replaced by the letter /l/:* This form is also used uniquely in the ALG and TUN dialects unlike the EGY one. Let us take the following examples of using of this form: أفعى */Âafςa/ ‘snake’* → لفعى /*lafςa*/, أرض /*ÂaarD*/ ‘earth’ → لرض /*larD*/. We note that the given examples are also exceptions where we use the same form for both definite and indefinite.
- *The glottal stop is replaced by the letter /h/:* opposite to the EGY dialect, the ALG and TUN ones use this form to pronounce in some cases the glottal stop, like in the words أجّالة *Âaj~aAlaħ* /*Âajja:la*/ ‘widow’ → هجّالة *hajjaAlaħ* /hajja:la/,أمّالا *Âam~aAlaA* /*Âamma:laA*/ ‘however’ → همّالا *ham~aAlaA* /hamma:laA/.

Unlike the Egyptian dialect, the Algerian dialect elides many short vowels in unstressed contexts. This feature characterizes also the other Maghreb dialects. This is the case of the following words: MSA جمل *jamal* ‘Camel’ (and EGY /*gamal*/) becomes ALG /*jmal*/. In addition, this feature introduce an interesting element to distinguish the Maghreb dialects from the EGY one, this element is the presence of a succession of two consonants at the beginning of the word which introduces a specific particularity in the verb scheme ‘*fςal’* in ALG instead of ‘*faςal’* in EGY, like in the verb MSA قتل /*qatal*/ ‘he killed’ (and EGY /*’atal*/) becomes ALG /*qtal*/.

The MSA diphthongs *ay* and *aw* are generally reduced uniformly to /i:/ and /u:/. For example, let us take the words: حيط */HayT/* 'wall' becomes ALG */Hi:T/*, لون */lawn/* 'color' becomes ALG /lu:n/. We note that this particularity is found in the younger generation speakers; however, older speakers still retain them in some words and contexts, for instance the word عود stills pronounced /çawd/ 'horse' by some old speakers.

Another feature of ALG dialect, shared with the TUN one, is the pronunciation of the MSA /a:/: in some words it is realized as /e:/ and in others remains /a:/. For example, the word جَمَال /jam:al/ 'beauty' with this signification is pronounced with /a:/ but it is realized with /e:/ in the word جْمَال /jme:l/ meaning 'camels'.

4.2 Morphological Variations

ALG dialect has also some morphological aspects that are different from that of the MSA, and closer to that of Maghreb dialects. These aspects consist essentially on a simplification of some inflexions and inclusion of new clitics as follow:

As regards the inflexion, in ALG dialect, like other Arabic ones, the casual endings in nouns and verbs mood are lost. We note that the indicative mood is the one which is used as default unlike the other moods that are not used. Moreover, the dual and the feminine plural disappeared; they are assimilated to the masculine in the plural form. For example, the word شَكَرْتُنَّ *šakartun~a* 'they (fem.pl.) thank' is normalized in the ALG dialect in شْكَرْتُوا *škar-tuwA* 'they thank'. In addition, the first and the second person of the singular form are conjugated in the same way in the dialect, e.g., in MSA we say شَكَرْتُ *šakartu* 'I thank' and شَكَرْتَ *šakarta* 'you thanks', these two forms are normalized in ALG dialect in the following unique form: شْكَرْت *škart* 'I/you thank'. This simplification can lead to some ambiguities in ALG.

The ALG dialect modifies the interne form of the verbs when it does their flexion in imperfective form. It introduces a gemination in the first radical letter and moving to this radical the vowel of the second one. This modification is applied only in the plural form and the 2nd person of feminine singular. For example, in ALG the verb 'to thank' in 3rd person of masculine singular is يُشْكُرْ *yu-škur* (he is thanking) and in 3rd person of masculine plural we have: يُشْكُرُوا *yuš~ukr-uwA* (they are thanking) but in EGY the same case have the form: يُشْكُرُوا *yuškur-uwA*. To enforce this statement we refer to (Souag, 2005) work where they defend that: "*As is common in Algeria, when normal short vowel elision would lead to another short vowel being in an open syllable, we have slight lengthening on the first member so as to change the stress:* يضرب *yaDṛab 'he hits' → yaD~arbuwA* يضربوا *"they hit",*ركبة *rukba 'knee' →* ركبتي *ruk~ubtiy 'my knee'*; this gemination need not occur, however, if the consonant to be geminated is one of the sonorants r, ṛ, l, n, although for younger speakers it often does. I have the impression that these compensatory geminates are not held as long as normal geminates; this needs further investigation."

Otherwise, ALG dialect uses, like the other Arabic dialects, only the suffix ين /yn/ to form the regular plural. However, the ALG elides the short vowels in plural forms like in the following examples: مْلْحَدْ *mulHad* 'unbeliever', in the plural form مْلْحْدِين *mulHdiyn*, مُهَنْدِسْ *muhandis* 'engineer', pl. مُهَنْدْسِين *muhandsiyn.* But in some dialects, like the EGY one, they don't elide the short vowel, for instance the plural of مُهَنْدِسْ *muhandis* 'engineer' in EGY is مُهَنْدِسِين *muhandisiyn.* But for some exception, like for the active participle [1A2i3] → [1A23-iyn] (Gadalla, 2000), this elision is maintained whatever the dialect like for the word صَايِمْ *SaAyim* 'fasting' → صَايْمِين *SaAymiyn.*

Cohen (1912) describes the emphatic suffix تيك /–tiyk/ as a characteristics of the Muslim Algiers dialect that is used to express adverbs ending with –a like in for the words قَانَا *gana* 'also' which becomes *ganaAtiyk*, زعما *zaçma* 'supposedly' which becomes *zaçmaAtiyk*.

For the form استفعل [Aista12a3] which exists in the different dialects, the ALG introduces in addition a new variant of this form. This variant is سفعل [*ssa-12a3*] and it is used essentially by the speakers of the west of Algeria (Marçais, 1902). For example, let us take the verb اِسْتَكْلَفْ *Aistaklaf* 'take care of' can be also used like سَّكْلَفْ *ssaklaf* or سَكْلَفْ *saklaf.*
Another feature of the ALG dialect is the insertion of vowel /i:/ between the stem and the consonantal suffixes of the perfect form of the primary geminate verb, e.g in MSA the verb شدَّ/شددت *šad~a/šadadtu* 'he/I pulled' becomes in ALG شدّ/شدّيت *šad~/šad~iyt*. This feature is also present in the other Arabic dialects.

The passive voice in classical Arabic uses vowel changes and not verb derivation but in ALG as in many Arabic dialects, the passive form is obtained by prefixing the verb with one the following elements:

- t- / tt-, for example : تبنى *tabnaý* 'it was built', ترفد *ttarfad* 'it was lifted'
- n-, for instance : نفتح *nftah* 'it opened'
- /tn- / or /nt/, e.g., نتكل *ntkal* 'was edible', تنقتل *tnaqtal* 'to be killed'. We note that this last element is specific for the ALG dialect.

The ALG dialect uses the particle «n» for the first person of singular like the other Maghreb dialects. This particle is generally absent from the Mashreq dialects like EGY one. In those dialects the «n» is substituted by the «a» like shown in the following example: نكتب /naktab/ 'I write' in ALG while the equivalent of it in EGY is اكتب /*Aaktib*/.

Like several dialects (EGY and TUN), ALG include the clictics, that are reduced forms of the MSA words, e.g., the demonstrative proclitic + ه *ha*+ which strictly precedes with the definite article +ال *Al*+ is related to the MSA demonstrative pronounsهذا *haðaA* and هذه *haðihi*, e.g.; (MSA → ALG) هذه الدنيا *haðihi AldunyaA* → *haAldinyaA* 'this life'.

Several dialects include the proclitic +ع, *ça*+ a reduced form of the preposition على/*çalaý*/ 'on/upon/about/to'. For example, (MSA → ALG) على/*çalaý* الطاولة *AlTaAwilaħ*/ → عالمايدة *çaAlmaAydaħ* 'on the table'. The same interpretation is valid for the proclitics +ف *+fa* and +م *m*+; which are the reduced form of the prepositions في *fiy* 'in' and من *min* 'from' respectively. Also, several dialect include the non-MSA negation circum-clitic+ما *mA*+ ش+ *+š*. For example ما قريتش *mA qriyteš* 'I haven't read'.

Furthermore, ALG almost lost all of the nominal dual forms, which are replaced with the word زوج *zudwj* /zu:dj/ 'two' with the plural form, e.g., (MSA→ ALG) كتابين *kitaAbayn* → زوج كتب *zuwdj ktub* 'two books'

4.3 Orthographic Variations

The orthographic variation in writing of Arabic dialects words is due to two reasons: i) the non-existence of an orthographic standard for Arabic dialects because these varieties are not codified and normalized, and ii) the phonological differences between MSA and Algerian dialect (ALG). For these dialects words can be spelled phonologically or etymologically using their corresponding MSA form. This fact creates some inconsistency among dialect writers. For example, the corresponding word to 'gold' can be written دهب *dhab* or ذهب *ðhab*. In addition, in some cases the phonology or underlying morphology is reflected by some regular phonological assimilation writing, e.g. طوموبيل *Tuwmuwbiyl* 'cars' is also written as طونوبيل *Tuwnuwbiyl*, إسماعيل *AismaAçiyl*, 'Ismaël' is also written as إسماعين *AismaAçiyn*, من بعد *min baçd* 'after' is also written as مم بعد *mim baçd*. Furthermore, these different spelling can conduce to some semantic confusion, like for شربو *šrbw* may be شربوا *šarbuwA* 'they drank' or شربه *šarbuh* 'he drank it'. Finally, the shortened long vowels, can be spelled long or short, for instance, شافوها/شفوها *šAfw+hA/ šfw+hA* 'they saw her, and مجابش *majaAbaš* 'he didn't bring' ماجابش *mAjaAbaš*.

4.4 Lexical Variations

As presented in Section 3, the Algerian dialect, like other Arabic dialects, has been influenced, over centuries, by other languages like Berber, Turkish, Italian, Spanish and French. Table 1 shows some examples of borrowed words[2] in ALG.

Words	Translation	Transliteration	Origin
فكرون	a tortoise	*Fakruwn*	Berber
شلاغم	Moustache	*šliAyam*	
قرجومة	a throat	*Qarjuwmaħ*	
تقاشير	Socks	*tqaAšiyr*	Turkish
سكارجي	a drunkard	*sukaArjiy*	
زردة	Feast	*Zardaħ*	
فيشطة	Party	*fiyšTaħ*	Italian
زبلة	Foul	*Zablaħ*	
صوردي	Money	*Suwrdiy*	
سيمانة	a week	*siymaAnaħ*	Spanish
سبردينة	Snickers	*Spardiynaħ*	
سُكويلة	a school	*Sukwiylaħ*	
طابلة	Table	*TaAblaħ*	French
تيليفون	Phone	*Tiyliyfuwn*	
فرملي	Nurse	*Farmliy*	

Table 1: The origin and the meaning of some borrowed words used in ALG.

5 Algerian Arabic CODA Guidelines

In this section we present a mapping of the CODA convention for the Algerian dialect. The CODA convention is presented and its goals and

[2] We refer to (Guella, 2011) for more examples.

principals are described in details in (Habash et al, 2012a). An example of Algerian CODA is presented in Table 5.

5.1 CODA Guiding Principles

We summarize the main CODA design elements (Habash et al., 2012a, Eskander et al., 2013):

- CODA is an internally consistent and coherent convention for writing Dialectal Arabic.
- CODA is created for computational purposes.
- CODA uses the Arabic script.
- CODA is intended as a unified framework for writing all Arabic dialects.
- CODA aims to strike an optimal balance between maintaining a level of dialectal uniqueness and establishing conventions based on MSA-DA similarities.

CODA is designed respecting many principles:

1. CODA is an Ad Hoc convention which uses only the Arabic script characters including the diacritics used for writing MSA.
2. CODA is consistent as it associates to each DA word a unique orthographic form that represents its phonology and morphology.
3. CODA uses and extends the basic MSA orthographic decisions (rules, exceptions and ad hoc choices), e.g., using Shadda for phonological gemination or spelling the definite article morphemically.
4. CODA generally preserves the phonological form of dialectal words given the unique phonological rules of each dialect (e.g., vowel shortening), and the limitations of Arabic script (e.g., using a diacritic and a glide consonant to write a long vowel).
5. CODA preserves DA morphology and syntax.
6. CODA is easy to learn and write.
7. The CODA principles are the same for all the dialects, however each dialect will have its proper CODA map. This unique map respects the phonology and the morphology of the considered dialect.
8. CODA is not a purely phonological representation. Text in CODA can be read perfectly in dialect given the specific dialect and its CODA map.

5.2 Algerian CODA

As we said above, CODA principles are applicable for all dialects but with a specific map for each dialect. Hence, in this section we present the map of the Algerian dialect (ALG) to CODA by summarizing the specific CODA guidelines for ALG. Firstly we chose a variant of the ALG which is the one used in the media as default. This variant represents the dialect of the capital city Algiers and follows the same orthographic rules as MSA by taking into accounts all the following exceptions and extensions.

5.3 Phonological Extensions

Long Vowels In ALG CODA the long vowel /e:/, which do not exist in MSA, will be written as *ay* or *iA* depending on its MSA cognate: *ay* or *aA*, respectively. In MSA orthography, the sequence *iA* is not possible, hence using words with *aA* MSA cognates can be a good solution for ALG. This orientation is suitable since the basic non-diacritical form of the word is preserved, for instance, دار *daAr* /da:r/ 'turn' and *diAr* /de:r/ 'do'. This extension is present also in Tunisian CODA unlike the Egyptian one.

Vowel Shortening Like the EGY and TUN CODA, the ALG long vowels are written in long form. In some cases, which are shortened in certain cases such as when adding affixes and clitics even if it is writing long. For example, ماجابهاش *mA jAb+hA+š* 'he did not forghets for her' and تقول لهم *tquwl lhm* /tqullhum/ 'you tell them' (not تقلهم *tqulhm*). This vowel shorting can be also considered in words with two long vowels. Phonologically, in DA, even if the two long vowels are written, only one is allowed in a word, in other terms, it should be only one stressed syllable in each phonological word. For instance, صايمين *SaAymiyn* 'fasting' (not صيمين *Saymiyn*).

5.4 Phono-Lexical Exceptions

The Algerian "qaf" The letter (ق) /q/ is used to represent the four following consonants: /q/, /g/ (like TUN), /k/ and (') (like EGY). The table 2 gives some examples of exceptional pronunciation for /g/.

CODA		Pronunciation	English
بقرة	*baqraħ*	/bagra/	Cow
قاناتيك	*qaAnaAtiyk*	/ga :na :ti :k/	so ...
قاوري	*qiAwriy*	/ge:wriy/	foreign

Table 2: ALG exceptional pronunciation examples

Consonant with Multiple Pronunciations
In ALG we use the MSA forms to write consonants with multiple pronunciations. The used MSA form has to be closer to the considerate

consonant if it has a corresponding MSA cognate. We give in Table 3 some examples. Like TUN CODA, the ALG one has more variations than the ones addressed in EGY CODA as for the former the efforts were focused on Cairene Arabic. Hence, ALG seems to have more MSA-like pronunciations where MSA spelling is simply the same as ALG.

Hamza Spelling Hamzated MSA cognate may not be spelled in ALG CODA in a way corresponding to the MSA cognate. In other words, the glottal stop will be spelled phonologically. This feature is also present in EGY and TUN CODA. However, when Hamza is pronounced in ALG, we apply the same MSA spelling rules. Furthermore, the glottal stop phoneme, appearing in many MSA words, has disappeared in ALG, like in the words: فاس *fAs* 'pickaxe' (not like MSA فأس *faÂs*), ذيب *Diyb* 'wolf' (not like MSA ذئب *Diŷr*). In addition, words starting with Hamzated Alif are not seen in ALG CODA, e.g, الارض *AlAarD* /larD/ 'earth' (not لرض *larD*).

CODA		Pronunciations	English
عجوز	*ςjuwz*	/ςadju:z/, /ςzu:z/ /ςju:z/	old women
ثاني	*θaAniy*	/fa:niy/, /θa:niy/	Also
صدر	*Sadr*	/sadr/, /Sadr/	Chest
قهوة	*qahwaħ*	/qahwa/, /gahwa/, /kahwa/, /'ahwa/	Coffee
غسل	*γsal*	/γsal/,/xsal/	he washed
غالي	*γaliy*	/γaa:li/, /qaa:li/	Expensive
فاسدة	*faAsdaħ*	/fa:zda/, /fa:sda/	Corrupt
ذهب	*ðhab*	/ðhab/, /dhab/ /vhab/	Gold
هبط	*hbaT*	/hbaT/, /HbaT/	he descended

Table3: examples of multiple pronunciations in ALG.

Definite Article If the word contains the article Al (ال), we must distinguish between the sun and the moon letters. In the case of the sun letters, the "L" is silent and the letter that follows is doubled (gemination) in pronunciation and in writing, e.g., النّهار *AlnnhAr* 'day' (not انّهار *AnnhAr*). Conversely, with the moon letters, the 'A' is not pronounced, the "L" of the article is pronounced and the letter that follows is not doubled, neither in pronunciation nor in writing, e.g., القمر *Alqmar* 'the moon' (not لقمر *lqmar*) (Saadane and Semmar, 2012; Biadsy et al., 2009).

N of Number Construct The ALG CODA adds the phoneme /n/ after some numerals in construct cases, e.g.,سطاشن طابلة *sTaAšn TaAblaħ* '16 tables' whereas the number 16 is pronounced alone سطاش *sTaAš*. This exception is valid for Number Construct forms with number between 11 and 19 preceding a noun in the singular. This property is also valid in TUN CODA.

5.5 Morphological Extensions

Attached clitics ALG dialect, as many other dialects, uses almost all the attached clitics in MSA, the definite article ال+ *Al+*, the future particle proclitic ح+ *Ha+* (expressed in east of Algeria like Annaba city), the coordinating conjunction و + *w+*, the negation particle enclitic ش+ *+š*. In addition ALG uses the new attached clitics reduced forms of the MSA, e.g., ع+ *ς+*, م+ *m+*, ه+ *h+*, ف+ *f+*. The following table illustrates some examples of these clitics where we consider the word وكليناهالكم *wikliynaAhaAlkum* 'and we have eaten your food'

Enclitics			Suffixes	Stem	Proclitics
كم	ل	ها	نا	كلي	و
kum	*l*	*haA*	*naA*	*kliy*	*wi*

Table 4: Tokenization of the word وكليناهالكم *wikliynaAhaAlkum*

Separated Clitics The spelling rule for the indirect object enclitics and the negation proclitic ما mA is preserved in the ALG CODA map. This map puts a separation using a space between the negation particle and the indirect object, e.g., ما جاب لكمش *mA jAb lkumš* /ma+jab+lkum+š/ 'he did not give/com you'.

5.6 Lexical Exceptions

The ALG CODA, like the TUN and EGY ones, contains a list of Algerian dialect words that have a specific ad hoc spelling. This specific spelling may be inconsistent with the map of CODA introduced above and can be spelled commonly in different ways. These exceptions include for instance:

- The demonstratives هذوك *haðuwk* (not هاذوكة *haðukaħ*) 'that', هكذا *hakðaA* 'like this' (not هاكذا *haAkðaA*, or هكدا *hakdaA* or هاكدا *haAkdaA*)
- The preposition 'I know' is expressed with the phrase عْلَى بَالِي *ςlaý baAliy* (not عمبالي *ςambaAliy*, or عن بالي *ςan baAliy*, or علبالي *ςlabaAliy*)

Raw Text	مرحبا بكم في بلاتو حصة برنامج الخط لحمر لنهار اليومة والي يتزامن مع عيد المرأة. إنشاء الله ڨاع النساء الي راهم يشوفو فينا إنشاء الله أيام سعيده وجميلة فحياتهم. إنشاء الله يتهناو ب ماليهم، ب والديهم وولادهم. قبل منروحو للموضوع نتاع اليومة والي خصصناه للمرأة ف الجزاير وكيفاش راهي عايشة خلونا نرحبو بالضيوف تع لبرنامج.
	mrHbA bkm fy plAtw HSħ brnAmj AlxT lHmr lnhAr Alywmħ wlly ytzAmn mç çyd AlmrÂħ. ĂnšA' Allh gAç AlnsA' Aly rAhm yšwfw fynA ĂnšA' Allh ÂyAm sçydh wjmylħ fHyAthm. ĂnšA' Allh ythnAw b mAlyhm, b wAldyhm wwlAdhm. qbl mnrwhw llmwDwç ntAç Alywmħ wAly xSSnAh llmrÂħ f AljzAyr wkyfAš rAhy çAyšħ xlwnA nrhbw bAlDywf tç lbrnAmj.
CODA	مرحبا بكم في بلاتو حصة برنامج الخط الحمر لنهار اليوم واللي يتزامن مع عيد المراة. انشا الله قاع النسا اللي راهم يشوفوا فينا انشا الله ايام سعيدة وجميلة فحياتهم. انشا الله يتهناوا بماليهم، بوالديهم وولادهم. قبل ما نروحوا للموضوع تاع اليوم واللي خصصناه للمراة فالجزاير وكفاش راهي عايشة خلونا نرحبوا بالضيوف تاع البرنامج.
	mrHbA bkm fy blAtw HSħ brnAmj AlxT AlHmr lnhAr Alywm wAlly ytzAmn mç çyd AlmrAħ, AnšA Allh qAç AlnsA Aly rAhm yšwfwA fynA AnšA Allh AyAm sçydħ wjmylħ fHyAthm. AnšA Allh ythnAwA bmAlyhm, bwAldyhm wwlAdhm. qbl mA nrwhwA llmwDwç tAç Alywm wAlly xSSnAh llmrAħ fAljzAyr wkfAš rAhy çAyšħ xlwnA nrhbwA bAlDywf tAç AlbrnAmj.
English	Hello everyone, in « The Red Line » daily show, which coincides with the Women's Day. God willing, for all the women who watch this show, they may have happy and beautiful days in their lives. God willing, and they will rejoice in their families, parents and children. Before addressing the topic of the day, where we focus on women in Algeria and how they are living, let's welcome to our program's guests.

Table 5: An example sentence in ALG

- The adverbs زعمة *zaçmaħ* (not زعما *zaçma*) 'supposedly', ضركة *Durkaħ* (not ضركا *Durka*) 'now', ڨانة *gaAnaħ* (not ڨانا *gaAna*) 'also'

In addition, in influence and integration of foreign words from other languages, like French, Berber or Italian, have emerged new phonemes like /g/, /p/ or /v/. These phonemes are used to express sounds that do not exist in MSA, but in CODA we will use the following Arabic characters: /q/, /b/ and /f/ to express respectively g, p and v. For example, جافال *jaAfiAl* 'detergent', كافي kaAvi 'stupid', بوبية *puwpiyaħ* 'doll', قيدون *qiyduwn* 'handlebar'.

6 Conclusions and Future Work

We presented in this paper a set of guidelines towards a conventional orthography for Algerian Arabic. We discussed the various challenges of working with Algerian Arabic and how we address them. In the future, we plan to use the developed guidelines to annotated collections of Algerian Arabic texts, in a first step towards developing resources and tools for Algerian Arabic processing.

Acknowledgment

The first author was supported by the DGCIS (Ministry of Industry) and DGA (Ministry of Defense): RAPID Project 'ORELO', referenced by N°142906001. The second author was supported by DARPA Contract No. HR0011-12-C-0014. Any opinions, findings and conclusions or recommendations expressed in this paper are those of the authors and do not necessarily reflect the views of DARPA. We would like to thank Bilel Gueni, Emad Mohamed and Djamel Belarbi for helpful feedback.

References

Abdenour Arezki. 2008. *Le rôle et la place du français dans le système éducatif algérien*. Revue du Réseau des Observatoires du Français Contemporain en Afrique, (23), 21-31.

Mohamed Benrabah. 1999. *Langue et pouvoir en Algérie: Histoire d'un traumatisme linguistique*. Seguier Editions.

Fadi Biadsy, Nizar Habash and Julia Hirschberg. 2009, *Improving the Arabic Pronunciation Dictionary for Phone and Word Recognition with Linguistically-Based Pronunciation Rules*, The 2009 Annual Conference of the North American Chapter of the ACL, pages 397–405, Boulder, Colorado.

Marcel Cohen. 1912. *Le parler arabe des Juifs d'Alger*. Champion :Paris.

Yacine Derradji, Valéry Debov, Ambroise Queffélec, Dalila S. Dekdouk and Yasmina C. Benchefra. 2002. *Le français en Algérie : lexique et dynamique des langues*, Ed. Duclot, AUF, 2002, 590 p.

Ramy Eskander, Nizar Habash, Owen Rambow and Nadi Tomeh. 2013. Processing Spontaneous Orthography. In Proceedings of Conference of the North American Association for Computational Linguistics (NAACL), Atlanta, Georgia.

Charles A. Ferguson. 1959. *Diglossia*. Word-Journal of the International Linguistic Association, 1959, vol. 15, no 2, p. 325-340.

Hassan A. Gadalla. 2000. *Comparative Morphology of Standard and Egyptian Arabic* (Vol. 5). Lincom Europa.

Noureddine Guella. 2011. *Emprunts lexicaux dans des dialectes arabes algériens*. Synergies Monde arabe, 8, 81-88.

Nizar Habash, Abdelhadi Soudi and Tim Buckwalter. 2007. *On Arabic Transliteration*. Book Chapter. In *Arabic Computational Morphology: Knowledge-based and Empirical Methods*. Editors Antal van den Bosch and Abdelhadi Soudi.

Nizar Habash. 2010. *Introduction to Arabic Natural Language Processing*. Synthesis Lectures on Human Language Technologies, Graeme Hirst, editor. Morgan & Claypool Publishers.

Nizar Habash, Mona Diab and Owen Rambow. 2012a. *Conventional Orthography for Dialectal Arabic*. In: Proceedings of the Language Resources and Evaluation Conference (LREC), Istanbul.

Nizar Habash, Ramy Eskander and Abdelati Hawwari. 2012b. *A Morphological Analyzer for Egyptian Arabic*. In the Proceedings of the Workshop on Computational Research in Phonetics, Phonology, and Morphology (SIGMORPHON) in the North American chapter of the Association for Computational Linguistics (NAACL), Montreal, Canada.

Salima Harrat, Karima Meftouh, Mourad Abbas and Kamel Smaïli. 2014. *Grapheme To Phoneme Conversion-An Arabic Dialect Case*. In Spoken Language Technologies for Under-resourced Languages.

Salima Harrat, Karima Meftouh, Mourad Abbas and Kamel Smaili. 2014. *Building Resources for Algerian Arabic Dialects*. Corpus (sentences), 4000(6415), 2415.

Salima Harrat, Karima Meftouh, Mourad Abbas, Salma Jamoussi, Motaz Saad, and Kamel Smaili. 2015. *Cross-Dialectal Arabic Processing*. In Computational Linguistics and Intelligent Text Processing (pp. 620-632). Springer International Publishing.

Khawla T. Ibrahimi. 1997. *Les Algériens et leur (s) langue (s): éléments pour une approche sociolinguistique de la société algérienne*. Éds. El Hikma.

Khawla T. Ibrahimi, K. 2006. *L'Algérie: coexistence et concurrence des langues*. L'Année du Maghreb, (I), 207-218.

Mustafa Jarrar, Nizar Habash, Diyam Akra and Nasser Zalmout. 2014. *Building a Corpus for Palestinian Arabic: a Preliminary Study*. *ANLP 2014*, 18.

Mohamed Maamouri, Tim Buckwalter and Christopher Cieri. 2004. *Dialectal Arabic telephone speech corpus: Principles, tool design, and transcription conventions*. In NEMLAR International Conference on Arabic Language Resources and Tools, Cairo (pp. 22-23).

William Marçais. 1902. *Le dialecte arabe parlé à Tlemcen: grammaire, textes et glossaire* (Vol. 26). E. Leroux.

Philippe Marçais. 1956. *Le parler arabe de Djidjelli: Nord constantinois, Algérie* (Vol. 16). Librairie d'Amérique et d'Orient Adrien-Maisonneuve.

Dalila Morsly. 1986. *Multilingualism in Algeria.* The Fergusonian Impact: In Honor of Charles A. Ferguson on the Occasion of His, 65.

Houda Saadane, Aurélie Rossi, Christian Fluhr and Mathieu Guidère. 2012. *Transcription of Arabic names into Latin.* In Sciences of Electronics, Technologies of Information and Telecommunications (SETIT), 2012 6th International Conference on (pp. 857-866). IEEE.

Houda Saadane and Nasredine Semma. 2013. *Transcription des noms arabes en écriture latine.* Revue RIST| Vol, 20(2), 57.

Lameen Souag. 2005. *Notes on the Algerian Arabic dialect of Dellys.* Estudios de dialectología norteafricana y andalusí, 9, 1-30.

Ines Zribi, Rahma Boujelbane, Abir Masmoudi, Mariem Ellouze, Lamia Belguith, and Nizar Habash. 2014. *A Conventional Orthography for Tunisian Arabic.* In Proceedings of the Language Resources and Evaluation Conference (LREC), Reykjavik, Iceland.

A Pilot Study on Arabic Multi-Genre Corpus Diacritization Annotation

Houda Bouamor,[1] **Wajdi Zaghouani,**[1] **Mona Diab,**[2] **Ossama Obeid,**[1]
Kemal Oflazer,[1] **Mahmoud Ghoneim,**[2] **and Abdelati Hawwari** [2]
[1]Carnegie Mellon University in Qatar; [2]George Washington University
{hbouamor,wajdiz,owo}@qatar.cmu.edu; ko@cs.cmu.edu
{mtdiab,mghoneim,abhawwari}@gwu.edu

Abstract

Arabic script writing is typically underspecified for short vowels and other mark up, referred to as diacritics. Apart from the lexical ambiguity found in words, similar to that exhibited in other languages, the lack of diacritics in written Arabic script adds another layer of ambiguity which is an artifact of the orthography. Diacritization of written text has a significant impact on Arabic NLP applications. In this paper, we present a pilot study on building a diacritized multi-genre corpus in Arabic. We annotate a sample of non-diacritized words extracted from five text genres. We explore different annotation strategies: *Basic* where we present only the bare undiacritized forms to the annotators, *Intermediate* (Basic forms+their POS tags), and *Advanced* (automatically diacritized words). We present the impact of the annotation strategy on annotation quality. Moreover, we study different diacritization schemes in the process.

1 Introduction

One of the characteristics of writing in Modern Standard Arabic (MSA) is that the commonly used orthography is mostly consonantal and does not provide full vocalization of the text. It sometimes includes optional diacritical marks (henceforth, diacritics or vowels). Diacritics are extremely useful for text readability and understanding. Their absence in Arabic text adds another layer of lexical and morphological ambiguity. Naturally occurring Arabic text has some percentage of these diacritics present depending on genre and domain. For instance, religious text such as the Quran is fully diacritized to minimize chances of reciting it incorrectly. So are children's educational texts. Classical poetry tends to be diacritized as well. However, news text and other genre are sparsely diacritized (e.g., around 1.5% of tokens in the United Nations Arabic corpus bear at least one diacritic (Diab et al., 2007)).

From an NLP perspective, the two universal problems for processing language that affect the performance of (usually statistically motivated) NLP tools and tasks are: (1) sparseness in the data where not enough instances of a word type are observed in a corpus, and (2) ambiguity where a word has multiple readings or interpretations. Undiacritized surface forms of an Arabic word might have as many as 200 readings depending on the complexity of its morphology. The lack of diacritics usually leads to considerable lexical ambiguity, as shown in the example in Table 1, a reason for which diacritization, aka vowel/diacritic restoration, has been shown to improve state-of-the-art Arabic automatic systems such as speech recognition (ASR) (Kirchhoff and Vergyri, 2005) and statistical machine translation (SMT) (Diab et al., 2007). Hence, diacritization has been receiving increased attention in several Arabic NLP applications.

In general, building models to assign diacritics to each letter in a word requires a large amount of annotated training corpora covering different topics and domains to overcome the sparseness problem. The currently available diacritized MSA corpora are generally limited to the newswire genres (as distributed by the LDC) or religion related texts such as the Quran or the Tashkeela corpus.[2] In this paper we present a pilot study where we annotate a sample of non-diacritized text extracted from five different text genres. We explore different annotation strategies where we present the data to the annotator in three modes: **Basic** (only forms with no diacritics), **Intermediate** (Basic forms+POS tags), and **Advanced** (a list of forms that is automatically diacritized). We show the impact of the annotation strategy on the annota-

[2]Tashkeela is publicly available at: http://sourceforge.net/projects/tashkeela/

Proceedings of the Second Workshop on Arabic Natural Language Processing, pages 80–88,
Beijing, China, July 26-31, 2015.

Undiacritized	Diacritized	Buckwalter[1]	English
ذكر	ذَكَرَ	/*akara/	he mentioned
ذكر	ذُكِرَ	/*ukira/	it/he was mentioned
ذكر	ذَكَّرَ	/*ak ~ara/	he reminded
ذكر	ذُكِّرَ	/*uk ~ira/	it was reminded
ذكر	ذَكَرٌ	/*akaruN/	male
ذكر	ذِكْرٌ	/*ikaruN/	prayer

Table 1: Possible pronunciations and meanings of the undiacritized Arabic word **kr* ذكر

tion quality. It has been noted in the literature that complete diacritization is not necessary for readability Hermena et al. (2015) as well as for NLP applications, in fact, (Diab et al., 2007) show that full diacritization has a detrimental effect on SMT. Hence, we are interested in eventually discovering an effective optimal level of diacritization. Accordingly, we explore different levels of diacritization. In this work, we limit our study to two diacritization schemes: FULL and MIN. For FULL, all diacritics are explicitly specified for every word. For MIN, we explore what a minimum and optimal number of diacritics that needs to be added in order to disambiguate a given word in context would be with the objective of making a sentence easily readable and unambiguous for any NLP application.

The remainder of this paper is organized as follows: In Section 2 we describe Arabic diacritics and their usage; In Section 3, we give an overview of the automatic diacritization approaches conducted mainly on news data and for a targeted application; We present the dataset used in our experiments in Section 4, followed by a description of the annotation procedure 5; Our analysis of the fully diacritized data, FULL, is provided in Section 6; In Section 7, we present a preliminary exploration of a MIN diacritization scheme; We finally draw some conclusions in Section 8.

2 Arabic Diacritics

Arabic script consists of two classes of symbols: letters and diacritics. Letters comprise long vowels such as A, y, w as well as consonants. Diacritics, on the other hand, comprise short vowels, gemination markers, nunation markers, as well as other markers (such as hamza, the glottal stop, which appears in conjunction with a small number of letters, e.g., أ, إ, آ, etc., dots on letters, elongation and emphatic markers)[3] which in all, if present, render a more or less precise reading of a word. In this study, we are mostly addressing three types of diacritical marks: short vowels, nunation, and shadda (gemination). Short vowel diacritics refer to the three short vowels in Modern Standard Arabic (MSA)[4] and a diacritic indicating the explicit absence of any vowel. The following are the three vowel diacritics exemplified in conjunction with the letter م/m: مَ/ma (fatha), مُ/mu (damma), مِ/mi (kasra), and مْ/mo (no vowel aka sukuun). Nunation diacritics can only occur word finally in nominals (nouns, adjectives) and adverbs. They indicate a short vowel followed by an unwritten n sound: مًا/mAF,[5] مٌ/mN and مٍ/mK. Nunation is an indicator of nominal indefiniteness. The shadda is a consonant doubling diacritic: مّ/m~(/mm/). The shadda can combine with vowel or nunation diacritics: مُّ/m~u or مٌّ/m~uN.

Functionally, diacritics can be split into two different kinds: **lexical diacritics** and **inflectional diacritics** (Diab et al., 2007) .

Lexical diacritics: distinguish between two lexemes.[6] We refer to a lexeme with its citation

[3]Most encodings do not count hamza as a diacritic and the dots on letters are obligatory, other markers are truly optional hence the exclusion of all these classes from our study.

[4]All reference to Arabic in this paper is specifically to the MSA variant.

[5]Buckwalter's transliteration symbols for nunation, F, N and K, are pronounced /an/, /un/ and /in/, respectively.

[6]A lexeme is an abstraction over inflected word forms which groups together all those word forms that differ only in terms of one of the inflectional morphological categories

form as the lemma. Arabic lemma forms are third masculine singular perfective for verbs and masculine singular (or feminine singular if no masculine is possible) for nouns and adjectives. For example, the diacritization difference between the lemmas كَاتِب/kAtib/'writer' and كَاتَب/kAtab/'to correspond' distinguishes between the meanings of the word (lexical disambiguation) rather than their inflections. Any of diacritics may be used to mark lexical variation. A common example with the shadda (gemination) diacritic is the distinction between Form I and Form II of Arabic verb derivations. Form II, indicates, in most cases, added causativity to the Form I meaning. Form II is marked by doubling the second radical of the root used in Form I: أَكَل/Akal/'ate' *vs.* أَكَّل/Ak~al/'fed'. Generally speaking, however, deriving word meaning through lexical diacritic placement is largely unpredictable and they are not specifically associated with any particular part of speech.

Inflectional diacritics: distinguish different inflected forms of the same lexeme. For instance, the final diacritics in كِتَابُ/kitAbu/'book [nominative]' and كِتَابَ/kitAba/'book [accusative]' distinguish the syntactic case of 'book' (e.g., whether the word is subject or object of a verb). Additional inflectional features marked through diacritic change, in addition to syntactic case, include voice, mood, and definiteness. Inflectional diacritics are predictable in their positional placement in a word. Moreover, they are associated with certain parts of speech.

3 Related Work

The task of diacritization is about adding diacritics to the canonical underspecified written form. This task has been discussed in several research works in various NLP areas addressing various applications.

Automatic Arabic Diacritization Much work has been done on recovery of diacritics over the past two decades by developing automatic methods yielding acceptable accuracies. Zitouni et al. (2006) built a diacritization framework based on maximum entropy classification to restore missing diacritics on each letter in a given word. Vergyri and Kirchhoff (2004) worked on automatic diacritization with the goal of improving automatic speech recognition (ASR). Different algorithms for diacritization based mainly on morphological analysis and lexeme-based language models were developed (Habash and Rambow, 2007; Habash and Rambow, 2005; Roth et al., 2008). Various approaches combining morphological analysis and/or Hidden Markov Models for automatic diacritization are found in the literature (Bebah et al., 2014; Alghamdi and Muzaffar, 2007; Rashwan et al., 2009). Rashwan et al. (2009) designed a stochastic Arabic diacritizer based on a hybrid of factorized and un-factorized textual features to automatically diacritize raw Arabic text. Emam and Fischer (2011) introduced a hierarchical approach for diacritization based on a search method in a set of dictionaries of sentences, phrases and words, using a top down strategy. More recently, Abandah et al. (2015) trained a recurrent neural network to transcribe undiacritized Arabic text into fully diacritized sentences. It is worth noting that all these approaches target full diacritization.

Impact of Diacritization in NLP Applications Regardless of the level of diacritization, to date, there have not been many systematic investigations of the impact of different types of Arabic diacritization on NLP applications. For ASR, Kirchhoff and Vergyri (2005) presented a method for full diacritization, FULL, with the goal of improving state of the art Arabic ASR. Ananthakrishnan et al. (2005) used word-based and character-based language models for recovering diacritics for improving ASR. Alotaibi et al. (2013) proposed using diacritization to improve the BBN/AUB DARPA Babylon Levantine Arabic speech corpus and increase its reliability and efficiency. For SMT, there is work on the impact of different levels of partial and full diacritization as a preprocessing step for Arabic to English SMT (Diab et al., 2007). Recently, Hermena et al. (2015) examined sentence processing in the absence of diacritics and contrasted it with the situation where diacritics were explicitly present in an eye-tracking experiment for readability. Their results show that readers benefited from the disambiguating diacritics. This study was a MIN scheme exploration focused on heterophonic-homographic target verbs that have different pronunciations in active and

such as number, gender, aspect, voice, etc. Whereas a lemma is a conventionalized citation form.

	Size in words	GOLD annotation
ATB News	2,478	Yes
ATB BN	3,093	Yes
ATB WebLog	3,177	Yes
Tashkeela	5,172	Yes
Wikipedia	2,850	No
Total	16,770	-

Table 2: The size of the data for annotation per corpus genre

passive.

In this work we are interested in two components: annotating large amounts of varied genres type corpora with diacritics as well as investigating various strategies of annotating corpora with diacritics. We also investigate two levels of diacritization, a full diacritization, FULL, and an initial attempt at a general minimal diacritization scheme, MIN.

4 Corpus Description

We conducted several experiments on a set of sentences that we extracted from five corpora covering different genres. We selected three corpora from the currently available Arabic Treebanks from the Linguistic Data Consortium (LDC). These corpora were chosen because they are fully diacritized and had undergone significant quality control, which will allow us to evaluate the annotation accuracy as well as our annotators understanding of the task.

ATB newswire: Formal newswire stories in MSA.[7]

ATB Broadcast news: Scripted, formal MSA as well as extemporaneous dialogue.[8]

We extend our corpus and include texts covering various topics beyond the commonly-used news topics:

ATB Weblog: Discussion forum posts written primarily in MSA and contained in the 70K words Gale Arabic-English Parallel Aligned Treebank.[9]

Tashkeela: a classical Arabic vocalized text corpus, collected using automatic Web crawling methods from Islamic religious heritage (mainly classical Arabic books). This corpus contains over 6 million words fully diacritized. For our study we include a subset of 5k words from this corpus.

Wikipedia: a corpus of selected abstracts extracted from a number of Arabic Wikipedia articles[10].

We select a total of 16,770 words from these corpora for annotation. The distribution of our dataset per corpus genre is provided in Table 2. Since the majority of our corpus is already fully diacritized, we strip all the diacritics prior to annotation.

5 Annotation Procedure and Guidelines

Three native Arabic annotators with good linguistic background annotated the corpora samples described in Section 4 and illustrated in Table 2, by adding the diacritics in a way that helps a reader disambiguate the text or simply articulate it correctly. Diab et al. (2007), define six different diacritization schemes that are inspired by the observation of the relevant naturally occurring diacritics in different texts. We adopt the FULL diacritization scheme, in which all the diacritics should be specified in a word (e.g., سَتُرَمَّمُ الجُدرَانُ/saturammu AlojidorAnu/"The walls will be restored").

5.1 Annotation Procedure

We design the following three strategies: (i) **Basic**, (ii) **Intermediate**, and, (iii) **Advanced**. These strategies are defined in order to find the best annotation setup that optimizes the annotation efforts and workload, as well as assessing the annotator skills in building reliable annotated corpora.

Annotators were asked to fully diacritize each word. They were assigned different tasks in which

[7]ATB Part 1 Version 4.1 Catalog No: LDC2010T1

[8]Arabic Treebank Broadcast News v1.0 Catalog No: LDC2012T07

[9]Catalog No : LDC2014T08.

[10]`http://ar.wikipedia.org/`

English	The ITU is the second oldest international organization that still exists.			
Buckwalter	*AlAtHAd Aldwly llAtSAlAt hw vAny >qdm tnZym EAlmy mA zAl mwjwdA.*			
Basic	الاتحاد الدولي للاتصالات هو ثاني أقدم تنظيم عالمي ما زال موجودا.			
Intermediate	الاتحاد/NN الدولي/Adj ل/Prep الاتصالات/NN هو/Pron ثاني/Adj أقدم/VV تنظيم/NN عَالمي/Adj مَا/Pron زَال/VV موجودًا/Adj ./Punc			
Advanced	**Word**	**MADAMIRA candidates**	**Word**	**MADAMIRA candidates**
	الاتحاد →	[الَاِتِّحَادُ، الَاِتِّحَادِ، الَاِتِّحَادَ]	تنظيم →	[تَنظِيمٍ ، تَنظِيمِ ، تَنظِيمِ]
	الدولي →	[الدُّوَلِيُّ، الدَّولِيُّ، الدُّوَلِيِّ]	عالمي →	[عَالَمِيٍّ، عَالَمِيٌّ، عَالَمِيّ]
	للاتصالات →	[لِلاِتِّصَالَاتِ، لِلاِتِّصَالَاتِ، لِلاِتِّصَالَات]	ما →	[مَا، مَا]
	هو →	[هُوَ، هُوَ]	زال →	[زَالَ]
	ثاني →	[ثَانِي، ثَانِي، ثَانِي]	موجودا →	[مَوجُوداً، مَوجُودَا]
	أقدم →	[أَقدَمَ، أُقَدِّمُ، أَقَدَّمُ]	. →	[.]

Table 3: Examples of a sentence (along with its English translation and Buckwalter transliteration) as presented to the annotator, in the Basic, Intermediate and Advanced annotation modes.

we vary the level and/or the text genre as follows:

	Annot$_1$	Annot$_2$	Annot$_3$
Text1	Basic	Advanced	Intermediate
Text2	Advanced	Basic	Intermediate
Text3	Basic	Advanced	Intermediate
Text4	Basic	Intermediate	Advanced
Text5	Intermediate	Advanced	Basic

Table 4: Data distribution per annotator and per annotation strategy.

Basic: In this mode, we ask for annotation of words where all diacritics are absent, including the naturally occurring ones. The words are presented in a raw tokenized format to the annotators in context. An example is provided in Table 3.

Intermediate: In this mode, we provide the annotator with words along with their POS information. The intuition behind adding POS is to help the annotator disambiguate a word by narrowing down on the diacritization possibilities. For example, the surface undiacritized spelling consonantal form for the Arabic word بين/byn could have the following possible readings: بَيَّنَ/bay~ina/'made clear|different', when it is a verb or بَيْنَ/bayona/'between' when it corresponds to the adverb. We use MADAMIRA (Pasha et al., 2014), a morphological tagging and disambiguation system for Arabic, for determining the POS tags.

Advanced: In this mode, the annotation task is formulated as a selection task instead of an editing task. Annotators are provided with a list of automatically diacritized candidates and are asked to choose the correct one, if it appears in the list. Otherwise, if they are not satisfied with the given candidates, they can manually edit the word and add the correct diacritics. This technique is designed in order to reduce annotation time and especially reduce annotator workload. For each word, we generate a list of vowelized candidates using MADAMIRA (Pasha et al., 2014). MADAMIRA is able to achieve a lemmatization accuracy 99.2% and a diacritization accuracy of 86.3%.

We present the annotator with the top three candidates suggested by MADAMIRA, when possible. Otherwise, only the available candidates are provided, as illustrated in Table 3. Each text genre (Text1→5) is assigned to our annotators (Annot$_1$, Annot$_2$ and Annot$_3$) in the three different modes. Table 4 shows the distribution of data per annotator and per mode. For instance, Text1 is given to Annot$_1$ in Basic mode, to Annot$_2$ in Advanced mode and to Annot$_3$ in Advanced mode. Hence, each text genre is annotated 3 times in 3 modes by the 3 annotators.[11]

[11] Different tasks were assigned based on the availability of the annotators since some annotators can afford more hours per week than others.

	News	BN	WebLog	Tashkeela	Wiki
Basic	32.23	33.59	37.13	42.86	46.16
Intermediate	31.86	33.07	35.02	39.79	39.00
Advanced	5.58	4.36	3.16	4.92	1.56

Table 5: IAA in terms of WER

	News	BN	Weblog	Tashkeela	Wiki
Basic	68.36	69.01	62.50	68.03	66.14
Intermediate	78.05	76.31	73.77	69.25	71.48
Advanced	**98.00**	**94.59**	**88.88**	**73.10**	**95.23**

Table 6: Annotations accuracy for the different corpora per mode

5.2 Guidelines

We provided annotators with detailed guidelines, describing our diacritization scheme and specifying how to add diacritics for each annotation strategy. We described the annotation procedure and specified how to deal with borderline cases. We also provided in the guidelines many annotated examples to illustrate the various rules and exceptions.

We extended the LDC guidelines (Maamouri et al., 2008) by adding some diacritization rules: The shadda mark should not be added to the definite article (e.g., اللَيمون/'lemon' and not اللّيمون); The sukuun sign should not be indicated at the end of silent words (e.g., مِن/'from'); The letters followed by a long Alif, should not be diacritized as it is a deterministic diacritization (القَوَاعِد/'the rules'); Abbreviations are not diacritized (كم/'km', كغم/'kg'). We also added an appendix that summarized all Arabic diacritization rules.[12]

6 Annotation Analysis and Results

In order to determine the most optimized annotation setup for the annotators, in terms of speed and efficiency, we test the results obtained following the three annotation strategies. These annotations are all conducted for the FULL scheme. We first calculated the number of words annotated per hour, for each annotator and in each mode. As expected, following the Advanced mode, our three annotators could annotate an average of 618.93 words per hour which is double those annotated in the Basic mode (only 302.14 words). Adding POS tags to the Basic forms, as in the Intermediate mode, does not accelerate the process much. Only +90 more words are diacritized per hour compared to the basic mode.

Then, we evaluated the Inter-Annotator Agreement (IAA) to quantify the extent to which independent annotators agree on the diacritics chosen for each word. For every text genre, two annotators were asked to annotate independently a sample of 100 words. We measured the IAA between two annotators by averaging WER (Word Error Rate) over all pairs of words. The higher the WER between two annotations, the lower their agreement. The results given in Table 5, show clearly that the Advanced mode is the best strategy to adopt for this diacritization task. It is the less confusing method on all text genres (with WER between 1.56 and 5.58). We note that Wiki annotations in Advanced mode garner the highest IAA with a very low WER.

We measure the reliability of the annotations by comparing them against gold standard annotations. In order to build the gold Wiki annotations, we hired two professional linguists, provided them with guidelines and asked them to fully diacritize the sentences. We compute the accuracy of the annotations obtained in each annotation mode and report results in Table 6 by measuring the pairwise similarity between annotators and the gold annotations.

The best result is obtained on the ATB-news dataset using the Advanced mode (annotation based on MADAMIRA's output). This is not surprising as MADAMIRA is partly trained on this corpus for diacritization. The accuracy of 98.0 obtained on this corpus validates our intuition be-

[12] The guidelines are available upon request.

hind using this annotation strategy. It is not surprising that Basic is the most difficult mode for our annotators. These are not trained lexicographers, though they possess an excellent command of MSA they are at a level where they need the Advanced mode. Furthermore, adding the POS information in the Intermediate mode helps significantly over the Basic mode, but it is still less accurate than annotations obtained in the Advanced mode.

The accuracy of the annotations for Tashkeela corpus in all the modes is very low compared to the other corpora, especially in the Advanced mode. Tashkeela was parsed with MADAMIRA and the annotations were presented to the annotators. So the results of MADAMIRA tagging are lower, hence the choice was among bad diacritized candidates. By observing the the number of edits done in the Advanced mode, we realize that annotators tend to not to edit (only 194 edits in total) in order to render a correct form of diacritization, this fits perfectly with the notion of tainting in annotation. It is always a trade off between quality and efficiency.

It is worth noting that the Basic mode shows that the Weblog corpus was the hardest one for the annotators in terms of raw accuracy. Further analysis is needed to understand why this is the case.

7 MIN annotation scheme: Preliminary study

This is a diacritization scheme that encodes the most relevant differentiating diacritics to reduce confusability among words that look the same (homographs) when undiacritized but have different readings. Our hypothesis in MIN is that there is an optimal level of diacritization to render a text unambiguous for processing and enhance its readability.

Annotating a word with the minimum diacritics needed to render it readable and unambiguous in context is subjective and depends on the annotator's understanding of the task. It also depends on the definition of the MIN scheme in the guidelines. We describe here a preliminary study aiming at exploring this diacritization scheme and measuring Inter-annotator agreement between annotators for such a task using the Basic mode.

We select a sample of 100 sentences (comprising 3,527 words) from the ATB News corpus and processed them with MADAMIRA. We, then assign it to four annotators including a lead annotator for providing a gold standard.[13] This task is done using the advanced mode.

We measure the IAA for this task using WER. We obtain an average WER of 27%, which reflects a high disagreement between annotators in defining the minimum number of diacritics to be added. The WER are shown in Table 9.

Annot$_1$	27.44
Annot$_2$	24.74
Annot$_3$	27.92
Average	27.15

Table 9: IAA WER scores against gold (Annot$_4$) for the MIN annotation scheme

An observation of some cases of disagreement of the examples in Table 7 and Table 8 shows a variable interpretation of what should be the MIN diacritization scheme. For Example, there is clear confusion about the letters to diacritize in the case of conjunctions and prepositions (such as: كَمَا/'as well' and عَلَى/'on'). In some other cases there is a disagreement of which diacritics to mention such as the word بِحمامات/'with baths' in Table 7 written in four different ways by the four annotators (بحَمَامَات, بِحَمَّامَاتٍ, بِحَمَامَات, بِحَمَّامَاتِ).

The outlier annotator (Annot$_1$) has been detected based on a large number of cases in which he disagree with the rest. For example, the words ضفاف/'banks' and خصوصا/'especially' in the sentence given in Table 7, were erroneously fully diacritized, while adding a fatha on the second letter is enough to disambiguate these words.

By design we meant for the guidelines to be very loose in attempt to discover the various factors impacting what a possible MIN could mean to different annotators. The main lessons learned from this experiment is: first, this is a difficult task since every annotator can have a different interpretation of what is a minimum diacritization. Second, we also noticed that the same annotator could be inconsistent in his interpretation. Third, we believe that the educational and cultural background of the annotator plays an important role in the various MIN scheme interpretations. However,

[13] Annot$_4$ is the lead annotator

English	And the spread of the phenomenon of building chalets equipped with steam baths especially on lake banks.
Annot$_1$	كَمَا إِنتَشَرَت ظاهرة بنَاء شاليهات مُجَهَّزَةٍ بِحَماماتِ بُخارٍ علَى ضِفافِ البُحَيراتِ خُصوصًاً .
Annot$_2$	كَمَا إِنتَشَرَت ظاهرة بنَاء شاليهَات مجهزة بِحَمّاماتِ بخار علَى ضفاف البحيرات خصوصَا .
Annot$_3$	كَمَا انتشرت ظاهرة بنَاء شاليهات مجهزة بحمامات بخار علَى ضفاف البحيرات خصوصَا .
Annot$_4$	كَمَا إِنتَشَرَت ظاهرة بِنَاءِ شاليهات مُجَهَّزَةٍ بِحَمّاماتٍ بخار عَلَى ضفاف البُحَيراتِ خصوصَا .

Table 7: An example showing a sentence with low average IAA (WER: 44.87).

English	And Dick Brass promised the readers by saying: we will put in your hands story books. And you will find in it the sound, the image and the text.
Annot$_1$	وَوَعَدَ ديك برَاس القرَاء بقوله : سنضع بَينَ ايديكم كتبًا تَحكي . وستجدون فيهَا الصوت وَالصورة وَالنص .
Annot$_2$	وّعد ديك برَاس القرَاء بقوله : سنضع بين ايديكم كتبًا تّحكي . وستجدون فيهَا الصوت وَالصورة وَالنص .
Annot$_3$	وَوَعَدَ ديك برَاس القرَاء بقوله : سنضع بَينَ أَيدِيكُم كتبًا تّحكي . وَسَتَجِدُونَ فيهَا الصوت وَالصورة وَالنص .
Annot$_4$	وَوَعَدَ ديك برَاس القرَاء بقوله : سنضع بَينَ ايديكم كتبًا تّحكِي . وَسَتَجِدُونَ فيهَا الصوت وَالصورة وَالنص .

Table 8: An example showing a sentence with higher average IAA (WER: 16.66).

this provides an interesting pilot study into creating guidelines for this task.

8 Conclusion

We described a pilot study to build a diacritized multi-genre corpus. In our experiments, we annotated a sample of non-diacritized words that we extracted from five text genres. We also explored different annotation strategies, and we showed that generating automatically the diacritized candidates and formulating the task as a selection task, accelerates the annotation and yields more accurate annotations. We also conducted a preliminary study for a minimum diacritization scheme and showed the difficulty in defining such a scheme and how subjective this task can be. In the future, we plan to explore the minimum scheme more deeply.

Acknowledgements

We thank Nizar Habash and anonymous reviewers for their valuable comments and suggestions. We also thank all our dedicated annotators: Noor Alzeer, Anissa Jrad, Samah Lakhal, Jihene Wafi, and Hoda Ibrahim. This publication is made possible by grant NPRP-6-1020-1-199 from the Qatar National Research Fund (a member of the Qatar Foundation).

References

Gheith A Abandah, Alex Graves, Balkees Al-Shagoor, Alaa Arabiyat, Fuad Jamour, and Majid Al-Taee. 2015. Automatic Diacritization of Arabic Text using Recurrent Neural Networks. *International Journal on Document Analysis and Recognition (IJDAR)*, 18(2):1–15.

Mansour Alghamdi and Zeeshan Muzaffar. 2007. KACST Arabic Diacritizer. In *The First International Symposium on Computers and Arabic Language*, pages 25–28.

Y.A. Alotaibi, A.H. Meftah, and S.A. Selouani. 2013. Diacritization, Automatic Segmentation and Labeling for Levantine Arabic Speech. In *Digital Signal Processing and Signal Processing Education Meeting (DSP/SPE), 2013 IEEE*, pages 7–11, Napa, CA.

Sankaranarayanan Ananthakrishnan, Shrikanth Narayanan, and Srinivas Bangalore. 2005. Automatic Diacritization of Arabic Transcripts for Automatic Speech Recognition. In *Proceedings of the 4th International Conference on Natural Language Processing*, pages 47–54.

Mohamed Bebah, Amine Chennoufi, Azzeddine Mazroui, and Abdelhak Lakhouaja. 2014. Hybrid Approaches for Automatic Vowelization of Arabic Texts. *International Journal on Natural Language Computing (IJNLC)*, 3(4).

Tim Buckwalter. 2002. Buckwalter Arabic Morphological Analyzer Version 1.0. Technical Report LDC2002L49, Linguistic Data Consortium.

Mona Diab, Mahmoud Ghoneim, and Nizar Habash. 2007. Arabic Diacritization in the Context of Statistical Machine Translation. In *Proceedings of MT-Summit*, Copenhagen, Denmark.

Ossama Emam and Volker Fischer. 2011. Hierarchical Approach for the Statistical Vowelization of Arabic Text. US Patent 8,069,045.

Nizar Habash and Owen Rambow. 2005. Arabic Tokenization, Part-of-Speech Tagging and Morphological Disambiguation in One Fell Swoop. In *Proceedings of the 43rd Annual Meeting of the Association for Computational Linguistics*, pages 573–580, Ann Arbor, Michigan.

Nizar Habash and Owen Rambow. 2007. Arabic Diacritization through Full Morphological Tagging. In *Human Language Technologies 2007: The Conference of the North American Chapter of the Association for Computational Linguistics; Companion Volume, Short Papers*, pages 53–56, Rochester, New York.

Ehab Hermena, Denis Drieghe, Sam Hellmuth, and Simon P Liversedge. 2015. Processing of Arabic Diacritical Marks: Phonological–Syntactic Disambiguation of Homographic Verbs and Visual Crowding Effects. *Journal of Experimental Psychology. Human Perception and Performance*, 41(2):494–507.

Katrin Kirchhoff and Dimitra Vergyri. 2005. Cross-Dialectal Data Sharing for Acoustic Modeling in Arabic Speech Recognition. *Speech Communication*, 46(1):37–51.

Mohamed Maamouri, Ann Bies, and Seth Kulick. 2008. Enhancing the Arabic Treebank: a Collaborative Effort toward New Annotation Guidelines. In *LREC*. Citeseer.

Arfath Pasha, Mohamed Al-Badrashiny, Ahmed El Kholy, Ramy Eskander, Mona Diab, Nizar Habash, Manoj Pooleery, Owen Rambow, and Ryan Roth. 2014. MADAMIRA: A Fast, Comprehensive Tool for Morphological Analysis and Disambiguation of Arabic. In *In Proceedings of the 9th International Conference on Language Resources and Evaluation*, Reykjavik, Iceland.

Mohsen Rashwan, Mohammad Al-Badrashiny, Mohamed Attia, and Sherif Abdou. 2009. A Hybrid System for Automatic Arabic Diacritization. In *The 2nd International Conference on Arabic Language Resources and Tools*, Cairo, Egypt.

Ryan Roth, Owen Rambow, Nizar Habash, Mona Diab, and Cynthia Rudin. 2008. Arabic Morphological Tagging, Diacritization, and Lemmatization Using Lexeme Models and Feature Ranking. In *Proceedings of ACL-08: HLT, Short Papers*, pages 117–120, Columbus, Ohio.

Dimitra Vergyri and Katrin Kirchhoff. 2004. Automatic Diacritization of Arabic for Acoustic Modeling in Speech Recognition. In *Proceedings of the Workshop on Computational Approaches to Arabic Script-based Languages*, pages 66–73. Association for Computational Linguistics.

Imed Zitouni, Jeffrey S. Sorensen, and Ruhi Sarikaya. 2006. Maximum Entropy Based Restoration of Arabic Diacritics. In *Proceedings of the 21st International Conference on Computational Linguistics and 44th Annual Meeting of the Association for Computational Linguistics*, pages 577–584, Sydney, Australia.

Annotating Targets of Opinions in Arabic using Crowdsourcing

Noura Farra
Columbia University
New York, NY 10027, USA
noura@cs.columbia.edu

Kathleen McKeown
Columbia University
New York, NY 10027, USA
kathy@cs.columbia.edu

Nizar Habash
New York University
Abu Dhabi, UAE
nizar.habash@nyu.edu

Abstract

We present a method for annotating targets of opinions in Arabic in a two-stage process using the crowdsourcing tool Amazon Mechanical Turk. The first stage consists of identifying candidate targets "entities" in a given text. The second stage consists of identifying the opinion polarity (positive, negative, or neutral) expressed about a specific entity. We annotate a corpus of Arabic text using this method, selecting our data from online commentaries in different domains. Despite the complexity of the task, we find high agreement. We present detailed analysis.

1 Introduction

An important task in subjectivity analysis of text is the identification of targets - also often called *topics* or *subjects* - of opinionated text. Knowledge of the target is important for making sense of an opinion (e.g in *'The **will of the people** will prevail over the **regime's brutality**'*, the opinion is positive towards 'the people' and negative towards 'the regime'). An opinion system which can identify both targets and polarities of opinions, and which can summarize the opinions of writers towards different targets, will be more informative than one which only identifies the overall sentiment of the text. This problem has started gaining interest in the product review domain (Hu and Liu, 2004; Qiu et al., 2011), news and social media (Kim and Hovy, 2006; Jiang et al., 2011), and in general language and discourse (Wilson, 2008; Ruppenhofer et al., 2008; Somasundaran and Wiebe, 2009).

Annotating targets of opinion is a difficult and expensive task, requiring definition of what constitutes a target, whether targets are linked to opinion expressions, and how the boundaries of target spans should be defined (e.g **'the people'** vs. **'the will of the people'** or **'the regime'** vs. **'the regime's brutality'**), a problem which annotators often disagree on (Pontiki et al., 2014; Kim and Hovy, 2006; Somasundaran et al., 2008). Additionally, it is not always straightforward to attribute a target to a specific opinion phrase. Consider for example the following statement:

*'The Lebanese PM said he was convinced that there would be a consensus on **the presidential election**, because since the moment the US and Iran had reached an understanding in the region, things were starting to look positive.'*

Which is the opinion expression that leads us to believe that the PM is optimistic about the target **presidential election**? Is it *'convinced'*, *'consensus'*, *'reached an understanding'*, or *'look positive'*, or a combination of the above? Such decisions are difficult for annotators to agree on; many studies have noted these challenges (Stoyanov and Cardie, 2008; Ruppenhofer et al., 2008) which can make the task complex.

Compared to the amount of resources available for sentiment and subjectivity analysis, there is much less annotated data available for this more fine-grained type of analysis. Due to the difficulty of the task, most of the available datasets of fine-grained subjectivity have been annotated by trained annotators or expert linguists, making the process slower and more expensive.

In this work, we consider annotation of targets using a sequence of simple crowdsourced substeps. We focus on Arabic, where subjectivity analysis is of growing interest, and where there are no publicly available resources for fine-grained opinion analysis. We assume targets of opinions to be noun phrase entities: people, places, things or ideas. We develop a two-stage annotation process for annotating targets of opinions using Amazon Mechanical Turk. In the first, annotators list all

Proceedings of the Second Workshop on Arabic Natural Language Processing, pages 89–98,
Beijing, China, July 26-31, 2015. ©2014 Association for Computational Linguistics

important 'entities', and in the second, they choose the polarity expressed (positive, negative, or neutral) towards any given entity. We select online data from multiple domains: politics, sports, and culture; and we provide a new publicly available resource for Arabic by annotating it for targets of opinions along with their polarities. Finally, we evaluate the quality of the data at different stages, obtaining majority agreement on sentiment for 91.8% of entities in a corpus of 1177 news article comments. We also find that the morphology and grammar of Arabic lends itself to even more variations in identifying the boundaries of targets.

Section 2 describes related annotation work. Section 3 describes the Amazon Mechanical Turk tasks design, the data selection, and the annotation process. In Section 4, we examine and analyze the annotations, evaluate the inter-annotator agreement, and provide detailed examples. We conclude in section 5.

2 Related Work

2.1 Annotating Targets in English

Fine-grained subjectivity annotation in the English language has recently started gaining interest, where annotation can include opinion targets, opinion sources, or phrase-level opinion expressions. One of the early datasets collected for identifying opinion targets is that of (Hu and Liu, 2004), where product features (e.g price, quality) were annotated in customer reviews of consumer electronics. These consisted of mostly explicit product features annotated by one person.

Also in the product review domain, the SemEval Task on aspect feature mining in 2014 (Pontiki et al., 2014) was concerned with finding aspect features of products with the polarities towards them. The products (e.g 'restaurant') and coarse-grained features (e.g 'service') were provided to annotators, who identified the aspects (e.g 'waiter') and the corresponding sentiment.

The MPQA corpus is an in-depth and general-purpose resource for fine-grained subjectivity annotations (Wiebe et al., 2005; Wilson, 2008), containing annotations of opinion expressions at the phrase level while specifying polarities, sources, and target spans. The annotation scheme links each subjective expression to one or more attitudes, which in turn can have one or more or no targets. The target annotations include the full target spans, but do not necessarily identify target entities within the span. Stoyanov and Cardie (2008) extended part of the MPQA corpus by annotating it for 'topics', arguing that 'targets' refer to the syntactic span of text that identifies the content of an opinion, while 'topic' is the real-world object or entity corresponding to the primary subject of the opinion. Using trained annotators, they identify 'topic clusters', which group together all opinions referring to the same topic. In parallel with this work, part of the MPQA corpus was recently annotated for entity-level targets (Deng and Wiebe, 2015) by specifying target entities within the MPQA span, leading to the annotation of 292 targets by two annotators. The entities were anchored to the head word of the noun phrase or verb phrase that refers to the entity or event. In our work, we only consider noun phrase entities, and we consider the noun phrase itself as an entity.

Other fine-grained annotation studies include that of Toprak et al. (2010) who enrich target and holder annotations in consumer reviews with measures such as relevancy and intensity, and Somasundaran et al. (2008) who perform discourse-level annotation of opinion frames, which consist of opinions whose targets are described by similar or contrasting relations.

In these studies, the annotation was usually done by trained individuals or someone who has knowledge and experience in the task. Our study is different in that it utilizes crowdsourcing for the annotation process, and it focuses on the marking of important entities and concepts as targets of opinions in the more noisy online commentary genre. We view targets as 'real-world entities', similar to the topics discussed by Stoyanov and Cardie (2008), and the targets in (Deng and Wiebe, 2015), and we annotate multiple targets in the text.

Carvalho et al. (2011) also annotated targets in online commentary data; here targets were considered to be human entities, namely political and media personalities. This annotation was done by one trained annotator where agreement was computed for a portion of the data. Another related task was that of Lawson et al. (2010) who describe a Mechanical Turk annotation study for annotating named entities in emails, with favorable agreement results. The tasks for identifying the spans of and labeling the named entities were grouped in a single Human Intelligence Task (HIT).

2.2 Annotation Studies in Arabic

Abdul-Mageed and Diab (2011) performed a

sentence-level annotation study for Modern Standard Arabic (MSA) newswire data which covered multiple domains including politics, sports, economy, culture, and others. Both the domains and the sentence-level sentiment were annotated by two trained annotators. Our data also comes from different domains, but it is from the genre of online commentaries, which have greater prevalence of dialect, imperfect grammar, and spelling errors. Also, to select less prevalent domains from our comments corpus, we used topic modeling.

There have been other MTurk studies in Arabic; among them Zaidan and Callison-Burch (2011) who annotated dialectness, Denkowski et al. (2010) who annotated machine translation pairs, and Higgins et al. (2010) who annotated Arabic nicknames. To the best of our knowledge, there are no known studies for target or topic annotation for Arabic.

3 Annotation Process

We describe the crowdsourcing process for annotating targets of opinions, including the choices which motivated our design, the tasks we designed on Amazon Mechanical Turk, and the way we selected our data.

3.1 Scope and Decisions

We assume targets of opinions to be nouns and noun phrases representing entities and concepts, which could be people, places, things, or important ideas. Consider for example:

'It is great ***that so many people showed up to the protest.****'*

The full target span is marked in bold, but the actual entity which receives the positive opinion is **'the protest'**. We are interested in such entities; for example, entities could be politicians, organizations, events, sports teams, companies, products, or important concepts and ideas such as 'democracy' or entities representing ideological belief.

Given the complexity of the task, we annotate targets without specifying opinion expressions that are linked to them, as in (Pontiki et al., 2014; Hu and Liu, 2004), although the dataset can be extended for this purpose to provide richer information for modeling. We assume the availability of an Arabic opinion lexicon, to identify the opinion words. We don't consider targets of *subjective-neutral* judgments (e.g *"I expect it will rain tomorrow"*). For this corpus, we are interested only in targets of polar **positive or negative** opinions; everything else we regard as neutral. Moreover, since our data comes from online commentaries, we assume that in the majority of cases, the opinion holder is the writer of the post.

3.2 Amazon Mechanical Turk Tasks

Instead of asking annotators to directly identify targets of opinions, which we believed to be a much harder task, we broke the annotation into two stages, each in a different series of HITs (Human Intelligence Tasks). The task guidelines were presented in Modern Standard Arabic (MSA) to guarantee that only Arabic speakers would be able to understand and work on them. Many of the insights in the task design were gained from an extensive pilot study.

Task 1: Identifying Candidate Entities Given an article comment, annotators are asked to list the main nouns and noun phrases that correspond to people, places, things, and ideas. This task, or HIT, is given to three annotators and a few examples of appropriate answers are provided.

The answers from the three annotators are then combined by taking the intersection of common noun phrases listed by all three responses. If they only agree on a subset of the noun phrase, we choose the maximal phrase among agreed entities in order to determine the entity span. For example, if two annotators specify *the president* and a third specifies *the election of the president*, we keep *the election of the president*. The maximal noun phrase was also chosen by Pontiki et al. (2014) when resolving disagreements on target spans.

We allowed annotators to list references in the comment to the same entity (e.g *'The president'* and *'President Mubarak'*) as separate entities.

Insights from Pilot We asked specifically for the **main** noun phrases, after we found that annotators in the pilot over-generated nouns and noun phrases, listing clearly unimportant entities (such as اليوم 'today/this day', and السلام 'hello/the greeting'), which would make Task 2 unnecessarily expensive. They would also break up noun phrases which clearly referred to a single entity (such as separating كرسي *'the seat'* and الرئاسة *'the presidency'* from كرسي الرئاسة *'the presidency's seat'*), so we instructed them to keep such cases as a single entity. These reasons also support choosing the maximal agreeing noun phrase provided by annotators. By making these changes, the average number of entities resolved per comment was reduced from 8 entities in the pilot study to 6 entities in the full study.

We paid 30 cents for Task 1, due to its importance and due to the time it took workers to complete (2-3 minutes on average).

Task 2: Identifying Sentiment towards Entities In the second task (HIT), annotators are presented with an article comment and a single entity, and are asked to specify the opinion of the comment towards this entity, termed a 'topic' موضوع. The entities are chosen from the resolved responses in Task 1. The question is in multiple-choice form where they can choose from options: positive, negative, or neutral. Each HIT is given to five annotators, and the entities which are specified as **positive or negative** with majority agreement of 3 are considered to be **targets**. Entities with disagreement, or with neutral majority, are discarded as non-targets. In this question, we tell annotators that opinions can include sentiment, belief, feelings, or judgments, and that the **neutral** option should be selected if the comment reveals either no opinion or an unbiased opinion towards this particular entity. We provide multiple examples. For this task, we paid workers 5 cents per HIT, which took 30 seconds to 1 minute on average.

Insights from Pilot In our pilot study, we had an additional question in this HIT which asks annotators to specify the holder of the opinion, which could be the writer or someone else mentioned in the text. However, we removed this question in the final study due to the low quality of responses in the pilot, some of which reflected misunderstanding of the question or were left blank.

Additionally, we found that some annotators specified the overall sentiment of the comment rather than the sentiment about the topic. We thus emphasized, and included an additional English translation of the instruction that the opinion polarity should be about the specific **topic** and not of the whole comment.

We completed the full annotation study in five rounds of a few hundred comments each. For the first two rounds of annotation, we rejected all HITs that were clearly spamming the task or were not Arabic speakers. After that we created task qualifications and allowed only a qualified group of workers (5 for Task 1 and 10 for Task 2) to access the tasks, based on their performance in the previous tasks.

Domain	**# Comments**	**Distribution(%)**
Politics	596	51
Culture	382	32
Sports	199	17
Total	1177	100

Table 1: Distribution of article comments by domain

3.3 Data Selection

Our data is selected from the Qatar Arabic Language Bank (QALB) (Mohit et al., 2014; Zaghouani et al., 2014), which includes online commentaries to *Aljazeera* newspaper articles.

Topic Modeling We initially selected a random sample of data from the *Aljazeera* corpus, which contains mostly political data. In our pilot study and first annotation round, we found that this data was biased towards negative sentiment. We thus used topic modeling (Blei et al., 2003; McCallum, 2002) to select data from other domains which we thought might contain more positive sentiment. Upon applying a topic model specifying 40 topics to the *Aljazeera* corpus, we found a general "sports" topic and a general "culture" (language, science, technology, society) topic among the other political topics. We chose sports and culture comments by taking the top few hundred comments having the highest probability score for these topics, to guarantee that the content was indeed relevant to the domain. Table 1 shows the distribution of the final data used for annotation, consisting of 1177 news article comments.

Data Characteristics The average length of comments is 51 words, spanning 1-3 Arabic sentences. We do not correct the data for spelling errors; we annotate the raw text because we want to avoid any alteration that may affect the interpretation of sentiment, and we would like to keep the data as real as possible. However, it is possible to correct this output automatically or manually.

We performed a manual analysis of 100 comments from a randomly selected subset of the dataset and having the same domain distribution. We found that 43% of the comments contain at least one **spelling error** including typos, word merges and splits,[1] 15% contain at least one **dialect word**, 20% contain a **run-on sentence** not separated by any conjunction or punctuation, and 98% contain **subjective opinions** on any topic. We believe this is a good dataset for annotation because it contains real-world data, and many strong opinions on controversial topics.

4 Experimental Results

This section describes results and analyses of the crowdsourced annotations. We report the inter-annotator agreement at each of the two annotation stages, the distribution of the sentiment of collected targets by domain, and a manual analysis of our target entities. We also provide examples of our final annotations.

4.1 Inter-annotator agreement

Task 1: Agreement on Important Noun Phrases To compute the agreement between annotators on important entities in a HIT, we compute the average precision p_{HIT}. p_{HIT} is then averaged over all HITs to obtain the agreement.

$$p_{HIT} = \frac{1}{3} \cdot \left(\frac{\#matches}{\#phrases\_a1} + \frac{\#matches}{\#phrases\_a2} + \frac{\#matches}{\#phrases\_a3}\right)$$

An average precision of **0.38** was obtained using exact matching of entities and **0.75** using subset matching: i.e a match occurs if the three annotators all list a sub-phrase of the same noun phrase. (Recall that the final entities were chosen according to subset agreement.)

Our noun phrase agreement numbers are comparable to the target span subset agreement numbers of Somasundaran et al. (2008) in English discourse data, and lower than that of Toprak et al. (2010), who annotated targets in the consumer review domain. Note that besides the language difference, the task itself is different, since we annotate important noun phrases rather than opinion targets; a lower agreement on this task essentially indicates that fewer entities are being passed on to the next task for consideration as targets, the assumption being that only important entities will be agreed upon by all three annotators. Since we had three rather than two annotators, the agreement using exact match is expected to be low.

Domain	# Entities	Majority Agree (%)
Politics	3853	91.2
Culture	2271	95.8
Sports	1222	87.6
Total	**7346**	**91.8**

Table 2: Agreement on entity-level sentiment annotation

Task 2: Sentiment agreement Table 2 shows the annotator agreement for the task of identifying sentiment towards given entities. A majority agreement occurs when 3 out of 5 annotators of an entity agree on whether the sentiment towards it is positive, negative, or neutral. We see that the agreement (91.8%) is reasonably high. Abdul-Mageed and Diab (2011) have reported overall agreement of 88% for annotating sentence-level Arabic sentiment (as positive, negative, neutral, or objective) using two trained annotators. We note that after assigning our task to only the qualified group of workers, the annotator agreement increased from 80% and 88% in the first two annotation rounds, to 95% in the remaining rounds.[2]

Sentiment Distribution Table 3 shows the distribution of the sentiment of the final targets by domain. The final targets of opinions correspond to entities which were agreed to be **positive or negative by majority agreement.** We can see that the politics and sports domains are biased towards negative and positive sentiment respectively, while targets in the culture domain have a mostly even distribution of sentiment. We also note that overall, 95% of all comments had at least one target of opinion, and 41% of those comments had multiple targets with both positive and negative sentiment. This verifies our hypothesis about the sentiment diversity and need for finer-level opinion analysis for this dataset.

Finally, we found that the majority of targets are composed of 2 words (38% of targets), followed by 1-word targets (25% of targets), 3-word targets (18%), and 4-word targets (9%), while 10% of all targets are composed of more than 4 words.

4.2 Manual Analysis

We manually examined 200 randomly selected targets from our final dataset, and found a num-

[1]We don't count the different variations of *Alef* ا, ى/ي, or ه/ة, forms, which are often normalized during model training and evaluation.

[2]In the final dataset, we include the annotations organized by each annotation round. We mark the entities with disagreement as 'undetermined'.

Domain	**# Targets**	**(%) Pos**	**(%) Neg**
Politics	2448	30	70
Culture	1149	48	52
Sports	748	79	21
Total	**4345**	**43**	**57**

Table 3: Distribution of sentiment in final targets

Class	**Example**
Spelling errors **2.5%**	ارادت الشعب *"the people's will"*
Punctuation **5%**	منتجات ابل. *"Apple's products."*
Prep & Conj clitics **8.5%**	لمانشتر يونايتد *"to Manchester United"*
Non-noun phrases **3%**	البرشا بطل الدور الاسباني *"Barcelona (is) the champion of the Spanish league"*
Targets with sentiment **5.5%**	الشعب السوري الحر *"the free Syrian people"*
Propositional entities **3%**	تشجيع الباحثين *"encouraging researchers"*

Table 4: Target phrase observations

ber of observations, many of which are language-specific, that deserve to be highlighted. They are summarized in Table 4.

We first note orthographic observations such as spelling errors, which come mostly from the original text, and punctuations attached to targets, which may easily be stripped from the text. The punctuations result from our decision to take the maximal noun phrase provided by annotators.

Prepositional and conjunctional clitics result from Arabic morphology which attaches prepositions such as *l+* ل *(to)* and *b+* ب *(in)*, or conjunctions *w+* و *(and)* to the noun preceding them. They can be removed by tokenization (Habash, 2010), but we preserve them for completeness and their usefulness for allowing us to distinguish between different mentions of the same target.

Non-noun phrases mainly come from nominal sentences specific to Arabic syntax جملة اسمية ; these are problematic because they may be interpreted as either noun phrases or full sentences that begin with a nominal. We also observed a number of verbal phrase targets (e.g "نبلبل بالديموقراطية" *"we confuse democracy"*), but these were very few; the majority of this class of observations comes from verbless nominal phrases.

Targets containing sentiment words appear since sentiment words can be part of the noun phrase and are not always independent of the topic itself. As for propositional entities, they result from process nominals مصدر which can have a verbal reading (Green and Manning, 2010) but are correctly considered to be nouns. We find that they occur mostly in the culture domain, where more discussions occur about 'important concepts'.

We also found from our manual inspection that our final entity spans reasonably corresponded to what would be expected to be targets of opinions for the topic in context. From our 200 randomly selected targets, we found 6 cases where the polarity of the noun phrase potentially negated the polarity towards a shorter entity within the noun phrase. However, in most of these cases, the noun phrase resolved from the annotations correctly represents the actual target of opinion: e.g.*"depletion of **ozone**"* ثقب الاوزون, *"bombing of **houses**"* قصف المنازل, and *"methodology of teaching **Arabic**"* اسلوب تعليم العربية. We found one case *"absence of **Messi**"* غياب مسي, labeled negative, where it could be argued that either *Messi* (positive) or his absence (negative) is the correct target. We generally preferred target annotations which correspond to the topic or event being discussed in the context of the comment.

Examples We provide examples of the annotations, shown in Table 5. Note that we have preserved all spelling errors in the original Arabic text. As it is common in Arabic to write very long sentences, we have added punctuation to make the English translation more readable.

Example (1) is from the culture domain. We see that it summarizes the writer's opinions towards all important topics. Note that the direct reference to the target *"e-book"* الكتاب الالكتروني is the first mention (the second mention is preceeded by the preposition *to* ل). However, we generally assume that the opinion towards a target is deduced from the entire comment (i.e from both the phrase *'despite the popularity of the e-book'* and the phrase *'there is no place for an e-book in my dictionary'*). Ideally, the annotators should also have marked *traditional book* الكتاب التقليدي as a positive target; although the opinion expressed towards it is less direct, it can also be inferred by co-reference with *paper book* الكتاب الورقي.

Example (2) lists an entity that doesn't appear in the text *"(to) the Arab team the world cup"*

للمتخب العربي المونديال; this likely results from an error in Task 1 where the phrase got picked up as the maximal common noun phrase. The annotator might have meant that *Arab team in the world cup* is a topic that the writer feels positively about; however, our current annotation scheme only considers entities that strictly appear in the text. We also see that annotators disagreed on the polarity of the propositional entity *"either team qualifying"* تأهل الفريقين, likely because they were not sure whether it should be marked as neutral or positive. In addition, this example contains an over-generated target *"world cup"* المونديال, which would have been best marked as neutral.

Example (3) is from the politics domain. It correctly annotates multiple references of *the Iraqi government* and captures the sentiment towards important entities in the text. The target *"the only neighboring country"* الدولة الجارة الوحيدة can be considered an over-generation; a better interpretation might be to consider this phrase part of the opinion expression itself (*"the only neighboring country with whom we have ties that are not just based on interests* is Turkey"). Nonetheless, this extra annotation may provide helpful information for future modeling. Notice that the Arabic comment for this example, in addition to being long, has no punctuation other than the period ending the sentence. It is common in Arabic to encounter such constructions, whereby conjunctions and transitional words are enough to determine the separation between clauses or sentence phrases. We have added punctuation to the English translation of this example.

We generally found that the annotations were a good representation of the diverse opinions of online writers, correctly covering sentiment towards essential targets and mostly complying with our definition of entities. The annotations contain some errors, but these are expected in a crowdsourcing task, especially one that relies so heavily on subjective interpretation. We noticed that annotators tended to over-generate targets rather than miss out on essential targets. We believe that even annotation of secondary targets may prove useful for future modeling tasks.

5 Conclusions

We developed a two-stage method for annotating targets of opinions using Amazon Mechanical Turk, where we consider targets to be noun phrase entities. This method was applied to Arabic, yielding a new, publicly available resource for fine-grained opinion analysis.[3] We found high agreement on the task of identifying sentiment towards entities, leading to the conclusion that it is possible to carry out this task using crowdsourcing, especially when qualified workers are available.

Unlike some of the previous work, our focus was on annotating target entities rather than the full target spans; and we developed a unique approach for identifying these entities using Amazon Mechanial Turk. The first task involves marking important entities, while the second task involves finding targets by assessing the sentiment towards each entity in isolation. We found that although the agreement was generally high for both tasks, it was not as high for the entity identification task as it was for the second and easier task of finding sentiment towards entities.

We also found that the morphological complexity of Arabic, as well as the variation in acceptable syntax for noun phrases, creates additional annotation challenges for deciphering the boundaries of entities. We also anticipate that the long structure of Arabic comments will create interesting challenges for future modeling tasks.

In the future, we hope to extend this dataset by mapping the targets to specific opinion phrases and identifying which targets refer to repeated mentions (e.g *the team*) or aspects (e.g *defense*) of the same target (e.g *the Algerian team*), in addition to annotating conflicting sentiment towards the same entity. We also hope to create a manually reviewed version of the corpus corrected for spelling errors and non-noun phrase targets.

6 Acknowledgments

This work was made possible by grant NPRP 6-716-1-138 from the Qatar National Research Fund (a member of the Qatar Foundation). The statements made are solely the responsibility of the authors. We thank anonymous reviewers for their helpful comments. We would also like to thank Debanjan Ghosh, Owen Rambow, and Ramy Eskander for helpful discussions and feedback. We thank the AMT annotators for all their hard work, insightful questions, and for continuing to participate in multiple rounds of our annotation tasks.

[3]The corpus is available and can be downloaded from www.cs.columbia.edu/~noura/Resources.html

	Example Comment
Example (1) Domain: Culture	رغم انتشار **الكتاب الألكتروني** الا ان **الكتاب الورقي** اثبت وجوده. احب **الكتاب المطبوع** .. حتى تقليب صفحاته أجد بها متعة.. والأجمل عند قراءته وهو بين يدي .. لا أحتمل **قراءة الكتاب من خلال الشاشة** .. لا أستطيع الاستمرار في تحمل وهج الضوء والصداع.. الكتاب التقليدي أقراءه في المكتبة في القطار في الطائرة على الشاطئ في الحديقة في اي مكان أرتاح فيه .. لامكان للكتاب الألكتروني في قاموسي.
English Translation	Despite the popularity of **the e-book**, **the paper book** has proven itself. I like **the printed book**... I even find a pleasure in turning its pages ... and it is nice is to read it while it is in my hands ... I cannot stand **reading a book through a screen** ... I cannot bear the glare of light and the headaches...I can read a traditional book in the library on the train in the airplane on the beach in the garden in anywhere I am comfortable .. there is no place for the e-book in my dictionary.
Annotated Targets	**negative:** the e-book الكتاب الالكتروني **positive:** the paper book الكتاب الورقي **positive:** the printed book الكتاب المطبوع **negative:** reading a book through a screen قراءة الكتاب من خلال الشاشة
Example (2) Domain: Sports	**المنتخبان المصري والجزائري** هما منتخبان قويان. والدعم الدي حضي به **المنتخب الجزائري** بالمناسبة جعل الكل مثوثر ولايوجد فرق في تأهل الفريقين و ا تمنى ان يتأهل **الفريق الجزائري** الي **المونديال** لأنني احب **الفريق الجزائري** الى جانب المنتخب المصري . والمهم التمثيل الجيد و ا تمنى ان يكون **للمتخب العربي** احسن تمثيل في **المونديال** .
English Translation	**The Egyptian and Algerian teams** are strong teams. The support gained by the **Algerian team** for this occasion has made everyone nervous and there is no difference in either team qualifying and I hope that **the Algerian team** gets qualified to **the world cup** because I like **the Algerian team** alongside the Egyptian team. The important thing is good representation and I hope that **the Arab team** will be best represented in **the world cup**.
Annotated Targets	**positive:** The Egyptian and Algerian teams المنتخبان المصري والجزائري **positive:** the Algerian team 'elect' المنتخب الجزائري **positive:** the Algerian team الفريق الجزائري **positive:** the world cup المونديال **positive:** (to) the Arab team the world cup للمتخب العربي المونديال **undetermined:** either team qualifying تأهل الفريقين
Example (3) Domain: Politics	مع الاسف **الحكومة العراقية** لا يفتهم من السياسة شيء لأن **الدولة الجارة الوحيدة** التي تربطنا معها اكثر من مصالح من الموارد الطبيعية كالمياه الى مصالح صناعية هي **تركيا** فعلينا ان نقوي علاقتنا معها لانها اصبحت تنافس الدول الاوربية لنستفاد منها ولكن **حكومة المالكي الفاشلة** لا يهمهم التطور وقد رجع **العراق** بظل هؤلاء مئات السنين الى الخلف.
English Translation	Unfortunately **the Iraqi government** understands nothing of politics because **the only neighboring country** with whom we have ties that are not just based on interests - such as natural resources like water and industrial interests - is **Turkey**, so we have to strengthen our relationship with it because it is now a competitor with European nations, we should benefit from it but **Maliki's failed government** cares nothing for progress and **Iraq** has gone back hundreds of years because of these people.
Annotated Targets	**negative:** the Iraqi government الحكومة العراقية **positive:** the only neighboring country الدولة الجارة الوحيدة **positive:** Turkey تركيا **negative:** Maliki's failed government حكومة المالكي الفاشلة **negative:** Iraq العراق

Table 5: Examples of Annotations. The original spelling errors are preserved.

References

Muhammad Abdul-Mageed and Mona T Diab. 2011. Subjectivity and sentiment annotation of modern standard Arabic newswire. In *Proceedings of the 5th Linguistic Annotation Workshop*, pages 110–118. Association for Computational Linguistics.

David M Blei, Andrew Y Ng, and Michael I Jordan. 2003. Latent dirichlet allocation. *the Journal of machine Learning research*, 3:993–1022.

Paula Carvalho, Luís Sarmento, Jorge Teixeira, and Mário J Silva. 2011. Liars and saviors in a sentiment annotated corpus of comments to political debates. In *Proceedings of the 49th Annual Meeting of the Association for Computational Linguistics: Human Language Technologies: short papers-Volume 2*, pages 564–568. Association for Computational Linguistics.

Lingjia Deng and Janyce Wiebe. 2015. Mpqa 3.0: An entity/event-level sentiment corpus.

Michael Denkowski, Hassan Al-Haj, and Alon Lavie. 2010. Turker-assisted paraphrasing for English-Arabic machine translation. In *Proceedings of the NAACL HLT 2010 Workshop on Creating Speech and Language Data with Amazon's Mechanical Turk*, pages 66–70. Association for Computational Linguistics.

Spence Green and Christopher D Manning. 2010. Better Arabic parsing: Baselines, evaluations, and analysis. In *Proceedings of the 23rd International Conference on Computational Linguistics*, pages 394–402. Association for Computational Linguistics.

Nizar Y Habash. 2010. Introduction to Arabic natural language processing. *Synthesis Lectures on Human Language Technologies*, 3(1):1–187.

Chiara Higgins, Elizabeth McGrath, and Lailla Moretto. 2010. MTurk crowdsourcing: a viable method for rapid discovery of Arabic nicknames? In *Proceedings of the NAACL HLT 2010 Workshop on Creating Speech and Language Data with Amazon's Mechanical Turk*, pages 89–92. Association for Computational Linguistics.

Minqing Hu and Bing Liu. 2004. Mining and summarizing customer reviews. In *Proceedings of the tenth ACM SIGKDD international conference on Knowledge discovery and data mining*, pages 168–177. ACM.

Long Jiang, Mo Yu, Ming Zhou, Xiaohua Liu, and Tiejun Zhao. 2011. Target-dependent twitter sentiment classification. In *Proceedings of the 49th Annual Meeting of the Association for Computational Linguistics: Human Language Technologies-Volume 1*, pages 151–160. Association for Computational Linguistics.

Soo-Min Kim and Eduard Hovy. 2006. Extracting opinions, opinion holders, and topics expressed in online news media text. In *Proceedings of the Workshop on Sentiment and Subjectivity in Text*, pages 1–8. Association for Computational Linguistics.

Nolan Lawson, Kevin Eustice, Mike Perkowitz, and Meliha Yetisgen-Yildiz. 2010. Annotating large email datasets for named entity recognition with mechanical turk. In *Proceedings of the NAACL HLT 2010 Workshop on Creating Speech and Language Data with Amazon's Mechanical Turk*, pages 71–79. Association for Computational Linguistics.

Andrew K McCallum. 2002. {MALLET: A Machine Learning for Language Toolkit}.

Behrang Mohit, Alla Rozovskaya, Nizar Habash, Wajdi Zaghouani, and Ossama Obeid. 2014. The first QALB shared task on automatic text correction for Arabic. In *Proceedings of the EMNLP 2014 Workshop on Arabic Natural Language Processing (ANLP)*, pages 39–47, Doha, Qatar, October. Association for Computational Linguistics.

Maria Pontiki, Haris Papageorgiou, Dimitrios Galanis, Ion Androutsopoulos, John Pavlopoulos, and Suresh Manandhar. 2014. Semeval-2014 task 4: Aspect based sentiment analysis. In *Proceedings of the 8th International Workshop on Semantic Evaluation (SemEval 2014)*, pages 27–35.

Guang Qiu, Bing Liu, Jiajun Bu, and Chun Chen. 2011. Opinion word expansion and target extraction through double propagation. *Computational linguistics*, 37(1):9–27.

Josef Ruppenhofer, Swapna Somasundaran, and Janyce Wiebe. 2008. Finding the sources and targets of subjective expressions. In *LREC*.

Swapna Somasundaran and Janyce Wiebe. 2009. Recognizing stances in online debates. In *Proceedings of the Joint Conference of the 47th Annual Meeting of the ACL and the 4th International Joint Conference on Natural Language Processing of the AFNLP: Volume 1-Volume 1*, pages 226–234. Association for Computational Linguistics.

Swapna Somasundaran, Josef Ruppenhofer, and Janyce Wiebe. 2008. Discourse level opinion relations: An annotation study. In *Proceedings of the 9th SIGdial Workshop on Discourse and Dialogue*, pages 129–137. Association for Computational Linguistics.

Veselin Stoyanov and Claire Cardie. 2008. Annotating topics of opinions. In *LREC*.

Cigdem Toprak, Niklas Jakob, and Iryna Gurevych. 2010. Sentence and expression level annotation of opinions in user-generated discourse. In *Proceedings of the 48th Annual Meeting of the Association for Computational Linguistics*, pages 575–584. Association for Computational Linguistics.

Janyce Wiebe, Theresa Wilson, and Claire Cardie. 2005. Annotating expressions of opinions and emotions in language. *Language resources and evaluation*, 39(2-3):165–210.

Theresa Ann Wilson. 2008. *Fine-grained subjectivity and sentiment analysis: recognizing the intensity, polarity, and attitudes of private states*. ProQuest.

Wajdi Zaghouani, Behrang Mohit, Nizar Habash, Ossama Obeid, Nadi Tomeh, Alla Rozovskaya, Noura Farra, Sarah Alkuhlani, and Kemal Oflazer. 2014.

Large scale Arabic error annotation: Guidelines and framework. In Nicoletta Calzolari, Khalid Choukri, Thierry Declerck, Hrafn Loftsson, Bente Maegaard, Joseph Mariani, Asuncion Moreno, Jan Odijk, and Stelios Piperidis, editors, *Proceedings of the Ninth International Conference on Language Resources and Evaluation (LREC'14)*, Reykjavik, Iceland, May. European Language Resources Association (ELRA). ACL Anthology Identifier: L14-1721.

Omar F Zaidan and Chris Callison-Burch. 2011. The Arabic online commentary dataset: an annotated dataset of informal Arabic with high dialectal content. In *Proceedings of the 49th Annual Meeting of the Association for Computational Linguistics: Human Language Technologies: short papers-Volume 2*, pages 37–41. Association for Computational Linguistics.

Best Practices for Crowdsourcing Dialectal Arabic Speech Transcription

Samantha Wray, Hamdy Mubarak, Ahmed Ali
Qatar Computing Research Institute
Hamad Bin Khalifa University
Doha, Qatar
{swray,hmubarak,amali}@qf.org.qa

Abstract

In this paper, we investigate different approaches in crowdsourcing transcriptions of Dialectal Arabic speech with automatic quality control to ensure good transcription at the source. Since Dialectal Arabic has no standard orthographic representation, it is very challenging to perform quality control. We propose a complete recipe for speech transcription quality control that includes using output of an Automatic Speech Recognition system. We evaluated the quality of the transcribed speech and through this recipe, we achieved a reduction in transcription error of 1.0% compared with 13.2% baseline with no quality control for Egyptian data, and down to 4% compared with 7.8% for the North African dialect.

1 Introduction

Crowdsourcing is the process of segmenting a complex task into smaller units of work and distributing them among a large number of non-expert workers at a lower cost and for less time than professional companies.

The usage of popular crowdsource platforms such as Amazon Mechanical Turk (MTurk) and CrowdFlower (CF) for the acquisition, transcription, and annotation of speech data has been well demonstrated (Evanini et al., 2010; Parent and Eskenazi, 2010; Zaidan and Callison-Burch, 2011; Novotney and Callison-Burch, 2010; Marge et al., 2010b), among others. However, using crowdsourcing for the transcription of speech for languages with nonstandard orthographies is less explored, especially with regards the development of quality control protocols in the absence of established writing standards.

Although the writing system of Modern Standard Arabic (MSA) is standardized, the varieties of Dialectal Arabic (DA) are written without standard orthography, typically by utilizing the writing system of MSA. In this paper, we present best practices for crowdsourcing transcriptions of report and conversational DA and present results of experiments varying automatic quality control parameters that led to the creation of these best practices. We show that comparing output from an MSA-based Automatic Speech Recognition (ASR) system trained on a minimal amount of DA to output from a human transcriber outperforms other methods of quality control and results in low rates of data attrition. We show that utilizing a forgiving edit distance algorithm to compare ASR and user transcripts retains natural variation in orthographic usage without sacrificing quality.

This paper is organized as follows: in Section 2 we discuss issues in crowdsourcing written DA, with particular reference to the usage of nonstandard orthography. Section 3 outlines the utilization of professional transcription for DA and compares it in general terms to the usage of crowdsourcing for the same task. The DA audio data used in this study is described in detail in Section 4. Crowdsourcing experiments are detailed in Section 5, and best practices based on the results of these experiments are presented in Section 6. Section 7 summarizes our findings.

2 Challenges in Crowdsourcing DA

The nonstandard features of the written form of DA complicate efforts for designing effective quality control in crowdsourcing because many typical methods are not effective, as we outline here.

2.1 Overview of DA

MSA is the variety used for formal communication, and written materials such as books, newspapers, etc. while DA varieties are used for daily communication between people in the Arab world.

Proceedings of the Second Workshop on Arabic Natural Language Processing, pages 99–107,
Beijing, China, July 26-31, 2015.

Nowadays, there are many available resources for MSA such as corpora, morphological analyzers, Part Of Speech taggers, parsers, and so forth. However, there is still a need to build such resources for DA.

MSA resources do not typically perform well for handling DA. Darwish et al. (2014) showed that there are differences between MSA and the Egyptian dialect of DA at almost all levels: lexical, morphological, phonological, and syntactic.

Another challenge for DA is the nonstandard orthography, and words may be written in many different ways. For example, the future marker in Egyptian DA can be spelled with two different MSA characters: ه or ح . (For a complete overview of these issues, see Eskander et al. (2013)). There are some proposed rules for standardizing DA such as the Conventional Orthography for Dialectal Arabic (CODA) (Habash et al., 2012) which is very useful for many applications like ASR, and natural language processing (NLP). Although these effective tools and others (such as Zribi et al. (2014)) exist for training annotators to write DA in a particular way and for automatic normalization of text after the fact, our aims are to obtain a transcribed speech corpus which exhibits natural orthographic variation among speakers, so normalization tools would not be appropriate for this task.

2.2 Quality Control in Crowdsourcing

Crowdsourcing is now considered a promising alternative to the employment of transcription experts to create large corpora of transcribed speech in languages such as English (Lee and Glass, 2011; Marge et al., 2010b; Marge et al., 2010a; Hämäläinen et al., 2013), Spanish (Audhkhasi et al., 2011), Swahili, Amharic (Gelas et al., 2011), Korean, Hindi, and Tamil (Novotney and Callison-Burch, 2010).

One of the main challenges in crowdsourcing is quality control. There is great incentive to performing automatic quality control as opposed to leaving the cleaning of data to post-processing. Automatic quality control which issues warning messages to a user or rejects submission of spammy data reduces overall data attrition.

A typical way of performing automatic quality control is the usage of a gold standard to be used as test questions. Users having low quality with respect to these questions will be excluded and their work will be rejected.

Sprugnoli et al. (2013) compared different automatic quality control methods for crowdsourcing speech transcription for Italian and German:

- **The iterative dual pathway method**
  In this method, the speech segment is randomly assigned to four annotators in two independent pathways. When four transcriptions, two from each pathway, match each other, the segment is considered as transcribed correctly. The key advantage of this method is to have accurate transcriptions without having explicit quality control or preparing test questions.

- **The gold standard method**
  In this method, at least 10% of the segments are transcribed by experts and this is used to distinguish between trusted and untrusted transcribers.

These quality control methods cannot be applied to DA because there is no standard orthography and it may happen in many cases that there will not be exact match between annotators (first method) nor with the gold standard (second method). Figure 1 shows real transcription outputs for the same speech segment in which there is no single match between the whole transcription among transcribers because words in colors are written differently and all are correct.

احنا ناس طيبين وملناش اي مسؤولية

ما نحنا ناس طيبين ومالناش اى مسؤولية

احنا ناس طيبين وملناش اى مسئولية

احنا ناس طيبيين ومالناش اى مسؤليه

احنا ناس طيبين مالناش اي مسؤلية

Figure 1: Non Standard Orthography for transcribing DA

For the current study, we utilize CF which draws users from worker channels including microworking and rewards sites. CF has a robust userbase in the Arab world, and users can be selected by country of origin, which is an attractive option for studies which focus on regional DA varieties. CF also allows users to obtain a High Quality status, which allows task designers to target only High Quality users for a task. The opposing setting is High Speed which allows any user in the targeted country to complete the task. CF also has a built-in gold standard system which performs quality control. However, options for fuzzy text matching using the built-in system are extremely limited, and as outlined earlier, exact matching will not suffice for DA's nonstandard orthography.

Automatic quality control for translation and transcription tasks which do not rely on typical gold standard or multi-pass quality control methods include utilizing a series of checks which prevent submissions with text similar to the instructions of the task (Gelas et al., 2011) or which violate set word minimum/maximum sizes (Gelas et al., 2011), using a support vector machine (SVM) classifier to determine if a transcript is of good or poor quality (Lee and Glass, 2011), comparing to a language model built from an existing text corpus (Gelas et al., 2011; Zaidan and Callison-Burch, 2011) and utilizing vocabulary size of transcript (Lee and Glass, 2011).

For the current study, we employ typical gold standard question quality control, as well as two other methods: one which does not rely on the audio content, and one which does. The former relies on comparing a user's transcript to expected norms for legal Arabic text (following Gelas et al. (2011) for Swahili and Amharic.) The latter utilizes ASR output of each audio segment. This was explored by Lee and Glass (2011) in the form of integration of auxiliary features from ASR including the Word Error Rate (WER) for the top N best, as well as Phoneme Error Rate (PER) for the same number of hypotheses. They used these features as a form of automatic quality control to reject transcripts which deviated from expected input. One reason for such a system to perform reasonably is access to mature ASR such as for English in this case. However, for the current study Arabic ASR is still facing major challenges, and performance for DA ASR systems is behind even compared to MSA ASR, to say nothing of more mature ASR systems such as English and French. WER for Arabic ASR are appreciably higher than WER for these mature systems. (See Section 4.2 for a detailed look at Arabic ASR). Thus, in the current study, we quantify transcription quality based on edit distance from the expected string itself instead of relying on WER.

3 Crowdsourcing versus Transcription House

To determine the potential advantages in cost and speed of transcribing using CF, we submitted several tasks of Egyptian DA audio totaling approximately 10 min of speech and selected the High Speed option, which allows every user in the selected country to participate. We collected 5 transcripts for each item. On average, the task was completed after 3 hours from its launch and the total cost was USD 7. Our calculated cost of transcribing 1 hour of speech is USD 42 taking 18 hours.

When we transcribed the same audio using a professional company, the cost was USD 300 and it took 4 days. Furthermore, only one transcript per audio segment was provided.

It's clear from this comparison that using crowdsourcing reduces the cost and time significantly. Another important benefit is having multiple transcriptions and different writings which is very useful for building resources for DA such as corpora and morphological analyzers.

The high quality of data from crowdsourcing when compared to professional experts has been well explored not only here but also by Zaidan and Callison-Burch (2011) and Williams et al. (2011), and many others.

4 Data

The data for this study took two forms: the speech audio to submit for transcription and automatic transcription of that audio from an ASR system.

4.1 DA Speech Data

Audio for the transcription task was taken from debate and news programs uploaded to Al Jazeera's website between June 2014 and January 2015.

The audio underwent a series of preprocessing steps before being submitted to CF for transcription. Voice Activation Detection was performed to remove non-speech audio such as music or white noise, followed by processing using the LIUM SpkDiarization toolkit, which is a software package dedicated to speaker segmentation and clustering, diarization, and speaker linking within the same episode (Meignier and Merlin, 2010). The output from LIUM segmentation is typically small chunks of audio files containing information about speaker ID, and duration of utterance.

In addition, a crucial preprocessing step took place: classification of dialect group. This was performed using human computation, which also occurred via CF. Utterances underwent dialect classification by 3-9 annotators per audio file into five broad Arabic dialect groups: Modern Standard Arabic (MSA), Egyptian (EGY), Levantine (LEV), North African/Maghrebi (NOR), and Gulf (GLF). (For more details about this process, see Wray and Ali (2015).) For the current study, we used audio segments which had been classified as EGY with at least 75% agreement between annotators.

Egyptian data was chosen as a test case to perform experiments and determine best practices for transcription for several reasons. First, EGY as a category consists of a smaller and potentially less diverse set of dialects than a more geographically spread category. For example, the category NOR contains speech from Morocco, Libya, Tunisia, Algeria, and Mauritania. Because CF allows restriction of tasks to users in specific countries, by selecting Egypt using the platform and presenting annotators with audio from the EGY category, there was a greater chance of the transcriber speaking the same dialect as the speaker in the audio clip when compared to other dialect categories. Secondly, the demographics of the classification task (Wray and Ali, 2015) showed that approximately 40% of users of CF in the Arab world who participated were located in Egypt, meaning that focusing on EGY audio and Egyptian annotators allowed us to complete multiple iterations of transcription tasks with a quick turnover. We found that the amount of users in Egypt contributed to an average of 287 transcripts per hour as opposed to an average of 3 transcripts per hour for users in the Levant, for example. Finally, there were significantly more audio segments classified with high levels of inter-annotator agreement as EGY when compared to other dialect categories.

4.2 ASR Transcripts

All of the speech data was automatically transcribed using the QCRI Advanced Transcription System (QATS) (Ali et al., 2014c). This Arabic ASR system is a grapheme-based system with sequential Deep Neural Network (DNN) for Acoustic Modeling (AM) with feature space Maximum Likelihood Linear Regression (fMLLR) adaption for the first pass. A tri-gram Language Model (LM) is used for recognition and a four-gram LM is used for LM rescoring. The AM was trained using about 400 hours Broadcast News (BCN) data, containing a mix of MSA and DA (Walker et al., 2013). The LM was trained using a six year worth archive of Al Jazeera print news as well as some web crawling. The lexicon for the ASR is 1.2M words, with an Out Of Vocabulary (OOV) rate of 2.5% on the test set.

We evaluated the ASR system using a test set taken from Ali et al. (2014b), with the resulting Word Error Rate (WER) shown in Table 1. The WER for report data is 12.35% which is largely MSA data, and 29.8% for conversational speech containing a mix of DA and MSA. The combined WER for the mix of both report and conversational data is 25.4%. More details about the grapheme dialectal Arabic system can be found here (Ali et al., 2014a).

Rep.	Conv.	Comb.
12.35%	29.8%	25.4%

Table 1: Grapheme Arabic ASR System WER

Once automatic transcriptions were obtained, we also generated phoneme-level transcriptions using a phoneme-based Arabic ASR (Ali et al., 2014b) in order to split the audio into short segments. We have found for human transcription, it is better to keep speech segments short (3-6 sec) for a transcriber not to get confused or discouraged with a long segment. To split the audio, we used the phoneme-level output and cut at periods of silence of at least 300 milliseconds.

5 Transcription Experiments

To guide our ideas for the development of possible protocols for quality control to test, we first submitted approximately two hours of EGY audio to CF for transcription by users in Egypt over the course of a month and observed what kinds of errors existed in poor quality transcripts in the results. Examples of poor quality transcripts are shown in Table 2.

After development of potential quality control methods (covered in detail in subsection 5.1), we ran experiments to test their efficiency. To de-

Transcription	Case
ليهتحليهتنحليتنحليتنل	word len >MAX_LEN
تتتتتتتت	repeated letters
قغف غعفغ فغق	same keyboard row
ا ثغ اق اق	word len <MIN_LEN
بلاتؤبغ خسعء	invalid char n-gram
ةكنثال	letter ة must appear at the end of word
نعم	# words <MIN_WORDS
...... ——	non-Arabic characters
قم بكتابة رقم الملف	copy from job instructions
والله منور يا باشا	irrelevant text not related to audio segment

Table 2: Types of poor transcription

Figure 2: User view of single audio file and text box. The red flag contains a warning against writing gibberish, which has been entered in the input box.

termine the highest performing protocol for quality control, we sampled 100 new audio segments of the EGY data described in Section 4 and submitted them to CF for transcription by users in Egypt. The 100 segments were submitted eight times: once for both High Quality and High Speed users for each of the four conditions described in the following section.

For each segment, five separate transcripts were collected from five different users. Users were presented with an audio button which they could press to listen to the audio an unlimited number of times, and a text box for entering the transcript. Users were directed to write as precisely as possible, to heed the item ID number, and to avoid using non-Arabic characters. Five items were presented per page, and completion of a page resulted in USD .05 compensation. An example of a single item as viewed by a user is shown in Figure 2.

5.1 Quality Control Parameters

Baseline Under the baseline condition, no quality control was performed. Users received direction on completion of the transcription tasks, but the input box did not issue a warning regardless of what the user typed into the box. Any text input was accepted by the system and users did not have a minimum set time required to be spent on the page, so they could submit after only a few seconds on the page.

Surface checks For this condition, we enabled a validation system that served two purposes: 1) a red notification flag with a warning to carefully follow directions appeared above the input box 2) the user was prevented from submitting the information entered on the page until whatever had triggered the warning was rectified. We accomplished this by using Javascript in CF's customization window to repurpose an existing CF validator (of which there are many, for example: must be a phone number) in order to satisfy our own conditions and display our own warning message. An example warning flag is shown in Figure 2.

The checks which triggered a flag under this condition were:

- 4 or more identical characters in a row
- fewer than 15 total characters
- url (to prevent copying and pasting of url into input box)
- lack of space character
- text from question display text (to prevent copying and pasting of task text into input box)

In addition to these checks, the user was required to spend a minimum of 40 seconds on the page before being allowed to submit. This time minimum was determined by observing the speed of completion of good quality transcripts from our original two hours of audio submitted during pilot work. We observed that users who submitted a page any quicker than this tended to submit spammy transcripts. Note that the Surface Checks condition did not rely on the existence of any gold standard or expected transcripts.

Expert-annotated checks Adopting traditionally-used methods of gold standard questions in crowdsource tasks, we obtained transcripts of 20% of the audio from a native speaker of Egyptian. These transcripts were incorporated into a validator which would issue a warning flag as described in the previous condition. We used Equation 1 in order to determine when to raise a warning flag and alert the user to be more careful:

$$diff(transcription) = \frac{dist}{refLen} \cdot 100 \qquad (1)$$

where $dist$ refers to Levenshtein edit distance[1] between the transcript and the reference (spaces are treated as characters), and $refLen$ refers to the length (in characters) of the expert-provided reference.

If $diff(transcription) \leq Threshold$, the transcript will be accepted.

$$Threshold = \begin{cases} 70\% & \text{for human transcript} \\ 80\% & \text{for ASR transcript} \end{cases}$$

When $Threshold$ = 70%, this means there should be at least 30% overlap with the reference. These thresholds were selected empirically based on observations of the number of different variations of writing words in DA.

Users were not aware which items would be compared to an existing transcript. If the item did not have an existing transcript (the remaining 80% of the data), the **surface checks** previously outlined were utilized.

ASR checks Recall that word-level transcripts were produced automatically by ASR (see Section 4). The ASR check condition also involved issuing a warning flag, but in contrast with the previous condition, every audio segment was compared to an expected input, and this time the expected transcript was produced by ASR. String overlap was also calculated using Equation 1, but to account for the higher WER for the ASR output than a human transcript, we lowered the threshold of overlap to 20% in comparison with the 30% overlap for expert-produced transcripts.

[1]JavaScript implementation taken from: `https://gist.github.com/andrei-m/982927`

Because every item was compared to an automatic transcript, no other checks were utilized in this condition.

5.2 Results

A total of 149 users participated in the transcription tasks of EGY audio. The average WER for each user was calculated based on comparing each transcript to the four other user-provided transcripts for each item. As shown in Figure 3, there were different distributions of above-average and below-average users across conditions. In Figure 3, users were binned based on their personal average compared to the the averages of the whole sets.

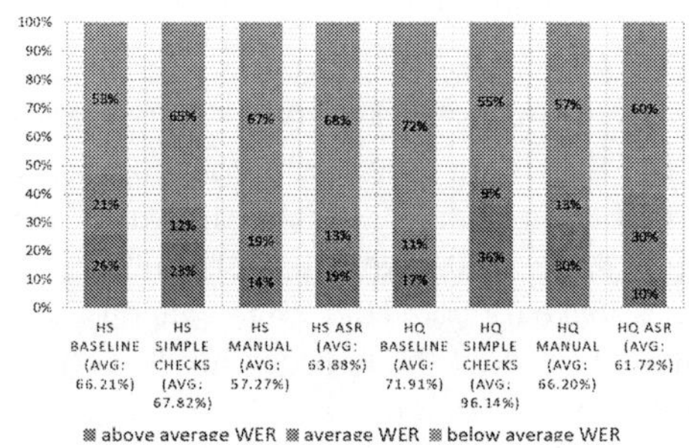

Figure 3: Average user WER for EGY audio across conditions

Given that the average WER for all conditions was very high, it was necessary to get a more complete picture about the true quality of the transcripts. (For comparison, typical WER for crowd-sourced transcripts written in languages with standard orthography are around 5-25% (Parent and Eskenazi, 2010)). Therefore, the performance of the four quality control methods was evaluated by manually counting the number of poor quality transcripts accepted after five transcriptions from five different users had been collected for each of the 100 segments. Poor quality for our purposes was defined in the following two ways:

- Error: a transcript which was irrelevant, or gibberish. An irrelevant transcript contained valid Arabic text with no relation to the audio segment, and a gibberish transcript is one which contained strings of characters not considered to be a legal Arabic sequence.

- Partial: a transcript which was truncated with respect to the appropriate output, for example a user who only wrote the first 3 words of a 6 word utterance.

Results comparing the four possible methods are shown in Table 3.

These results show that using ASR output as a comparison for every item outperformed other quality control methods for both High Speed and High Quality transcribers. In comparison to the baseline no quality control condition, the ASR check with only 20% string overlap between the transcription and the ASR output resulted in a total gain of 12.2% in error-free transcripts in the High Speed condition. The ASR comparison method is also a far more effective quality control method than using a human-annotated gold standard. Not only does ASR require less effort on the part of the researcher because it is automatically produced and does not require consulting a native speaker, it also outperforms the traditional use of interspersing gold standard questions which have been annotated by an expert (1% of transcripts with errors vs. 7.4% of transcripts with errors for High Speed users.) Overall, the highest performing option was using High Quality transcribers and the ASR output check, which resulted in 0.4% total errors, a reduction of 7.2% when compared to the baseline and 14.6% when compared to the worst performing condition.

It is interesting to note also that Surface Checks did not always result in cleaner data. Although for High Speed transcriptions, the total errors were reduced from 13.2% in the baseline to 10% by using Surface Checks, this trend did not continue for the High Quality condition. In fact, the total percentage of poor quality transcripts increased from 7.6% to 15%. Recall that 23% of users had above-average WER in the Simple Checks condition. However, further analysis showed that these users contributed 27% of the data. If an error-prone user happens to be prolific, and checks are not sufficient to stop the user's submissions, their errors may be over-represented.

5.3 NOR Speech Replication

To test the possibility of generalizing this method and utilizing it outside of Egypt, we replicated the experiments on another dialect group with a larger geographic spread. We selected 100 segments of NOR and submitted it under the four conditions on the High Speed option. The expert-annotated transcripts were written by a native speaker of Algerian. The CF task was then restricted to users in Morocco, Algeria, and Tunisia. Results of this replication are shown in Table 4.

As shown in Table 4, using the ASR output and comparing to every user input as a method of quality control shows that ASR still outperforms other methods of quality control for NOR audio just as for EGY audio. Compared to a baseline rate of 7.8% of poor quality transcripts, quality control using the ASR transcripts resulted in reduction to 4% total errors. Note again that Surface Checks resulted in a higher total percentage of poor quality transcripts from the 7.8% baseline to 9.4%. Higher still is the traditionally employed method of inserting random human-annotated transcripts for comparison as a gold standard, which has a total of 13.6% total of poor transcripts. As expected, these iterations happened to exhibit prolific above-average WER users (contributing 17% of the data for the Simple Checks condition and 19% of the data for the manual test questions condition, compared to z 15% of the data for the baseline condition and 15% of the data for the ASR condition.) However, even taking user variation into account, the ASR condition outperformed the baseline by 3.8%.

6 Best Practices

Based on the results presented in subsections 5.2 and 5.3, we have determined a working list of best practices for using a crowdsourcing platform such as CF for transcription of DA data:

- Segment audio files into smaller segments (from 3 seconds to 6 seconds each) such that transcription of each audio segment has a few words (more than 2 words, but less than 1 line of text).

- Restrict tasks to users in specific countries to match the required language skills needed for dialectal transcription.

- Perform dialect classification tasks or start with data for which the dialect is already known. When coupled with targeting users in a particular region, this will decrease the likelihood that a user is transcribing a dialect they are unfamiliar with.

EGY speech - 100 segments				
	Baseline	**Surface Checks**	**Manual edit distance**	**ASR edit distance**
High Speed				
Errors	1.6%	2.8%	1.2%	**0.6%**
Partial	11.6%	7.2%	6.2%	**0.4%**
Total	13.2%	10.0%	7.4%	**1.0%**
High Quality				
Errors	4.0%	12.2%	1.2%	**0.0%**
Partial	3.6%	2.8%	3.4%	**0.4%**
Total	7.6%	15.0%	4.6%	**0.4%**

Table 3: Percent of low quality transcripts across automatic quality control conditions

NOR speech - 100 segments				
	Baseline	**Surface Checks**	**Manual edit distance**	**ASR edit distance**
High Speed				
Errors	5.2%	3.6%	7.6%	**2.6%**
Partial	2.6%	5.8%	6.0%	**1.4%**
Total	7.8%	9.4%	13.6%	**4.0%**

Table 4: Percent of low quality transcripts across automatic quality control conditions

- Assign each audio segment an ID and ask annotators to write the ID and the transcript.
- Use JavaScript-defined or similar code for validation to check user input. First, check that the input ID is a valid ID. Then ASR output matched with the ID can be used to detect invalid transcription. In using this option, the acceptance threshold when using string matching should be lower than of human-written gold transcriptions to accommodate any limitations in ASR.
- Utilize automatic feedback to warn users to be more careful when they do not submit text that conforms to desired norms. In addition to simply warning, utilize automatic methods of preventing submission of poor data.
- Do not completely rely on quality control messages which do not refer to the content of the audio. Usage of quality control checks which aim to restrict input to a possible string of Arabic without consideration for the audio segment itself may result in the propagation of errors from irrelevant text
- After each job, generate statistics about the quality of all users (for example, how much agreement with other transcribers by calculating WER across transcriptions) and use the results to block low quality users from participating in future transcription tasks.

7 Summary

In this paper, we have shown that using the output of a publicly available ASR system trained on MSA and DA with an edit distance algorithm with a low threshold is an effective form of quality control in crowdsourcing transcriptions of a non-standard variety, namely Egyptian DA. We have also demonstrated the ability of using the same methodology on another dialect group, specifically North African DA. Currently, we are working to replicate our methods across all DA dialect groups to create a multi-dialectal DA speech corpus with both automatic and manual transcriptions.

References

Ahmed Ali, Hamdy Mubarak, and Stephan Vogel. 2014a. Advances in dialectal arabic speech recognition: A study using twitter to improve egyptian asr. In *International Workshop on Spoken Language Translation (IWSLT 2014)*, pages http–workshop2014.

Ahmed Ali, Yifan Zhang, Patrick Cardinal, Najim Dahak, Stephan Vogel, and Jim Glass. 2014b. A Complete Kaldi Recipe For Building Arabic Speech Recognition Systems. In *Spoken Language Technology Workshop (SLT), 2014 IEEE.*

Ahmed Ali, Yifan Zhang, and Stephan Vogel. 2014c. Qcri advanced transcription system (qats). In *Spoken Language Technology Workshop (SLT), 2014 IEEE.*

Kartik Audhkhasi, Panayiotis Georgiou, and Shrikanth S Narayanan. 2011. Accurate transcription of broadcast news speech using multiple noisy transcribers and unsupervised reliability metrics. In *Acoustics, Speech and Signal Processing (ICASSP), 2011 IEEE International Conference on*, pages 4980–4983. IEEE.

Kareem Darwish, Hassan Sajjad, and Hamdy Mubarak. 2014. Verifiably Effective Arabic Dialect Identification. *EMNLP-2014.*

Ramy Eskander, Nizar Habash, Owen Rambow, and Nadi Tomeh. 2013. Processing spontaneous orthography. In *HLT-NAACL*, pages 585–595.

Keelan Evanini, Derrick Higgins, and Klaus Zechner. 2010. Using Amazon Mechanical Turk for transcription of non-native speech. In *Proceedings of the NAACL HLT 2010 Workshop on Creating Speech and Language Data with Amazon's Mechanical Turk*, pages 53–56. Association for Computational Linguistics.

Hadrien Gelas, Solomon Teferra Abate, Laurent Besacier, and François Pellegrino. 2011. Quality assessment of crowdsourcing transcriptions for African languages. In *Interspeech.*

Nizar Habash, Mona T Diab, and Owen Rambow. 2012. Conventional Orthography for Dialectal Arabic. In *LREC*, pages 711–718.

Annika Hämäläinen, Fernando Pinto Moreira, Jairo Avelar, Daniela Braga, and Miguel Sales Dias. 2013. Transcribing and annotating speech corpora for speech recognition: A three-step crowdsourcing approach with quality control. In *First AAAI Conference on Human Computation and Crowdsourcing.*

Chiaying Lee and James Glass. 2011. A transcription task for crowdsourcing with automatic quality control. In *Interspeech*, pages 3041–3044.

Matthew Marge, Satanjeev Banerjee, and Alexander I Rudnicky. 2010a. Using the Amazon Mechanical Turk for transcription of spoken language. In *Acoustics Speech and Signal Processing (ICASSP), 2010 IEEE International Conference on*, pages 5270–5273. IEEE.

Matthew Marge, Satanjeev Banerjee, and Alexander I Rudnicky. 2010b. Using the Amazon Mechanical Turk to transcribe and annotate meeting speech for extractive summarization. In *Proceedings of the NAACL HLT 2010 Workshop on Creating Speech and Language Data with Amazon's Mechanical Turk*, pages 99–107. Association for Computational Linguistics.

Sylvain Meignier and Teva Merlin. 2010. Lium spkdiarization: an open source toolkit for diarization. In *CMU SPUD Workshop*, volume 2010.

Scott Novotney and Chris Callison-Burch. 2010. Cheap, fast and good enough: Automatic speech recognition with non-expert transcription. In *Human Language Technologies: The 2010 Annual Conference of the North American Chapter of the Association for Computational Linguistics*, HLT '10, pages 207–215, Stroudsburg, PA, USA. Association for Computational Linguistics.

Gabriel Parent and Maxine Eskenazi. 2010. Toward better crowdsourced transcription: Transcription of a year of the let's go bus information system data. In *Spoken Language Technology Workshop (SLT), 2010 IEEE*, pages 312–317. IEEE.

Rachele Sprugnoli, Giovanni Moretti, Matteo Fuoli, Diego Giuliani, Luisa Bentivogli, Emanuele Pianta, Roberto Gretter, and Fabio Brugnara. 2013. Comparing two methods for crowdsourcing speech transcription. In *Acoustics, Speech and Signal Processing (ICASSP), 2013 IEEE International Conference on*, pages 8116–8120. IEEE.

Kevin Walker, Christopher Caruso, Kazuaki Maeda, Denise DiPersio, and Stephanie Strassel. 2013. *GALE Phase 2 Arabic Broadcast Conversation Speech.* Linguistics Data Consortium.

Jason D Williams, I Dan Melamed, Tirso Alonso, Barbara Hollister, and Jay Wilpon. 2011. Crowdsourcing for difficult transcription of speech. In *Automatic Speech Recognition and Understanding (ASRU), 2011 IEEE Workshop on*, pages 535–540. IEEE.

Samantha Wray and Ahmed Ali. 2015. Crowdsource a little to label a lot: Labeling a Speech Corpus of Dialectal Arabic. In *Interspeech.* (in press).

Omar F Zaidan and Chris Callison-Burch. 2011. Crowdsourcing translation: Professional quality from non-professionals. In *Proceedings of the 49th Annual Meeting of the Association for Computational Linguistics: Human Language Technologies-Volume 1*, pages 1220–1229. Association for Computational Linguistics.

Ines Zribi, Rahma Boujelbane, Abir Masmoudi, Mariem Ellouze, Lamia Belguith, and Nizar Habash. 2014. A Conventional Orthography for Tunisian Arabic. In *Proceedings of the Language Resources and Evaluation Conference (LREC), Reykjavik, Iceland.*

Joint Arabic Segmentation and Part-Of-Speech Tagging

Shabib AlGahtani
Research and Development
Ministry of Interior
Riyadh, Saudi Arabia
shabib@moi.gov.sa

John McNaught
National Centre for Text Mining
University of Manchester
Manchester, United Kingdom
John.McNaught@manchester.ac.uk

Abstract

Arabic has a very complex morphological system, though a very structured one. Character patterns are often indicative of word class and word segmentation. In this paper, we explore a novel approach to Arabic word segmentation and part-of-speech tagging relying on character information. The approach is lexicon-free and does not require any morphological analysis, eliminating the factor of dictionary coverage. Using character-based analysis, the developed system yielded state-of-the-art accuracy comparing favourably with other taggers that involve external resources.

1 Background

Part-of-speech (POS) tagging is the process of assigning a morphosyntactic role to each word in a text and hence is considered to be a crucial step that highly affects subsequent NLP tasks. The POS tagging task differs in complexity from one language to another. For instance, in languages that lack space delimitation, word boundaries must be found before tagging. With respect to Modern Standard Arabic (MSA), the importance of POS tagging is even larger due to MSA characteristics that impose a number of processing challenges. For example, POS tagging is vital for Arabic named entity recognition, due to the absence of capitalization in proper nouns. In Semitic languages including Arabic, the phenomenon of clitic attachment is another challenge adding to POS tagging complexity. The process of finding the boundaries between the lemma and the clitics attached to it is called word tokenization or segmentation. Ambiguity can arise both in segmentation and in tagging for each segment. The two tasks are closely bound in a sense that finding the correct tagging requires the correct segmentation in advance.

In this paper, we introduce a novel approach to joint Arabic tagging and segmentation relying on character patterns, adopting a character-based method. Our work is inspired mainly by Asian language processing especially Chinese character-based processing (Qian and Liu 2012). In Chinese, text is a stream of characters (symbols) that could be interpreted differently based on their context where one symbol could be an independent word or part of a word. However, there is no space delimiting feature in Chinese while it exists in Arabic between words that are a combination of segments. Arabic examples given in this paper will be transliterated using the Buckwalter transliteration scheme[1].

2 Arabic Language

The main feature of MSA that affects processing is the total or partial absence of diacritical marks that historically represented vowels, adding more complexity to both syntactic and semantic analysis. This is due to the fact that diacritics reduce the number of possible classes of the word. This feature is not present in English, but can be imagined by dropping vowels from words. For example, dropping the vowel from *is* would result in three possible interpretations: *us*, *is* and *as*. Still, vowels would have to be restored by the context to decide on the correct word.

One critical aspect of Arabic writing today is spelling errors. Common sources of spelling error were studied in (Shaalan et al. 2003), and categorized as errors of hearing, writing, morphology, etc. More details of Arabic characteristics are demonstrated in (AlGahtani 2012).

3 Arabic Morphology

Arabic derivational morphology is based on the principle of roots and patterns to generate open-

[1]http://www.qamus.org/transliteration.htm

Proceedings of the Second Workshop on Arabic Natural Language Processing, pages 108–117,
Beijing, China, July 26-31, 2015.

class stems. A root (called radical) is a sequence of consonants, commonly triliteral (Beesley 2001).

Arabic has a complex morphological system that makes it a highly inflected language, with the presence of prefixation, suffixation, inflectional and derivational processes. Although it has a complex system, it is strongly structured (Kiraz 2002). Arabic also has a rich morphological system, where words are explicitly marked for case, gender, number, definiteness, mood, person, voice, tense and other morphological features (Maamouri et al. 2006).

An Arabic word is composed of stem plus affixation to indicate tense, gender and number. In addition to affixes, clitics are attached to the beginning, the end or to both. Clitics are segments that represent an independent syntactic role: mainly conjunctions, prepositions and pronouns. Prepositions and conjunctions are attached to the beginning of the word and pronouns at the end (Diab et al. 2004). Clitics are composed of general Arabic characters that could be part of the stem, and hence pose problems for tokenization. To appreciate the problem of clitic attachment in English, we use the example illustrated in (AlGahtani et al. 2009). Consider passing English text through a noisy channel with the possibility of dropping the space delimiter between words, resulting in word concatenation. Assume the following (noisy) sentence is received:

Those cars uselessfuel.

The wordform *useless* has two interpretations as it is a candidate that might have been formed by concatenation due to noise; one interpretation is correct and the other is the result of concatenating the words *use* and *less.* If we use the POS tagging information of the previous word *cars*, it would be more sensible to choose the interpretation *use less*, since verbs are more likely to follow nouns than adjectives.

Bar-Haim et al. (2005) refer to each unit of the word that represents an independent tag as a segment. In Arabic, the word [ولدك ,wldk, your child] has three valid segmentations; wld+k, w+ld+k and w+l+dk. Each of these corresponds to a number of POS tagging annotations; for example, the segmentation w+ld+k, might have the POS tagging sequence of CC+NN+PRP$. Combining both the segmentation with the tagging information constitutes a full analysis; w/CC+ld/VBD+k/PRP. These two tasks are bound together in such a way that the correct tagging analysis always encodes the correct segmentation. Multiple analysis of the following sentence is illustrated in Table 1:

[قرأ ولدك الكتاب , qr> wldk AlktAb,
Your child read the book]

word	Translation	Full Analysis
qr>	read	qr>/VBD
wldk	your boy	wld/NN +k/PRP$
	and diverted you	w/CC+ld/VBD +k/PRP
	and to demolish	w/CC+l/IN +dk/NN
AlktAb	the book	AlktAb /NN

Table 1: Sample sentence analysis

Given the clitic attachment feature in Arabic, the POS tag of a word could be compound in nature, leading to tagset extension which, in turn, adds more complexity to this task. Also, this adds the problem of data sparseness (fewer forms with specific compound tags).

4 Previous Work

Recent advances in POS tagging have introduced the concept of bidirectional learning, which has resulted in the now state-of-the-art accuracy of above 97% for English. Bidirectional learning uses previous and successive context explicitly to find the tag of the current word. One instance of bidirectional learning is the bidirectional dependency network proposed and discussed in (Toutanova et al. 2003), which yielded 97.20% on the WSJ corpus. Moreover, the same concept was also adopted to develop a biomedical text tagger, discussed in (Tsuruoka et al. 2005). Their results showed the robustness of the tagger when tested on different genres. Another instance of bidirectional learning is the perceptron-like guided learning explained in (Shen et al. 2007), which also yielded comparable results.

In Arabic POS tagging, Khoja (2001) used a hybrid technique of statistical and rule-based analysis with a morphosyntactic tagset. Later, Support Vector Machines were used to separately implement a character based word-tokenizer and a POS tagger with a collapsed tagset of the Arabic Tree Bank, achieving scores of 99.7% and 95.5% on word-tokenization and tagging respectively (Diab et al. 2004). An enhancement of this system is discussed in (Diab 2009). With the help of the rich morphological features of Arabic, Habash and Rambow were able to tackle both tokenization and tagging in one step, achieving an accuracy of 97.5% (Habash and

Rambow 2005). Later, their system was extended in (Habash et al. 2009). An HMM Hebrew tagger was ported to Arabic, yielding an accuracy of 96.1% (Mansour et al. 2007). Transformation-based Learning has been investigated in (AlGahtani et al. 2009) yielding comparable results.

A recent morphological analyzer and POS tagger was implemented and discussed in (Sawalha and Atwell 2010). With 22 morphological features, their tool produces all possible analyses of Arabic words including lemma, root, pattern and vowelization (adding diacritical marks).

MADAMIRA discussed in (Pasha et al. 2014) is a hybrid system that combines aspects of MADA (Habash and Rambow 2005) and AMIRA (Diab 2009). Their system was blind-tested on part of the standard split highlighted in (Diab et al. 2013).

The performance of the systems discussed in this brief review are given if the tool has been tested on a standard dataset although not standard settings.

Selecting the most appropriate tagger for an application is quite difficult given these taggers have not been benchmarked due to the lack of standard test data which was not defined until recently. However, we expect character-based approaches to be more portable to different text genres. Most taggers developed for Arabic employ lexicons either directly or implicitly by using morphological analyzers. To our knowledge, there is no state of the art accuracy tagger that is lexicon free.

5 Joint segmentation and tagging Approach

Most taggers attempt to find the correct segmentation of a word before tagging, i.e., sequential processing. Sequential processing limits transfer and sharing of knowledge between different levels of analysis. Moreover, errors committed at any level of analysis will propagate to the subsequent levels. Word-based and segment-based techniques are highly affected by noise such as degraded text in the Web where people do not follow standard writing. Character-based approaches are very robust techniques and more efficient with unknown words due to their capability of capturing internal word patterns. Spelling errors are thus more tolerated in such approaches.

Given the rich morphology of Arabic that is encoded in a very structured system, a character-based approach would be appropriate to capture external and internal patterns. Also, given that clitics are always at the boundary and tagging of the word is governed by patterns, a joint approach will be used for both tasks.

To achieve the target of this study, we focus on the character as the unit of analysis. The aim is to find the word boundaries and find the correct POS of the word jointly. We model the problem as a sequence tagging problem, using machine learning. The learning algorithm's goal is to build a probability model; the model's goal in the decoding phase is to find the best sequence of character tags given raw text characters.

In the segmentation task, the appropriate representation is the same as used for boundary detection: IOB representation discussed in (Kudo and Matsumoto 2001). The IOB scheme was successfully applied to Arabic segmentation by (Diab et al. 2004). We investigate both IOB (Inside, Outside, Begin) and the more comprehensive IOBES (Inside, Outside, Begin, End, Single). The only modification is that the O indicator will not be used as each character should have a tag. In POS tagging, the tagset is the Arabic collapsed tagset[2].

segment (s)	t(s)	char (c)	t(c)
w	CC	w	S-CC
b	CC	b	S-CC
ktAbAt	NNS	k	B-NNS
		t	I-NNS
		A	I-NNS
		b	I-NNS
		A	I-NNS
		t	E-NNS
hm	PRP$	h	B-PRP$
		m	E-PRP$

Table 2: Arabic segment vs. character tagging of "wbktAbAthm"

Since the two tasks are bound, the joint segmentation and tagging is done by merging the tagsets of both tasks. Extending the POS tagset with character position indicators used in IOBES adds 4 subcategories to each tag. For instance, the NN tag will be extended to S-NN, B-NN, I-NN and E-NN. We also use a special character tag for the space delimiter. Table 2 illustrates the tagging of segments vs. characters, where s, c

[2]http://www.ircs.upenn.edu/arabic/Jan03release/arabic-POStags-collapse-to-PennPOStags.txt

and t represent segment, character and tag, respectively.

We use maximum entropy modeling to build our tagging model. Maximum entropy modeling has been widely used in various NLP tasks including POS tagging. It is known for its ability to combine features from diverse knowledge sources successfully. Given a sequence of words:

$$w = \{w_1, w_2, w_3, \dots, w_{n-1}, w_n\}$$

we try to find the best POS sequence:

$$t = \{t_1, t_2, t_3, \dots, t_{n-1}, t_n\}$$

by splitting the words into their characters:

$$c = \{c_1, c_2, c_3, \dots, c_{n-1}, c_n\}$$

then finding the best sequence of tags for characters:

$$tc = \{tc_1, tc_2, tc_3, \dots, tc_{n-1}, tc_n\}$$

Finally, we reconstruct the word POS tags from character tags.

In the decoding phase, character tags will be evaluated using gold standard (GS) annotations. The elementary decision of the tagger is finding the tag of each character from a tagset of (4 x 27) possible tags: t(c) in Table 2.

Beam search with window size 5 is used to find the best sequence of character tags for the whole sentence and to assist in ignoring inadmissible sequences i.e. 'Inside' tag following 'End' (E-NN, I-NN).

After decoding, the bare tags of the segments are constructed from the character tagging sequence. The position indicator is stripped of the tag and if a middle character has the position indicator "B" or "S" that means it is a start of a new segment and a plus sign "+" is inserted.

As per Arabic writing, some letters might change based on their position in the word. Feminine indicator 'p' is changed to 't' when connected to a pronoun. Such a case does not receive special processing in our approach since the tagger tries to find the POS tag of a sequence of characters without attempting to find the standard form of the word. If the tagger has never seen this word form in training, it still has the chance of correctly tagging it using its features and the features of surrounding characters. The only preprocessing we do is in the case of omission such as omitting 'A' from determiner 'Al' when connected to a preposition 'l' producing 'll'. We replace any 'll' in the input text with 'lAl'. This rule of transformation will fail in very rare cases i.e. when a word starts with letter 'l'.

We use a Java implementation available in the openNLP project[3] which has been used extensively in NLP tasks.

The feature set used is a combination of lexical and contextual features of the stream of characters, focusing on the current character. For instance, consider character (*H*) in the word *wb>bHAvhm* underlined in the following sentence:

"$ArkwA bHwrhm wb>bHAvhm fy Alm&tmr"

"شاركوا بحضورهم وبأبحاثهم في المؤتمر"

which translates as: "participated with their attendance and with their researches in the conference".

feature	description	value
c_i	curr char	H
c_{-1}	prev char	b
c_{-2}	prev char	>
$c_{i-1}c_i$	prev, curr char	bH
$c_{i-2}c_{i-1}$	prev prev, prev char	>b
$c_{i-2}c_{i-1}c_i$	prev prev, prev, curr	>bH
$c_{i-1}c_ic_{i+1}$	prev,curr,next	bHA
c_{+1}	next char	A
c_ic_{i+1}	curr,next char	HA
$c_{i+1}c_{i+2}$	next, next next char	Av
$c_ic_{i+1}c_{i+2}$	curr,next,next next char	HAv
c_0	leading char	w
c_0c_1	leading bigram	wb
$c_0c_1c_2$	leading trigram	wb>
c_n	trailing char	m
c_nc_{n-1}	trailing bigram	hm
$c_nc_{n-1}c_{n-2}$	trailing trigram	vhm
tc_{i-1}	tag of prev char	I-NN
tc_{i-2}	tag of prev prev char	I-NN
tb_{i-1}	bare tag of prev char	NN
tb_{i-2}	bare tag of prev prev char	NN
w_i	curr word	wb>bHAvhm
w_{i-1}	prev word	bHDwrhm
w_{i+1}	next word	fy
tw_{n-1}	tag of prev word	IN+VBN
tw_{n-2}	tag of prev prev word	VBD

Table 3: Feature set example

Table 3 gives a list of the features generated for that character, assuming previous context preceding this character has already been processed. Here, w, c, tw, tc, tb, i, n represent word,

[3]http://maxent.sourceforge.net/

character, word tag, character tag, bare tag, index of character and last character.

6 Experiments

6.1 Corpus

The corpus used in our experiments is the Arabic Tree Bank (ATB) which is a standard data set developed by the Linguistic Data Consortium (LDC)[4]. It is manually annotated with morphology syntactic features. The Treebank has gone through a number of revisions. Although previous studies involved the same corpus, different splits were used. The most common parts used in previous studies are ATB 1,2,3 as noted by (Diab et al. 2013) where a standard split was also defined. Table 4 shows details of parts used in this experiment following Diab et al. (2013) guidelines.

Part	Version	LDC Catalog	Source
ATB1	4.1	LDC2010T13	AFP
ATB2	3.1	LDC2011T09	Ummah
ATB3	3.2	LDC2010T08	Annahar

Table 4: Corpus ATB parts

The total number of words is some 738k. The annotations include morphological analysis and syntactic trees of sentences. For our task, only the morphological analysis is needed. We first mapped the morphological analysis annotation to the Arabic collapsed tagset distributed with ATB, which comprises 24 tags. We maintained two versions of the same corpus: **uns**egmented **c**orpus (UNSC) and **seg**mented **c**orpus (SEGC). The format in the unsegmented version is a full word level one (compound tag) whereas, in the segmented version, single tags are produced. Assigning extended tags to word characters occurs in the training phase where each word is split into its characters then tags assigned as described.

Table 5 shows the number of words in both segmented and unsegmented format. A word list was built from each version. The format of the word list is simply each word with the possible tags and their frequencies. The word list size varies in both given the generative behaviour of Arabic. Tag-per-word measure is given to appreciate the complexity of the task, showing 1.8 in the segmented corpus. Almost half of the corpus was ambiguous in the sense that a word was tagged with at least two different tags. We note also that a word could be formed by up to 6 segments although very rarely.

	SEGC	UNSC
corpus size (k)	738.89	637.02
tag-per-word	1.862	1.539
ambiguous token (%)	49.33	36.85
word list size (k)	46.529	68.031
ambiguous tokens (%)	11.13	8.64
Word count per number of tags	1=41348 2=4456 3=600 4=103 5=19 6=3	1=62148 2=5176 3=593 4=94 5=16 6=4

Table 5: Corpus ambiguity analysis

6.2 Settings

In order to evaluate the performance of our approach, experiments were conducted on each version of the corpus. Each experiment was performed on segmented text (GS segmentation provided in corpus) and on the unsegmented version. The unsegmented text is the primary goal of this approach, i.e, performing segmentation and tagging simultaneously.

Division	Doc	Document_Range
ATB1_TRAIN	568	20000715_AFP_ARB.0074 20001115_AFP_ARB.0128
ATB1_TEST	95	20001115_AFP_ARB.0129 20001115_AFP_ARB.0236
ATB2_TRAIN	400	UMAAH_UM.ARB_20020224-a.0005 - UMAAH_UM.ARB_backissue_34-a.0013
ATB2_TEST	51	UMAAH_UM.ARB_backissue_34-a.0014 - UMAAH_UM.ARB_backissue_40-e.0025
ATB3_TRAIN	480	ANN20020215.0001 ANN20021115.0033
ATB3_TEST	61	ANN20021115.0034 ANN20021215.0045

Table 6: Standard split (Diab et al. 2013)

The split used is the same setting detailed in (Diab et al. 2013). The training set was a combination of the three training set parts. The test set was formed likewise, as in Table 6. We followed the exact setting, excluding the development part as it was not required for our model.

We firstly constructed baselines for the two corpus versions, by assigning the most frequent

[4] https://www.ldc.upenn.edu

tag in the training set to corresponding test set tokens and tagging OOV tokens as NN. Most frequent tags were extracted from a word list built from the training set to produce the analysis.

In the first experiment, a statistical tagging model was produced using the joint segmentation and tagging approach detailed in section 5. In this experiment, we evaluate our approach on the two versions of the corpus. The segmented corpus is already segmented using the GS segmentation provided in the corpus, thus only testing of POS tagging accuracy is actually performed. The full evaluation of our joint approach is carried out by testing on the unsegmented corpus.

As the ATB was generated from different sources and annotated at different times, presumably by different annotators, in our second experiment we measured the performance on different parts only with respect to the unsegmented corpus. The performance is measured on each ATB part independently with its corresponding split.

Finally, a confusion matrix and error analysis was produced.

6.3 Results and discussion

The baseline tagger, which tags each token with the most frequent tag, achieved 91.02% and 88.34% on segmented and unsegmented corpora, respectively.

The results of the joint approach are shown in Table 7, which provides details of results obtained at each stage of the first experiment on segmented and unsegmented versions of the corpus. The performance is comparable to the state of the art, achieving an accuracy of 95.54% and 94.29%, on segmented and unsegmented corpora, respectively, yielding 4.5% and 6.95% improvements over the baseline.

	SEGC	UNSC
Size	664.95k	573.11k
Train set	590.82k	509.23k
Test set	74.13k	63.87k
OOV	4.14%	8.49%
Baseline POS	91.02%	88.34%
OOV Baseline acc.	30.09%	13.74%
Joint POS acc.	95.54%	94.29%
Joint SEG acc.	100 GS	99.36%
Joint OOV acc.	75.89%	73.811%
Joint POS acc. no lex	-----	93.00%
Joint SEG acc. no lex	-----	99.13
tag set count	27	186

Table 7: Experimental results

The difference in unknown words percentage between the two versions demonstrates the higher data sparseness in the unsegmented text, which is consistent with the fact that sparseness is increased due to clitic attachment.

The number of OOV items in the unsegmented corpus was double that of the segmented corpus, interestingly; guessing accuracy of unknown words in both experiments is almost equal, above 70%. The OOV guessing as NN in the baseline on the segmented corpus was double the accuracy of that on the unsegmented one. This was probably the cause of degradation by 3% in performance of the baseline between the two versions.

Original tagging inconsistency of the ATB dataset is present in some tokens, e.g., month names are tagged as either NN or NNP, which is also a cause of degradation.

The segmentation module achieved an accuracy of 99.4% on the unsegmented corpus, while segmented corpus evaluation used the gold standard segmentation. Segmentation accuracy was calculated as number of words correctly segmented over the total number of words. The result is comparable to what has been achieved by other systems. The superior accuracy of the segmentation was achieved due to the low number of words having multiple segmentations in the corpus.

Disabling lexical features (word, previous word, next word) had higher effect on tagging than segmentation performance. The accuracy degradation was 1.29% in tagging and 0.23% in segmentation.

Applying IOBES representation performed slightly better than IOB, with 0.2% difference in tagging accuracy. Table 7 results are achieved using the IOBES scheme.

The results of testing the model on each part independently are shown in Table 8. The model trained on the whole training set is tested on the test set of each part. Then a single model is built from each training set of each part and tested on the test set of the given part. The highest scores are in bold showing the best tagging was achieved on ATB1 and best segmentation on ATB2.

Train/Test	Task	ATB1	ATB2	ATB3
per-part	**POS**	**94.37**	93.75	93.03
	SEG	99.24	**99.29**	99.12
all parts	**POS**	**95.45**	95.09	93.44
	SEG	99.53	**99.64**	99.23

Table 8: Testing results per part

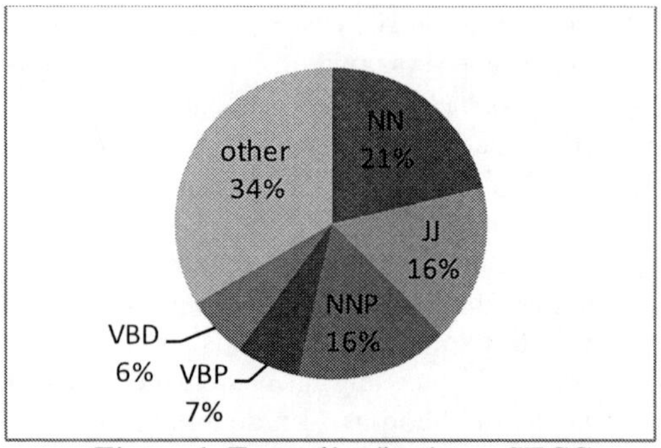

Figure 1: Error distribution – SEGC

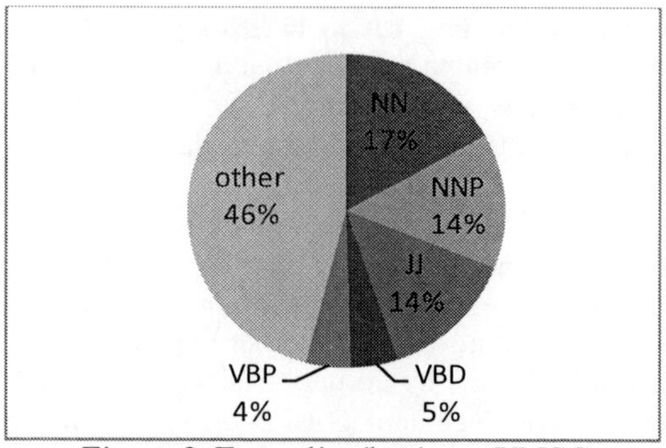

Figure 2: Error distribution – UNSC

	total error	largest target	total count	relative
NN	685	JJ	20867	3.28
JJ	524	NN	6106	8.58
NNP	513	NN	5967	**8.60**
VBP	211	NN	2663	7.92
VBD	206	NN	3047	6.76

Table 9: Most errorneous classes – SEGC

	total error	largest target	total count	relative
NN	612	JJ	16342	3.74
NNP	503	NN	5421	9.28
JJ	498	NN	5854	8.51
VBD	173	NN	1772	**9.76**
VBP	167	NN	2018	8.28

Table 10: Most errorneous classes – UNSC

To determine the highest ambiguous classes, we generated the confusion matrix of our tagger errors. The pie charts in Figure 1 and Figure 2 show the largest classes of the errors committed by the tagger in the two experiments. The three largest classes NN, JJ and NNP constitute almost half of the errors. The NN error rate is affected by the frequency of occurrence of that class in the corpus. Also, nouns share most of adjective and some verb forms.

Given that this measure is affected by the frequency of specific tags, we calculated the relative error where the number of errors is divided by the total number of occurrences of the given class (last columns of Table 9 and Table 10). On the segmented corpus, the NNP class has the highest relative error followed by JJ. This was due to the general case of Arabic proper nouns that are in the form of general nouns or adjectives. Arabic proper noun characteristics are highlighted in (AlGahtani 2012). Adjectives share most morphological features with nouns, such as gender and number indicators.

On the unsegmented version, the highest relative error was VBD and NNP. Errors in tagging VBD are attributed to verbs sharing the exact form of writing with nouns apart from a different vowelization, which is not present in written MSA. The largest error target class was tagging NN as JJ, followed by the remaining five classes tagged as NN affected by the dominating number of NN in the corpus.

The other analysis we carried out was to find the most erroneous tokens in our experiments. The list of the highest 10 tokens are in Table 11 and Table 12. These tokens were highly ambiguous in terms of the number of tags they could be assigned. The tables show each token with possible tags and frequency. The ones having unique tags but that were mistagged are due to the use of "_" as token/tag separator by our training algorithm implementation, which will be reconsidered in a future experiment.

The token "hA" was in the list due to being used as possessive pronoun or personal pronoun based on its preceding token. If the preceding token is mistagged, it will also be mistagged as a result. The rule is when the preceding token is a verb then the following pronoun is a personal pronoun and if the preceding token is a noun then it is possessive.

We have not been able to compare this work with previous work due to different settings used. The only published work that applied the splits highlighted in (Diab et al. 2013) was (Pasha et al. 2014). However, another tagset was used and their test was only on part of the test set, 25k blindly selected from the test set. Mapping from the ATB tagset to their tagset was not feasible.

token	error/all	tag	frequency
f	56/226	CC	1094
		NN	199
		RP	688
		IN	17
An	53/867	IN	7124
		VBP	693
		NN	36
		NNP	3
lA	45/274	RP	1921
		VBP	350
		CC	77
		UH	15
		NNP	5
mA	45/335	WP	2047
		IN	801
		RP	145
		NN	37
		VBP	15
l_	33/33	IN	223
mn	32/1356	IN	9978
		WP	303
		RP	23
h	27/1234	PRP$	5721
		PRP	4630
		RP	1
		NN	1
AlvAny	27/76	ADJNUM	158
		NNP	152
		JJ	9
hA	23/1160	PRP$	4466
		PRP	4122
		DT	4
		VBP	2
		UH	1
w	22/4644	CC	35983
		IN	196
		NN	77

Table 11: Most erroneous tokens – SEGC

7 Future Work

The study has showed that our approach succeeded in performing segmentation and tagging jointly. The tagger designed performs comparably to state of the art taggers for Arabic POS tagging, without knowledge-deep features, as well as being lexicon-free. This approach is applicable to any concatenating language such as the Semitic family languages.

token	error /all	tag	frequency
An	36/643	IN	5586
		VBP	303
		NN	36
		NNP	3
l_	33/33	IN	33
mA	32/268	WP	1672
		IN	763
		RP	93
		NN	37
		VBP	12
mn	27/1209	IN	8972
		WP	192
		RP	22
lA	27/188	RP	1363
		VBP	246
		CC	58
		UH	15
AlvAny	26/72	ADJNUM	150
		NNP	136
		JJ	9
Al_	18/18	DT	171
<n	16/49	IN	2098
		NN	9
wlA	16/63	CC+RP	419
		CC+VBP	88
		CC+CC	19
		IN+RP	2
b_	15/15	IN	15

Table 12: Most erroneous tokens – UNSC

To improve our tagger, we plan to have a wider context of features. Also, we plan to apply it in other tasks such as morphological analysis and named entity recognition.

Acknowledgments

We would like to acknowledge the support of Ilya Ahtaridis, from LDC, for providing upgrades of ATB versions.

References

AlGahtani, S., W. Black, and J. McNaught. 2009. 'Arabic Part-of-Speech Tagging Using Transformation-Based Learning'. In *Proceedings of the Second International Conference on Arabic Language Resources and Tools*. Cairo, Egypt.: The MEDAR Consortium. <http://www.elda.org/medar-conference/pdf/43.pdf>.

AlGahtani, S. 2012. 'Arabic Named Entity Recognition: A Corpus-Based Study'. University of Manchester. <http://www.manchester.ac.uk/escholar/uk-ac-man-scw:158690>.

Beesley, K. 2001. 'Finite-State Morphological Analysis and Generation of Arabic at Xerox Research: Status and Plans in 2001'. In *ACL Workshop on Arabic Language Processing: Status and Perspective*, 1:1–8. Toulouse, France. <http://www.xrce.xerox.com/Research-Development/Publications/2001-0094/%28language%29/eng-GB>.

Diab, M. 2009. 'Second Generation AMIRA Tools for Arabic Processing: Fast and Robust Tokenization, POS Tagging, and Base Phrase Chunking'. In *Proceedings of the MEDAR'09 Conference*. Cairo, Egypt. <www.elda.org/medar-conference/pdf/56.pdf>.

Diab, M., K. Hacioglu, and D. Jurafsky. 2004. 'Automatic Tagging of Arabic Text: From Raw Text to Base Phrase Chunks'. In *Proceedings of HLT-NAACL 2004: Short Papers*, 149–152. <http://dl.acm.org/citation.cfm?id=1614022>

Diab, Mona, Nizar Habash, Owen Rambow, and Ryan Roth. 2013. 'LDC Arabic Treebanks and Associated Corpora: Data Divisions Manual'. *arXiv Preprint arXiv:1309.5652*. <http://arxiv.org/abs/1309.5652>.

Habash, N., and O. Rambow. 2005. 'Arabic Tokenization, Part-of-Speech Tagging and Morphological Disambiguation in One Fell Swoop'. In *Proceedings of the 43rd Annual Meeting on Association for Computational Linguistics*, 573–580doi:10.3115/1219840.1219911. . <http://dl.acm.org/citation.cfm?id=1219911>

Habash, N., O. Rambow, and R. Roth. 2009. 'Mada+Tokan: A Toolkit for Arabic Tokenization, Diacritization, Morphological Disambiguation, Pos Tagging, Stemming and Lemmatization'. In *Proceedings of the 2nd International Conference on Arabic Language Resources and Tools (MEDAR)*. Cairo, Egypt. <www.elda.org/medar-conference/pdf/24.pdf>.

Bar-Haim, R., K. Sima'an, and Y. Winter. 2005. 'Choosing an Optimal Architecture for Segmentation and POS-Tagging of Modern Hebrew'. In *Proceedings of the ACL Workshop on Computational Approaches to Semitic Languages*, 39–46. <http://dl.acm.org/citation.cfm?id=1621796>

Khoja, S. 2001. 'APT: Arabic Part-of-Speech Tagger'. In *Proceedings of the Student Workshop at NAACL-2001*, 20–25. <https://nats-www.informatik.uni-hamburg.de/intern/proceedings/2001/naacl/srw/pdf/srw-06.pdf>.

Kiraz, G. 2002. 'Computational Nonlinear Morphology: With Emphasis on Semitic Languages'. *Computational Linguistics* 28 (4): 576–58doi:10.1162/coli.2002.28.4.576. . <http://dx.doi.org/10.1162/coli.2002.28.4.576>.

Kudo, T., and Y. Matsumoto. 2001. 'Chunking with Support Vector Machines'. In *Proceedings of the Second Meeting of the North American Chapter of the Association for Computational Linguistics on Language Technologies*, 1–8. <http://dx.doi.org/10.3115/1073336.1073361>.

Maamouri, M., A. Bies, and S. Kulick. 2006. 'Diacritization: A Challenge to Arabic Treebank Annotation and Parsing'. In *Proceedings of the Conference of the Machine Translation SIG of the British Computer Society*. <http://papers.ldc.upenn.edu/NLTSG/DiacritizationArabicTreebank.pdf>.

Mansour, S., K. Sima'an, and Y. Winter. 2007. 'Smoothing a Lexicon-Based Pos Tagger for Arabic and Hebrew'. In *Proceedings of the 2007 Workshop on Computational Approaches to Semitic Languages: Common Issues and Resources*, 97–103. <http://dl.acm.org/ft_gateway.cfm?id=1654593&type=pdf&CFID=95957381&CFTOKEN=73775663>.

Pasha, A, M. Al-Badrashiny, M. Diab, A. El Kholy, R. Eskander, N. Habash, M. Pooleery, O. Rambow, and R. Roth. 2014. 'Madamira: A Fast, Comprehensive Tool for Morphological Analysis and Disambiguation of Arabic'. In *Proceedings of the Language Resources and Evaluation Conference (LREC), Reykjavik, Iceland*. <http://www.lrec-conf.org/proceedings/lrec2014/pdf/593_Paper.pdf>

Qian, X, and Y. Liu. 2012. 'Joint Chinese Word Segmentation, POS Tagging and Parsing'. In *Proceedings of the 2012 Joint Conference on Empirical Methods in Natural Language Processing and Computational Natural Language Learning*, 501–511. <http://dl.acm.org/citation.cfm?id=2391007>.

Sawalha, M., and E. S. Atwell. 2010. 'Fine-Grain Morphological Analyzer and Part-of-Speech Tagger for Arabic Text'. In *Proceedings of the Seventh Conference on International Language Resources and Evaluation ((LREC'10))*, 1258–1265. Valleta, Malta. <http://www.lrec-conf.org/proceedings/lrec2010/pdf/282_Paper.pdf>

Shaalan, K., A. Allam, and A. Gomah. 2003. 'Towards Automatic Spell Checking for Arabic'. In *Proceedings of the 4th Conference on Language Engineering ((ELSE '03))*, 240–247. Cairo, Egypt: Egyptian Society of Language Engineering. <http://www.claes.sci.eg/NARIMS_upload/CLAESFILES/3847.pdf>.

Shen, L., G. Satta, and A. Joshi. 2007. 'Guided Learning for Bidirectional Sequence Classification'. In

Proceedings of the 45th Annual Meeting of the Association of Computational Linguistics, 45:760–767. Prague, Czech Republic. <http://acl.ldc.upenn.edu/P/P07/P07-1096.pdf>.

Toutanova, K., D. Klein, C.D. Manning, and Y. Singer. 2003. 'Feature-Rich Part-of-Speech Tagging with a Cyclic Dependency Network'. In *Proceedings of the 2003 Conference of the North American Chapter of the Association for Computational Linguistics on Human Language Technology (NAACL '03)*, 1:173–180. Edmonton, Canada. <http://dx.doi.org/10.3115/1073445.1073478>.

Tsuruoka, Y., Y. Tateishi, J.D. Kim, T. Ohta, J. McNaught, S. Ananiadou, and J. Tsujii. 2005. 'Developing a Robust Part-of-Speech Tagger for Biomedical Text'. *Advances in Informatics* 3746. Lecture Notes in Computer Science: 382–392. <http://dx.doi.org/10.1007/11573036_36>.

Multi-Reference Evaluation for Dialectal Speech Recognition System: A Study for Egyptian ASR

Ahmed Ali[1,2], **Walid Magdy**[1], **Steve Renals**[2]
[1]Qatar Computing Research Institute, HBKU, Doha, Qatar
[2]University of Edinburgh, Edinburgh EH8 9AB, UK
{amali,wmagdy}@qf.org.qa, {ahmed.ali, s.renals}@ed.ac.uk

Abstract

Dialectal Arabic has no standard orthographic representation. This creates a challenge when evaluating an Automatic Speech Recognition (ASR) system for dialect. Since the reference transcription text can vary widely from one user to another, we propose an innovative approach for evaluating dialectal speech recognition using Multi-References. For each recognized speech segments, we ask five different users to transcribe the speech. We combine the alignment for the multiple references, and use the combined alignment to report a modified version of Word Error Rate (WER). This approach is in favor of accepting a recognized word if any of the references typed it in the same form. Our method proved to be more effective in capturing many correctly recognized words that have multiple acceptable spellings. The initial WER according to each of the five references individually ranged between 76.4% to 80.9%. When considering all references combined, the Multi-References MR-WER was found to be 53%.

1 Introduction

Arabic Automatic Speech Recognition (ASR) is a challenging task because of the lexical variety and data sparseness of the language. Arabic can be considered one of the most morphologically complex languages (Diehl et al., 2012). With more than 300 million people speaking Arabic as a mother tongue, it is counted as the fifth most widely spoken language. Modern Standard Arabic (MSA) is the official language amongst Arabic native speakers. In fact, MSA is used in formal events, such as newspapers, formal speech, and broadcast news.

Nevertheless, MSA is rarely used in day-to-day communication. The vast majority of Arabic speakers use Dialectal Arabic (DA) in everyday communication (Cotterell and Callison-Burch, 2014). DA has many differences from MSA in morphology, phonology and the lexicon. A significant challenge in dialectal speech recognition is diglossia, in which the written language differs considerably from the spoken vernaculars (Elmahdy et al., 2014). Variance among different Arabic dialects such as Egyptian, Levantine or Gulf has been considered similar to the variance among Romance languages (Holes, 2004). There are many varieties of dialectal Arabic distributed over the 22 Arabic countries, often several variants of the Arabic language within the same country.

In natural language processing (NLP), researchers have aggregated dialectal Arabic into four regional language groups: Egyptian, Maghrebi, Gulf (Arabian Peninsula), and Levantine (Cotterell and Callison-Burch, 2014; Al-Sabbagh and Girju, 2012; Darwish and Magdy, 2014).

Most ASR systems are trained and tuned by minimizing WER, which counts word errors at the surface level. It does not consider the contextual and syntactic roles of a word, which are often critical for tasks like Machine Translation (MT), particularly in the end-to-end Speech Translation (ST) scenarios.

In a study by (He et al., 2011) , they showed that WER is not the optimal metric for a speech recognizer trained for a speech translation task. They developed a BLEU-optimized approach for training the scale parameters of a log-linear based speech translation system. In their study, they got better results using the new measure, although WER were found to be higher in the intermediate step of the speech recognition.

Dialectal Arabic can be viewed as an example of a language with no orthographic rules, since

Proceedings of the Second Workshop on Arabic Natural Language Processing, pages 118–126,
Beijing, China, July 26-31, 2015. ©2014 Association for Computational Linguistics

there is no academies in DA nor enough amount of language resources, such as no standard lexicon or clear rules for writing. In a study by (Habash et al., 2012) in which they presented Conventional Orthography for Dialectal Arabic CODA, they explain the design principles of CODA and provide description of CODA, and use the Egyptian dialect as an example, which has been presented mainly for the purpose of developing DA computational models.

In a similar study by (Ali et al., 2014a), they studied the best practices for writing Egyptian orthography. They conducted experiments on both Acoustic Model (AM), Language Model (LM), and guidelines for transcribing Egyptian speech. They released guidelines for transcribing Egyptian speech for what is called augmented Conventional Orthography for Dialectal Arabic augmented-CODA. They also reported gain in Egyptian speech recognition when augmented-CODA is followed in transcribing Egyptian speech data.

Unlike previous work by (Habash et al., 2012; Ali et al., 2014a), where they studied the best practices for writing DA, in this paper, we propose an evaluation method that accepts the variations in transcribing dialectal Arabic. We use multiple references, up to five different transcriptions per utterance, to evaluate the performance of the speech recognition engine. The main idea is to learn from the crowd and use multi-references to vote for each word in the recognized output. This is, in a way, similar to BLUE score used in MT, where multiple translation could be accepted for one source sentence. Here, we submit our speech data on a crowdsourcing platform, and ask for five different transcriptions for each speech segment. These five transcriptions typically capture the different acceptable variations of the Arabic dialect, where we then use them as our multiple references to calculate *multi-reference* WER (MR-WER).

The rest of the paper is organized as follows: In section 2, we describe dialectal speech recognition; section 3, we discuss the details of the multi-reference WER, and the proposed method evaluate dialectal ASR; section 4, we elaborate the data used in this experiment; section 5, we discuss the experiment and the results; and section 6 is for conclusion and future work.

2 Dialectal Speech Recognition

Large Vocabulary Speech Recognition (LVCSR) has been studied thoroughly in well-developed languages such as English, French, and Spanish. Also, MSA has obtained good results over the past decade as a result of GALE project, as well as more attention is paid to Arabic Broadcast domain(Diehl et al., 2012; Mangu et al., 2011; Cardinal et al., 2014; Ali et al., 2014b).

Dialectal Arabic ASR could be seen as under-resourced as it is lacking the basic component to have a decent system, such as enough labeled speech data for training, a lexicon, and a Natural Language Processing (NLP) pipeline for phonetic systems. Moreover, DA Arabic lacks standard orthography for writing. The absence of clear definition for right and wrong spelling has led to many representations for each word.

In our Arabic ASR, we use a grapheme-based system using sequential Deep Neural Network for the acoustic modelling. Although, conventionally, a phoneme system always outperforms a grapheme system, so a valid question is why do we choose grapheme system here?

We have found that WER in the grapheme system has increased by less than 1% relative to conversational speech compared to the phoneme system, which could be explained as conversational speech being mainly dialectal Arabic in most cases, and grapheme models will outperform phoneme models. Mainly, the NLP pipeline for phonetic system is not mature enough for dialectal Arabic, and is still facing challenges such as dicratization, and phonetization. The other amusing feature in the grapheme system is having a 1:1 ratio between the number of types, and the number pronunciation in the lexicon, compared to 1:4 in the phoneme-based system. This enables us to increase the lexicon size from 500K words to more than 1.2M words for the same text in the Language Model (LM) with small impact on memory. This has reduced the Out Of Vocabulary (OOV) from 3.9% to 2.5%, which also enables us to have more coverage for dialectal words that have not been measured precisely at this stage.

3 Applying Multi-Reference Evaluation for ASR

In this section, we discuss the reason for proposing our new methodology of evaluating ASR, particularly DA ASR, using multiple references instead of the standard method of using only one reference. In addition, we introduce our methodology for applying multi-reference to ASR evaluation.

3.1 The Concept of Multi-Reference Evaluation

One of the tasks that uses multi-reference evaluation is Machine Translation (MT). The main reason here is that many translations in the target language are fully valid for a given sentence in the source language. Thus, the MT research community found it more appropriate when evaluating an MT system to compare the automatic translation to more than one possible manual reference translations, typically translated by different language experts, to have a less biased evaluation to one translation. Therefore, most of the MT evaluation scores are designed to accept multiple references (Papineni et al., 2002).

ASR is treated differently, since the speech recognition is seen to have a single exact match to a specific string, and one reference should be sufficient to transcribe or judge what is spoken in the speech segment. This assumption is valid in most of the spoken languages. However, for languages with no standard orthographic representation such as Dialectal Arabic, there are many different ways to write a given spoken word. Table 1 shows an example for an Egyptian speech segment, which presents the transcription of one sound track from four different transcribers. As shown, many of the words presented has various spellings among the four transcribers. In addition, there are some words that are written by some transcribers but neglected by the others, such as the word "آه"(Ah) and "يعني"(yEny), that could be seen by some people as noise or filler and not worthy of writing. The variations in spelling the same words are clear in the shown example, such as {"ده"(dh),"دا"(dA)} and {"احنا"(AHnA),"نحن"(nHn), "إحنا"(AHnA)}.

Table 2 presents some additional samples of Arabic dialect words that have multiple acceptable spellings. These examples illustrate the problem of comparing an ASR output to only one reference that picks one of many possible spellings of a dialect Arabic word.

Accordingly, we propose introducing a multi-reference evaluation methodology for ASR tasks that targets languages with no standardized orthography. Similar to BLEU score in MT, multi-reference increases the likelihood of accepting an automatic translation (speech recognition), if any of the manual translations (transcriptions) agreed with it in some portions.

3.2 Multi-References Alignment to Recognized Speech Text

Our approach here is to extend the current alignment used when performing ASR evaluation between recognized text and one reference text to allow alignment between the recognized text and N references.

For a recognized text $Rec = \{w'_1, w'_2, ... w'_{|Rec|}\}$, and a set of N references: $Ref1 = \{w_{11}, w_{12}, ... w_{1|Ref1|}\}$ to $RefN = \{w_{N1}, w_{N2}, ... w_{N|RefN|}\}$, we perform the following steps:

- For each word in Rec, list all the words in $Ref1$ to $RefN$ that are aligned to it. Note, that some references may not include any corresponding word for some of the words in Rec, which is counted as an insertion. The output of this process will be an array of size N of reference words for each recognized word.
  e.g.: $w'_3 \rightarrow [\ w_{12}, w_{23}, \text{<INS>}, ..., w_{N4}\ ]$
- The previous step effectively captures insertions, substitutions, and correct recognition. However, deletions would not be handled, since there is no corresponding word in the Rec to the deleted words in the reference. In addition, different number of deletions could exist across different references. To map deletions effectively across multiple references, for each reference, we map any non-aligned word to the recognized text to a "deletion pointer" (<DEL>) with a counter to the position of the last aligned word in Rec. For example, if two deletions are detected for one reference after 3 aligned words with Rec, the words in reference would be mapped to {"03-01 <DEL>", "03-02 <DEL>"} in the Rec. If another deletion is detected after the fifth word in Rec, it will be mapped to "05-01 <DEL>". For deletion pointers that are mapped to some of the references only, those reference that has nothing deleted would be assigned to "NULL". See Table 3 as an example.

For example shown in Table 1, the ASR system produced the following sentence:

Different Transcription
نعم اه طبيعي إن دة أصلاً إحنا في وضع غير قانوني بالمرة غير دستوري بالمرة وضع nEm Ah TbyEy <n dp >SlAF <HnA fy wDE gyr qAnwny bAlmrp gyr dstwry bAlmrp wDE
نعم اه طبيعي دا أصلا يعني أحنا فى وضع غير قانوني بالمرة غير دستوري بالمرة اه وضع nEm Ah TbyEy dA >SlA yEny >HnA fY wDE gyr qAnwny bAlmrp gyr dstwry bAlmrp Ah wDE
نعم نعم اه هو طبيعي ده اصلا احنا في وضع غير قانوني بالمره غير دستوري بالمره وضع Ah hw TbyEy dh ASlA AHnA fy wDE gyr qAnwny bAlmrh gyr dstwry bAlmrh wDE
نعم هو طبيعى دا أصلا يعنى نحن فى وضع غير قانونى بالمره غير دستورى بالمره وضع nEm hw TbyEY dA >SlA yEnY nHn fY wDE gyr qAnwnY bAlmrh gyr dstwrY bAlmrh wDE

Table 1: Different transcriptions for the same utterance

“أعطى بإن دا أصلا يعني إحنا في وضع غير قانوني بالمر غير دستوري بالمر واضح أه فيه انقلاب”.
The alignment algorithm with the four references would produce the alignments shown in Table 3. As shown, now each word in the recognition is aligned to N references, which maximize the likelihood of finding a possible match that is accepted by one of the references.

3.3 Calculating MR-WER

Using the multi-aligned references, the number of correct, insertions, substitutions, and deletions are calculated as follows:

- **C** (Correct): is the number of recognized words that has a match in any of the aligned reference words.
- **S** (Substitutions): is the number of recognized words that has alignment to at least one reference words, but none of them matches it.
- **I** (Insertions): is the number of recognized words that is not aligned to any reference word. i.e. all corresponding alignments are “<INS>”.
- **D** (Deletions): is the number of “<DEL>” instances in the *Rec* that has no “NULL” alignment in any of the references. The main reason for not counting deletions that has no corresponding word in one of the references is for the following assumptions: if one of the reference transcriptions decided that one of the spoken words is not worth transcribing, then the ASR should not be penalized for missing it. We can refer to example like the word “اه”(Ah) and “يعني”(yEny) where some of the transcribers considered them as a noise, and they decided not to write it.

Based on the counts of C, S, I, and D, MR-WET is calculated according to the following equation:

$$WER = \frac{S + D + I}{(S + D + C)}$$

In the case of multi transcriptions per reference, the length of the transcription varies from one reference to another which means that the deletion count is different among different transcriptions as shown in Table 3. By look at examples in this table, we can see that first reference has 16 words, the second one has 17 words, the third 17, and the fourth 16, we can see the number of words varies from one example to another. More specifically, the second transcriber decided to add the word “اه”(Ah) which none of the other three references considered it as a valid word. We can also see the third reference decided to add the word “نعم”(nEm) at the beginning which no one else added.

By applying the same WER equation mentioned above, we can see that reference 1 will have WER

Translation	Valid Spellings	Buckwalter
He was not	ماكانش	mAkAn$
	ماكنش	mAkn$
	ما كانش	mA kAn$
	مكنش	mkn$
I told him	قولتله	qwltlh
	قولت له	qwlt lh
	قلتله	qltlh
	قلت له	qlt lh
In the morning	على الصبح	ElY AlSbH
	علي الصبح	Ely AlSbH
	ع الصبح	E AlSbH
	عالصبح	EAlSbH
	عصّبح	ESbH

Table 2: Sample of phrases with multiple valid spellings

Index	Rec	$Ref1$	$Ref2$	$Ref3$	$Ref4$
(00-1)	<DEL>	NULL	NULL	نعم	NULL
(00-2)	<DEL>	نعم	نعم	نعم	نعم
(01)	أعطى	اه	اه	اه	هو
(02)	بإن	طبيعي	طبيعي	هو	طبيعى
(03)	دا	إن	دا	طبيعي	دا
(04)	أصلا	دة	أصلا	ده	أصلا
(05)	يعني	أصلاً	يعني	اصلا	يعنى
(06)	إحنا	إحنا	أحنا	احنا	نحن
(07)	في	في	فى	في	في
(08)	وضع	وضع	وضع	وضع	وضع
(09)	غير	غير	غير	غير	غير
(10)	قانوني	قانوني	قانوني	قانوني	قانونى
(11)	بالمر	بالمرة	بالمرة	بالمره	بالمره
(12)	غير	غير	غير	غير	غير
(13)	دستوري	دستوري	دستوري	دستوري	<INS>
(14)	بالمر	<INS>	<INS>	<INS>	<INS>
(15)	واضح	<INS>	<INS>	<INS>	<INS>
(16)	أه	<INS>	بالمرة	<INS>	دستورى
(17)	فيه	بالمرة	اه	بالمره	بالمره
(18)	انقلاب	وضع	وضع	وضع	وضع
WER	MR:52%	75%	59%	88%	68%

Table 3: Alignment applied between a recognized text (Rec) and four different references

75%, reference 2 58%, reference 3 87%, and finally reference 4 will have 78% WER.

The MR-WER will have better results than any of the references distinctively, the MR-WER will be calculated as follow: :

$$MR - WER = \frac{6+1+2}{(6+1+10)}$$

Which is 52.6% WER, obviously, this is lower than the the lowest WER in any of the references.

4 Data

The data used in our experimentation comes from Broadcast News BCN domain; particularly, Aljazeera Arabic news channel. The nature of the data is debates and news programs which were uploaded to Al Jazeera in the duration between June 2014 and January 2015. All the speech data have gone through the pre-processing steps before being submitted to the used crowdsource platform [1] for transcription. Pre-processing included: removing non-speech audio such as music or white noise, followed by speaker segmentation and clustering, diarization, and speaker linking within the same episode. In addition to this, a dialect classification was performed using human computation, which also occurred via crowdFlower platform. Utterances underwent dialect classification by 3-9 annotators per audio file into five broad Arabic dialect groups: Modern Standard Arabic (MSA), Egyptian (EGY), Levantine (LEV), North African/Maghrebi (NOR), and Gulf (GLF). For the current study, we used audio segments which had been classified as EGY with at least 75% agreement between annotators.

In this study, Egyptian data was chosen as a test case to take advantage of the fact that the classification pre-processing showed us that approximately 40% of users of the crowdsource platform in the Arab world are located in Egypt, meaning that focusing on EGY audio and Egyptian annotators allowed us to complete transcription fairly quickly. Furthermore, there were significantly more audio segments classified with high levels of inter-annotator agreement as EGY when compared to other dialect categories. Finally, EGY as a category contains a potentially less diverse set of dialects than a more geographically spread regional category.

We have asked for five references for 2765 speech segments (utterances), representing 4.8 hours, with speech segments of an average length between 4-6 seconds. Our results are based on these five files or sometimes mentioned as five references. This does not necessary mean five different annotators. It is mainly five transcription representations that have come from more than one annotator. Allocating transcription tasks to annotators and randomize the data to make sure one single editor did not write the same sentence more

[1] http://www.crowdFlower.com

than once was managed through the crowdFlower platform.

5 Experimentation

Our experiments are designed to address the following research questions:

1. How many references should be used in the multi reference
2. What is the inter-reference agreement? How good is the crowdsource data? Do we need to filter bad transcription for the MR-WER evaluation?
3. How many times do we need to see correct word to count it correct?

5.1 Number of References

We have evaluated the speech recognition using various number of N reference transcriptions, where N ranged from 1 to 5. We have used all the combinations between reference transcriptions in cases when $N > 1$ to validate our findings. As shown in Table 4, for every experiment, we report the minimum, maximum and average MR-WER for each number of transcriptions we use. We conclude from this experiments two findings:

1. The WER reduces considerably when we increase the number of transcriptions from one reference to five references, and may be there is potential to reduce the WER more if there are more transcriptions (although we can see the reduction in MR-WER between four and five references is not significant). The multi-reference evaluation has taken the error from an average WER of 80.8% to 53.5%. The 33% difference in performance are possibly happening due to various ways of writing DA not really due to bad ASR.
2. The variance in WER reduces noticeably when we increase the number of references. For example if you look at Figure3, the WER for five single references varies from 76.4% to 80.9%, with a absolute difference of 3.7% which is high error margin, for two references, the absolute difference is 3.4%, and in three references is 1.9% and in five references, it is only 0.5%. Obviously, we have only one WER for five transcriptions, as there is no combination between multiple transcriptions. Possible explanation for this nice reduction is error margin is that multi reference is capable to capture some of the variations in transcription, and make the reported error rate more robust.

# Re.f	One	Two	Three	Four	Five
Min.	78.5%	65.5%	59.3%	55.8%	53.5%
Av.	80.8%	66.7%	60.0%	56.0%	
Max.	82.2%	68.9%	61.2%	56.3%	
# Exp.	5	10	10	5	1

Table 4: MR-WER for various number of references per experiment.

5.2 What is the inter-reference agreement

The transcribed data is suffering from a very limited quality control that have been applied to it, which raised an important question: what is the inter-annotator agreement in this transcription task? This is a difficult question to ask in language with no clear orthographic rules. In most of the cases, if we consider exact string matches between different transcriptions even if it is perfect, the inter-annotator agreement is almost zero as shown in Table 4.

We evaluated WER for every transcription file with the other four files. For every utterance in each reference, there will be four WER for the same utterance in the other four files, the WER will be averaged. Each file has 2760 utterances, corresponding to 4.8 hours. We split the 2760 averaged WER values into four bins, WER 0-25%, WER 25-50%, WER 50-75% and anything more than 75%. We plot the results as seen in figure 1. It is clear from the aforementioned figure that there is a great deal of missmatch between the five references. Partially, this is due to bad transcription coming from some of the crowd source contributors, that we did not apply quality check at this stage.

As an attempt to quantify the bad transcriptions issue, and their impact on our experiment, we did some cleaning up for the data by removing any utterance that has more than 90% WER across the other four annotators. This is a very simple way assuming the majority of the transcription are correct, and may be invalid in a case where there is a single good transcription and the other four are bad, which has not been noticed in our corpus.

This experiment has reduced the number of utterances as shown in Table 5, so $Ref1$ has gone from 2765 utterances to 1824, $Ref2$ from 2765 to 2160 .. etc. Also, we plot the clean data as shown in 2 To evaluate the impact of data cleaning on the MR-WER, we run the same algorithm as explained in section 3.3 on the clean data, and we found that the MR-WER for the five references actually has increased from 53.5% to 54.2%.

This is an interesting finding to say that by cleaning the evaluation data, the MR-WER has not got any better, which could be explained because removing the potentially noisy data did not impact the MR-WER rather than removing some of the examples that could help in finding alternatives for Dialectal words. Also, it is fair to say that the proposed method is robust for the noisy data.

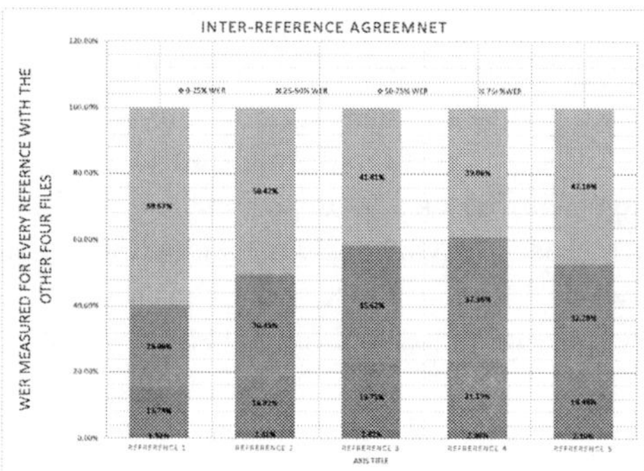

Figure 1: Inter-reference agreement for the full data

$Ref1$	$Ref2$	$Ref3$	$Ref4$	$Ref5$
1824	2160	2351	2414	2193

Table 5: Number of utterances per file after removing outlier transcriptions.

5.3 Counting Correct Words

In the case of single reference, the algorithm will loop over the solo reference, and check each word; insertion, deletion, substitution or correct. However, in the MR scenario, someone can argue that the algorithm in acting like cherry picking and looking for correct word in any of the references to make the WER look better rather than validating these findings. Basically, the spirit for this algorithm is try to find the recognized word in any

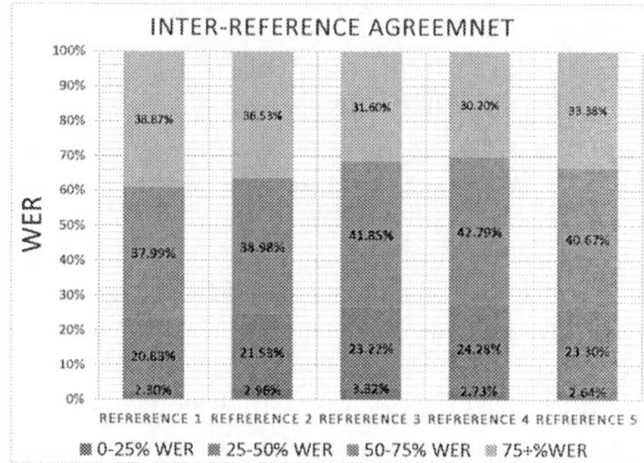

Figure 2: Inter-reference agreement after removing outlier transcriptions

of the references, obviously minding the position in text as explained in section 3.

To address this concern, we explore the impact in MR-WER when the algorithm asks for more than one evidence that a word is correct, i.e the same word occurred in same position in more than one reference. We evaluated correct word counting in 1+ (standard), 2+ and 3+ occurrences. Obviously, we apply N number of times seeing the word correct if there is N number of references or more.

We can see it clear in the alignment algorithm as shown in Table 3. The proposed MR-WER for the example in this table is 52.6%. In row index 03, the word "دا" (dA) will count correct for count 1+, and 2+, but not 3+. Row index 06, the word "إحنا" (ehnA) will count correct only in the 1+ count..etc.

The MR-WER for the example of at least two correct will be: 56.25% as the number of correct will reduce to 9 instead of 10. Same in the case of three correct examples or more, the MR-WER will be 64.28% as the number of correct examples will be 7. Table 6 can show that the MR-WER is going high when we ask for more than one occurrence in the reference for correct word. It is also notable in the case of five references, when the algorithms ask for at least two or three counts for the correct word, the MR-WER is 65.5%, and 77.5% respectively compared to 80.8% average WER in the case of single reference. This is an evidence that while asking for more than one proof in the reference for each correct word, the MR-WER is still outperforming the standard WER when we average it over five references.

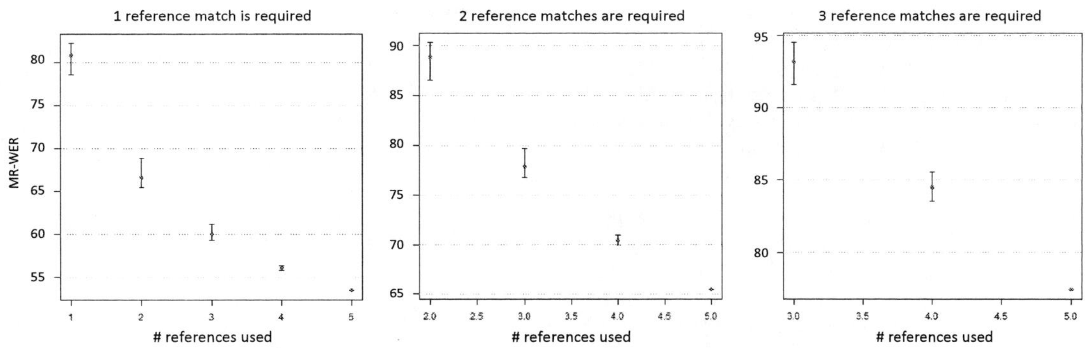

Figure 3: MR-WER for counting correct once or more

	One	Two	Three	Four	Five
1+	80.8%	66.7%	60.0%	56.0%	53.5%
2+	NA	88.8%	77.8%	70.4%	65.5%
3+	NA	NA	NA	84.5%	77.5%

Table 6: MR-WER for counting correct once or more.

6 Conclusion

In this paper, we have presented an innovative way for measuring the accuracy for speech recognition system in non-standard orthographic language; Multi-Reference Word Error Rate (MR-WER). Figure 3 summarized our findings in the multi reference approach applied on Dialectal Arabic (DA). We were able to report 53% MR-WER for five references collectively, while for the same test set the standard WER was between 76.4% to 80.9% when it used the same five references individually. We plan to extend this work to learn from multiple transcription the best orthography to improve the robustness of the computational models. Also, the usage of multi-reference in tuning, and training, similar to the proposed usage in evaluation.

References

[Al-Sabbagh and Girju2012] Rania Al-Sabbagh and Roxana Girju. 2012. Yadac: Yet another dialectal arabic corpus. In *LREC*, pages 2882–2889.

[Ali et al.2014a] Ahmed Ali, Hamdy Mubarak, and Stephan Vogel. 2014a. Advances in dialectal arabic speech recognition: A study using twitter to improve egyptian asr. In *International Workshop on Spoken Language Translation (IWSLT 2014)*, pages http–workshop2014.

[Ali et al.2014b] Ahmed Ali, Yifan Zhang, Patrick Cardinal, Najim Dahak, Stephan Vogel, and Jim Glass. 2014b. A complete kaldi recipe for building arabic speech recognition systems. In *Spoken Language Technology Workshop (SLT), 2014 IEEE.*

[Cardinal et al.2014] Patrick Cardinal, Ahmed Ali, Dehak, Najim, Yu Zhang, Al Hanai, Tuka, Yifan Zhang, James Glass, and Stephan Vogel. 2014. Recent advances in asr applied to an arabic transcription system for al-jazeera. In *INTERSPEECH.*

[Cotterell and Callison-Burch2014] Ryan Cotterell and Chris Callison-Burch. 2014. A multi-dialect, multi-genre corpus of informal written arabic. In *Proceedings of the Language Resources and Evaluation Conference (LREC).*

[Darwish and Magdy2014] Kareem Darwish and Walid Magdy. 2014. Arabic information retrieval. *Foundations and Trends in Information Retrieval*, 7(4):239–342.

[Diehl et al.2012] Frank Diehl, Mark JF Gales, Marcus Tomalin, and Philip C Woodland. 2012. Morphological decomposition in Arabic ASR systems. *Computer Speech & Language*, 26(4):229–243.

[Elmahdy et al.2014] Mohamed Elmahdy, Mark Hasegawa-Johnson, and Eiman Mustafawi. 2014. Development of a tv broadcasts speech recognition system for qatari arabic.

[Habash et al.2012] Nizar Habash, Mona T Diab, and Owen Rambow. 2012. Conventional orthography for dialectal arabic. In *LREC*, pages 711–718.

[He et al.2011] Xiaodong He, Li Deng, and Alex Acero. 2011. Why word error rate is not a good metric for speech recognizer training for the speech translation task? In *Acoustics, Speech and Signal Processing (ICASSP), 2011 IEEE International Conference on*, pages 5632–5635. IEEE.

[Holes2004] Clive Holes. 2004. *Modern Arabic: Structures, functions, and varieties.* Georgetown University Press.

[Mangu et al.2011] Lidia Mangu, Hong-Kwang Kuo, Stephen Chu, Brian Kingsbury, George Saon, Hagen Soltau, and Fadi Biadsy. 2011. The ibm 2011 gale arabic speech transcription system. In *Automatic Speech Recognition and Understanding (ASRU), 2011 IEEE Workshop on*, pages 272–277. IEEE.

[Papineni et al.2002] Kishore Papineni, Salim Roukos, Todd Ward, and Wei-Jing Zhu. 2002. Bleu: a method for automatic evaluation of machine translation. In *Proceedings of the 40th annual meeting on association for computational linguistics*, pages 311–318. Association for Computational Linguistics.

Arib@QALB-2015 Shared Task: A Hybrid Cascade Model for Arabic Spelling Error Detection and Correction

Nouf AlShenaifi[1], Rehab AlNefie[2], Maha Al-Yahya[3] and Hend Al-Khalifa[4]
[1,2]Computer Science Department and [3,4]Information Technology Department
College of Computer and Information Sciences
King Saud University
Riyadh, Saudi Arabia
{[1]noalshenaifi|[3]malyahya|[4]hendk}@ksu.edu.sa,
{[2]rehhb@hotmail.com}

Abstract

In this paper we present the Arib system for Arabic spelling error detection and correction as part of the second Shared Task on Automatic Arabic Error Correction. Our system contains many components that address various types of spelling error and applies a combination of approaches including rule based, statistical based, and lexicon based in a cascade fashion. We also employed two core models, namely a probabilistic-based model and a distance-based model. Our results on the development and test set indicate that using the correction components in cascaded way yields the best results. The overall recall of our system is 0.51, with a precision of 0.67 and an F1 score of 0.58.

1 Introduction

In last year's shared task on Automatic Arabic Error Correction of the Arabic NLP Workshop (QALB-2014 shared task), a diverse set of approaches were presented including pipeline, hybrid and cascade. These approaches used different techniques such as supervised learning, rule and/or lexicon based, and statistical language modeling. Furthermore, systems presented used several external resources, namely, Arabic Gigaword, AraComLex dictionary, Arabic Wikipedia and Aljazeera articles, to name but a few.
The QALB-2015 shared task is an extension of the first QALB-2014 shared task [1] that occurred last year. QALB-2014 handled errors in comments written by Arabic native speakers in Aljazeera articles [2]. This year's competition includes two subtasks, and, in addition to Arabic native speakers errors, also includes correction of texts written by new learners of Arabic language [3]. The test written by Arabic native subtask includes Alj-train-2014, Alj-dev-2014, Alj-test-2014 texts from QALB-2014. The L2 subtask includes L2-train-2015 and L2-dev-2015. This data was released for the development of the systems.
To build on the previous efforts, we present in this paper, the design and implementation of the Arib system to address the problem of Arabic spelling errors detection and correction. Hence, the name Arib [أريب] is an Arabic word that means a person who is bright, skilled, intelligent and insightful.
Arib will employ a hybrid cascade model as an approach with distance and probability-based techniques that reuse a large scale dataset complied from different external resources.
This paper is organized as follows: section 2 presents related work, section 3 shows how we compiled the necessary language resources for our system, section 4 highlights the main components of our proposed system, section 5 presents our experiments on the system, section 6 reports the obtained results and section 7 concludes the paper with final remarks and future directions.

2 Related Work

The task of Arabic spelling errors detection and correction generally addresses errors such as edit errors, add, split, merge, punctuation, orthographical, dialectal, and other error types. Depending on the techniques used for the task, systems designed for the error detection and correction task utilize language resources such as textual corpora and dictionaries.
One of the earliest studies on Arabic spelling detection and correction is the work conducted by Al-Fedaghi and Amin [4]. The system built

Proceedings of the Second Workshop on Arabic Natural Language Processing, pages 127–132,
Beijing, China, July 26-31, 2015. ©2014 Association for Computational Linguistics

detects all four error types edit, add, split, and merge and employs the technique of reducing the words to their original roots to identify spelling errors. Dictionaries used in this system are arranged according to Arabic word roots. The work presented in [5] describes a system which uses an Arabic morphological analyzer, lexicon, and heuristics to detect five types of errors: reading, hearing, touch-type, morphological errors and editing errors. Another similar system that uses the Arabic Web Dictionary (AWD) is presented in [6]. The system used dictionary lookup, morphological analysis and regular expressions to detect the four error types as well as punctuation errors. Other dictionaries used for the Arabic spelling errors detection and correction task include: Ayaspell [7], and AraComLex [8] [9].

Arabic language corpora have been used for spelling error detection and correction. Using a corpus to support the task by providing a resource for training machine-learning based spell-checking systems. Popular corpora used in Arabic spelling error detection and correction systems include: QALB corpus [10], Muaidi [11], and the Arabic Gigaword. The QALB corpus is a large Arabic corpus of manually corrected sentences, it is considered as a "Spelling-error corpus" for Arabic. Systems which used the corpus for the task of error detection and correction include [12], [13], [14], [7], [15], [8], and [16]. The Muaidi corpus has been used in the work presented in [17]. The corpus is a personally built corpus containing a set of 101,987 word types. The Arabic Gigaword corpus is a large corpus of Arabic text from Arabic news sources, developed by the Linguistic Data Consortium. The work described in [9] uses the Gigaword corpus to support the task of spelling error detection and correction.

Techniques and tools reported in the literature for supporting the Arabic spelling errors detection and correction task include morphological analysis [12] [5] [4] [6] [18] [15] [16], regular expressions [6] [13], heuristics (rules) [5] [14] [7] [15] [8] [16], finite state transducer with edit distance [9] [8], statistical character level transformation [14], N-gram scores [17] [8], conditional random fields [14] [8], and Naïve Base [15].

Similar to systems described in the literature, Arib utilizes language resources such as dictionaries and corpora as well as the application of different techniques to support the task of Arabic spelling error detection and correction.

3 Language Resources

An important component of any spelling errors detection and correction system is the compilation of a large scale dictionary that can be used to cover most Arabic words for the sake of detecting the misspelled word. So in order to build this dictionary we reverse-engineered the QALB corpus by replacing the wrong words from the annotated text with the correct words in the final text. We also used several other corpuses, namely: KSU corpus of classical Arabic [19], Open Source Arabic Corpora (OSAC) [20], Al-Sulaiti Corpus [21], and KACST Arabic Corpus [22]. These corpuses were compiled into one complete corpus, we then used KHAWAS tool (KACST Arabic Corpora Processing Tool) [23] to extract the words with their frequencies. This final step helped in building a huge dictionary that was used later on in our system (See Fig.1).

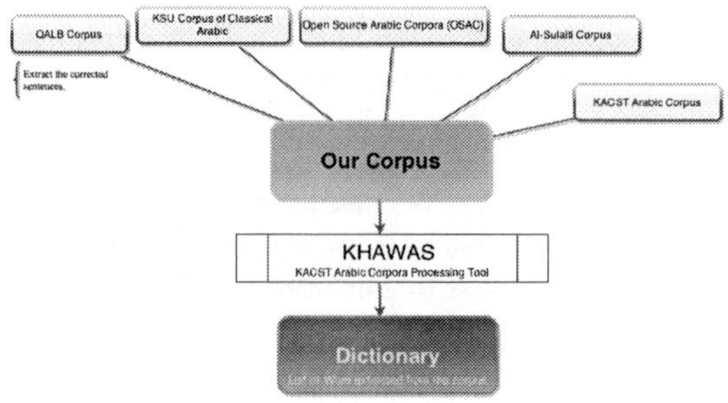

Fig. 1: Dictionary List of Arib.

4 Our Approach

The design of Arib is based on a hybrid cascade approach to spelling errors detection and correction. By cascade we mean that the original Arabic text passes through several components before a final result is returned. Each component participates in identifying spelling errors and recommending a correction. The final result is a compiled collection of all spelling errors identified and the suggested corrections. Our system can cover a range of spelling errors. Errors that are discovered by Arib include: edit, add, split, merge, punctuation, phonological, and common mistakes. The general architecture and major components of Arib system are shown in Fig. 2.

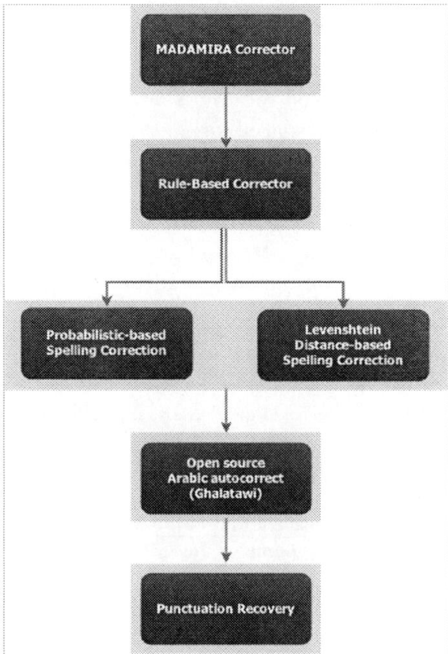

Fig. 2: The general architecture of Arib.

4.1 MADAMIRA Corrector

MADAMIRA [24] is a system developed for morphological analysis and Disambiguation of Arabic text. Since the organizers of the shared task provided the data pre-processed with MADAMIRA, we used the features generated by MADAMIRA to support the spelling error detection and correction. The output of MADAMIRA includes an analysis and correction of the spelling mistakes in the word (Alf)(أ) and terminal (Yaa)(ى). Spelling errors of this type can easily and accurately be detected and corrected using this component.

4.2 Rule-Based Corrector

In this component knowledge of common spelling error patterns are represented as rules that can be applied to provide a correction. All rules are applied to the misspelled word to generate possible corrections. These rules were created through analysis of samples of the QALB Shared Task Dataset and from Arabic language expert who summarized common misspellings of Arabic new learners.

Examples of the extracted rules:

- Replace the English punctuation marks by the Arabic ones (e.g.: replace ',' by '،').
- All numbers are separated from words.
- Fix the Speech effects characters.
- Remove extra characters by eliminating a sequence of three or more of the same characters. (e.g.: replace 'آميييييييين' (Āmyyyyyyyn) by 'آمين' (Āmyn)).
- Insert a space after all words end by a Ta-Marbouta characters (ة)(p) if it is attached to the following word.
- Insert a space after "ElY, ALY" (على، إلى) (On, For) preposition if it is attached to the following word.
- Merge the lone occurrences of the conjunction "W, FA" (and) (و، ف) with the following word.

4.3 Probabilistic-Based Spelling Correction

This component scans the text for spelling errors using Bayes probability theory, and is based on the algorithm by Peter Norvig for spell checking [25], [26]. It is classified as a probabilistic technique, thus it computes the probability that a given word is the correction for a misspelled work. This component uses our customized dictionary, with word frequencies extracted from KHAWAS to enumerate all possible corrections for the misspelled word. In order to find a correction of misspelled word from all possible corrections we chose the candidate word with the highest probability. For example, the misspelled non-word "تزاب" "tzAb" could be corrected to "تراب" "trAb" (Soil) or "تراث" "trAv" (Heritage), in this component we suggest the correction based on the probabilities.

4.4 Levenshtein-Distance-based Spelling Correction

This component implements the Symmetric Delete Spelling Correction (FAROO) algorithm, a robust algorithm for error detection and correction based on the edit distance using (Damerau-Levenshtein) distance measure [27]. A dictionary entry is selected to be the correction based on its edit distance to the misspelled word. The algorithm works by generating words with an edit distance of <=2 from each dictionary word, and adds them both to the dictionary. Words are generated with an edit distance of <=2 from the input words, and they are searched in the dictionary.

4.5 Open Source Arabic autocorrect (Ghaltawi)

Ghalatawi [28] is an open source Arabic spelling errors detection and correction system available online [28]. The system discovers common spelling errors and uses a dictionary lookup and regular expressions. It is written in Python and has been integrated as a cascade within our development.

4.6 Puctuation Recovery

This component runs a set of rules against the input to determine the absence of periods, semicolon and commas in a given Arabic text. Rules on punctuation are extracted from Arabic language resources and modeled within this component. Previous works mentioned that it is always better to keep the existing punctuation marks in the text [15], so we keep the current punctuation marks (period, comma, question mark, exclamation mark, colon, semicolon, parentheses, and quotation mark) and attempt only to insert the missing marks. The output of this component is the final output of the system.

5 System Experiments

As we previously mentioned, Arib consists of several components designed to tackle different types of errors. For the submissions to the second shared task, we submitted three versions of the system. We refer to these as Arib-1, Arib-2, and Arib-3.

Table.1 shows the component of our system and which components are incorporated in each version.

Component	System Run		
	Arib-1	Arib-2	Arib-3
MADAMIRA	•	•	•
Rule-Based	•	•	•
Probabilistic		•	•
Distance	•		•
Ghaltawi	•	•	•
Punctuation	•	•	•

Table.1: The three output runs of Arib.

6 Results and Discussion

With a view to evaluate the performance of our system, we used the M2 Scorer [29], the official scorer of the shared task.
Table.2 reports the performance results of Arib on the development and test set Alj-dev-2014, Alj-test-2014, L2-dev-2015, and L2-test-2014.
Table.3 reports the performance results of Arib as each system component is added.

	Precision	Recall	F-measure
Arib Result	0.6658	0.5108	0.5781

Table.2: Performance results of Arib.

Component	System Performance		
	Precision	Recall	F-measure
MADAMIRA	0.6615	0.3671	0.4722
+Rule-Based	0.6719	0.4212	0.5178
+Probabilistic	0.6521	0.4471	0.5305
+Distance	0.6650	0.5092	0.5768
+Ghaltawi	0.6658	0.5108	0.5781

Table.3: Performance results of Arib with the respect of each system component.

Table.4 reports the performance results of Arib on the test set for the 2nd QALB Shared Task Alj-test-2015 and L2-test-2015.

System	Test Set	Precision	Recall	F-measure
Arib-1	Alj-test-2015	64.50	56.50	60.23
Arib-2		67.56	51.61	58.51
Arib-2	L2-test-2015	50.08	22.30	30.86
Arib-3		48.79	24.57	32.68

Table.4: Performance results of Arib on Alj-test-2015 and L2-test-2015

Results from the evaluation show that the Arib performed well as each component is added to the system.

7 Conclusion and Further Research

In this paper, we described a hybrid cascade approach for Arabic Spelling detection and correction system for participation in the second shared task on Automatic Arabic Error Correction. Our approach combines rule-based linguistic techniques with probabilistic-based and Distance-based Spelling Correction techniques. We experiment with our system using different configurations of the developed components. Results of the experiments show encouraging results.

Future work involves further enhancements to the system including developing more intelligent techniques to correct split and merge errors. Moreover, use more advanced techniques for the sake of punctuation corrector including machine learning techniques and semantic text analysis technology.

Reference

[1] B. Mohit, A. Rozovskaya, N. Habash, W. Zaghouani, and O. Obeid., "The First QALB Shared Task on Automatic Text Correction for Arabic," in Proceedings of EMNLP Workshop on Arabic Natural Language Processing, Doha, Qatar, 2014.

[2] W. Zaghouani, B. Mohit, N. Habash, O. Obeid, N. Tomeh, A. Rozovskaya, N. Farra and S. Alkuhlani, and K. Oflazer., "Large Scale Arabic Error Annotation: Guidelines and Framework," in Proceedings of the Ninth International Conference on Language Resources and Evaluation (LREC'14), 2014.

[3] W. Zaghouani, N. Habash, H. Bouamor, A. Rozovskaya, B. Mohit, A. Heider, and K. Oflazer., "Correction Annotation for Non-Native Arabic Texts: Guidelines and Corpus," in Proceedings of the Ninth Linguistic Annotation Workshop, Association for Computational Linguistics, 2015, pp. 129–139.

[4] Al-Fedaghi, S. and Amin, A., "Automatic correction of spelling errors in Arabic," J-Univ. KUWAIT Sci., vol. 19, no. 2, p. 175, 1992.

[5] K. Shaalan, Amin Allam, and Abdullah Gomah, "Towards automatic spell checking for Arabic," 2003.

[6] Rachidi T., M. Bouzoubaa, L. ElMortaji, B. Boussouab, and A. Bensaid, "Arabic user search Query correction and expansion," in Proc. of COPSTIC'03, Rabat December 11--13, 2003.

[7] Djamel Mostefa, Omar Asbayou, and Ramzi Abbes, "TECHLIMED system description for the Shared Task on Automatic Arabic Error Correction," in EMNLP, Doha, Qatar.

[8] Mona Diab, Mohammed Attia, and Mohamed Al-Badrashiny, "GWU-HASP: Hybrid Arabic Spelling and Punctuation Corrector," in EMNLP, Doha, Qatar, 2014.

[9] Attia, Mohammed, Pavel Pecina, and Younes Samih, "Improved Spelling Error Detection and Correction for Arabic," in COLING, 2012.

[10] B. Mohit, "QALB: Qatar Arabic language bank," Qatar Found. Annu. Res. Forum Proc., p. ICTP 032, Nov. 2013.

[11] Muaidi H, "Extraction Of Arabic Word Roots: An Ap- proach Based on Computational Model and Multi-ackpropagation Neural Networks.," PhD Thesis, De Mont- fort University, UK, 2008.

[12] Y. Hassan, M. Aly, and A. Atiya, "Arabic Spelling Correction using Supervised Learning," ArXiv14098309 Cs, Sep. 2014.

[13] Taha Zerrouki, Khaled Alhowaity, and Amar Balla, "Auto-correction of arabic common errors for large text corpus," in EMNLP, Doha, Qatar, 2014.

[14] H. Mubarak and K. Darwish, "Automatic Correction of Arabic Text: a Cascaded Approach," ANLP 2014, p. 132, 2014.

[15] A. R. N. Habash and R. E. N. F. W. Salloum, "The Columbia System in the QALB-2014 Shared Task on Arabic Error Correction," ANLP 2014, p. 160, 2014.

[16] Michael Nawar and Moheb Ragheb, "Fast and Robust Arabic Error Correction System," in EMNLP, Doha, Qatar, 2014.

[17] H. Muaidi and R. Al-Tarawneh, "Towards Arabic Spell-Checker Based on N-Grams Scores," Int. J. Comput. Appl., vol. 53, no. 3, pp. 12–16, Sep. 2012.

[18] B. Haddad and M. Yaseen, "Detection and Correction of Non-Words in Arabic: A Hybrid Approach," Int. J. Comput. Process. Lang., vol. 20, no. 04, pp. 237–257, Dec. 2007.

[19] Alrabiah, M., Al-Salman A. and Atwell, E., "The design and construction of the 50 million words KSUCCA King Saud University Corpus of Classical Arabic," in Proceedings of the Second Workshop on Arabic Corpus Linguistics (WACL-2), Lancaster University, UK, 2013.

[20] Saad, M. and Ashour, W., "OSAC: Open Source Arabic Corpora," in Proceedings of the 6th International Symposium on Electrical and Electronics Engineering and Computer Science (EEECS'10), European University of Lefke, Cyprus, pp. 118-123, 2010.

[21] Al-Sulaiti, Latifa; Atwell, Eric. “The design of a corpus of contemporary Arabic,” International Journal of Corpus Linguistics, vol. 11, pp. 135-171, 2006.

[22] Al-Thubaity, A., “A 700M+ Arabic corpus: KACST Arabic corpus design and construction,” Language Resources and Evaluation, pp. 1-31, 2014.

[23] “Ghawwas: An open source system for Arabic corpora processing.”[Online]. Available: http://sourceforge.net/projects/ghawwasv4/. [Accessed: 1-June-2015].

[24] A. Pasha, M. Al-Badrashiny, M. T. Diab, A. E. Kholy, R. Eskander, N. Habash, M. Pooleery, O. Rambow, and R. Roth, “MADAMIRA: A Fast, Comprehensive Tool for Morphological Analysis and Disambiguation of Arabic,” in Proceedings of the Ninth International Conference on Language Resources and Evaluation (LREC-2014), Reykjavik, Iceland, May 26-31, 2014, 2014, pp. 1094–1101.

[25] “How to Write a Spelling Corrector.” [Online]. Available: http://norvig.com/spell-correct.html. [Accessed: 28-May-2015].

[26] T. Segaran and J. Hammerbacher, Beautiful Data: The Stories Behind Elegant Data Solutions. O’Reilly Media, Inc., 2009.

[27] “1000x Faster Spelling Correction algorithm | FAROO Blog.” [Online]. Available: http://blog.faroo.com/2012/06/07/improved-edit-distance-based-spelling-correction/. [Accessed: 28-May-2015].

[28] “غلطاوي:التصحيح التلقائي العربي Ghalatawi:Arabic AutoCorrect.” [Online]. Available: http://ghalatawi.sourceforge.net/. [Accessed: 28-May-2015].

[29] D. Daniel, and H. Ng., “Better evaluation for grammatical error correction,” in Proceedings of the 2012 Conference of the North American Chapter of the Association for Computational Linguistics: Human Language Technologies. Association for Computational Linguistics, 2012.

[30] A. Rozovskaya, H. Bouamor N. Habash, W. Zaghouani, O. Obeid, and B. Mohit., “The Second QALB Shared Task on Automatic Text Correction for Arabic,” in Proceedings of ACL Workshop on Arabic Natural Language Processing, Beijing, China, 2015

CUFE@QALB-2015 Shared Task: Arabic Error Correction System

Michael Nawar Ibrahim
Computer Engineering Department
Cairo University
Giza, Egypt
michael.nawar@eng.cu.edu.eg

Moheb M. Ragheb
Computer Engineering Department
Cairo University
Giza, Egypt
moheb.ragheb@eng.cu.edu.eg

Abstract

In this paper we describe the implementation of an Arabic error correction system developed for the WANLP-2015 shared task on automatic error correction for Arabic text. We proposed improvements to a previous statistical rule based system, where we use the words patterns to improve the error correction, also we have used a statistical system the syntactic error correction rules. The system achieves an F-score of 0.7287 on the Alj-test-2015 dataset, and an F-score of 0.3569 on the L2-test-2015 dataset.

1 Introduction

This paper presents improvements to a previously developed rule-based probabilistic system (Nawar and Ragheb, 2014). We first make use of a unique Arabic feature, which is the word pattern to extract more rules for the system. Also, we have proposed a probabilistic Arabic grammar analyzer instead of a simple rule-based one proposed in the previous work.

This shared task was on automatic Arabic text correction. For this task, the Qatar Arabic Language Bank (QALB) corpus (Rozovskaya et. al, 2015) was provided. It is an extension of the first QALB shared task (Mohit et al., 2014) that took place last year. QALB-2014 addressed errors in comments written to Aljazeera articles by native Arabic speakers (Zaghouani et al., 2014). This year's competition includes two tracks, and, in addition to errors produced by native speakers, also includes correction of texts written by learners of Arabic as a foreign language (L2) (Zaghouani et al., 2015). The native track includes Alj-train-2014, Alj-dev-2014, Alj-test-2014 texts from QALB-2014. The L2 track includes L2-train-2015 and L2-dev-2015. This data was released for the development of the systems. The systems were scored on blind test sets Alj-test-2015 and L2-test-2015.

The proposed framework could be described as a probabilistic rule-based framework. During the training of this framework, we extracted error correction rules and compute a probability to each rule as shown later in section 3. The extracted rules are then sorted based on their probabilities. And during the test, we apply the rules from the highest probability to the lowest probability one by one, on the entire test data till a stopping criteria is satisfied. During the algorithm we have some kind of heuristic to estimate the F-score after each rule is apply. The stopping criteria for the algorithm is that the estimated F-score start to decrease.

This paper is organized as follow, in section 2, an overview of the related work in the field of error correction is discussed. In section 3, the proposed system and its main components are explained. The improvements in the correction rules are discussed in section 4. The evaluation process is presented in section 5. Finally, concluding remarks and future work are presented in section 6.

2 Related Work

During the last two decades, there was an increasing interest in the problem of error correction, and most of the work done in that field, is made for English language (Kukich, 1992; Golding and Roth, 1999; Carlson and Fette, 2007; Banko and Brill, 2001). Recently, Arabic spelling correction has also received considerable interest. Ben Othmane Zribi and Ben Ahmed, (2003) have reduced the number of alternatives to a wrong word by about 75%. Haddad and Yaseen (2007) used a unique Arabic language feature, word root-pattern relationship, to locate, reduce and rank the most probable correction

Proceedings of the Second Workshop on Arabic Natural Language Processing, pages 133–137,
Beijing, China, July 26-31, 2015. ©2014 Association for Computational Linguistics

candidates in Arabic derivative words to improve the process of error detection and correction. Hassan et al. (2008) proposed an error correction system that use a finite state automata to propose candidate corrections for wrong words, then assign a score to each candidate and choose the best correction based on the context. Shaalan et al. (2010) developed an error correction system to Arabic learners. Alkanhal et al. (2012) have developed an error correction system that emphasizes on space insertion and deletion errors.

Last year, in the QALB 2014 shared task, multiple systems for text error correction were proposed. Jeblee et al. (2014) proposed a pipeline consisting of rules, corrections proposed by MADAMIRA (Pasha et al., 2014), a language model for spelling mistakes, and a statistical machine-translation system. Rozovskaya et al. (2014) used multiple approaches to correct the wrong word including: corrections proposed by MADAMIRA, a Maximum Likelihood model trained on the training data, regular expressions; a decision-tree classifier for punctuation errors trained on the training data, an SVM character-level error correction model, a Naïve Bayes classifier trained on the training data and the Arabic Gigaword corpus, and finally, they analyzed the results to find the best combination of correction technique that produce the best result.

3 The Proposed System

This paper is an extension to the work by Nawar and Ragheb (2014). The main system idea is explained by the algorithm, in figure 1. The algorithm has two inputs: the set of sentences that need to be modified T[1..n], and the set of correction rules C[1..m] that could be applied to text. The algorithm has one single output: the set of modified sentences T'[1..n]. The algorithm could be divided into two main component: the initialization and the main loop.

First, the initialization part of the algorithm starts from line 1 to line 8. In the first line, the sentences are copied from T[1..n] to T'[1..n]. In line number 2, the number of errors in the test set T[1..n] is expected using the rate of errors in the train set (#error / #words). In lines 3 to 8, the variables used in the algorithm are initialized to zero.

The variable Pattern[1..n] holds the patterns of the words in the sentences T[1..n]. For example, the pattern of ("كاتب","kAtb", "writer") is ("فاعل","fAEl) and the pattern of ("مكتب","mktb", "office") is ("مفعل","mfEl"). For the extraction of the word pattern, we assign for each stem in the stem table of the morphological analyzer (BAMA v2) an appropriate pattern, then we assign the word a pattern based on its stem pattern, prefix and suffix. For example, we assign for the stem ("ستخدم", "stxdm") the pattern ("ستفعل", "stfEl"), and when we analyze the word ("مستخدمين", "mstxdmyn", "users") – that have a prefix ("م","m") and a suffix ("ين", "yn") – we assign to it the pattern ("مستفعلين", "mstfElyn"), and when we analyze the word ("يستخدمون", "ystxdmwn", "they use")–that have a prefix ("ي","y") and a suffix ("ون", "wn") – we assign to it the pattern ("يستفعلون", "ystfElwn"). We don't assign a pattern to a word if the word is Arabized (nouns borrowed from foreign languages) like ("كمبيوتر", "kmbywtr", "computer") or ("أمريكا", ">mrykA", "America"), or if the word is fixed (words used by Arabs, and do not obey the Arabic derivation rules) like ("هذا", "h*A", "this") or ("كل", "kl", "every").

```
Input: T[1..n], C[1..m]
Output: T'[1..n]
1: T' = T
2: Gold Edits = #Words in Test * # Gold Edits in
Train / # Words in Train
3: Correct Edits = 0
4: Performed Edits = 0
5: Precision = 0
6: Recall = 0
7: Old F-score = 0
8: F-score = 0
9: Pattern[1..n] = Extract Patterns of T
10: Do
11:      T' = T
12:      Old F-score = F-score
13:      Get next correction "c" with the highest
         probability "p" from C
14:      Apply the correction "c" on T
15:      Update Patterns based on "c"
16:      N = number of changes between T and
         T'
17:      Performed Edits = Performed Edits + N
18:      Correct Edits = Correct Edits + p * N
19:      Precision = Correct Edits / Performed
         Edits
20:      Recall = Correct Edits / Gold Edits
21:      F-score = 2*Precision*Recall / (Preci-
         sion+Recall)
22: while F-score > Old F-score do
23: return T'
```

Figure 1: Proposed Algorithm

The main loop of the algorithm starts from line 10 to line 22. In line 10, the loop begins, and the sentences are copied from T[1..n] to T'[1..n] and the F-score is copied to old F-score, in lines 11 and 12. Then the first not applied correction with the highest probability to be correct is correct is chosen in line 13. In line 14, the correction is applied on the text T[1..n], and in line 15 the Patterns[1..n] is updated based on the corrections performed. Then we calculate the number of changes between T[1..n] and T'[1..n], in line 16. And based on the expected number of changes, we update the expected number of performed edits in line 16. Also, we update the expected number of the correct edits based on the number of change and the probability of a change to be correct in line 17. In lines 19 to 21, we calculate the expected precision, recall and F-score based on the expected gold edits, performed edits, and correct edits calculated at lines 2, 16, and 17. If the F-score is higher than the old F-score, which means that applying the correction c on the text T[1..n] will increase the expected F-score, then go to line 10 and start a new iteration in the loop. And if the F-score is lower than the old F-score, which means that applying the correction c on the text T[1..n] will decrease the expected F-score, then exit the loop and return the modified text T'[1..n].

To calculate the correctness probability of a rule, we apply the rule to the training set, then we calculate the number of correct edits, and the number of performed edits, finally we calculate the probability as the ratio between the correct and the performed edits. For example, let's consider the rule to be a simple edit rule as shown below:

RULE: Replace the word **W1** by the word **W2**.

W1	W2	Correct Edits	Performed Edits	p
امريكا AmrykA	أمريكا >mrykA	785	786	0.99
اميركا AmyrkA	أمريكا mrykA	25	54	0.46
اميركا AmyrkA	أميركا >myrkA	29	54	0.54
لان lAn	لأن l>n	690	702	0.98
اسرائيل AsrA}yl	إسرائيل <srA}yl	1087	1088	0.99
ان An	إن <n	1507	9359	0.16

Table 1: Examples of Correction Rules Precisions

The calculation of the correctness probability is the same when applied to more complex rules. One naïve method to generate rules, is to extract all edit rules from the training set and, calculate their probabilities, and finally adding them to the rules file. The algorithm will deal with multiple edit rules with the same first word (W1) by ignoring the rules with smaller probability. For example, ("اميركا", "AmyrkA") if it is going to be modified, it will always be edited to ("أميركا", ">myrkA").

4 Correction Rules

After we have discussed the main idea of algorithm, in the following subsections we will discuss some of the extracted corrections rules based on the word pattern and the syntactic error correction rules. These rules and their probabilities are compiled by analyzing the training data.

4.1 Patterns Corrections Rules

We have modified the morphological analyzer, BAMA-v2.0 (Buckwalter Arabic morphological analyzer version 2.0) (Buckwalter, 2010), to be able to assign an appropriate pattern to each word.

These patterns will be used to make rules based on the words patterns. For example, removing the unnecessary determinant ("ال", "Al"), or adding necessary determinant ("ال", "Al") which are common errors in the second language text. Another example, these patterns could be used to correct errors based on type mismatch between masculine or feminine words. Also, it could be used to correct errors on count mismatch is plural or dual or singular words. Finally, simple punctuation rules could be put based on the words patterns.

4.2 Syntactic Errors Corrections

The syntactic errors are the most difficult error to correct. For this task we apply a statistical grammatical analyzer to assign simple grammatical tag to the words. And based on these tags, we apply different correction rules. For example, nouns are genitive if they occur after a preposition ("حرف جر"," Hrf jr"), or if they are possessives ("مضاف إليه", "mDAf <lyh") or if they are adjectives ("نعت", "nEt") of genitive nouns, or if they are conjunction ("معطوف", "mETwf") with genitive noun, or if they are appositions ("بدل", "bdl") to genitive noun. And based on these facts the following simple rule could be applied.

RULE: Plural and Dual genitive nouns that end with ("ون", "wn") or ("ان", "An") should end with ("ين", "yn").

For the construction of this grammatical system, we used the data provided by Ibrahim 2015. To assign an appropriate grammatical tag to the tokens, the classifier training and testing could be characterized as follow:

Input: A sequence of transliterated Arabic tokens processed from left-to-right with break markers for word boundaries.

Context: A window of -3/+3 tokens centered at the focus token.

Features: The 7 tokens themselves, POS tag decisions for tokens within context, the base phrase chunk for tokens within the context, the root of the words within the context,, the pattern of the words within the context, whether the word is definite or not, whether the word is feminine or not, and whether the word is plural or dual or singular.

Classifier: CRF suite classifier.

5 Results and discussion

For the evaluation of the system, we used the M2 scorer by Dahlmeier and Ng (2012). When we evaluated the system with the Alj-dev-2014 dataset, we have reached an F-score of 0.6872; and F-score of 0.6668 on Alj-test-2014 dataset and an F-score of 07287 when evaluated on Alj-test-2015 dataset. For the second language, the system achieved an F-score of 0.5673 on L2-dev-2015 dataset, and an F-score of 0.3569 on the L2-test-2015 dataset.

The proposed algorithm is very fast compared to traditional error correction algorithm, since that the algorithm ranks the rules during the training time, and applies one rule at the time until the expected F-score decreases. But as a direct result to the design of the algorithm, and its concern in maximizing the overall F-score of the test set, the algorithm may apply the rule with the highest probability till it saturates, i.e. it applies the rule to the first few errors and stops if this is going to decrease the expected value for the F-score.

Also, one can notice, that this algorithm may apply correction rules with probability less than 0.5 (which means that applying this rule is expected to cause more errors than correcting wrong word), it all depends on the value of the precision and the recall. Although that seems to be a little bit not logical but this could be justified by its ability to maximize the F-score. This is not an issue from the algorithm, this problem arises from the properties of the F-score. This shows the problem in using the F-score for evaluating the text error correction systems, and it opens the doors for researchers to find a new metric to measure the performance of the text error correction systems.

Another problem in the F-score as an evaluation metric for the error correction systems is that if a word contains more than one error, if you correct one of these errors and not the others the entire word is considered wrong. An example of a word that contains one syntax error and anther syntactic error is: ("العراقون", "AlErAqwn") in the context ("مع العراقون", "mE AlErAqwn"). The word should be corrected to ("العراقيين", "AlErAqyyn"), but if it is corrected to ("العراقيون", "AlErAqywn") which means the syntax error is handled and the syntactic is not, the entire word will be considered as wrong.

6 Conclusions and Future Work

In this paper we have improved a previously proposed system for text correction for Arabic. The proposed algorithm has has the potential to be further improved. As a future work, the punctuation error correction might need to be further improved. And finally, the rules used in the framework could be extended by further analysis of the training data. As a future work, we can merge the proposed algorithm with other error correction technique, and use it as an acceptance-rejection scheme for the other error correction algorithm. Another future work, is to propose another evaluation metric for the text error correction systems.

References

Mohamed I. Alkanhal, Mohammed A. Al-Badrashiny, Mansour M. Alghamdi, and Abdulaziz O. AlQabbany. 2012. Automatic Stochastic Arabic Spelling Correction with Emphasis on Space Insertions and Deletions. *IEEE Transactions on Audio, Speech & Language Processing*, 20:2111–2122.

Michele Banko and Eric Brill, 2001. Scaling to very very large corpora for natural language disambiguation. In *Proceedings of 39th Annual Meeting of the Association for Computational Linguistics*. Toulouse, France.

Chiraz Ben Othmane Zribi and Mohammed Ben Ahmed. 2003. Efficient Automatic Correction of Misspelled Arabic Words Based on Contextual Information. In *Proceedings of the Knowledge-*

Based Intelligent Information and Engineering Systems Conference, Oxford, UK.

Tim Buckwalter. 2010. Buckwalter Arabic Morphological Analyzer Version 2.0. Linguistic Data Consortium, University of Pennsylvania, 2002. LDC Catalog No.: LDC2004L02. ISBN 1-58563-324-0.

Andrew Carlson and Ian Fette. 2007. Memory-based context-sensitive spelling correction at web scale. In *Proceedings of the IEEE International Conference on Machine Learning and Applications (ICMLA)*.

Daniel Dahlmeier and Hwee Tou Ng. 2012. Better evaluation for grammatical error correction. In *Proceeding of the 2012 Conference of the North American Chapter of the Association for Computational Linguistics: Human Language Technologies*.

Andrew R. Golding and Dan Roth. 1999. A Winnow based approach to context-sensitive spelling correction. *Machine Learning*, 34(1-3):107–130.

Bassam Haddad and Mustafa Yaseen. 2007. Detection and Correction of Non-Words in Arabic: A Hybrid Approach. *International Journal of Computer Processing Of Languages (IJCPOL)*.

Ahmed Hassan, Sara Noeman, and Hany Hassan. 2008. Language Independent Text Correction using Finite State Automata. In *Proceedings of the International Joint Conference on Natural Language Processing (IJCNLP 2008)*.

Karen Kukich. 1992. Techniques for Automatically Correcting Words in Text. *ACM Computing Surveys*, 24(4).

Arfath Pasha and Mohamed Al-Badrashiny and Ahmed El Kholy and Ramy Eskander and Mona Diab and Nizar Habash and Manoj Pooleery and Owen Rambow and Ryan Roth. 2014. MADAMIRA: A Fast, Comprehensive Tool for Morphological Analysis and Disambiguation of Arabic. In Proceedings of the Ninth International Conference on Language Resources and Evaluation (LREC)

Alla Rozovskaya, Nizar Habash, Ramy Eskander, Noura Farra, and Wael Salloum. 2014. The Columbia System in the QALB-2014 Shared Task on Arabic Error Correction. In Proceedings of EMNLP Workshop on Arabic Natural Language Processing: QALB Shared Task.

Alla Rozovskaya, Nizar Habash, Wajdi Zaghouani, Ossama Obeid, and Behrang Mohit. 2015. The Second QALB Shared Task on Automatic Text Correction for Arabic. In *Proceedings of ACL workshop on Arabic Natural Language Processing*. Beijing, China.

Khaled Shaalan, Rana Aref, and Aly Fahmy. 2010. An approach for analyzing and correcting spelling errors for non-native Arabic learners. In *Proceedings of Informatics and Systems (INFOS).*Ibrahim, Michael Nawar. 2015. Statistical Arabic Grammar Analyzer. *Computational Linguistics and Intelligent Text Processing. Springer International Publishing. 187-200.*

Behrang Mohit, Alla Rozovskaya, Nizar Habash, Wajdi Zaghouani, and Ossama Obeid, 2014. The First shared Task on Automatic Text Correction for Arabic. In *Proceedings of EMNLP workshop on Arabic Natural Language Processing*. Doha, Qatar.

Nawar, Michael N., and Moheb M. Ragheb. 2014. Fast and robust arabic error correction system. *ANLP 2014. 143.*

Wajdi Zaghouani, Behrang Mohit, Nizar Habash, Ossama Obeid, Nadi Tomeh, Alla Rozovskaya, Noura Farra, Sarah Alkuhlani, and Kemal Oflazer. 2014. Large Scale Arabic Error Annotation: Guidelines and Framework. In *Proceedings of the Ninth International Conference on Language Resources and Evaluation (LREC'14)*, Reykjavik, Iceland.

Wajdi Zaghouani, Nizar Habash, Houda Bouamor, Alla Rozovskaya, Behrang Mohit, Abeer Heider, and Kemal Oflazer. 2015. Correction Annotation for Non-Native Arabic Texts: Guidelines and Corpus. In *Proceedings of the Ninth Linguistic Annotation Workshop*, Denver, Colorado, USA. *Association for Computational Linguistics. 129-139.*

GWU-HASP-2015@QALB-2015 Shared Task: Priming Spelling Candidates with Probability[1]

Mohammed Attia, Mohamed Al-Badrashiny, Mona Diab
Department of Computer Science
The George Washington University
{Mohattia;badrashiny;mtdiab}@gwu.edu

Abstract

In this paper, we describe our system HASP-2015 (Hybrid Arabic Spelling and Punctuation Corrector) in which we introduce significant improvements over our previous version HASP-2014 and with which we participated in the QALB-2015 Second Shared Task on Arabic Error Correction. Our system utilizes probabilistic information on errors and their possible corrections in the training data and combine that with an open-source reference dictionary (or word list) for detecting errors and generating and filtering candidates. We enhance our system further by allowing it to generate candidates for common semantic and grammatical errors. Eventually, an n-gram language model is used for selecting best candidates. We use a CRF (Conditional Random Fields) classifier for correcting punctuation errors in a two-pass process where first the system learns punctuation placement, and then it learns to identify punctuation types.

1 Introduction

In this paper we describe our system for Arabic spelling error detection and correction, HASP-2015 (Hybrid Arabic Spelling and Punctuation Corrector). We introduce significant improvements to our previous version HASP-2014 (Attia et al., 2014). We participate with HASP-2015 in the QALB-2015 Second Shared Task on Arabic Error Correction (Rozovskaya et al., 2015).

The problem of Arabic spelling error correction has been investigated in a number of papers (Haddad and Yaseen, 2007; Alfaifi and Atwell, 2012; Hassan et al., 2008; Attia et al., 2012; Alkanhal et al., 2012). Significant contributions were also introduced in the 2014 Shared Task on Arabic Error Correction (Mohit et al., 2014) including (Rozovskaya et al., 2014; Nawar and Ragheb, 2014; Jeblee et al., 2014; and Mubarak and Darwish, 2014).

The QALB-2015 shared task is an extension of the first QALB shared task (Mohit et al., 2014) that took place in 2014. QALB-2014 addressed errors in comments written to Aljazeera articles by native Arabic speakers (Zaghouani et al., 2014). This year's competition includes two tracks, and, in addition to errors produced by native speakers, also includes correction of texts written by learners of Arabic as a foreign language (L2) (Zaghouani et al., 2015). The native track includes Alj-train-2014, Alj-dev-2014, Alj-test-2014 texts from QALB-2014. The L2 track includes L2-train-2015 and L2-dev-2015. This data was released for the development of the systems. The systems are scored on blind test sets Alj-test-2015 and L2-test-2015. Our system is ranked third and fourth on the Alj and L2, respectively.

The shared task data deals with "errors" in the general sense which comprise: a) punctuation errors; b) non-word errors; c) real-word spelling errors; d) grammatical errors (related to case, number and gender); and, e) affective variations such as elongation (kashida) and speech effects such as character multiplication for emphasis. Our previous system, HASP-2014, handles only types (a), (b), and (e) errors. We extend our systemt HASP-2015 to provide coverage for and address types (d) and (e) spelling errors.

[1] This work was supported by the Defense Advanced Research Projects Agency (DARPA) Contract No. HR0011-12-C-0014, BOLT program with subcontract from Raytheon BBN.

Proceedings of the Second Workshop on Arabic Natural Language Processing, pages 138–143,
Beijing, China, July 26-31, 2015.

2 Our Methodology

Our system uses a pipeline of four components: 1) regular expression normalization for deterministic errors, 2) A discriminative classifier for punctuation errors, 3) Spelling detection and handling, and, 4) Post-processing for fixing common system errors.

For punctuation errors, we use a classifier in a two-pass process where first the system learns punctuation placement, and then it learns to identify punctuation types. The reason for this staging is that learning six punctuation types at once could be problematic for the classifier, and we hypothesize that splitting the task of placement from identification, where in the first step it makes a binary decision of whether or not to insert a punctuation mark, and in the second step it predicts the type of that punctuation mark.

In HASP-2014, we only rely on a reference dictionary (or word list) for detecting errors and generating candidates. The candidates were generated according to the edit distance between the erroneous word and possible candidates.

In HASP-2015, we generate probabilistic information from the training data on errors and their possible corrections and utilize this information in detecting errors and generating candidates. The reference dictionary is relegated to as a back-off function when no probabilistic information is available in the training data. Our system is able to detect and generate candidates for common semantic and grammatical errors. Candidates and their probabilistic scores are passed an n-gram language model for selecting best candidates. Our system is explained in detail in the next section.

For organizational purposes, we divide errors into two types: a) nonverbal errors which include affective variations, punctuation, word merges and word splits; and b) verbal errors, which include non-word error, real-word error, grammatical errors, and dialectal words/expressions. In other words, verbal errors are related to the alphabetical buildup of words, and non-verbal errors go beyond this alphabetical buildup.

3 Nonverbal Errors

Nonverbal errors include affective variations, punctuation errors, word merges and word splits.

3.1 Affective Variations

There are many instances in the shared task's data that can be treated using simple and straightforward conversion via regular expression replace rules. We estimate that these instances cover 10% of the non-punctuation errors in the development set. In HASP, we use deterministic heuristic rules to normalize the text, including the removal of speech effects, such as الرجاااال AlrjAAAAl 'men' which is converted to الرجال AlrjAl, the removal of decorative kashida, e.g. دمـــاء dm__A' 'blood', and the conversion of Hindi digits (٠١٢٣٤٥٦٧٨٩) into Arabic digits [0-9].

3.2 Punctuation Errors

Punctuation errors constitute 40% of the errors in the QALB Arabic data. In HASP-2015, we continue to handle the six basic punctuation marks: comma, colon, semi-colon, exclamation mark, question mark, and period.

For classification, we use a Conditional Random Field, CRF++ classifier (Lafferty et al. 2001) with window size 5. The features we use are extracted from the 'column' file in the QALB shared task data, which includes preprocessing with MADAMIRA morphological disambiguator (Pasha et al., 2014). In HASP-2015, we split the task of the classifier into two subtasks: placement and identification.

Experiment	R	P	F
Baseline	45.70	76.01	57.08
Pass_II + Alj_Training	52.11	72.33	60.58
Pass_II + Merge_Training	**52.17**	**72.38**	**60.63**

Table 1. CRF Pass II results for Alj

Experiment	R	P	F
Baseline	13.87	20.57	16.57
Pass_II + Alj_Training	37.38	30.53	33.61
Pass_II + Merge_Training	**33.98**	**33.73**	**33.86**

Table 2. CRF Pass II results for L2

Pass I: Placement

The placement subtask is a binary classification task where the classifier decides whether a punctuation mark (regardless of the type) should be included or not. We use five features in this process:

(1) The original word, that is the word as it appears in the text without any further processing, (e.g., للتشاور llt$Awr 'for consulting');
(2) Stem. We use the Penn Arabic Treebank (PATB) tokenization (e.g., ل+التشاور l+Alt$Awr) and strip off the clitics (e.g., التشاور Alt$Awr);
(3) Kulick (Kulick et al., 2011) POS tag (e.g., IN+DT+NN);
(4) Buckwalter POS tag (e.g., PREP+DET+NOUN+CASE_DEF_GN) as produced by MADAMIRA;
(5) Classes to be predicted: punc_after and NA.

Pass II: Identification

This stage uses the same set of features of the placement stage in addition to its output to determine the type of punctuation mark to be placed. The predicted class is one of the following seven: colon_after, comma_after, exclmark_after, period_after, qmark_after, semicolon_after, and NA.

This two-pass process shows significant improvement over the baseline for Alj and L2 data as illustrated in Table 1 and 2.

2.3 Word Merges

Merged words are when the space(s) between two or more words is deleted, such as هذاالنظام h*AAlnZAm 'this system', which should be هذا النظام h*A AlnZAm. These errors constitute 3.67% and 3.48% of the error types in the shared task's development and training data, respectively. We use Attia et al.'s (2012) algorithm for dealing with merged words, $l - 3$, where l is word length.

Moreover, we found out that common merge errors and their correction can conveniently be learned from the training data, leading to significant improvement as shown in the final results. Here are some examples of frequent merge errors:

- yArb يارب "O Lord" → yA rb
- EbdAllh عبدالله"Abdullah"→Ebd Allh

2.4 Word Splits

Beside the problem of merged words, there is also the problem of split words, where one or more spaces are inserted within a word, such as صم ام Sm Am 'valve' (the correct form is صمام SmAm). This error constitutes 6% of the shared task's found in the training and development sets. We found that the vast majority of instances of this type of error involve the clitic conjunction *waw* "and", which should be represented as a word prefix. Therefore, we opted to handle this problem in our work in a partial and shallow manner using deterministic rules by the reattachment of the separated conjunction morpheme *waw* و w "and" to the succeeding word.

4 Verbal Errors

Verbal errors include non-word errors, real-word errors, grammatical errors, and dialectal words/expressions.

4.1 Error Detection

The method for detecting spelling errors have usually varied according to the type of error. A non-word spelling error is typically defined as (adapted from Brill, and Moore, 2000): given an alphabet Σ, a reference dictionary D consisting of strings in Σ^*, a given word is a spelling error s if $s \in \Sigma^*$ and $s \notin D$.

For real-word errors, a reference dictionary will not help, as both the error and the correction are valid words in isolation. Instead, a language model, for example, is used to estimate the likelihood of words in a certain context, and words that fall below a certain threshold are considered as a possible error. POS bigrams and tri-grams have also been used for that purpose (Kukich, 1992).

We employ a single algorithm to detect all types of spelling errors, whether non-word, semantic, grammatical or dialectal. Our algorithm for error detection is to find words in the training data where $n(P(s \mid c)) > P(s \mid s')$, where s is a spelling error, c is the correction, n is a threshold and s` is s considered as a candidate. This translates to the probability of c given s times n is greater than the probability of s' given s. In our system, we set the threshold $n = 2$ which effectively mean that a semantic error is only considered when the probability of the correction is more than half the probability of the reference word. The threshold estimation is an empirical question determined by the robustness of the language model and the quantity of noise in the training data.

In HASP-2015, the reference dictionary is not totally discarded, but used as a back-off resource to cover instances not included in the training data. We use AraComLex Extended, an open-source reference dictionary (or word list) of 9.2M full-formed words (Attia et al., 2012) as our backup reference dictionary.

4.2 Candidate Generation

Correcting spelling errors is ideally treated as a probabilistic problem formulated as (Kernigan, 1990; Norvig, 2009; Brill, and Moore, 2000):

$$argmax_c \, P(s \mid c) \, P(c)$$

Here $P(c)$ is the probability that c is the correct word (or the language model), and $P(s \mid c)$ is the probability that s is typed when c is intended (the error model or noisy channel model), $argmax_c$ is the scoring mechanism that computes the correction c that maximizes the probability.

In HASP-2014, we ranked candidates according to their edit distance score using the finite state compiler, foma (Hulden, 2009), but in HASP-2015, we rank candidates according to their probability, $(s \mid c)$, as derived from the training data, and we pass candidates along with their probability scores to the language model. Again, the edit distance candidates and their ranking are used when no probability information is available from the training data. The following are some illustrative examples of the statistical information extracted from the training data for the various error types.

Non-word errors:
An ان "that" >n#7781; <n#1485; |n#29
AlA الا "but" <lA#1442; >lA#225

Semantic errors:
Alhm الهم "worry" Alhm#20; Allhm#17
Ely علي "on" ElY#818; Ely#318

Grammatical errors:
mjrmyn مجرمين "criminals" mjrmyn#31; mjrmwn#16
lyl ليل "night" lyl#34; lylA#16

Dialectal words:
bs بس "but" lkn#67; fqT#27
AHnA احنا "we" nHn#65; >HnA#9

Additionally, we use some generic rules to generate candidates for possible dialectal errors:

- Add *A* after final *w* as in آمنوا *|manuw* "they believe",
- Remove the colloquial aspectual clitic particle *b* before the perfective initials *n, y, t*.

5 Error Correction and Final Results

For error correction, namely selecting the best solution among the list of candidates, we use an n-gram language model (LM), as implemented in the SRILM package (Stolcke et al., 2011). We use the 'disambig' tool for selecting candidates from a map file where erroneous words are provided with a list of possible corrections. We also use the 'ngram' utility in post-processing for deciding on whether a split-word solution has a better probability than a single word solution. Our tri-gram language model is trained on the Arabic Gigaword Corpus, 5th edition (Parker et al., 2011) and a corpus crawled from Al-Jazeera (Attia et al.; 2012).

For the LM disambiguation we use the '-fb' option (forward-backward tracking), and we provide candidates with probability scores collected from the QALB training data. Both of the forward-backward tracking and the probability scores in tandem yield better results than the default values. We evaluate the performance of our system against the gold standard using the *Max-Match* (M^2) method for evaluating grammatical error correction by Dahlmeier and Ng (2012).

Our best f-score is obtained by priming candidates from the training data, adding Al-Jazeera corpus to Gigaword 5, and using the two-pass CRF punctuation prediction. Table 3 and 4 show the results on Alj and L2 development sets respectively. Table 5 shows the results on Alj and L2 test sets.

#	Experiment	R	P	F
1	Baseline (HASP'14)	52.98	75.47	62.25
2	Prime non-word candidates from the training set	55.26	77.40	64.48
3	Include real-word candidates from the training data	57.87	77.03	66.09
4	Prime merge errors from the training set	58.67	77.70	66.86
5	Post-processing	58.80	77.83	66.99
6	Two-pass punctuation correction	60.40	76.57	67.53
7	3 gram LM and adding Al-Jazeera corpus to Gigaword	**60.59**	**76.65**	**67.68**

Table 3. Results for Alj-test-2014 (dev set)

#	Experiment	R	P	F
1	Baseline	22.27	56.80	31.99
2	3 gram LM and adding Al-Jazeera corpus to Gigaword	**22.35**	**57.17**	**32.14**

Table 4. System results for L2-dev-2015

#	Experiment	R	P	F
1	Alj-test-2015	67.51	74.69	70.92
2	L2-test-2015	23.32	55.66	32.87

Table 5. System results for the test sets

For the baseline, we use the older version of our system (HASP-2014), and the results show significant improvement in performance. The biggest two gains in performance, as shown in Table 3, came from experiments 2 and 3 when candidates and their probabilities were extracted from the training data and used to supplement candidates generated from the reference dictionary using edit distance. Experiment 3, i.e. using real-word candidate allowed our system to handle semantic and grammatical errors, a domain which was beyond the scope of the previous version. Dialectal errors were included in Experiment 2 dealing with non-word candidates. It is to be noted the system can benefit from a larger training set if that becomes available in the future.

The slight improvements gained by experiments 4 through 7 are an indication of the dimensions along which future improvements might be achieved. These dimensions include better way of handling merge errors, post-processing for correcting system-specific errors, better handling of punctuation errors, and better selection of data for training the language model.

It is also to be noted that the gold data suffers from instances of inconsistency. For example لابد lAbd "must" is split as two words لا بد lA bd in 64% of the cases, while مازال mAzAl "still" is split in 32% of the cases.

Moreover, while conducting error analysis we found many errors in the manual annotation of the gold development data. For example, اللذي All*y "who" is incorrectly corrected as الذى Al*Y while the correct correction is الذي Al*y and many more errors are not detected at all in the gold data, such as انكم، Ankm "you" and الملتحدة AlmltHdp for المتحدة AlmtHdp "united". In total, we automatically found over 200 errors in the gold development data, but with manual checking it is found that some of the instances are incorrectly reported. However, we assume that more investigation of the consistency and accuracy of the gold data can lead to better performance and better evaluation of the systems participating in the shared task.

6 Conclusion

We have described our system HASP for the automatic correction of spelling and punctuation mistakes in Arabic. To our knowledge, this is the first system to handle punctuation errors. We utilize and improve on an open-source full-form dictionary, introduce a better algorithm for handing merged word errors, tune the LM parameters, and combine the various components together, leading to cumulative improved results.

References

Alkanhal, Mohamed I., Mohamed A. Al-Badrashiny, Mansour M. Alghamdi, and Abdulaziz O. Al-Qabbany. (2012) Automatic Stochastic Arabic Spelling Correction With Emphasis on Space Insertions and Deletions. IEEE Transactions on Audio, Speech, and Language Processing, Vol. 20, No. 7, September 2012.

Attia, Mohammed, Mohamed Al-Badrashiny, Mona Diab. GWU-HASP: Hybrid Arabic Spelling and Punctuation Corrector. Proceedings of the EMNLP 2014 Workshop on Arabic Natural Langauge Processing (ANLP), pages 148–154, October 25, 2014, Doha, Qatar.

Attia, Mohammed, Pavel Pecina, Younes Samih, Khaled Shaalan, Josef van Genabith. 2012. Improved Spelling Error Detection and Correction for Arabic. COLING 2012, Bumbai, India.

Brill, Eric and Moore, Robert C. (2000) An improved error model for noisy channel spelling correction. Proceedings of the 38th Annual Meeting of the Association for Computational Linguistics, Hong Kong, pp. 286–293.

Dahlmeier, Daniel and Ng, Hwee Tou. 2012. Better evaluation for grammatical error correction. In Proceedings of NAACL.

Haddad, B., and Yaseen, M. (2007) Detection and Correction of Non-Words in Arabic: A Hybrid Approach. International Journal of Computer Processing of Oriental Languages. Vol. 20, No. 4.

Hassan, A, Noeman, S., and Hassan, H. (2008) Language Independent Text Correction using Finite State Automata. IJCNLP. Hyderabad, India.

Hulden, M. (2009) Foma: a Finite-state compiler and library. EACL '09 Proceedings of the 12th Conference of the European Chapter of the Association for Computational Linguistics. Association for Computational Linguistics Stroudsburg, PA, USA

Jeblee, S., Bouamor, H., Zaghouani, W., and Oflazer, K. 2014. CMUQ@QALB-2014: An SMT-based System for Automatic Arabic Error Correction. In Proceedings of EMNLP Workshop on Arabic Natural Language Processing: QALB Shared Task.

Kulick Seth. Exploiting separation of closed-class categories for Arabic tokenization and part-of-speech tagging. In Graham Katz and Mona Diab, editors, Special Issue on Arabic Computational Linguistics, ACM Transactions on Asian Language Information Processing. 2011.

Kernigan, M., Church, K., Gale W. (1990). A Spelling Correction Program Based on a Noisy Channel Model. AT & T Laboratories, 600 Mountain Ave., Murray Hill, NJ.

Kukich, Karen. (1992) Techniques for automatically correcting words in text. Computing Surveys, 24(4), pp. 377–439.

Lafferty, John, Andrew McCallum, and Fernando Pereira. (2001) Conditional random fields: Probabilistic models for segmenting and labeling sequence data, In Proceedings of the International Conference on Machine Learning (ICML 2001), MA, USA, pp. 282-289.

Mohit, Behrang, Alla Rozovskaya, Nizar Habash, Wajdi Zaghouani, and Ossama Obeid, 2014. The First QALB Shared Task on Automatic Text Correction for Arabic. In Proceedings of EMNLP workshop on Arabic Natural Language Processing. Doha, Qatar.

Mubarak, H. and Darwish, K. 2014. Automatic Correction of Arabic Text: a Cascaded Approach. In Proceedings of EMNLP Workshop on Arabic Natural Language Processing: QALB Shared Task.

Nawar, M. and Ragheb, M. 2014. Fast and Robust Arabic Error Correction System. In Proceedings of EMNLP Workshop on Arabic Natural Language Processing: QALB Shared Task.

Ng, Hwee Tou, Siew Mei Wu, Yuanbin Wu, Christian Hadiwinoto, and Joel Tetreault. (2013) The CoNLL-2013 Shared Task on Grammatical Error Correction. Proceedings of the Seventeenth Conference on Computational Natural Language Learning: Shared Task, pages 1–12, Sofia, Bulgaria, August 8-9 2013.

Norvig, P. (2009) Natural language corpus data. In Beautiful Data, edited by Toby Segaran and Jeff Hammerbacher, pp. 219- "-242. Sebastopol, Calif.: O'Reilly.

Och, Franz Josef, Hermann Ney. (2003) A Systematic Comparison of Various Statistical Alignment Models. In Computational Linguistics, volume 29, number 1, pp. 19-51 March 2003.

Parker, R., Graff, D., Chen, K., Kong, J., and Maeda, K. (2011) Arabic Gigaword Fifth Edition. LDC Catalog No.: LDC2011T11, ISBN: 1-58563-595-2.

Pasha, Arfath, Mohamed Al-Badrashiny, Ahmed El Kholy, Ramy Eskander, Mona Diab, Nizar Habash, Manoj Pooleery, Owen Rambow, Ryan Roth. (2014) MADAMIRA: A Fast, Comprehensive Tool for Morphological Analysis and Disambiguation of Arabic. In Proceedings of the 9th International Conference on Language Resources and Evaluation (LREC 2014), Reykjavik, Iceland.

Rozovskaya, Alla, Houda Bouamor, Nizar Habash, Wajdi Zaghouani, Ossama Obeid and Behrang Mohit. (2015) The Second QALB Shared Task on Automatic Text Correction for Arabic. Proceedings of ACL Workshop on Arabic Natural Language, Beijing, China.

Rozovskaya, A., Habash, N., Eskander, R., Farra, N., and Salloum, W. (2014) The Columbia System in the QALB-2014 Shared Task on Arabic Error Correction. In Proceedings of EMNLP Workshop on Arabic Natural Language Processing: QALB Shared Task.

Stolcke, A., Zheng, J., Wang, W., and Abrash, V. (2011) SRILM at sixteen: Update and outlook. in Proc. IEEE Automatic Speech Recognition and Understanding Workshop. Waikoloa, Hawaii.

Zaghouani, Wajdi, Habash, Nizar, Bouamor, Houda, Rozovskaya, Alla, Mohit, Behrang, Heider, Abeer and Oflazer, Kemal. 2015. Correction Annotation for Non-Native Arabic Texts: Guidelines and Corpus. Proceedings of The 9th Linguistic Annotation Workshop, Denver, Colorado, USA, pp. 129-139.

Zaghouani, Wajdi, Behrang Mohit, Nizar Habash, Ossama Obeid, Nadi Tomeh, Alla Rozovskaya, Noura Farra, Sarah Alkuhlani, and Kemal Oflazer. 2014. Large Scale Arabic Error Annotation: Guidelines and Framework. In Proceedings of the Ninth International Conference on Language Resources and Evaluation (LREC'14), Reykjavik, Iceland.

QCMUQ@QALB-2015 Shared Task: Combining Character level MT and Error-tolerant Finite-State Recognition for Arabic Spelling Correction

Houda Bouamor[1], **Hassan Sajjad**[2], **Nadir Durrani**[2] **and Kemal Oflazer**[1]
[1]**Carnegie Mellon University in Qatar**
hbouamor@qatar.cmu.edu, ko@cs.cmu.edu
[2]**Qatar Computing Research Institute**
{hsajjad,ndurrani}@qf.org.qa

Abstract

We describe the CMU-Q and QCRI's joint efforts in building a spelling correction system for Arabic in the QALB 2015 Shared Task. Our system is based on a hybrid pipeline that combines rule-based linguistic techniques with statistical methods using language modeling and machine translation, as well as an error-tolerant finite-state automata method. We trained and tested our spelling corrector using the dataset provided by the shared task organizers. Our system outperforms the baseline system and yeilds better correction quality with an F-score of 68.12 on L1-test-2015 testset and 38.90 on the L2-test-2015. This ranks us 2nd in the L2 subtask and 5th in the L1 subtask.

1 Introduction

With the increased usage of computers in the processing of various languages comes the need for correcting errors introduced at different stages. Hence, the topic of text correction has seen a lot of interest in the past several years (Haddad and Yaseen, 2007; Rozovskaya et al., 2013). Numerous approaches have been explored to correct spelling errors in texts using NLP tools and resources (Kukich, 1992; Oflazer, 1996). The spelling correction for Arabic is an understudied problem in comparison to English, although small amount of research has been done previously (Shaalan et al., 2003; Hassan et al., 2008). The reason for this is the complexity of Arabic language and unavailability of language resources. For example, the Arabic spell checker in Microsoft Word gives incorrect suggests for even simple errors. First shared task on automatic Arabic text correction (Mohit et al., 2014) has been established recently. Its goal is to develop and evaluate spelling correction systems for Arabic trained either on naturally occurring errors in text written by humans or machines. Similar to the first version, in this task participants are asked to implement a system that takes as input MSA (Modern Standard Arabic) text with various spelling errors and automatically correct it. In this year's edition, participants are asked to test their systems on two text genres: (i) news corpus (mainly newswire extracted from Aljazeera); (ii) a corpus of sentences written by learners of Arabic as a Second Language (ASL). Texts produced by learners of ASL generally contain a number of spelling errors. The main problem faced by them is using Arabic with vocabulary and grammar rules that are different from their native language.

In this paper, we describe our Arabic spelling correction system. Our system is based on a hybrid pipeline which combines rule-based techniques with statistical methods using language modeling and machine translation, as well as an error-tolerant finite-state automata method. We trained and tested our spelling corrector using the dataset provided by the shared task organizers Arabic (Rozovskaya et al., 2015). Our systems outperform the baseline and achieve better correction quality with an F-score of 68.42% on the 2014 testset and 44.02 % on the L2 Dev.

2 Data Resources

QALB: We trained and evaluated our system using the data provided for the shared task and the m2Scorer (Dahlmeier and Ng, 2012). These datasets are extracted from the QALB corpus of human-edited Arabic text produced by native speakers, non-native speakers and machines (Zaghouani et al., 2014). The corpus contains a large

Proceedings of the Second Workshop on Arabic Natural Language Processing, pages 144–149,
Beijing, China, July 26-31, 2015. ©2014 Association for Computational Linguistics

	Train 14	%	Dev 14	%	L2 Train	%	L2 Dev	%
Word Count	925,643	-	48,471	-	51,483	-	29,475	-
Total Errors	306,757	33.14	16,659	34.37	13,206	25.65	7,293	24.74
Word errors	187,040	60.97	9,878	59.30	9,417	71.30	5,193	71.20
Punctuation Errors	618,886	39.03	6,781	40.70	3,789	28.70	2,100	28.79
Error per type								
Split	10,869	3.48	612	3.67	255	1.93	110	1.51
Add_before	99,258	32.36	5,704	34.24	3,721	28.17	2,067	28.34
Delete	6,778	2.21	338	2.03	576	4.36	324	4.44
Edit	169,769	55.34	8,914	53.51	8,009	60.64	4,434	60.79
Merge	18,267	5.95	994	5.97	662	5.01	380	5.21
Add_after	20	0.01	2	0.01	1	-	-	-
Move	427	0.14	13	0.08	132	0.9	102	1.39

Table 1: Statistics on Error Types in the QALB 2014 and 2015 datasets

dataset of manually corrected Arabic sentences. QALB covers a variety of errors, and is not just limited to typical spelling errors. For instance, train and dev-2014 data and up to 28% on the 2015 data provided in this Shared Task (See Table[1] 1).

Arabic Wordlist for Spellchecking: We used a list of 9-million Arabic words (Attia et al., 2012). The words are automatically generated from the AraComLex open-source finite state transducer. The entire list is validated against Microsoft Word spell checker.[2]

Monolingual Arabic corpus: Additionally, we used the GigaWord Arabic corpus and the News commentary corpus as used in state-of-the-art English-to-Arabic machine translation system (Sajjad et al., 2013b) to build different language models (character-level and word-level LMs). The complete corpus consists of 32 million sentences and approximately 1,700 million tokens. Due to computational limitations, we were able to train our language model only on 60% of the data which we randomly selected from the whole corpus.

3 Our Approach

Our automatic spelling corrector consists of a hybrid pipeline that combines five different and complementary approaches: (i) a morphology-based corrector; (ii) a rule-based corrector; (ii) an SMT(statistical machine translation)-based corrector; and (d) an error-tolerant finite-state automata approach.

Our system design is motivated by the diversity of the errors contained in our train and dev datasets (See Table 1). It was very challenging to design one system to handle all of the errors. We propose several expert systems each tacking a different kind of spelling errors. For example, we built a character-level machine translation system to handle cases of space insertion and deletion affecting non-clitics, as this part is specifically treated by the rule-based module. To cover some remaining character-level spelling mistakes, we use a Finite-State-Automata (FSA) approach. All our systems run on top of each other, gradually correcting the Arabic text in steps.

3.1 MADAMIRA Corrections (Morph)

MADAMIRA (Pasha et al., 2014) is a tool, originally designed for morphological analysis and disambiguation of MSA and dialectal Arabic texts. MADAMIRA employs different features to select, for each word in context, a proper analysis and performs Alif and Ya spelling correction for the phenomena associated with its letters. The task organizers provided the shared task data preprocessed with MADAMIRA, including all of the features generated by the tool for every word.

Similar to Jeblee et al. (2014), we used the corrections proposed by MADAMIRA and apply them to the data. We show in Section 4 that while the correction candidate proposed by MADAMIRA may not be necessarily correct, it performs at a very high precision.

[1]Part of the statistics reported in Table 1 is taken from Diab et al. (2014)

[2]The list is freely available at: http://sourceforge.net/projects/arabic-wordlist/

Original	**Source**	ألذي شاهدته في أليوتوب هو ان ...‘
	Target	الذي شاهدته في اليوتوب هو أن ...
	English	*which I have seen in Youtube is that*
Characters	**Source**	أ ل ذ ي # ش ا ه د ت ه #ف ي #أ ل ي و ت و ب #ه و #ا ن # ...
	Target	ا ل ذ ي #ش ا ه د ت ه #ف ي #ا ل ي و ت و ب #ه و #أ ن # ...

Table 2: Preparing the training and tuning and test corpus for alignment

3.2 Rule-based Corrector (Rules)

The MADAMIRA corrector described above does not handle splits and merges; In addition to that, we use the rule-based corrector described in (Rozovskaya et al., 2014). The rules were created through analysis of samples of the 2014 training data. We also apply a set of rules to reattach clitics that may have been split apart from the base word. After examining the train dataset, we realized that 95% of word merging cases involve "و/w/'and'" attachment. Furthermore, we removed duplications and elongations by merging a sequence of two or more of the same character into a single instance.

3.3 Statistical Machine Translation Models

An SMT system translate sentence from one language into another. An alignment step learns mapping from source into target. A phrase-based model is subsequently learned from the word-alignments. The phrase-based model along with other decoding features, such as language and reordering models[3] are used to decode the test sentences. We will use the SMT framework for spell checker where error sentences act as our source and corrections act as a target in the training data.

Phrase-based error correction system (PBMT): The available training data from the shared task consists of parallel sentences. We build a phrase-based machine translation using it. Since the system learns at phrase-level, we hope to identify and correct different errors, especially the ones that were not captured by MADAMIRA.

Character-based error correction system (CBMT): There has been a lot of work in using character-based models for Arabic transliteration to English (Durrani et al., 2014c) and for conversion of Arabic dialects into MSA and vice verse (Sajjad et al., 2013a; Durrani et al., 2014a). The conversion of Arabic dialects to MSA at character-level can be seen as a spelling correction task where small character-level changes are made to convert a dialectal word into an MSA word. We also formulate our correction problem as a character-level machine translation problem, where the pre-processed incorrect Arabic text is considered as the source, and our target is the correct Arabic text provided by the Shared task organizers.

The goal is to learn correspondences between errors and their corrections. All the train data is used to train our the phrase-based model. We treat sentences as sequences of characters instead, as shown in Table 2. Our intuition behind using such model is that it may capture and correct: (i) split errors, occurring due to the deletion of a space between two words, and (ii) merge errors occurring due to the insertion of a space between two words by mistake; (iii) common spelling mistakes (hamzas, yas, etc).

We used the Moses toolkit (Koehn et al., 2007) to create a word and character levels model built on the best pre-processed data (mainly the feat14 tokens extracted using MADAMIRA described in 3.1). We use the standard setting of MGIZA (Gao and Vogel, 2008) and the grow-diagonal-final as the symmetrization heuristic (Och and Ney, 2003) of MOSES to get the character to character alignments. We build a 5-gram word and character language models using KenLM (Heafield, 2011).

3.4 Error-tolerant FST (EFST)

We adapted the error-tolerant recognition approach developed by Oflazer (1996). It was originally designed for the analysis of the agglutinative morphology of Turkish words and used for dictionary-based spelling corrector module. This error-tolerant finite-state recognizer identifies the strings that deviate mildly from a regular set of

[3] See (Durrani et al., 2014b) for more on state-of-the-art PBSMT and features used within.

	Alj-test-2014			L2-dev-2015		
	Precision	Recall	F1	Precision	Recall	F1
	Single Systems					
Morph	**78.33**	31.27	44.69	46.46	12.97	20.28
Rules	56.92	8.51	14.81	55.84	3.02	5.72
PBMT	73.29	50.18	59.58	53.20	21.10	30.34
CBMT	71.96	57.74	64.07	57.60	29.57	39.07
EFST	38.05	26.94	38.05	47.24	8.21	13.99
	System Combinations					
Morph+PBMT	72.94	55.14	62.80	56.55	24.57	34.26
Morph+CBMT	71.22	60.18	65.24	58.12	30.46	39.98
Morph+EFST	72.19	35.05	47.19	42.49	14.24	21.34
Morph+CBMT+Rules	70.45	65.55	67.91	58.21	34.35	43.20
Morph+CBMT+Rules+EFST	70.14	**66.79**	**68.42**	58.73	35.20	44.02

Table 3: System results on the QALB 2014 test set (left) and L2 dev set (right).

strings recognized by the underlying FSA. For example, suppose we have a recognizer for a regular set over a, b described by the regular expression (aba + bab)*, and we want to recognize the inputs that are slightly corrupted, for example, abaaaba may be matched to abaaba (correcting for a spurious a), or babbb may be matched to babbab (correcting for a deletion), or ababba may be matched to either abaaba (correcting a b to an a) or to ababab (correcting the reversal of the last two symbols). This method is perfect for handling mainly transposition errors resulting from swapping two letters , or typing errors of neighboring letters in the keyboard.

We use the Foma library (Hulden, 2009) to build the finite-state tranducer using the Arabic Word-list as a dictionary.[4] For each word, our system checks if the word is analyzed and recognized by the finite-state transducer. It then generates a list of correction candidates for the non-recognized ones. The candidates are words having an edit distance lower than a certain threshold. We score the different candidates using a LM and consider the best one as the possible correction for each word.

4 Evaluation and Results

We experimented with different configurations to reach an optimal setting when combining different modules. We evaluated our system for precision, recall, and F measure (F1) against the devset reference and the test 2014 set. Results for various system configurations on the L2 dev and test 2014 sets are given in Table 3. The results clearly show different modules are complementry. For instance, combining Morph and PBMT improves the results by +3.22 compared to only using the PBMT model, on last year's test set.

We achieved our best F-measure value with the following configuration: using CBMT system after applying the clitic re-attachment rules. These were then passed through the EFST. Using this combination we are able to correct 66.79% of the errors on the 2014 test set with a precision of 70.14%. Our system outperforms the baseline for the L2 data as well with an F-measure of 44.02% compared to (F1=20.28% when we use the Morph module).

5 QCMUQ@QALB-2015 Results

We present here the official results of our system (Morph+CBMT+Rules+EFST) on the 2015 QALB test set (Rozovskaya et al., 2015). The official results of our QCMUQ are presented in Table 4. These results rank us 2nd in the L2 subtask and 5th in the L1 subtask.

	P	R	F1
L1-test-2015	71.39	65.13	**68.12**
L2-test-2015	50.37	31.68	**38.90**

Table 4: The QCMUQ Official results on the 2015 test set.

[4]Foma is an open-source finite-state toolkit that implements the Xerox lexc and xfst utilities.

6 Conclusion and Future work

We described our system for automatic Arabic text correction. Our system combines rule-based methods with statistical techniques based on SMT framework and LM-based scoring. We additionally used finite-state-automata to do corrections. Our best system outperforms the baseline with an F-score of 68.12 on L1-test-2015 testset and 38.90 on the L2-test-2015. In the future, we want to focus on correcting punctuation errors, to produce a more accurate system. We plan to experiment with different combination methods similar to the ones used for combining MT outputs.

Acknowledgements

This publication was partly made possible by grants NPRP-4-1058-1-168 from the Qatar National Research Fund (a member of the Qatar Foundation).

References

Mohammed Attia, Pavel Pecina, Younes Samih, Khaled Shaalan, and Josef van Genabith. 2012. Improved Spelling Error Detection and Correction for Arabic. In *Proceedings of COLING 2012: Posters*, pages 103–112, Mumbai, India.

Daniel Dahlmeier and Hwee Tou Ng. 2012. Better Evaluation for Grammatical Error Correction. In *NAACL HLT '12 Proceedings of the 2012 Conference of the North American Chapter of the Association for Computational Linguistics: Human Language Technologies*, pages 568–572.

Mona Diab, Mohammed Attia, and Al-Badrashiny Mohamed. 2014. GWU-HASP: Hybrid Arabic Spelling and Punctuation Corrector. In *Proceedings of the EMNLP 2014 Workshop on Arabic Natural Language Processing (ANLP)*, Doha, Qatar.

Nadir Durrani, Yaser Al-Onaizan, and Abraham Ittycheriah. 2014a. Improving Egyptian-to-English SMT by mapping Egyptian into MSA. In *Computational Linguistics and Intelligent Text Processing*, pages 271–282, Khatmandu, Nepal. Springer Berlin Heidelberg.

Nadir Durrani, Barry Haddow, Philipp Koehn, and Kenneth Heafield. 2014b. Edinburgh's phrase-based machine translation systems for WMT-14. In *Proceedings of the ACL 2014 Ninth Workshop on Statistical Machine Translation*, WMT '14, pages 97–104, Baltimore, MD, USA.

Nadir Durrani, Hassan Sajjad, Hieu Hoang, and Philipp Koehn. 2014c. Integrating an unsupervised transliteration model into statistical machine translation. In *Proceedings of the 15th Conference of the European Chapter of the ACL*, EACL '14, Gothenburg, Sweden.

Qin Gao and Stephan Vogel. 2008. Parallel Implementations of Word Alignment Tool. In *Software Engineering, Testing, and Quality Assurance for Natural Language Processing*, pages 49–57. Association for Computational Linguistics.

Bassam Haddad and Mustafa Yaseen. 2007. Detection and Correction of Non-words in Arabic: a Hybrid Approach. *International Journal of Computer Processing of Oriental Languages*, 20(04):237–257.

Ahmed Hassan, Sara Noeman, and Hany Hassan. 2008. Language Independent Text Correction using Finite State Automata. In *Proceedings of the Third International Joint Conference on Natural Language Processing (IJCNLP 2008)*, pages 913–918, Hyderabad, India.

Kenneth Heafield. 2011. KenLM: Faster and smaller language model queries. In *Proceedings of the Workshop on Statistical Machine Translation (WMT'11)*, Edinburgh, UK.

Mans Hulden. 2009. Foma: A finite-state compiler and library. In *Proceedings of the 12th Conference of the European Chapter of the Association for Computational Linguistics: Demonstrations Session*, EACL '09, pages 29–32, Stroudsburg, PA, USA. Association for Computational Linguistics.

Serena Jeblee, Houda Bouamor, Wajdi Zaghouani, and Kemal Oflazer. 2014. Cmuq@qalb-2014: An smt-based system for automatic arabic error correction. In *Proceedings of the EMNLP 2014 Workshop on Arabic Natural Language Processing (ANLP)*, pages 137–142, Doha, Qatar, October. Association for Computational Linguistics.

Philipp Koehn, Hieu Hoang, Alexandra Birch, Christopher Callison-Burch, Marcello Federico, Nicola Bertoldi, Brooke Cowan, Wade Shen, Christine Moran, Richard Zens, Christopher Dyer, Ondrej Bojar, Alexandra Constantin, and Evan Herbst. 2007. Moses: Open Source Toolkit for Statistical Machine Translation. In *Proceedings of the 45th Annual Meeting of the Association for Computational Linguistics Companion Volume Proceedings of the Demo and Poster Sessions*, pages 177–180, Prague, Czech Republic.

Karen Kukich. 1992. Techniques for Automatically Correcting Words in Text. *ACM Computing Surveys (CSUR)*, 24(4):377–439.

Behrang Mohit, Alla Rozovskaya, Nizar Habash, Wajdi Zaghouani, and Ossama Obeid. 2014. The First QALB Shared Task on Automatic Text Correction for Arabic. In *Proceedings of EMNLP Workshop on Arabic Natural Language Processing*, Doha, Qatar, October.

Franz Josef Och and Hermann Ney. 2003. A Systematic Comparison of Various Statistical Alignment Models. In *Computational Linguistics*, page 1951.

Kemal Oflazer. 1996. Error-tolerant Finite-state Recognition with Applications to Morphological Analysis and Spelling Correction. *Comput. Linguist.*, 22(1):73–89, March.

Arfath Pasha, Mohamed Al-Badrashiny, Mona Diab, Ahmed El Kholy, Ramy Eskander, Nizar Habash, Manoj Pooleery, Owen Rambow, and Ryan M Roth. 2014. MADAMIRA: A fast, comprehensive tool for morphological analysis and disambiguation of Arabic. In *Proceedings of the Language Resources and Evaluation Conference*, LREC '14, pages 1094–1101, Reykjavik, Iceland.

Alla Rozovskaya, Kai-Wei Chang, Mark Sammons, and Dan Roth. 2013. The University of Illinois System in the CoNLL-2013 Shared Task. In *Proceedings of the Seventeenth Conference on Computational Natural Language Learning: Shared Task*, pages 13–19, Sofia, Bulgaria, August. Association for Computational Linguistics.

Alla Rozovskaya, Nizar Habash, Ramy Eskander, Noura Farra, and Wael Salloum. 2014. The columbia system in the qalb-2014 shared task on arabic error correction. In *Proceedings of the EMNLP 2014 Workshop on Arabic Natural Language Processing (ANLP)*, pages 160–164, Doha, Qatar, October. Association for Computational Linguistics.

Alla Rozovskaya, Houda Bouamor, Nizar Habash, Wajdi Zaghouani, Ossama Obeid, and Behrang Mohit. 2015. The Second QALB Shared Task on Automatic Text Correction for Arabic. In *Proceedings of ACL Workshop on Arabic Natural Language Processing*, Beijing, China, July.

Hassan Sajjad, Kareem Darwish, and Yonatan Belinkov. 2013a. Translating dialectal Arabic to English. In *Proceedings of the 51st Annual Meeting of the Association for Computational Linguistics (Volume 2: Short Papers)*, ACL '13, pages 1–6, Sofia, Bulgaria.

Hassan Sajjad, Francisco Guzmn, Preslav Nakov, Ahmed Abdelali, Kenton Murray, Fahad Al Obaidli, and Stephan Vogel. 2013b. QCRI at IWSLT 2013: Experiments in Arabic-English and English-Arabic spoken language translation. In *Proceedings of the 10th International Workshop on Spoken Language Technology*, IWSLT '13, Heidelberg, Germany.

Khaled Shaalan, Amin Allam, and Abdallah Gomah. 2003. Towards Automatic Spell Checking for Arabic. In *Proceedings of the 4th Conference on Language Engineering, Egyptian Society of Language Engineering (ELSE)*, Cairo, Egypt.

Wajdi Zaghouani, Behrang Mohit, Nizar Habash, Ossama Obeid, Nadi Tomeh, Alla Rozovskaya, Noura Farra, Sarah Alkuhlani, and Kemal Oflazer. 2014. Large Scale Arabic Error Annotation: Guidelines and Framework. In *Proceedings of the Ninth International Conference on Language Resources and Evaluation (LREC'14)*, Reykjavik, Iceland.

QCRI@QALB-2015 Shared Task:Correction of Arabic Text for Native and Non-Native Speakers' Errors

Hamdy Mubarak, Kareem Darwish, Ahmed Abdelali
Qatar Computing Research Institute
Hamad Bin Khalifa University
Doha, Qatar
{hmubarak, kdarwish, aabdelali}@qf.org.qa

Abstract

This paper describes the error correction model that we used for the QALB-2015 Automatic Correction of Arabic Text shared task. We employed a case-specific correction approach that handles specific error types such as dialectal word substitution and word splits and merges with the aid of a language model. We also applied corrections that are specific to second language learners that handle erroneous preposition selection, definiteness, and gender-number agreement.

1 Introduction

In This paper, we provide a system description for our submissions to the Arabic error correction shared task (QALB-2015 Shared Task on Automatic Correction of Arabic) as part of the Arabic NLP workshop. The QALB-2015 shared task is an extension of the first QALB shared task (Mohit et al., 2014) which addressed errors in comments written to Aljazeera articles by native Arabic speakers (Zaghouani et al., 2014). The current competition includes two tracks, and, in addition to errors produced by native speakers, also includes correction of texts written by learners of Arabic as a foreign language (L2) (Zaghouani et al., 2015). The native track includes Alj-train-2014, Alj-dev-2014, Alj-test-2014 texts from QALB-2014. The L2 track includes L2-train-2015 and L2-dev-2015. This data was released for the development of the systems. The systems were scored on blind test sets Alj-test-2015 and L2-test-2015.

We submitted runs to the automatic correction of text generated by native speaker (L1) and non-native speakers (L2). For both L1 and L2, we employed a case-specific approach that is aided by a language model (LM) to handle specific error types such as dialectal word substitutions and word splits. We also constructed a list of corrections that we observed in the QALB-2014 data set and in the QALB-2015 training set. We made use of these corrections to generate alternative corrections for words. When dealing with L2 text, we noticed specific patterns of mistakes mainly related to gender-number agreement, phonetic spellings, and definiteness. As for punctuation recovery, we opted only to place periods at the end of sentences and to correct reversed question marks. We opted not to invest in punctuation recovery based on the mixed results we obtained for the QALB-2014 shared task (Mubarak and Darwish, 2014).

2 QALB L2 Corpus Error Analysis

The QALB corpus used for the task contains over two million words of manually corrected Arabic text. The corpus is composed of text that is produced by native speakers as well as non-native speakers (Habash et al., 2013). While annotating the corpus, Zaghouani et al. (2014) detailed various types of errors that were encountered and addressed - mainly L1. Additional proposed corrections for L2 errors were summarized with no details. Understanding the error types would shed light on their manifestations and help correct them properly. We inspected the training and development sets and noticed a number of potential issues that can be summarized as follows:

1. Syntax Errors due to first language influence: L2 learners may carry over rules from their native languages resulting in syntactic and morphological errors, such as:

(a) Definiteness: In Arabic syntax, a possessive case, idafa construct, which happens between two words, mostly requires that the first word be indefinite while the second be definite. Such as the case of "كتاب التلميذ" (ktAb Al-

Proceedings of the Second Workshop on Arabic Natural Language Processing, pages 150–154,
Beijing, China, July 26-31, 2015.

tlmy* [1] – "The book of the student"). Note, the first Arabic word doesn't contain the definite article "Al" while the second does. Erroneous application, or not, of the definite article was common. For example, the student may say: "كتاب تلميذ" (ktAb tlmy*) or "الكتاب التلميذ" (AlktAb Altlmy*).

(b) Gender-number agreement: Gender-number agreement is another common error type. The inflectional morphology of Arabic may: embed gender-number markers in verbs as in "أعجبتني المدينة" (>Ejbtny Almdynp – I liked the city) and the learner may write "أعجبني المدينة" (>Ejbny Almdynp) without the feminine marker; and the use of feminine singular adjectives with masculine plural inanimate nouns as in "مدن عظيمة" (mdn EZymp – great cities) and the learner may write "مدن عظيمون" (mdn EZymwn) or "مدن عظيمات" (mdn EZymAt).

(c) Prepositions: Mixing the usage of prepositions is another typical challenge for L2 learners, as it requires good understanding of spacio-temporal aspects of language. Thus, L2 learners tend to mix between these prepositions as in "وصلت في المدينة" (wSlt fy Almdynp – I arrived in the city) instead of "وصلت إلى المدينة" (wSlt ¡lY Almdynp – I arrived to the city).

2. Spelling errors: Grasping sounds is another challenging issue particularly given:

(a) Letter that sound the same but written differently, such as "ت" (t) and "ة" (p), may lead to erroneous spellings like "مبارات" (mbArAt – game) instead of "مباراة" (mbArAp). Other example letter pairs are "ص" (S) and "س" (s) and "ط" (T) and "ت" (t)

(b) Letters that have similar shapes but a differ number of dots on or below them. We noticed that L2 learners often confuse letter such as: "ج" (j), "ح" (H), and "خ (x); and "ص" (S) and "ض" (D). This may lead to errors such as "صبب الخادث" (Sbb AlxAdv) instead of "سبب الحادث" (sbb AlHAdv – the reason for the accident).

3 Word Error Correction

In this section we describe our case-specific error correction system that handles specific error types with the aid of a language model (LM) generated from an Aljazeera corpus. We built a word bigram LM from a set of 234,638 Aljazeera articles[2] that span 10 years. Mubarak et al. (2010) reported that spelling mistakes in Aljazeera articles are infrequent. We used this language model in all subsequent steps.

We attempted to address specific types of errors including dialectal words, word normalization errors, and words that were erroneously split or merged. Before applying any correction, we always consulted the LM. We handled the following cases in order (L2 specific corrections are noted):

• Switching from English punctuation marks to Arabic ones, namely changing: "?" → "؟" and "," → "،".

• Correcting errors in definite article (ال "Al") when it's preceded by the preposition (ل "l") ex: لالعمل "lAlEml" → للعمل "llEml".

• Handling common dialectal words and common word-level mistakes. To do so, we extracted all the errors and their corrections from the QALB-2014 (train, dev, and test) and the training split of the QALB-2015 data set. In all, we extracted 221,460 errors from this corpus. If an error had 1 seen correction and the correction was done at least 2 times, we used the correction as a deterministic correction. For example, the word (الاحداث "AlAHdAv" – the events) was found 86 times in this corpus, and in all cases it was corrected to (الأحداث "$Al > HdAv$"). There were 10,255 such corrections. Further, we manually revised words for which a specific correction was made in 60% or more of the cases (2,076 words) to extract a list of valid alternatives for each word. For example, the word (الامور "AlAmwr") appeared 157 times and was corrected to (الأمور "$Al > mwr$") in 99% of the cases. We ignored the remaining seen corrections. An example dialectal word is (اللي "Ally" – "this" or "that")

[1]Buckwalter transliteration

[2]http://www.aljazeera.net

which could be mapped to (الذي "Al*y"), (التي "Alty"), or (الذين "Al*yn"). An example of a common mistake is (إنشاء الله " > *n$A'Allh*" – "God willing") which is corrected to (إن شاء الله ">n $A' Allh"). When performing correction, given a word appearing in our list, we either replaced it deterministically if it had one correction, or we consulted our LM to pick between the different alternatives. When dealing with L2 data, we added 297 more deterministic errors (ex: وثم "wvm" was always corrected to ثم "vm").

• Handling split conjunctions (و "w") that should be concatenated with the next word (ex: و هناك "w HnAk" → وهناك "wHnAk").

• Handling errors pertaining to the different forms of *alef*, *alef maqsoura* and *ya*, and *ta marbouta* and *ha* as described in Table 1 and Table 2. We used an approach similar to the open suggested by Moussa et al. (Moussa et al., 2012), and we also added the following cases, namely attempting to replace: ؤ "&" with ؤو "&w" or ئو "}w"; and ئ "}" with يء "y'" or vice versa (ex: مرؤس "mr&s" → مرؤوس "mr&ws", قاريء "qAry'" → قارئ "qAr}"). To generate the alternatives for words, we normalized all the unique words in the Aljazeera corpus, and we constructed a reverse look-up table that has the normalized form as the key and a list of seen alternatives that could have generated the normalized form. The look-up table contained 905k normalized word entries with corresponding denormalized forms. When correcting, a word is normalized and looked-up in the table to retrieve possible alternatives. We used the LM to pick the best alternative in context. Table 2 shows examples from the look-up table for normalized words and their alternative corrections.

• Removing repeated letters. Often people repeat letters, particularly long vowels, for emphasis as in (أخيييراااا ">xyyyyrAAA") (meaning "at last"). We corrected for elongation in a manner similar to that of Darwish et al. (Darwish et al., 2012). When a long vowel is repeated, we replaced it with a either the vowel (ex. أخيرا ">xyrA" – finally) or the vowel with one repetition (ex. سعوديين "sEwdyyn" – Saudis) and scored it using the LM. This was expanded to consonants also (ex. بكثيررر "bkvyrrrr" → بكثير "bkvyr"). If a repeated *alef* appeared in the beginning of the word, we attempted to replace it with alef lam (ex. ااحضارة "AAHDArp" → الحضارة "AlHDArp" – "civilization"). A trailing alef-hamza-alef sequence was replaced by alef-hamza (ex. سماءا "smA'A" → سماء "smA'" (meaning "sky")). Also, we replaced (للل "lll") at the beginning of word by (لل "ll") (ex. لللغة "lllgp" → للغة "llgp").

• Handling grammar errors in verb suffixes to restore missing alef (ex. افعلو "AfElw" → افعلوا "AfElwA" – do (plural); سيفعلوا "syfElwA" → سيفعلون "syfElwn" – they will do; لتحفظون "ltHfZwn" → لتحفظوا "ltHfZwA" – that you may memorize/protect).

• Handling merges and splits. Often words are concatenated erroneously. Thus, we attempted to split all words that were at least 5 letters long after letters that don't change their shapes when they are connected to the letters following them, namely different alef forms, د "d", ذ "*", ر "r", ز "z", و "w", ة "p", and ى "Y" (ex: ياربنا "yArbnA" → يا ربنا "yA rbnA"). If the bigram was observed in the LM and the LM score was higher (in context) than when they were concatenated, then the word was split. Conversely, some words were split in the middle. We attempted to merge every two words in sequence. If the LM score was higher (in context) after the merge, then the two words would be merged (ex: انتصار ات "AntSAr At" → انتصارات "AntSArAt").

• Correcting out-of-vocabulary (OOV) words. For words that were not observed in the LM, we attempted replacing phonetically or visually similar letters and deleting/replacing letters that appear in dialectal words as shown in Table 3. Generated suggestions are scored in context using the LM. Many of these errors are common in the L2 data set.

• For L2 data only, as we mentioned earlier we observed errors pertaining to definiteness and gender-number agreement. We generated possible corrections as follows: words that start with definite article, we scored the word with and without a definite article. We did the same with words ending with ta marbouta (p). We also added other alternatives for the word by adding the definite article and/or that ta marbouta (for words without one or the other or neither). In all cases, we used the LM to select the most probable alternative in contexts.

Letter	Norm.	Example
أ، إ، آ	ا	أحمد ← احمد
>, <, |	A	$AHmd \leftarrow > Hmd$
		إقناع ← اقناع
		$AqnAE \leftarrow < qnAE$
		آمن ← امن
		$Amn \leftarrow \|mn$
ى	ي	قصوى ← قصوي
Y	y	$qSwy \leftarrow qSwY$
ة	ه	قيادة ← قياده
p	h	$qyAdh \leftarrow qyAdp$
ؤ، ئ	ء	مسؤول ← مسءول
&, }	’	ms&wl ← ms’wl
diacritics	$null$	مُثَقَّفٌ ← مثقف
		$mvqf \leftarrow muvaq fK$
kashida	$null$	كبيـــــــر ← كبير
		$kbyr \leftarrow kby\_r$

Table 1: Word Normalization.

4 Official Shared Task Experiments and Results

We submitted 1 run for L1 errors (QCRI-1-ALJ), and 2 runs for L2 errors (QCRI-1-L2, QCRI-2-L2) as follows:

1. QCRI-1-ALJ: case-based correction for L1 test.
2. QCRI-2-L1: case-based correction for L2 test file and also by adding alternatives for possible errors in the definite article ال "Al" and feminine mark ة "p" as described in section 3.
3. QCRI-1-L2: case-based correction for L2 test file with handling the definiteness or feminine marker.

Table 4 and Table 5 report the officially submitted results against the development set and test set in order, and Table 6 reports the results of the new system against the development set and test set of QALB 2014 shared task.

Word	Alternatives and Frequencies
اعلام	5 اعلام, 632 أعلام, 20352 إعلام
AElAm	$< ElAm$ 20352, $> ElAm$ 632, $AElAm$ 5
حضاره	1 حضاره, 1271 حضارة
HDArh	$HDArp$ 1271, $HDArh$ 1

Table 2: Word Alternatives.

Case	Example
ض، ظ	ظابط ← ضابط
Z, D	DAbT ← ZAbT
د، ذ	الدهب ← الذهب
d, *	Al*hb ← $Aldhb$
ب+	بيلعب ← يلعب
b+	ylEb ← bylEb
د+	ديلعب ← يلعب
d+	ylEb ← dylEb
ح+، ه+	حيكتب ← سيكتب
H+, h+	syktb ← Hyktb
هال+	هالبنت ← هذه البنت
hAl+	h*h Albnt ← hAlbnt
عال+	عالأرض ← على الأرض
EAl+	ElY AlArD ← EAlArD
ت، ط	اللاطينية ← اللاتينية
t, T	AllAtynyp ← AllATynyp
ج، ح، خ	التحصص ← التخصص
j, H, x	AltxSS ← AltHSS
ق، ك	دقتوراه ← دكتوراه
q, k	dktwrAh ← dqtwrAh
ال+ ... +ي	التخرجي ← التخرج
Al+ ... +y	Altxrj ← Altxrjy

Table 3: Phonetic, Dialectal, and L2 Errors

5 Conclusion

In this paper, we presented an automatic approach for correcting Arabic text based on handling specific error types. We handled common dialectal words, some dialectal morphological features, letter normalization errors (ex. alef, ta marbouta, etc.), and word splitting and merging. For the L2 corpus, we also corrected letters that L2 learners often confuse because of similarity in shape or sound, and we attempted to correct errors pertaining to definiteness and gender-number agreement. For punctuation recovery, we opted to put periods at the end of sentences. Preliminary experiments using fuzzy match using a character-based mod-

Run	P	R	F1
QCRI-1-ALJ (Alj-dev-2015)	84.2	49.8	62.6
QCRI-1-L2 (L2-dev-2015)	46.3	19.2	27.1
QCRI-2-L2 (L2-dev-2015)	57.6	16.3	25.4

Table 4: Official Results for Dev. Data

Run	P	R	F1
QCRI-1-ALJ (Alj-test-2015)	84.74	58.10	68.94
QCRI-1-L2 (L2-test-2015)	45.86	20.16	28.01
QCRI-2-L2 (L2-test-2015)	54.87	17.63	26.69

Table 5: Official Results for Test Data

els showed promising results(Sajjad et al., 2012; Durrani et al., 2014; Darwish et al., 2014). We intend to incorporate this development among others in our on-going research. The fuzzy match algorithm will correct cases like: (الأبعاء، يستخدنونها, Al>bEA' , ystxdnwnhA) to (الأربعاء، يستخدمونها, Al<rbEA' , ystxdmwnhA).

L2 learners present new spelling error types. Such types may not typical spelling errors as they may produce valid words that are erroneous in context. Hence employing a methodology to detect such cases will be of great help.Also, we plan to handle more grammar errors for cases like: numbers, case endings, gender-number agreement, irregular (broken) plurals, and Tanween errors (الممنوع من الصرف).

References

Kareem Darwish, Walid Magdy, and Ahmed Mourad. 2012. Language processing for arabic microblog retrieval. In *Proceedings of the 21st ACM international conference on Information and knowledge management*, pages 2427–2430. ACM.

Kareem Darwish, Ahmed M. Ali, and Ahmed Abdelali. 2014. Query term expansion by automatic learning of morphological equivalence patterns from wikipedia. In *SIGIR 2014 Workshop on Semantic Matching in Information Retrieval (SMIR)*, volume 1204, pages 24–29. CEUR-WS.

Nadir Durrani, Hassan Sajjad, Hieu Hoang, and Philipp Koehn. 2014. Integrating an unsupervised transliteration model into statistical machine translation. In *Proceedings of the 14th Conference of the European Chapter of the Association for Computational Linguistics, volume 2: Short Papers*, pages 148–153, Gothenburg, Sweden, April. Association for Computational Linguistics.

Run	P	R	F1
Alj-dev-2014	65.42	62.96	64.17
Alj-test-2014	65.79	61.94	63.81

Table 6: Results for QALB 2014 Data Sets

Nizar Habash, Behrang Mohit, Ossama Obeid, Kemal Oflazer, Nadi Tomeh, and Wajdi Zaghouani. 2013. Qalb: Qatar arabic language bank. In *Proceedings of Qatar Annual Research Conference (ARC-2013)*, Doha, Qatar.

Behrang Mohit, Alla Rozovskaya, Nizar Habash, Wajdi Zaghouani, and Ossama Obeid. 2014. The First QALB Shared Task on Automatic Text Correction for Arabic. In *Proceedings of EMNLP Workshop on Arabic Natural Language Processing*, Doha, Qatar, October.

Mohammed Moussa, Mohamed Waleed Fakhr, and Kareem Darwish. 2012. Statistical denormalization for arabic text. In *In Empirical Methods in Natural Language Processing*.

Hamdy Mubarak and Kareem Darwish. 2014. Automatic correction of arabic text: a cascaded approach. *Arabic NLP 2014 Workshop*.

Hamdy Mubarak, Mostafa Ramadan, and Ahmed Metwali. 2010. Spelling mistakes in arabic newspapers. In *Arabic Language and Scientific Researches conference*, Faculty of Arts, Ain Shams University, Cairo, Egypt.

Hassan Sajjad, Alexander Fraser, and Helmut Schmid. 2012. A statistical model for unsupervised and semi-supervised transliteration mining. In *Proceedings of the Association for Computational Linguistics*, ACL '12, pages 469–477, Jeju, Korea.

Wajdi Zaghouani, Behrang Mohit, Nizar Habash, Ossama Obeid, Nadi Tomeh, Alla Rozovskaya, Noura Farra, Sarah Alkuhlani, and Kemal Oflazer. 2014. Large scale arabic error annotation: Guidelines and framework. In *Proceedings of the Ninth International Conference on Language Resources and Evaluation (LREC'14)*, Reykjavik, Iceland, May.

Wajdi Zaghouani, Nizar Habash, Houda Bouamor, Alla Rozovskaya, Behrang Mohit, Abeer Heider, and Kemal Oflazer. 2015. Correction annotation for non-native arabic texts: Guidelines and corpus. In *Proceedings of The 9th Linguistic Annotation Workshop*, pages 129–139, Denver, Colorado, USA, June. Association for Computational Linguistics.

SAHSOH@QALB-2015 Shared Task: A Rule-Based Correction Method of Common Arabic Native and Non-Native Speakers' Errors

Wajdi Zaghouani
Carnegie Mellon University,
Doha, Qatar
wajdiz@cmu.edu

Taha Zerrouki
Bouira University,
Bouira, Algeria
t_zerrouki@esi.dz

Amar Balla
The National Computer
Science Engineering School
(ESI), Algiers, Algeria
a_balla@esi.dz

Abstract

This paper describes our participation in the QALB-2015 Automatic Correction of Arabic Text shared task. We employed various tools and external resources to build a rule based correction method. Hand written linguistic rules were added by using existing lexicons and regular expressions. We handled specific errors with dedicated rules reserved for non-native speakers. The system is simple as it does not employ any sophisticated machine learning methods and it does not correct punctuation errors. The system achieved results comparable to other approaches when the punctuation errors are ignored with an F1 of 66.9% for native speakers' data and an F1 of 31.72% for the non-native speakers' data.

1 Introduction

The Automatic Error Correction (AEC) is an interesting and challenging problem in Natural Language Processing. The existing methods that attempt to solve this problem are generally based on deep linguistic and statistical analysis. AEC tools can assist in solving multiple natural language processing (NLP) tasks like Machine Translation or Natural Language Generation. However, the main application of AEC is the building of automated spell checkers to be used as writing assistant tools (e.g. word-processing) or even for applications such as Mobile auto-completion and auto correction programs, post-processing optical character recognition tools or with the correction of large content site such as Wikipedia. Conventional spelling correction tools detect typing errors simply by comparing each token of a text against a dictionary of words that are known to be correctly spelled. Any token that matches an element of the dictionary, possibly after some minimal morphological analysis, is deemed to be correctly spelled; any token that matches no element is flagged as a possible error, with near-matches displayed as suggested corrections (Hirst 2005).

In this paper we describe our participation in the QALB-2015 shared task (Rozovskaya 2015) which is an extension of the first QALB shared task (Mohit et al. 2014) that took place last year. The QALB-2014 shared task was reserved to errors in comments written to Aljazeera articles by native Arabic speakers (Zaghouani et al. 2014; Obeid et al. 2013). The 2015 competition includes two tracks. The first track is dedicated to errors produced by native speakers and the second track includes correction of texts written by learners of Arabic as a foreign language (L2) (Zaghouani et al. 2015). The native track includes Alj-train-2014, Alj-dev-2014, Alj-test-2014 texts from QALB-2014. The L2 track includes L2-train-2015 and L2-dev-2015. This data was released for the development of the systems. The systems were scored on blind test sets Alj-test-2015 and L2-test-2015.

Our pipeline approach is based on a combination of pre-existing tools, hand written contextual rules and lexicons. Detecting and correcting such complex errors within the scope of a rule based approach require specific rules to be written in order to correctly analyze the dependencies between words in a given sentence. The remainder of this paper is organized as follows: Section 2 describes the related works. Section 3 presents our approach including the tools and resources used and finally in Section 4 we report the results obtained on the Development set.

Proceedings of the Second Workshop on Arabic Natural Language Processing, pages 155–160,
Beijing, China, July 26-31, 2015.

2 Related Works

The task of automatic error correction has been explored widely by many researchers in the past years especially for the English language. Many approaches have been used to build systems (hybrid, rule base, supervised and unsupervised machine learning…). These systems used various NLP tools and resources including pre-existing lexicons, morphological analyzers and Part of Speech Taggers. We cite for the English language early works done by (Church and Gale, 1991; Kukich, 1992; Golding, 1995; Golding and Roth, 1996). Later on we find (Brill and Moore, 2000; Fossati and Di Eugenio, 2007) and more recently Han and Baldwin, 2011; Dahlmeier and Ng 2012; Wu et al., 2013). For Arabic, this problem has been investigated in a couple of papers as in Shaalan et al. (2003) who presented his work on the specification and classification of spelling errors in Arabic. Later on, Haddad and Yaseen (2007) built a hybrid approach that used rules and some morphological features to correct non-words using contextual clues and Hassan et al. (2008) presented a language independent text correction method using Finite State Automata. More recently, Alkanhal et al. (2012) wrote a paper about a stochastic approach used for word spelling correction and Attia et al. (2012) created a dictionary of 9 million entries fully inflected Arabic words using a morphological transducer. Later on, they used a dictionary to build an error model by analyzing the various error types in the data. Moreover, Shaalan et al. (2012) created a model using unigrams to correct Arabic spelling errors and recently, (Pasha et al., 2014) created MADAMIRA, a morphological analyzer and a disambiguation tool for Arabic. Finally, Alfaifi and Atwell (2012) created a native and non-native Arabic learner's corpus and an error coding correction taxonomy made available for research purpose.

3 Our Approach

Our correction approach watches out for certain predefined "errors" as the user types, replacing them with a suggested "correction" depending on the corpus type L1 or L2. Therefore an error analysis was performed on the provided data set to find the most frequent error types per data set. We also located some external freely available resources listed in (Zaghouani 2014) such as Alfaifi L1 and L2 corpus (Alfaifi and Atwell 2013), The JRC-Names names (Steinberger et al. 2011) and the Attia list (Attia 2012).

3.1 Corpus Error Analysis

In order to better write our correction rules and to better understand the nature of errors in the L1 and L2 data, we performed a manual inspection on a sample taken from the Dev Sets of the shared task and we obtained the errors distribution shown in Table 1. While the errors committed by L1 speakers are mostly spelling errors such as the Hamza and Ta-Marbuta confusion, L2 speakers tend more to have difficulties with the following issues: the definiteness structure, the words agreement, the preposition usage and the correct word choice in the sentence. We used this analysis to optimize our rules for each corpus.

Rank	Native L1	Non-Native L2
#1	Hamza	Definiteness
#2	Ta-Marbuta / Ha Alif-Maqsura/Ya	Agreement
#3	Case Endings	Prrnaleposition
#4	Verbal Inflection	Hamza
#5	Conjunctions	Word Choice

Table 1: Most frequent errors observed in the Dev sets of the L1 and L2 Corpus. The errors are sorted from the most frequent to the least frequent

In Arabic, spelling confusion in Hamza forms is frequently found, e.g. the word إستعمال IstEmAl[1] "usage" must be written by a simple Alef ا, not Alef with Hamza below إ. This error can be classified as a kind of errors and not a simple error in a word as reported by (Shaalan, 2003, Habash, 2011). While typical common errors based on wrong letter spelling such as the confusion in the form of Hamza همزة, Daad ضادand Za ظاء, and the omission dots with Yeh ياء and Teh تاء are generally relatively easy to handle, the task is more challenging for grammatical and semantic errors. Previously, we created an Arabic auto correction tool to correct common mistakes in Wikipedia articles. The idea is to create a script that detects common spelling errors using a set of regular expressions and a word replacement list[2].

In a similar way, the system we are presenting in this paper is based primarily on:

---

[1] Buckwalter transliteration

[2] The script is named AkhtaBot, which is applied to Arabic wikipedia, the Akhtabot is available on http://ar.wikipedia.org/wiki/مستخدم:AkhtaBot

- Regular expressions used to identify errors and give a replacement.

- Replacement list that contains the misspelled word and the exact correction needed for each particular case. Furthermore, we used the following combination of tools and resources:

- **Arabic word list for spell checking**: This list contains 9 million Arabic words from AraComLex, an open-source finite state transducer (Attia 2012). The list[3] was validated against Microsoft Word spell checker tool. This list was used to check and replace wrongly spelled words.
- **JRC-Names[4]**: a list of 1.18 million person and 6,700 organization names (Steinberger et al. 2011). We used the list to correct and replace wrongly spelled named entities in the data set.
- **Alfaifi L1 and L2 corpus:** Used to observe the errors in context and to study the patterns of spelling errors made by native and non-native speakers. The corpus was created by (Alfaifi and Atwell 2013) and freely available[5].
- **A Python script** to generate the errors.
- **Hunspell** spellchecker program[6] combined with **Ayaspell**[7] dictionary (Hadjir 2009, Zerrouki, 2013).
- **Ghalatawi**[8] : Our spelling correction tool
- A **task dedicated script** to select the best suggestion from Hunspell correction suggestions to generate customized autocorrected list customized for each data set.

3.1 Regular Expressions

We use regular expression patterns to detect errors by using the Arabic verb forms (الأوزان AlOwzAn) and affixes. For example we can detect very common Hamza spelling errors with the Arabic verbs form VII which expresses a submission to an action or an effect as in the case of an animate being, it could mean an involuntary submission. This form reflects the meaning on two levels: reflexive (to let oneself be put through) and an agentless passive (non-reciprocal of form I). Using such a rule with a word such as INFIAL it انفعال should be written with Hamza Wasl, as the form إنفعال InfEAl is wrongly spelled. Moreover, we represent all forms with all possible affixes as shown in Table 2 and Table 3

Suffixes	Form	Prefixes
...ين، ات، ي، ان، ه، ها، هما، ك، كما kmA, k, hmA, h, An, y, At, yn…	انفعال	...ب، ال، و، ف f, w, Al, b

Table 2: Infi'aal verb forms with affixes

<table>
<tr><th># Example of rules for انفعال</th></tr>
<tr><td>ur'\b(إن|)(ال|)(ك|ب|)(و|ف|)(\w\w)ا(\w)(ين|ات|ة|تين)(|اي)\b'</td></tr>
<tr><td>ur'\b(إن|)(لل|)(و|ف|)(\w\w)ا(\w)(ين|ات|تين|ة)(|اي)\b'</td></tr>
<tr><td>ur'\b(إن|)(و|ف|)(\w\w)ا(\w)(ا|أ|آ)(|اي)\b'</td></tr>
</table>

Table 3: Sample rules for the Infi'al verb form

Furthermore, we have modeled the following spelling errors cases using regular expressions (c.f Table 4):
(1) words with the verb forms infi'al and ifti'al انفعال وافتعال ; (2) words with the letter Alif Maqsura followed by Hamza, for example سىئ s} will be corrected as سيء sy'. (3) words with Teh Marbuta misplaced or incorrectly merged, like in مدرسةالعلم mdrspAlElm to be corrected to مدرسة العلم mdrsp AlElm "school of knowledge".

<table>
<tr><th>Regular expressions</th><th>Replacements</th></tr>
<tr><td># removing kashida (Tatweel)</td><td></td></tr>
<tr><td>ur'([\u0621-\u063F\u0641-\u064A])\u0640+([\u0621-\u063F\u0641-\u064A])'</td><td>ur'\1\2'</td></tr>
<tr><td># rules for انفعال</td><td></td></tr>
<tr><td>ur'\b(إن|)(ال|)(ك|ب|)(و|ف|)(\w\w)ا(\w)(ين|ات|ة|تين)(|اي)\b'</td><td>ur'\1\2\3\ان4\ا5\6\7'</td></tr>
</table>

Table 4: Sample rules expressed by regular expressions.

3.2 Wordlist

Many common mistakes cannot be corrected using regular expressions only, such as confusion between the letter Dhad and the letter Za, and omitted dots on letter Teh and letter Yeh, as in the المكتبه* Almktbh "the library" and * فى fY "in", So we resort to build a list of common misspelled words.

To build our word list, we used the existing lexicons of correctly spelled 9M words by Attia

[3] The list available at: http: //sourceforge.net/projects/ arabic-wordlist/

[4] The list is available at : https://ec.europa.eu/jrc/en/language-technologies/jrc-names

[5] The corpus is available at http://www.arabiclearnercorpus.com

[6] Available at http://hunspell.sourceforge.net/

[7] Available at http://ayaspell.sourceforge.net.

[8] The Ghalatawi autocorrect program is available as an open source program at http://ghalatawi.sourceforge.net

(2012) and the JRC-Names named entities corpus (Steinberger et al. 2011) by generating errors for common letters errors, then filtering the results to obtain an autocorrected words list with no ambiguity. In order to build the list, first, we take a correct word list than we select candidate words from words starting with Hamza Qat' or Wasl , words ending by Yeh or Teh marbuta or Words containing the letter Dhad or Zah. Than we generate errors on words by replacing candidate letters by errors on purpose. Finally we check the spelling and eliminate the corrected words, because some modified words can be correct, for example, if we take the word ضل Dla , then modify it to ظل Zl, the modified word exists in the dictionary, then we exclude it from the auto corrected wordlist, and we keep only misspelled modified words as the examples in the word إسلام IslAm "islam", it can be written as اسلام AslAm "islam" by mistake since it has the same phonological construction.

3.3 Customized Wordlist for L1 and L2 Texts

We generated a case specific auto correction list for each corpus (L1 or L2). The following algorithm is applied to generate customized list from each corpus:

(1) Extract misspelled words from dataset by using Hunspell spellchecker. **(2)** Generate suggestions given by Hunspell. **(3)** Observe the suggestions to choose the best one in hypothesis that words have common errors on letters according to modified letters. **(4)** Exclude ambiguous cases. **(5)** The automatically generated word list is used to autocorrect the dataset instead of the default word list.

4 Evaluation

In order to evaluate the performance of our system, we used the data set provided in the shared task test (Alj-dev-2014 and L2-dev-2015). For this evaluation we have used two autocorrected word lists:

- A generic word list generated from Attia wordlist and the JRC corpus, this wordlist is used for general correction purposes.
- A customized wordlist based on each dataset L2-dev-2015, L2-test-2015, Alj-dev-2014 and Alj-test-2015 by generating a special word list according to each data set, in order to improve the results and avoid unnecessary replacement. The customized auto correction word list is built in the same way as the generic one, by replacing the source dictionary by misspelled words from QALB corpus (Zaghouani, 2014). We submitted only one run for each corpus type and the official results obtained on the Development sets and the Test sets are shown in Table 5 by using the M2 scorer (Dahlmeier et al 2012):

Data set	Precision	Recall	F1
Alj-dev-2014	71.40	32.10	44.30
Alj-test-2014	82.63	41.89	55.59
Alj-test-2015	81.88	40.24	53.97
L2-dev-2015	60.30	11.30	19.00
L2-test-2015	59.75	15.90	25.12

Table 5: Results on the Dev and Test sets

The relatively low results obtained were expected since we decided to ignore the punctuation errors and therefore our system is penalized by this decision. We estimate that punctuation errors represent more than 38% of the errors in the QALB data sets (L1 and L2). When the punctuation errors were removed from the evaluation, we noticed a significant improvement of the recall and the F1 score for L1 (+13 points) and for L2 (+6.6 points) as seen in table 6.

Data set	Precision	Recall	F1
Alj-test-2015	83.85	55.65	**66.90**
L2-test-2015	58.95	21.70	31.72

Table 6: Official Results on the Dev and Test sets with with punctuation errors ignored

5 Error Analysis

Our system failed to find the appropriate correction in many cases due to the limitations of the rule based systems in general. In this section, we will highlight some of the main errors not corrected by our system for both data sets. We will not discuss punctuation related errors as they are not handled by our system.

5.1 L1 Errors

- **Split and Merge errors:** Such as والجزيرةنت wAljzyrpnt "AljazeeraNet" it is not obvious to detect where the words should be split as in والجزيرة نت wAljzyrp nt "Aljazeera Net". Other words that should be merged are hard to detect as both words produced can be valid entries such as الفلس طيني Alfls Tyny that should be corrected to الفلسطيني AlflsTyny "the Palestinian" but both words wrongly produced are acceptable in this case.

- **Wrong Hamza spelling:** Such as أن On "indeed" and إن In "indeed". For these particular examples advanced rules may be required.

- **Ta-Marbuta / Ha errors:** These errors are practically frequent for the L1 corpus and they are not always corrected by our system in the cases of named entities.

- **Keyboard Typos:** Keyboard errors are very frequent and our system did not detect most of them due to the complexity of the issue, since the typo word could be correctly spelled like misspelling الباب AlbAb "the door" for البار AlbAr "The bar" .

5.2 L2 Errors

Many L2 detection errors are very similar to the L1 errors listed in the previous section, but some errors are mostly found in L2 texts such as the following:

- **Definiteness:** correcting definite errors with a rule based system could be very challenging without access to a parser. For instance errors such as missing definite article in المدينة منورة Almdynp mnwrp "The Madinah Munawwarah" are very frequent in L2 texts and our system failed to detect them most of the time since the word missing the definite article are correct as standalone words.

- **Gender and number agreement:**

The Gender-number agreement is another frequent error type where our system failed frequently to correct it such as in أخلاق سكانه جيد OxlAq skAnh jyd "morals of its inhabitants is good" with the wrong gender in the word جيد jyd "good" that should be corrected to جيدة jydp instead as it is related the feminine noun أخلاق OxlAq "morals".

- **Prepositions:** Non-native speakers are frequently confused in the preposition usage in Arabic. An advanced language level is usually required to master this. A frequent confusion in the usage of the wrong preposition في fy "in" in the following example. ذهبت في البيت *hbt fy Albyt "I went in the house" that should be corrected by our system to ذهبت إلى البيت . *hbt IlY Albyt "I went to the house"

- **Wrong Word choice:** L2 speakers have some difficulties with words that may be homophones but spelled in a different way such as in البقار يستريحون AlbqAr ystryHwn "the cow boys are resting" and it is obvious here that it is meant to be الأبقار يستريحون AlObqAr ystryHwn "the cows are resting". Again these cases show another limitation of rule based systems to detect correctly spelled wrong word choices.

6 Conclusion and Discussion

We presented a pipeline rule based approach for correcting Arabic text optimized for two native and non-native text types. We focused mainly on the most common errors made by native and non-native speakers such as the Hamza errors, The Ta-Marbuta and letter Ya. We also used complex regular expressions to correct splitting and merging errors. We also, used lexicons such as the Attia word list and the JRC-names to boost the results of our system. The correction of more complex errors was also tested such as the correction of phonological errors caused by a confusion and similarity of the words. For non-native speakers, we detected and corrected some of the errors related to the misuse of gender and number agreement and also for the wrong usage of the definite article.

The results obtained showed that our systems performs much better with native speakers texts, this is mainly due to the complex nature of some spelling errors of L2 learners. In the future, we plan to handle more complex errors for both native and non-native texts such as grammatical and case ending errors and also wrong word choice errors. We are also planning to integrate the MADAMIRA morphological analyzer in a post processing step to increase our recall.

7 Acknowledgements

This publication was made possible by grants NPRP-4-1058-1-168 from the Qatar National Research Fund (a member of the Qatar Foundation).

References

Alfaifi Abdullah and Atwell Eric. 2012. Arabic Learner Corpora (ALC): a taxonomy of coding errors. In Proceedings of the 8th International Computing Conference in Arabic (ICCA 2012)

Alfaifi, Abdullah and Atwell, Eric. 2013. Arabic Learner Corpus v1: A New Resource for Arabic Language Research. In proceedings of *the Second Workshop on Arabic Corpus Linguistics (WACL-2)*. Lancaster University, UK.

Alkanhal, Mohamed I., Mohamed A. Al-Badrashiny, Mansour M. Alghamdi, and Abdulaziz O. Al-Qabbany. 2012. Automatic Stochastic Arabic Spelling Correction With Emphasis on Space Insertions and Deletions. IEEE Transactions on Audio, Speech, and Language Processing, Vol. 20, No. 7, September 2012.

Attia, Mohammed, Pavel Pecina, Younes Samih, Khaled Shaalan, Josef van Genabith. 2012. Improved Spelling Error Detection and Correction for Arabic. COLING 2012, Bumbai, India.

Dahlmeier, Daniel and Ng, Hwee Tou. 2012. Better evaluation for grammatical error correction. In Proceedings of NAAC-HLT, Montreal, Canada.

Deorowicz S,, Marcin G. Ciura. 2005. Correcting Spelling Errors By Modeling Their Causes. Int. J. Appl. Math. Comput. Sci., 2005, Vol. 15, No. 2, 275–285

Golding and Roth. 1999. A Winnow based approach to Context-Sensitive Spelling Correction. In Machine Learning - Special issue on natural language learning, Volume 34 Issue 1-3, Feb. 1999.

Habash Nizar. 2010. Introduction to Arabic natural language processing. Synthesis Lectures on Human Language Technologies 3.1 (2010): 1-187

Habash Nizar, Ryan M. Roth. 2011. Using Deep Morphology to Improve Automatic Error Detection in Arabic Handwriting Recognition, ACL, page 875-884. The Association for Computer Linguistics, (2011)

Hadjir I .2009 .Towards an open source Arabic spell checker. MA thesis in Natural language processing, scientific and technique research center to Arabic language development.

Hammad M and Mohamed Alhawari. 2010. In Recent improvement of arabic language search, Google Arabia Blog, Google company, 2010 http://google-arabia.blogspot.com/.

Hassan Ahmed, Noeman Sara and Hassan Hany. 2008. Language Independent Text Correction using Finite State Automata. IJCNLP. Hyderabad, India.

Hirst Graeme and Alexander Budanitsky. 2005. Correcting real-word spelling errors by restoring lexical cohesion, Natural Language Engineering 11 (1): 87–111, 2005 Cambridge University Press

Mohit Behrang, Alla Rozovskaya, Wajdi Zaghouani, Ossama Obeid, and Nizar Habash. 2014. The First shared Task on Automatic Text Correction for Arabic. In Proceedings of EMNLP Workshop on Arabic Natural Language Processing, Doha, Qatar.

Obeid Ossama, Wajdi. Zaghouani, Behrang. Mohit, Nizar Habash, Kemal Oflazer and Nadi Tomeh. 2013. A Web-based Annotation Framework For Large-Scale Text Correction. In The Companion Volume of the Proceedings of IJCNLP 2013: System Demonstrations. Asian Federation of Natural Language Processing.

Pasha A., M. Al-Badrashiny, M. Diab, A. El Kholy, R. Eskander, N. Habash, M. Pooleery, O. Rambow, and R. Roth. 2014. MADAMIRA: A Fast, Comprehensive Tool for Morphological Analysis and Disambiguation of Arabic. In Proceedings of the Ninth International Conference on Language Resources and Evaluation (LREC).

Rozovskaya Alla, Houda Bouamor, Wajdi Zaghouani, Ossama Obeid, and Nizar Habash and Behrang Mohit. 2015. The Second QALB Shared Task on Automatic Text Correction for Arabic. In Proceedings of ACL Workshop on Arabic Natural Language Processing, Beijing, China.

Shaalan, Khaled, Amin Allam and Abdallah Gomah. 2003. Towards automatic spell checking for Arabic. In Proceedings of the Conference on Language Engineering, 2003 - claes.sci.eg

Steinberger, Ralf, Pouliquen, Bruno, Kabadjov, Mijail, Belyaeva, Jenya and van der Goot, Erik. 2011. JRC-NAMES: A Freely Available, Highly Multilingual Named Entity Resource. In Proceedings of the International Conference Recent Advances in Natural Language Processing, Hissar, Bulgaria.

Zaghouani, Wajdi. 2014. Critical survey of the freely available Arabic corpora. In Proceedings of the Workshop on Free/Open-Source Arabic Corpora and Corpora Processing Tools Workshop, LREC 2014, Reykjavik, Iceland.

Zaghouani Wajdi, Nizar Habash, Houda Bouamor, Alla Rozovskaya, Behrang Mohit, Abeer Heider, and Kemal Oflazer. 2015. Correction annotation for nonnative arabic texts: Guidelines and corpus. In Proceedings of The 9th Linguistic Annotation Workshop, pages 129–139, Denver, Colorado, USA, June. Association for Computational Linguistics.

Zaghouani Wajdi, Behrang Mohit, Nizar Habash, Ossama Obeid, Nadi Tomeh, Alla Rozovskaya, Noura Farra, Sarah Alkuhlani, and Kemal Oflazer. 2014. Large Scale Arabic Error Annotation: Guidelines and Framework. In Proceedings of the Ninth International Conference on Language Resources and Evaluation (LREC'14), Reykjavik, Iceland.

Zerrouki Taha. 2011. Improving the spell checking dictionary by users feedback. A meeting of experts check the spelling and grammar and composition automation, Higher Institute of Applied Science and Technology of Damascus, the Arab Organization for Education, Science and Culture, Damascus, April 18 to 20, 2011.

TECHLIMED@QALB-Shared Task 2015: a hybrid Arabic Error Correction System

Djamel Mostefa **Jaber Abualasal** **Omar Asbayou**

Mahmoud Gzawi **Ramzi Abbes**

Techlimed 42, rue de l'Université Lyon, France
{firstname.lastname}@techlimed.com

Abstract

This paper reports on the participation of Techlimed in the Second Shared Task on Automatic Arabic Error Correction organized by the Arabic Natural Language Processing Workshop. This year's competition includes two tracks, and, in addition to errors produced by native speakers (L1), also includes correction of texts written by learners of Arabic as a foreign language (L2). Techlimed participated in the L1 track. For our participation in the L1 evaluation task, we developed two systems. The first one is based on the spell-checker Hunspell with specific dictionaries. The second one is a hybrid system based on rules, morphology analysis and statistical machine translation. Our results on the test set show that the hybrid system outperforms the lexicon driven approach with a precision of 71.2%, a recall of 64.94% and an F-measure of 67.93%.

1 Introduction

Spell checking is an important task in Natural Language Processing (NLP). It can be used in a wide range of applications such as word processing tools, machine translation, information retrieval, optical character recognition etc. Automatic error correction tools on Arabic are underperforming in comparison with other languages like English or French. The lack of appropriate resources (e.g. publicly available corpora and tools) and the complexity of the Arabic language can explain this difference. Arabic is a challenging language for any NLP tool for many reasons. Arabic has a rich and complex morphology compared to other languages. Short vowels are missing in the texts but are mandatory from a grammatical point of view. Moreover, they are needed to disambiguate between several possibilities of words. Arabic is a rich language. It is characterised by its great number of synonyms and is a highly agglutinative, inflectional and derivational language that uses clitics (proclitics and enclitics). Arabic has many varieties. Modern Standard Arabic represents the variety of the news and formal speech. Classical Arabic refers to religious and classical texts. Dialectal Arabic has no standard rules for orthography and is based on the pronunciation. Therefore, a same word can be written using many different surface forms depending on the dialectal origin of the writer. Another very popular way of writing Arabic on the Internet and the social media like Facebook or Tweeter is to use "Arabizi", a Latinized form of writing Arabic using Latin letters and digits (Aboelezz 2009).

For our participation in this second QALB Shared Task, we tried to improve the systems we have developed for the first edition (Mostefa 2014). The first approach is a lexicon driven spell checker using Hunspell (Hunspell 2007). The second approach is a hybrid system based on correction rules, morphological analysis and statistical machine translation.

The paper is organized as follows: section 2 gives an overview of the automatic error correction evaluation task and resources provided by the organizers; section 3 describes the systems we have developed for the evaluations; and finally in section 4 we discuss the results and draw some conclusion.

Proceedings of the Second Workshop on Arabic Natural Language Processing, pages 161–165,
Beijing, China, July 26-31, 2015. ©2014 Association for Computational Linguistics

2 Task description and language resources

The QALB-2015 shared task (Rozovskaya 2015) is an extension of the first QALB shared task (Mohit 2014) that took place in 2014. QALB-2014 addressed errors in comments written to Aljazeera articles by native Arabic speakers (Zaghouani 2014).This year's competition includes two tracks, and, in addition to errors produced by native speakers, also includes correction of texts written by learners of Arabic as a foreign language (L2) (Zaghouani 2015). The native track includes Alj-train-2014, Alj-dev-2014, Alj-test-2014 texts from QALB-2014. The L2 track includes L2-train-2015 and L2-dev-2015. This data was released for the development of the systems. The systems were scored on blind test sets Alj-test-2015 and L2-test-2015.
The Alj-train-2014 set is made of 20,428 sentences for 1.1 M tokens.
The Alj-dev-2014 and Alj-test-2014 includes each around 1k sentences for 50k tokens
Finally, a test set Alj-test-2015 of 920 sentences for 48k tokens with no gold standard has to be corrected automatically for the evaluation campaign.
The evaluation metric is performed by comparing the gold standard with the hypothesis using the Levenshtein edit distance (Levenshtein 1966) and the implementation of the M2 scorer (Dahlmeier 2012). Then for each sentence Precision, Recall and F-measure are calculated.

3 System description

3.1 Rule-based system

For the rule-based system, we used the spell-checker Hunspell (Hunspell 2007) with different dictionaries and affix files.
The structure of Hunspell uses two files to define the spell checking of a language. The first file is a dictionary file that contains a stem list of the language. The second file is an affix file that maps the lemmas with their affixes. Affixes in Hunspell are divided into prefixes and suffixes, infixes are only included in the stems and spell checked in terms of proximity in lexical morphemes.
Dictionary and affix file in Hunspell is similar to the one depicted in Table 1 and Table 2

لدن/36	
نعفن/290	1246
تعفنان/273	1246

Table 1 Example of Hunspell dictionary

AF Tbcc # 36
PFX Tb 0 و .
SFX cc 0 ي .

Table 2 Example of Hunspell affix file

The dictionary contains the minimal words which are mapped with the affix rules.
The affix file contains mainly prefix and suffix rules that apply to the words of the dictionary. For instance, the rule of prefixation /Tb/ in Table 2 creates the word-form ولدن (wldn) while the rule of suffixation /cc/ creates ولدني (wldny).

For the evaluation, we used Hunspell with a modified version of the Hunspell Arabic dictionary and affix files version 3.2 (Ayaspell 2008).
We obtained a precision of 56.64% and a recall of 19.78% for an F-measure of 29.32% on the development set.
The results seem to be low but we have to consider that Hunspell does not correct the punctuation errors; many errors in the data include punctuation errors (around 30%).

3.2 Hybrid system based on SMT

For the second approach, we combined Statistical Machine Translation (SMT) system with morphological output of MADAMIRA (Pasha 2014) and some automatic rules to correct the text.
We build three different SMT systems based on the Moses toolkit (Koehn 2007) with different input for training the phrase-based translation models.
For the first system (Tech-1), we used the output of MADAMIRA morphological analyzer and the corrected texts to train a MADAMIRA/correct translation model. We used the text from the Alj-train-2014 data and apply corrections to build a parallel MADAMIRA/correct text corpus of 20,428 sentences and we train a phrase based translation model. The Alj-dev-2014 data is used for Moses to tune the translation models.
The second system (Tech-2) is the same as the previous one, but we added Alj-dev-2014 in the training data and used Alj-Test-2014 as development data for tuning the translation models.
The third system (Tech-3) uses the original erroneous text instead of the MADAMIRA output to build a parallel error/correct text corpus and we train a phrase based model. As for Tech-1, the Alj-dev-2014 data is used for Moses to tune the translation models.

For the word alignment, we used GIZA++ (Och 2003).

For the language model, we used corpora of newspapers publicly available and collected by Techlimed. The sources are coming from the Open Source Arabic Corpora (Saad 2010) (20M words), the Adjir corpus (Abdelali 2005) (147M words) and other corpora we collected from various online newspapers for a total of 300M words. The language model was created with the IRSTLM toolkit (Federico, 2008).

SMT System	TECH-1	TECH-2	TECH-3
MADAMIRA	Yes	Yes	No
Training data	Alj-train-2014	Alj-train-2014+Alj-dev-2014	Alj-train-2014
LM data	300 M	300 M	300 M
Rule correction	Yes	Yes	Yes

Table 3 System component description

For each system, we then applied the following rules:

- Convert eastern Arabic digits (٠١٢٣٤٥٦٧٨٩) into western Arabic digits (0 1 2 3 4 5 6 7 8 9).
- Separate numbers from word.
- Add a final stop at all sentence with no final punctuation.
- Remove duplicated punctuation marks, for instance ". !" ➔"!" or "!!!!"➔"!".

The results obtained on the development data (Alj-test-2014) and the evaluation set (Alj-test-2015) are given in the Table *4* and Table *5*.

System	P	R	F1
TECH-1	73.05	59.12	65.35
TECH-2	73.33	59.46	65.67
TECH-3	72.99	56.29	63.56

Table 4 Results on the development data (Alj-test-2014)

System	P	R	F1
TECH-1	71.08	64.74	67.76
TECH-2	71.20	64.94	67.93
TECH-3	69.99	60.41	64.85

Table 5 Results on the evaluation data (Alj-Test-2015)

The best system TECH-2 is obtained with the combination of MADAMIRA correction with the SMT system trained on 21k sentences and with correction rules. Table *6* describes the contribution of each component on the correction of TECH-2 on the evaluation data.

TECH-2	P	R	F1
MADAMIRA	80.33	39.98	53.39
+SMT	70.89	59.12	64.89
+Rule correction	71.20	64.94	67.93

Table 6 Performance of TECH-2 on the evaluation data (Alj-Test-2015) by component.

4 Error analysis and discussion

Some difficulties appear when we try to achieve and develop the automatic correction by spellchecker. These problems and difficulties are due not only to the complex morphological system of Arabic language, but also for many reasons, which concern the capacity of spellchecker system. The following list shows us types of problems and difficulties (the Buckwalter transliteration (Buckwalter 2002) is given for each Arabic word example).

Problem related to pronunciation similarities between the Hamza and Alif in some word such as إستعجال/إستقبل (<stEjAl/ <stqbl), which are respectively wrong versions of استعجال/استقبل. (AstEjAl/ Astqbl)

- Similar form problems leading to wrong word substitutions (i.e. incorrect substitution of words by one another): For example, words having similarities in form such as أن (>n) and إن (<n) are confused and ان (An), which does not exist in Arabic, is frequently used.
- Deverbal nouns ending ة/ـة: we notice that spellchecker does not respect Arabic forms of deverbal nouns, called Masdar in the Arabic grammatical tradition. As a result, it could not be able to correct words in which "ه/ـه" is wrongly used at the end of word position instead of ة/ـة (e.g. إبادة (<bAdp) having the deverbal form /?ifâlat/ إفالة (<fAlp) is written إباده/اباده (AbAdh/ <bAdh).
- The morphosyntaxic information are not taken into consideration: the use of morphosyntaxic information makes our system capable of correcting nouns beginning with de morpheme "ال" (definite article) and ending by "ه/ـه" by substituting

this latter by "ـة/ة". These information allow us to apply rules such as المشكله (Alm$klh)➔المشكلة (Alm$klp).

- Plural nouns: broken plural (called also irregular plural) are not controlled by specific or respected rules in spellchecker system (e. g. both forms أفاعيل (>fAEyl) and أفعال (>fEAl) like اساطيل (AsATyl) and اطفال (ATfAl), wrong spelling of أساطيل (>sATyl) and أطفال (>TfAl), are not corrected by spellchecker system. The correct plural forms are أفاعيل (>fAEyl) and أفعال (>fEAl) instead of افعال (AfEAl) and افعال (AfEAl) where we do not respect the rule relative to the Hamza أ in the beginning of the broken plural form.
- Precision problems (homophony): a word in Arabic language may have different forms like سوريا (swryA) and سورية (swryp). But it has the same pronunciation. In such cases, both versions should be taken as correct.
- The spelling is influenced by dialectical language: e,g the use of انو (Anw) rather than أنه (>nh).
- The repetition of the same letter in a word: e.g الجزيييرة; الجهاااد ; االمرسوم ; اللذي (Aljzyyyyrp; AljhAAAAd; AAlmrswm; Alll*y)
- The merging of two words: eg. اقتصادالبلد ; الثورةفسأحمل ; اقطعواالأمل (AqtSAdAlbld; Al-vwrpfs>Hml; AqTEwAAl>ml).

5 Conclusion

This paper has reported on the participation of Techlimed in the 2015 QALB Shared Task on Automatic Arabic Error Correction. We developed two approaches, one based on Hunspell and the other based on a hybrid SMT system.

The best results were obtained with the hybrid SMT system which was able to deal with the punctuation mark corrections. We also tested a hybrid system by combining Hunspell and the SMT system but did not get better results than the SMT system. Our perspective is to include the DiiNAR lexical database (Abbès 2004) and also a large dialectal corpus to improve the results.

References

Abbès, Ramzi Dichy, Joseph and Mohamed Hassoun. "The architecture of a standard arabic lexical database: some figures, ratios and categories from the Diinar. 1 source program." *In Proceedings of the Workshop on Computational Approaches to Arabic Script-based Languages.* Association for Computational Linguistics, 2004. 15–22.

Abdelali, Ahmed. *http://aracorpus.e3rab.com/.* 2005. http://aracorpus.e3rab.com/ (accessed 2015).

Aboelezz, Mariam. "Latinised arabic and connections to bilingual ability." *In Papers from the Lancaster University Postgraduate Conference in Linguistics and Language Teaching.* 2009.

Ayaspell. *Ayaspell Arabic dictionary project.* 2008. http://ayaspell.sourceforge.net.

Buckwalter, Tim. *Buckwalter Arabic Morphological Analyzer Version 1.0.* 2002. http://catalog.ldc.upenn.edu/LDC2002L49 (accessed 06 2015).

Dahlmeier, Daniel and Ng, Hwee Tou. "Better evaluation for grammatical error correction." *In Proceedings of the 2012 Conference of the North American Chapter of the Association for Computational Linguistics: Human Language Technologies.* Association for Computational Linguistics, 2012. 568–572.

Hunspell. *Hunspell.* 2007. http://hunspell.sourceforge.net/ (accessed 2015).

Koehn, Philipp Hoang, Hieu Birch, Alexandra Callison-Burch, Chris Federico, Marcello Bertoldi, Nicola Cowan, Brooke Shen, Wade Moran, Christine Zens, Richard Dyer, Christopher Bojar, Ondrej Constantin, Alexandra and Herbst. Evan. "Open source toolkit for statistical machine translation." *45th Annual Meeting of the ACL on Interactive Poster and Demonstration Sessions.* Association for Computational Linguistics, 2007. 177-180.

Levenshtein, Vladimir. "Binary codes capable of correcting deletions, insertions and reversals." *In Soviet physics doklady.* 1966. volume 10, page 707.

Mohit, Behrang Rozovskaya, Alla Habash, Nizar Zaghouani, Wajd and Obeid, Ossama. "The First QALB Shared Task on Automatic Text Correction for Arabic." *Proceedings of EMNLP Workshop on Arabic Natural Language Processing.* Doha, Qatar, 2014.

Mostefa, Djamel Asbayou, Omar and Abbes, Ramzi. "TECHLIMED System Description for the Shared Task on Automatic Arabic Error Correction." *Proceedings of EMNLP Workshop on Arabic Natural Language Processing.* Doha, Qatar, 2014.

Och, Franz Joseph and Ney, Hermann. "A systematic comparison of various statistical alignment models." *Computational Linguistics.* 2003. 29(1):19–51.

Pasha, Arfath Al-Badrashiny, Mohamed El Kholy, Ahmed Eskander, Ramy Diab, Mona Habash, Nizar Pooleery, Manoj Rambow,

Owen and Roth, Ryan. "MADAMIRA: A Fast, Comprehensive Tool for Morphological Analysis and Disambiguation of Arabic." *Proceedings of LREC'2014.* Reykjavik,, 2014.

Rozovskaya, Alla Bouamor, Houda Habash, Nizar Zaghouani, Wajdi Obeid, Ossama and Mohit, Behrang. "The Second QALB Shared Task on Automatic Text Correction for Arabic." *Proceedings of ACL Workshop on Arabic Natural Language.* Beijing, China, 2015.

Saad, Ashour and Motaz, Wesam. "Osac: Open source arabic corpora." *In 6th ArchEng Int. Symposiums, EEECS.* 2010. volume 10.

Zaghouani, Wajdi Habash, Nizar Bouamor, Houda Rozovskaya, Alla Mohit, Behrang Heider, Abeer and Oflazer, Kemal. "Correction Annotation for Non-Native Arabic Texts: Guidelines and Corpus." *Proceedings of The 9th Linguistic Annotation Workshop.* Denver, Colorado, USA: Association for Computational Linguistics, 2015. 129-139.

Zaghouani, Wajdi Mohit, Behrang Habash, Nizar Obeid, Ossama Tomeh, Nadi Rozovskaya, Alla Farra, Noura Alkuhlani, Sarah and Oflazer, Kemal. "Large scale arabic error annotation: Guidelines and framework." *In Proceedings of the Ninth International Conference on Language Resources and Evaluation (LREC'14).* Reykjavik, Iceland: European Language Resources Association (ELRA), 2014.

UMMU@QALB-2015 Shared Task: Character and Word level SMT pipeline for Automatic Error Correction of Arabic Text

Fethi Bougares[1] **and Houda Bouamor**[2]
[1]**Laboratoire d'Informatique de l'Université du Maine**
[2]**Carnegie Mellon University in Qatar**
fethi.bougares@lium.univ-lemans.fr, hbouamor@qatar.cmu.edu

Abstract

In this paper we present the LIUM (Laboratoire d'Informatique de l'Universit du Maine) and CMU-Q (Carnegie Mellon University in Qatar) joint submission in the Arabic shared task on automatic spelling error correction. Our best system is a sequential combination of two statistical machine translation systems (SMT) trained on top of the MADAMIRA output. The first is a Character-based one, used to produce a first correction at the character level. Characters are then glued to form the input to the second system working at the Word level. This sequential combination achieves an F_1 score of (**69.42**) that is better than the best F_1 score reported on the 2014 test set (**67.91**). The UMMU best submission to the QALB-15 shared task is **ranked first** over 10 submission on the L2 test condition and **second** over 12 submission on the L1 testsset.

1 Introduction

Errors such as incorrect spelling, word choice, or grammar, limit the effectiveness of NLP models: language errors are problematic when provided as input to NLP systems, which are often not robust enough to handle unexpected variations. The difficulty of spelling errors are language-dependent: the more complex the orthography, morphology, or syntax of a language, the more likely it is to have errors in aspects requiring complex human/machine processing. For morphologically rich languages such as Arabic, spelling errors are very frequent, even among native speakers (Shaalan, 2005). This is because Modern Standard Arabic (MSA), the unifying language of formal text, is not the native language of any Arab (Habash et al., 2008).[1] Arabic word morphology is agglutinative: particles and pronouns are written as part of a word (Habash, 2010). This adds an additional challenge to the writer (native or non native) and could be a principal source of spelling mistakes.

In this paper, we describe an approach performing a sequential combination of two statistical machine translation systems for automatic spelling error correction for Arabic. Our system learns models of correction by training on paired examples of errors and their corrections. The training, tuning and test data are provided by the Shared task organizers. Compared to the first edition of this shared task, this year's version proposes two sub-tasks tackling two text genres: (1) news corpus (news articles extracted from Aljazeera); (2) a corpus of sentences written by learners of Arabic as a Second Language. These two corpora are extracted from the QALB corpus (Zaghouani et al., 2014). We tested our system and showed that it performs well on both corpora.

The remainder of this paper is organized as follows. First, we review the main previous efforts for automatic spelling correction, in Section 3. We then give an overview of the various spelling mistakes done while writing an Arabic text, in Section 4. In Section 5, we detail our error correction system. We present in section 6 the results obtained for the different experiments we conducted using the shared task 2015 dev set. Before concluding, we section 7 details the UMMU official results on QALB-15 test set.

[1]MSA is a language that children learn at school and not innately from their parents

Proceedings of the Second Workshop on Arabic Natural Language Processing, pages 166–172,
Beijing, China, July 26-31, 2015.

2 QALB Shared Task Description

The goal of the QALB shared task is developing the of an automatic system for Arabic Error Correction. The QALB-2015 task is the extension of the first QALB shared task (Mohit et al., 2014) that took place last year. The QALB-2014 addressed errors in comments written to Aljazeera articles by native Arabic speakers (Zaghouani et al., 2014). This year's competition includes two tracks, and, in addition to errors produced by native speakers, also includes correction of texts written by learners of Arabic as a foreign language (L2) (Zaghouani et al., 2015). The native track includes Alj-train-2014, Alj-dev-2014, Alj-test-2014 texts from QALB-2014. The L2 track includes L2-train-2015 and L2-dev-2015. This data was released for the development of the systems. The systems were scored on blind test sets Alj-test-2015 and L2-test-2015.

3 Related Work

Automatic error detection and correction include automatic spelling checking, grammar checking and post-editing. Numerous approaches (both supervised and unsupervised) have been explored to improve the fluency of the text and reduce the percentage of out-of-vocabulary words using NLP tools, resources, and heuristics, e.g., morphological analyzers, language models, and edit-distance measure (Kukich, 1992; Oflazer, 1996; Zribi and Ben Ahmed, 2003; Shaalan et al., 2003; Haddad and Yaseen, 2007; Hassan et al., 2008; Habash, 2008; Shaalan et al., 2010). There has been a lot of work on error correction for English (e.g., (Golding and Roth, 1999)).

For Arabic, this issue was studied in various directions and in different research work. In 2003, Shaalan et al. (2003) presented work on the specification and classification of spelling errors in Arabic. Later on, Haddad and Yaseen (2007) presented a hybrid approach using morphological features and rules to fine tune the word recognition and non-word correction method. In order to build an Arabic spelling checker, Attia et al. (2012) developed semi-automatically, a dictionary of 9 million fully inflected Arabic words using a morphological transducer and a large corpus. They then created an error model by analyzing error types and by creating an edit distance ranker. Finally, they analyzed the level of noise in different sources of data and selected the optimal subset to train their system. Alkanhal et al. (2012) presented a stochastic approach for spelling correction of Arabic text. They used a context-based system to automatically correct misspelled words. First of all, a list is generated with possible alternatives for each misspelled word using the Damerau-Levenshtein edit distance, then the right alternative for each misspelled word is selected stochastically using a lattice search, and an n-gram method. Shaalan et al. (2012) trained a Noisy Channel Model on word-based unigrams to detect and correct spelling errors. Dahlmeier and Ng (2012) built specialized decoders for English grammatical error correction.

More recently, (Pasha et al., 2014) created MADAMIRA, a system for morphological analysis and disambiguation of Arabic, this system can be used to improve the accuracy of spelling checking system especially with Hamza spelling correction. A statistical machine translation model to train an error correction system was presented recently by Jeblee et al. (2014). In contrast to their approach, our system combines two level MT models: character level, then a word level.

4 Spelling errors in Arabic

Three types of Arabic word misspellings are defined in the literature: *typographic*, *cognitive* and *phonetic* errors (Haddad and Yaseen, 2007). The typographic errors corresponding to single word error misspelling represent 80% of all misspelling errors in Arabic (Ben Hamadou, 1994). Based on this study, the most common typographic editing errors that can be found in any Arabic text are the following:

Substitution: approximately, 41.5% of errors belong to substitution errors. In the case of (/لغب → لعب/, "he played"), for example, the letter /ع, E/ is mistakenly substituted by /غ, g/, which results in an incorrect word.

Deletion: approximately 23% of single errors are deletion errors. For example in /فح→ فتح /, "he opens", the letter /ت, t/ had been missed leading to an erroneous word.

Insertion: approximately 15% of the errors are insertion errors. For example, (in /المدرسة →

المدرسة/, "the school", the letter /د, d/ is erroneously inserted twice.

Transposition: swapping two letters represents 4% of the errors. i.e., (/تتشرك → تشترك/, "shares"), the letters /ش, $/ and /ت, t/ are swapped.
In addition to misspelling errors, different editing errors can occur in writing. Some can result in :

Merge: words accidentally merged with surrounding words: (الأمم المتحدة→الأممالمتحدة, United Nations)

Split: words mistakenly splitted (فقال→فقال, "he said")

Cognitive and phonetic errors: words generally coming from Arabic dialects: (لكن→لاكن, "but"),

5 SMT system for error correction

We formulate the error correction task as a translation problem where the source part is the text to be corrected and the target part is the correct text. Let's assume that we want to correct an erroneous sentence e to a correct sentence c, and $f_i(e, c)$ is such a model which calculates a probability that c is the correction of e. The goal of the system is to find the correction c^* defined as :

$$\begin{aligned} c^* &= \arg\max_c \ p(c|e) \\ &= \arg\max_c \ p(e|c)p(c) \end{aligned}$$

$p(e|c)$ is estimated in a translation model and $p(c)$ is the target-side language model. The $argmax$ is the task of the decoder and it represent the search for the best hypothesis in the space of possible correction c. The translation system is trained using the well known *MOSES* toolkit (Koehn et al., 2007). The system is constructed using data produced for the QALB shared task and described in Table 1 as follows: First, we generate the correct sentences[2] of the QALB training corpus then translation and reordering models are trained. The language model (LM) is trained on the correct side of the QALB data and a selected part of the Arabic Gigaword corpus.

In order to select the most appropriate amount of monolingual data, we employ data selection techniques based on cross-entropy criterion using *Xenc*[3] (Rousseau, 2013). The selected data is determined in such a way that the corresponding LM minimize the perplexity calculated on the development set. Selected part of each monolingual corpus is used to train an interpolated n-gram [4] back-off target LM using SRILM toolkit (Stolcke et al., 2011) with Kneser-Ney smoothing.

In this work, we propose to use two SMT systems trained with different translation unit (words and characters) as described previously. This was motivated by our intuition that each system will target a different pattern of errors and their combination may outperform the single system performance.

6 Experiments and results

We train four models depending on the used training unit and the nature source side (with or without pre-processing). Each system is evaluated independently and best systems are combined.

6.1 Data description

All our models are built using training, development and testing data provided by the shared task organizers and described in Table 1.

	# sentences	# tokens
Alj-train-2014	19,411	1.1M
L2-train-2015	310	46.3k
Alj-dev-2014	1,017	58.9K
Alj-test-2014	968	56.1k
L2-dev-2015	154	26.3k

Table 1: Train, dev and test data distribution

6.2 Baseline: MADAMIRA corrections

MADAMIRA (**?**) is a tool, originally designed for morphological analysis and disambiguation of MSA and dialectal Arabic texts. MADAMIRA employs different features to select, for each word in context, a proper analysis and performs Alif and Ya spelling correction for the phenomena associated with its letters.

The task organizers provided the shared task data preprocessed with MADAMIRA, including all of the features generated by the tool for every word. Similarly to Jeblee et al. (2014), we use the

[2] for that we used a modified version of the *m2scorer* script that could be distributed

[3] https://github.com/rousseau-lium/XenC

[4] we trained a 4-gram LM for word level and 9-gram LM for character level system

corrections proposed by MADAMIRA and apply them to the data. Table 2 gives the detailed scores obtained using MADAMIRA correction. While the candidates obtained may not necessarily be correct, MADAMIRA performs at a very high precision.

	Precision	Recall	F1
Alj-dev-2014	77.47	32.10	45.40
Alj-test-2014	**78.33**	31.27	44.69
L2-dev-2015	46.46	12.97	20.28

Table 2: F1-score on Dev14, Test14 and L2Dev obtained using MADAMIRA correction

6.3 SMT on raw data

We present here the results we obtained using the wod-level and character-level systems trained on raw non processed data. As shown in Table 3 and Table 4, these systems outperform the MADAMIRA baseline.

	Precision	Recall	F1
Alj-dev-2014	72.69	53.00	61.31
Alj-test-2014	73.80	52.69	61.48
L2-dev-2015	53.40	21.54	30.70

Table 3: Word level SMT for spelling error correction.

It is interesting to note that our character-level system performs better than the word-level one, both on the dev (66.12 *vs.* 61.31) and test sets. This could be explained by the fact that character level system takes advantage from its finer granularity.

	Precision	Recall	F1
Alj-dev-2014	73.19	60.29	66.12
Alj-test-2014	74.22	59.84	66.26
L2-dev-2015	57.08	29.34	38.76

Table 4: Character level SMT error correction.

6.4 SMT on MADAMIRA pre-processed data

The results obtained using MADAMIRA correction candidates (see Table 2) makes it a good start point which one can exploit in order to improve our SMT correction systems. For this we used MADAMIRA as pre-processing step of the SMT training data. Indeed, we re-train our systems over the MADAMIRA pre-processed data. Results for the character-level and word-level systems are presented in Table 5 and Table 6.

	Precision	Recall	F1
Alj-dev-2014	73.72	56.08	63.71
Alj-test-2014	74.33	55.84	63.77
L2-dev-2015	56.79	25.97	35.64

Table 5: Word level SMT error correction with MADAMIRA pre-process

	Precision	Recall	F1
Alj-dev-2014	74.15	61.86	67.45
Alj-test-2014	75.02	61.39	67.53
L2-dev-2015	58.55	30.51	40.12

Table 6: Character level SMT error correction with MADAMIRA pre-process.

As we expected, this combination yields better results (F-score of 40.12 on the L2-dev-2015 data set *vs.* 38.76, when using only the character-level system). It is not surprising that the character level system gives better results than the word level one when trained on the MADAMIRA pre-processed data (66.12 *vs.* 63.71 on Alj-dev-2014).

6.5 Sequential combination

Although the character level system outperforms the word level one, we still want to take benefits from the higher modeling level of word based system. For this we propose two combination setups: (i) *top-down sequential combination* and (ii) *bottom-up sequential combination.* [5] Both combination are performed using data pre-processed with MADAMIRA.

6.5.1 Top-down combination

In this setup, we first use the word-based SMT system. Then we re-translate its outputs using the character level system. The results obtained are given in Table 7. This combination yeilds better results than when using the character level system only (See Table 4).

6.5.2 Bottom-up combination

The Bottom-up combination consists in using the word-level system to re-translate the character

[5]We refer to word to be the top level since characters are of a finer granularity

	Precision	Recall	F1
Alj-dev-2014	69.96	63.18	66.40
Alj-test-2014	70.88	62.59	**66.48**
L2-dev-2015	53.61	31.58	**39.74**

Table 7: Top-down sequential combination

level outputs. Results are shown in Table 8. We obtain our best F1-scores with this setup.

	Precision	Recall	F1
Alj-dev-2014	71.63	66.68	**69.07**
Alj-test-2014	72.77	66.36	**69.42**
L2-dev-2015	56.72	34.80	**43.13**

Table 8: Bottom up sequential combination.

7 UMMU@QALB-2015 Results

In this section, we present the official results of our system on the 2015 QALB test set (Rozovskaya et al., 2015). We submitted two outputs UMMU-1 and UMMU-2. The UMMU-1 is the result of our best system on the dev data (see Table 8 for UMMU-1 dev results) and the UMMU-2 is the output of the Character level SMT without combination (see table 6 for UMMU-2 dev results). The official results of UMMU primary and secondary submissions are respectively presented on table 9 and 10. According to the results presented on Table 9 our system is ranked first in the L2 subtask and second in the L1.

	P	R	F1
L1-test-2015	70.28	71.93	**71.10**
L2-test-2015	54.12	33.26	**41.20**

Table 9: The UMMU Official results on the 2015 test set. First column shows the system rank according to the $F1$ score.

	P	R	F1
L1-test-2015	72.69	67.52	**70.01**
L2-test-2015	55.83	29.47	**38.58**

Table 10: The UMMU-2 results on the 2015 test-set.

Table 10 gives the results of the UMMU-2 submission. With regards to our UMMU-1 results we note that our character-level system has a higher precision and lower recall in both subtask. These findings show that our word-level system, when applied on the character-level outputs, improves the recall but decrease the precision. Thus, a better combination of our systems may improve the final F_1 score by avoiding the precision drop.

8 Conclusion and Future Work

We described our submission in the Arabic shared task on automatic spelling error correction. Our system is a sequential combination of two statistical machine translation systems (SMT). First a Character-based SMT system is used to perform lower level correction. Characters outputs of this systems are then glued and used as the input to the higher level system working at the Word level. This sequential combination allows to achieve a F_1 score of **71.10** on L1-test-2015 and **41.20** on L2-test-2015, which ranks us **2nd** in the L1 subtask and **1st** in the L2 subtask. We submitted is a three-stage system that benefits from a MADAMIRA pre-processing, a low level character based SMT system and a higher word-level SMT system. We showed the complementarity of the three stages. We also showed that at each step we our F1-score was improved. In future work, we would like to investigate the possibility of adding an additional layer that uses a neural network language model to estimate the probability in a continuous space and gives better generalization to unseen events.

Acknowledgements

This publication was partly made possible by grants NPRP-4-1058-1-168 from the Qatar National Research Fund (a member of the Qatar Foundation).

References

Mohamed I. Alkanhal, Mohamed Al-Badrashiny, Mansour M. Alghamdi, and Abdulaziz O. Al-Qabbany. 2012. Automatic Stochastic Arabic Spelling Correction With Emphasis on Space Insertions and Deletions. *IEEE Transactions on Audio, Speech & Language Processing*, 20(7):2111–2122.

Mohammed Attia, Pavel Pecina, Younes Samih, Khaled Shaalan, and Josef van Genabith. 2012. Improved Spelling Error Detection and Correction for Arabic. In *Proceedings of COLING 2012: Posters*, pages 103–112, Mumbai, India.

Abdelmajid Ben Hamadou. 1994. The Phases of Computational Analysis of Arabic Towards Detecting and Correcting Errors. In *Proceedings of the Second Conference for Arabization of Computers, in Arabic.*

Daniel Dahlmeier and Hwee Tou Ng. 2012. A Beam-Search Decoder for Grammatical Error Correction. In *Proceedings of the 2012 Joint Conference on Empirical Methods in Natural Language Processing and Computational Natural Language Learning*, pages 568–578, Jeju Island, Korea.

A. R. Golding and D. Roth. 1999. A Winnow Based Approach to Context-Sensitive Spelling Correction. *Machine Learning*, 34(1-3):107–130.

Nizar Habash, Owen Rambow, Mona Diab, and Reem Kanjawi-Faraj. 2008. Guidelines for Annotation of Arabic Dialectness. In *Proceedings of the LREC Workshop on HLT & NLP within the Arabic world*, Marrakech, Morocco.

Nizar Habash. 2008. Four Techniques for Online Handling of Out-of-Vocabulary Words in Arabic-English Statistical Machine Translation. In *Proceedings of ACL-08: HLT, Short Papers*, pages 57–60, Columbus, Ohio.

Nizar Habash. 2010. *Introduction to Arabic Natural Language Processing*, volume 3. Morgan & Claypool Publishers.

Bassam Haddad and Mustafa Yaseen. 2007. Detection and Correction of Non-words in Arabic: a Hybrid Approach. *International Journal of Computer Processing of Oriental Languages*, 20(04):237–257.

Ahmed Hassan, Sara Noeman, and Hany Hassan. 2008. Language Independent Text Correction using Finite State Automata. In *Proceedings of the Third International Joint Conference on Natural Language Processing (IJCNLP 2008)*, pages 913–918, Hyderabad, India.

Serena Jeblee, Houda Bouamor, Wajdi Zaghouani, and Kemal Oflazer. 2014. Cmuq@qalb-2014: An smt-based system for automatic arabic error correction. In *Proceedings of the EMNLP 2014 Workshop on Arabic Natural Language Processing (ANLP)*, pages 137–142, Doha, Qatar, October. Association for Computational Linguistics.

P. Koehn, H. Hoang, A. Birch, C. Callison-Burch, M. Federico, N. Bertoldi, B. Cowan, W. Shen, C. Moran, R. Zens, et al. 2007. Moses: Open source toolkit for statistical machine translation. In *Annual meeting-association for computational linguistics*, volume 45, page 2.

Karen Kukich. 1992. Techniques for Automatically Correcting Words in Text. *ACM Computing Surveys (CSUR)*, 24(4):377–439.

Behrang Mohit, Alla Rozovskaya, Nizar Habash, Wajdi Zaghouani, and Ossama Obeid. 2014. The First QALB Shared Task on Automatic Text Correction for Arabic. In *Proceedings of EMNLP Workshop on Arabic Natural Language Processing*, Doha, Qatar, October.

Kemal Oflazer. 1996. Error-Tolerant Finite-State Recognition with Applications to Morphological Analysis and Spelling Correction. *Computational Linguistics*, 22(1):73–89.

Arfath Pasha, Mohamed Al-Badrashiny, Mona Diab, Ahmed El Kholy, Ramy Eskander, Nizar Habash, Manoj Pooleery, Owen Rambow, and Ryan Roth. 2014. MADAMIRA: A Fast, Comprehensive Tool for Morphological Analysis and Disambiguation of Arabic. In *Proceedings of the Ninth International Conference on Language Resources and Evaluation (LREC'14)*, pages 1094–1101, Reykjavik, Iceland.

Anthony Rousseau. 2013. Xenc: an open-source tool for data selection in natural language processing. *Prague Bulletin of Mathematical Linguistics*, 100:73–82.

Alla Rozovskaya, Houda Bouamor, Nizar Habash, Wajdi Zaghouani, Ossama Obeid, and Behrang Mohit. 2015. The Second QALB Shared Task on Automatic Text Correction for Arabic. In *Proceedings of ACL Workshop on Arabic Natural Language Processing*, Beijing, China, July.

Khaled Shaalan, Amin Allam, and Abdallah Gomah. 2003. Towards Automatic Spell Checking for Arabic. In *Proceedings of the 4th Conference on Language Engineering, Egyptian Society of Language Engineering (ELSE)*, Cairo, Egypt.

Khaled Shaalan, Rana Aref, and Aly Fahmy. 2010. An Approach for Analyzing and Correcting Spelling Errors for Non-native Arabic Learners. In *Proceedings of The 7th International Conference on Informatics and Systems, INFOS2010, the special track on Natural Language Processing and Knowledge Mining*, pages 28–30, Cairo, Egypt.

Khaled Shaalan, Mohammed Attia, Pavel Pecina, Younes Samih, and Josef van Genabith. 2012. Arabic Word Generation and Modelling for Spell Checking. In *Proceedings of the Eighth International Conference on Language Resources and Evaluation (LREC-2012)*, pages 719–725, Istanbul, Turkey.

Khaled F Shaalan. 2005. Arabic GramCheck: A Grammar Checker for Arabic. *Software: Practice and Experience*, 35(7):643–665.

Andreas Stolcke, Jing Zheng, Wen Wang, and Victor Abrash. 2011. SRILM at sixteen: Update and outlook. In *Proceedings of the Automatic Speech Recognition and Understanding Workshop (ASRU)*, Décembre.

Wajdi Zaghouani, Behrang Mohit, Nizar Habash, Ossama Obeid, Nadi Tomeh, Alla Rozovskaya, Noura Farra, Sarah Alkuhlani, and Kemal Oflazer. 2014. Large Scale Arabic Error Annotation: Guidelines and Framework. In *Proceedings of the Ninth International Conference on Language Resources and Evaluation (LREC'14)*, Reykjavik, Iceland.

Wajdi Zaghouani, Nizar Habash, Houda Bouamor, Alla Rozovskaya, Behrang Mohit, Abeer Heider, and Kemal Oflazer. 2015. Correction annotation for non-native arabic texts: Guidelines and corpus. In *Proceedings of The 9th Linguistic Annotation Workshop*, pages 129–139, Denver, Colorado, USA, June. Association for Computational Linguistics.

Chiraz Zribi and Mohammed Ben Ahmed. 2003. Efficient Automatic Correction of Misspelled Arabic Words Based on Contextual Information. In *Proceedings of the Knowledge-Based Intelligent Information and Engineering Systems Conference*, pages 770–777, Oxford, UK.

Robust Part-of-Speech Tagging of Arabic Text

Hanan Aldarmaki and Mona Diab
Department of Computer Science
The George Washington University
{aldarmaki;mtdiab}@gwu.edu

Abstract

We present a new and improved part of speech tagger for Arabic text that incorporates a set of novel features and constraints. This framework is presented within the MADAMIRA software suite, a state-of-the-art toolkit for Arabic language processing. Starting from a linear SVM model with basic lexical features, we add a range of features derived from morphological analysis and clustering methods. We show that using these features significantly improves part-of-speech tagging accuracy, especially for unseen words, which results in better generalization across genres. The final model, embedded in a sequential tagging framework, achieved 97.15% accuracy on the main test set of newswire data, which is higher than the current MADAMIRA accuracy of 96.91% while being 30% faster.

1 Introduction

Part-of-speech (POS) tagging is an essential enabling technology and a precursor for most Natural Language Processing (NLP) tasks such as syntactic parsing, semantic role labeling, machine translation, and information extraction. POS tagging ranges in its complexity depending on the morphological richness of the targeted language. For morphologically rich languages, POS tagging poses a significant challenge, especially when moving away from formal textual genres to more informal genres. In this paper, we present a suite of linear supervised learning methods and features used to enhance POS tagging for Modern Standard Arabic (MSA) text using a relatively complex POS tag set. The novel POS tagger is presented within the context of the MADAMIRA suite framework (Pasha et. al., 2014). MADAMIRA is a combination of two well established approaches: AMIRA (Diab, 2009) and MADA (Roth et al, 2008). AMIRA is a relatively simple cascaded system that performs clitic segmentation, segmentation correction or normalization, and POS tagging as three separate steps performed sequentially, while MADA performs all three steps in one fell swoop. Both systems are based on supervised learning. However, the MADA approach relies on optimizing the results of a morphological analyzer while AMIRA does not rely on external resources. While the current MADAMIRA release only includes the MADA system, the goal is to combine both systems to improve MADAMIRA further. For the remainder of this paper, we will refer to the two systems as MD-MADA and MD-AMIRA, as both are presented within the MADAMIRA software suite.

In MD-AMIRA, POS tagging is implemented for MSA using linear classification with lexical features, and it results in reasonable accuracy within familiar contexts. However, the performance degrades when the model encounters words unseen in training. In this paper, we attempt to enhance the performance of this model, especially for unseen words, by including features from various external resources while maintaining the simplicity of the linear model. We refer to this enhanced model as MD-AMIRA+EX. Using a morphological analyzer, we extract morphological features as well as valid part-of-speech tags for input tokens. We also use these tags to impose soft constraints on the output. In addition, we include word clusters using two clustering methods applied to a large unlabeled data set. The basic POS tagging model and the additional features and constraints are described in Section 4.

MSA exhibits affixival and agglutinative morphology, where various forms of prepositions, articles, and pronouns are merged with words as clitics. A surface space-delimited word such as

Proceedings of the Second Workshop on Arabic Natural Language Processing, pages 173–182,
Beijing, China, July 26-31, 2015.

"wsyktbwnhA",[1] 'and they will write it', packs what would be considered several words in a language such as English. The different words are expressed as agglutinated morphemes or clitics broken up as follows: *"w+ s+ yktbwn +hA"*, 'and+ will+ write_plural +it_fem'. Due to limited amounts of labeled data, separating clitics from words, i.e. tokenization, is essential in reducing sparsity and enhancing the accuracy of POS tagging. In this paper, we address MSA tokenization as a precursor to POS tagging.

In MD-AMIRA, MSA tokenization is split into two steps: clitic segmentation and segmentation normalization. In the segmentation step, described in Section 3.1.1, we break each input word into segments corresponding to the clitics and the stem that make up that word. In MSA, some morphemes change in form as a result of affixation, and we render them to their original underlying forms in the segmentation normalization step, which is described in Section 3.1.2.

We evaluate the performance of the separate steps and the whole pipeline from tokenization to part-of-speech tagging in Sections 6 to 8. We show that this approach is robust and efficient as it compares to state of the art accuracy while exhibiting robust performance on unseen words.

2 Related Work

The sequential NLP process presented in this paper is adapted from the AMIRA toolkit, which is described in (Diab, 2009) and (Diab et al., 2004), and is publicly available. Another data-driven part-of-speech tagger for Arabic was presented in (Kopru, 2011), which uses an HMM to learn an efficient classifier using surface features.

The alternative approach is MADA, which relies on deep morphological analysis and disambiguation, as described in (Habah et al., 2005) and (Roth et al, 2008). Several SVM classifiers are trained to predict morphological features in the first stage. These features are then used to rank the morphological analyses retrieved from a dictionary, and the analysis with the highest score is taken as the final analysis for the given word. This deep analysis results in accurate and detailed tagging albeit slower than simple SVM methods. Finally, the problem of classification and incorporating structural constraints on the output is studied in (Punyakanok et al, 2005). This is related to the constrained POS tagging attempted here, where external inference is used to maintain consistency after learning. A related example of incorporating external resources to constrain the learned classifiers is presented in (Do and Roth, 2010)

[1] We transliterate Arabic text using Buckwalter romanization scheme: http://www.qamus.org

3 Approach

We adapt the AMIRA tagger approach by using linear support vector machines (SVM) as our basic classification machinery for both MD-AMIRA and MD-AMIRA+EX. We approach both Tokenization and POS tagging as classification problems. The basic models directly follow the implementation details described in (Diab, 2009).

3.1 Tokenization

3.1.1 Clitic Segmentation

Clitics are independent meaning-bearing units that are phonologically and orthographically merged with words, either as prefixes (proclitics) or suffixes (enclitics). Clitics are different from derivational or inflectional affixes, which either change the meaning or the syntactic role of their stems and are not segmented here. A word, in this context, refers to a stem and its inflectional and derivational affixes, and clitic segmentation is the process of separating clitics from words. Since clitics have their own meaning and part-of-speech tags, separating them reduces sparsity in the input space.

In MSA, a word can have up to three proclitics and one enclitic. Table 1 shows some of the word classes that serve as clitics in MSA.

Type	Category	Examples
Proclitic	Definite article	Al
Proclitic	Prepositions	b, l, k
Proclitic	Conjunctions	w, f
Proclitic	Future marker	s
Enclitics	Pronouns	h, hm, hmA, etc.

Table 1: Examples of clitics in MSA

Set up: Segmentation is modeled as a classification problem at the character level, where each character is given a tag. Similar to the AMIRA framework, we adopt an IOB chunk/segment tagging scheme. The tag set is defined as follows:

Tag set: {B-PRE, I-PRE, B-WORD, I-WORD, B-SUFF, I-SUFF, O}

WORD:	stem+inflectional affixes
PRE:	enclitic
SUFF:	proclitic
B- :	beginning of segment
I- :	Inside segment
O:	outside of segment (word boundaries)

The input consists of Buckwalter (BW) transliterated Arabic characters (Habah et al., 2007) with word boundary markers, preprocessed by digit normalization (converting all digits into '8') and removal of diacritics, if any. The features are as follows: (1) contextual features: [-5,+5] characters in context, the previous [-5, -1] tag decisions, and (2) lexical features: the whole space-delimited word, and character N-grams, N$\leq$4, within that word.

3.1.2 Segmentation Normalization

Segmentation normalization is a correction step that attempts to restore citation forms of some words that have been transformed as a result of the morphotactics of clitic affixation. This task aims to reduce sparsity in the input space, and is inspired by the AMIRA tokenization lemmatization step (Diab et al., 2004), but we include additional forms of normalization. More details on Arabic orthographic and morphological adjustment rules can be found in (El Kholy and Habash, 2010).

Some forms of correction are deterministic, such as restoring the definite article *"Al"* ('the') from its reduced form *"l"* when it's preceded by the preposition *"l"* ('for'). Another example is the restoration of the trailing *"n"* in prepositions such as *"mn"* (from') and *"En"* ('about') when followed by the suffix *"mA"* ('what'), as in *"mmA"* $\rightarrow$ *"mn+mA"*. These are cases of clitic lemmatization, and since they are observed on a closed class of tokens, they are easily addressed as a post-tokenization processing step.

On the other hand, segmentation of open-class word forms cannot be restored deterministically. In MSA, words that end with the feminine marker character Taa Marbuta *"p"*, are transformed into *"t"* when followed by suffixes, as in: *"klmp"* ('word') $\rightarrow$ *"klmt+h"* ('his word'). A stem that ends with a *"t"* could either be a transformed *"p"* or a word that originally ends with *"t"*, as in *"byt"* (house). The other type of word ending that is transformed in affixation is the character Alef Maqsura *"Y"*, which is transformed into *"y"* or *"A"* if followed by suffixes (e.g.: *"ElY"* ('on'), $\rightarrow$ *"Ely+h"* ('on him')). The problem is more complex for words that can correspond to multiple lemmas such as *"ESAhm"*, which could correspond to the verb *"ESY+hm"* ('disobeyed+them') or the noun *"ESA+hm"* ('stick +their').

The restoration of Taa Marbuta and Alef Maqsura is not a deterministic process and it requires both contextual information and/or deeper knowledge of the language. The segmentation normalization step attempts to achieve this type of correction by learning to distinguish these cases from contextual data as follows.

Set up: The problem of segmentation normalization is addressed as a classification problem on the token level cascaded from the prior segmentation step. The input consists of a list of tokens, with proclitic and enclitic markers–the '+' marker indicating a segmentation point. The feature vector consists of [-2,+2] tokens in context, character N-grams, N$\leq$4, for the current token, and the previous 2 tag decisions. Each token is assigned one of the following tags:

CIP:	Change trailing t to p
CIY:	Change trailing y or A to Y
NA:	Do nothing

4 Part of Speech Tagging

POS tagging is performed on the resulting tokenized text; that is, after performing clitic segmentation and segmentation normalization. The tag set used is a modified version of ERTS (Diab, 2007), which explicitly encodes several morphological features like determiner definiteness, gender, and number for nominals. We extend the tagset to include person, gender, number, and voice for verbs, and we refer to the new tagset as ERTS2. These fine-grained tags can be easily reduced to broad part-of-speech classes after prediction, which makes them suitable for a range of applications. They encode the full part-of-speech tag information provided in the LDC Arabic Treebank, excluding syntactic mood, syntactic case, and construct state definiteness. The following are some examples of ERTS2 tags, which illustrate the level of encoded details—refer to the appendix for a full listing of possible tags:

PV+3_MASC_SG: Third-person singular masculine perfective verb
IV_PASS+3_MASC_SG: Passive-voice masculine singular imperfective verb
ADJ+FEM_PL: Feminine plural adjective

The input to this classification problem consists of a list of digit-normalized tokens with explicit enclitic and proclitic affixes marked with '+' at segmentation points. The feature vector consists of [-2,+2] tokens in context, character N-grams, N$\leq$4, for the current token, the type of the current token {alpha, numeric}, and the previous 2 tag decisions.

We add two more components (constraints and features) over the MD-AMIRA POS tagging pipeline as follows.

4.1 ALMOR for Constrained Tagging

ALMOR (Habah, 2007) is a morphological analysis and generation system for MSA and dialectal Arabic. Given a word, ALMOR retrieves all possible analyses for that word and a list of characteristics, including part-of-speech tags, for each analysis. ALMOR constructs the analyses by generating all possible segmentations and verifying the validity and compatibility of the segments on an underlying database of valid stems and affixes.

In our POS tagging model, ALMOR is used as a source of external knowledge to constrain the statistical SVM tagger: the retrieved ALMOR part-of-speech tags are used as constraints on the SVM decision function by penalizing tags that do not appear in ALMOR analyses set. Given k tags, the POS tag y_i for a word w_i, as given by the original SVM decision function, is the tag with the maximum SVM score

$$\underset{y_i, i \in \{1,..,k\}}{\operatorname{argmax}} \ (\operatorname{score}(y_i))$$

Using ALMOR, we retrieve the set of possible part-of-speech tags, S_i, and penalize the tags that are not found in this set by reducing their SVM score. Accordingly, the final tag is given by the modified decision function:

$$\underset{y_i, i \in \{1,..,k\}}{\operatorname{argmax}} \ (\operatorname{score}(y_i) - \rho \, \mathrm{I}_{S_i^C}(y_i))$$

where I is the indicator function of the complement of S_i, and ρ is the penalty parameter. This modification is implemented only in the prediction step, so the experiment doesn't require re-training of the models.

4.2 Additional Features

The following sets of features were extracted from external resources and tested separately as well as in combination.

Morphological features: The top m part-of-speech tags from the set of analyses S_i, as described in the previous section, are used as features. The optimal number of tags, m, to include is tuned from the data. Additional morphological features extracted from ALMOR are voice, gender, person, and number.

Clustering features: We add cluster IDs retrieved from a large unlabeled dataset using two clustering methods: Brown clustering (Brown et al., 1992), and word2vec K-means clustering (Mikolov et. al., 2013).

Named-entity-related features: To support proper noun identification, we add binary features for exact and partial match in a gazetteer, and capitalization in the English gloss in any one of ALMOR analyses.

5 Experimental Set Up

5.1 Data set

The data sets used for training the models are LDC's Arabic Treebank (ATB) parts 1,2, and 3 (Maamouri et. al., 2004), which consist of MSA newswire data. The data is split as follows: 10% development set, 80% training set, and 10% test set. For cross-genre evaluation, we use the test set from ATB parts 5,6,7 and 10, which consist of MSA broadcast news and a small portion from the Weblog genres. The data sets are pre-processed using the approach described in (Habah et al., 2005) to correct annotation inconsistencies.

5.2 SVM Classification

Linear SVM classification is implemented using Cogent (Pasha et. al., 2014), a java utility and a wrapper around Liblinear (Fan et. al., 2008). Cogent pre-processes the input and converts text features into binary feature vectors for linear classification. In these experiments, Cogent is configured to keep a maximum of 100,000 features, so features are filtered to keep the maximum value within that range by removing the least frequent feature-value pairs. This limitation is imposed to keep the models more manageable during training and prediction.

6 Evaluation

The performance of our systems, MD-AMIRA and MD-AMIRA+EX, are evaluated and compared against the performance of MD-MADA (Pasha et. al., 2014), on the same tasks. MD-MADA produces highly sophisticated and accurate analysis of raw text, which includes a large number of morphological features reflecting the full spectrum of part-of-speech tags used in ATB, which is more specified than the ERTS2 tag set used in this work. Moreover, MD-MADA produces lemmas and their corresponding diacritization forms. We report comparative results on Tokenization and POS tagging using a subset of MD_-MADA outputs that correspond directly to our output specifications.

6.1 Clitic Segmentation

We evaluate the performance of MD-AMIRA as described in Section 3.1.1. Table 2 shows the overall performance of MD-AMIRA segmentation model compared with MD-MADA using the harmonic mean F-score metric. We perform clitic segmentation at the most detailed segmentation level, D3, which is ATB tokenization in addition to segmenting out the definite article Al (Habah et al., 2006). The overall F score of our linear segmentation is over 99 on ATB1-2-3 test set, comparable to the F score achieved by MD-MADA. Both models perform worse on cross-genre data, i.e. ATB5-6-7-10 test set, and MD-AMIRA performs worse on this set.

Model	F score on test set	
	ATB1-2-3	ATB5-6-7-10
MD-MADA	99.20	98.54
MD-AMIRA	99.24	97.76

Table 2: Overall segmentation performance on held-out test data

We report precision and recall results at the chunk level, PRE, WORD, SUFF in Figure 1. On ATB1-2-3 test set, MD-AMIRA has higher precision and lower recall rates over all segment types. On cross-genre data, MD-AMIRA precision drops for all types, with a notable drop in suffix segmentation. This set consists primarily of broadcast news transcriptions, and it includes filled pauses transcribed as ">h" ('uh'), which are not encountered in the formal newswire training data. In MD-AMIRA, the "h" in this interjection is incorrectly segmented as a possessive pronoun "+h", ('his'), and this is responsible for about 60% of the drop in suffix precision.

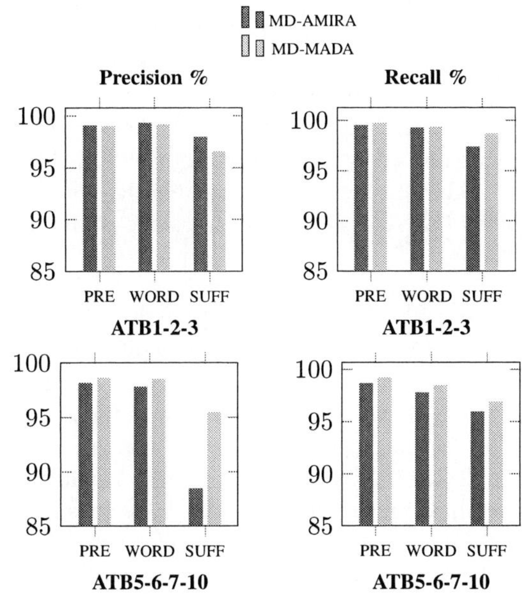

Figure 1: Chunk-level segmentation performance on held-out test data

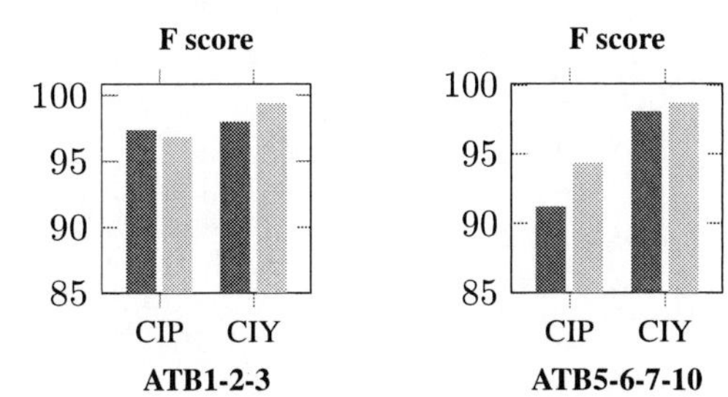

Figure 2: Segmentation Normalization performance on held-out test data

6.2 Segmentation Normalization

Figure 2 shows the performance of normalization conditions CIP and CIY using both systems on each test set. On ATB1-2-3 test set, the performance MD-AMIRA is comparable to MD-MADA. On cross-genre data, the performance of MD-AMIRA in CIP normalization is significantly lower than MD-MADA. Around half the errors in CIP identification are caused by words unseen in training since MD-AMIRA does not use any external resources in this step. Note that these results are evaluated after performing automatic segmentation with each system, so some errors are propagated from the clitic segmentation step.

7 Part of Speech Tagging

We first analyze the performance of the POS tagging module on the development set independently using gold tokenization. The purpose of this analysis is to tune the model without the effect of errors cascaded from automatic tokenization. In Section 8, we evaluate the performance of the finalized POS tagging model within the pipelined MD-AMIRA system and compare it with MD-MADA.

7.1 ALMOR Constrained Tagging

As discussed in Section 4.1, we modify the SVM scores to prioritize the tags retrieved by ALMOR. Figure 3 shows the performance as a function of ρ on the development set (the y-axis is divided and scaled for clarity). Without a constraint, the overall accuracy is 97.3%. Adding the constraints initially improves the overall accuracy, which peaks around $\rho = 1$, then drops considerably. Breaking up the accuracy on seen versus unseen words in training, the accuracy of unseen words increases generally, and is maximized around $\rho = 2$. For seen words, where the accuracy is close to 98% to start with, adding the constraints degrades performance.

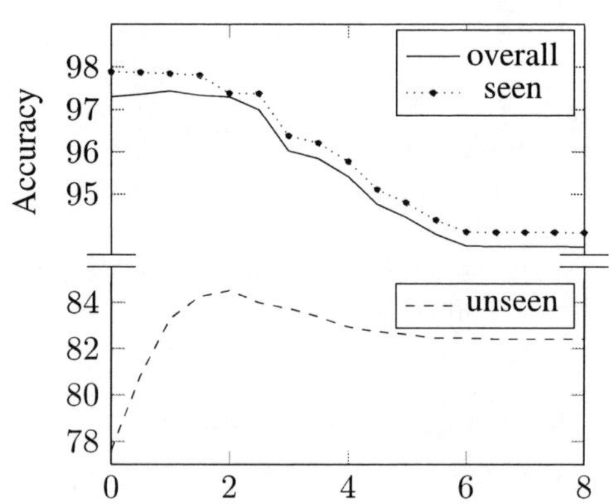

Figure 3: Accuracy as a function of ρ

Accordingly, we impose the constraints only on words that are unseen in training. This achieves an overall accuracy of 97.5%, which is a statistically significant improvement.[2]

7.2 ALMOR Tags as Features

An alternative use for the part-of-speech tags retrieved from ALMOR is to include the top m tags as features. Figure 4 shows the accuracy with m tags. Adding a single tag significantly improves the overall accuracy, which continues to improve up to $m = 4$. While adding more tags as features slightly improves the accuracy, limiting the number of retrieved tags improves the speed of the prediction model. Since the improvement beyond $m = 2$ is not statistically significant, we keep the number of tags at $m = 2$, which achieves an accuracy of 97.64%.

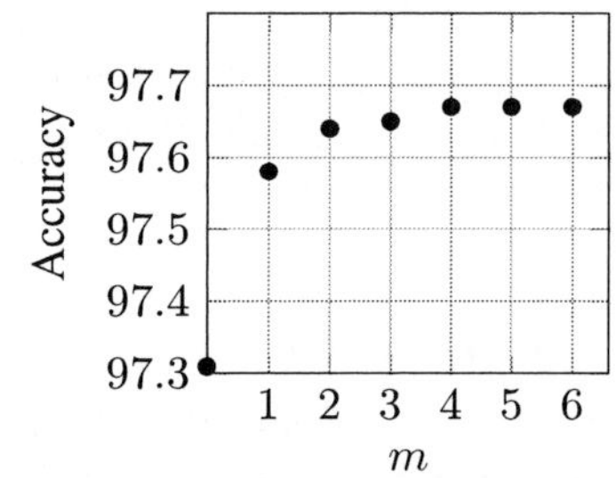

Figure 4: Accuracy as a function of m

7.3 Impact of additional features

In addition to POS tags, additional morphological features can be extracted from ALMOR analyses. We extracted the following set of features: number, gender, person, and voice, from the top two analyses, and included them as features on top of the basic set of lexical features.

We also experimented with a set of named-entity-related features: a binary feature for having a match in a set of gazetteers, and a binary feature for capitalization in the English gloss in one of ALMOR analyses (which is equivalent to having proper noun as one of the analyses). These features are added to help identify proper nouns. We tested these two sets of features separately, and the overall accuracy as well as the accuracy for unseen words are shown in Table 3.

Feature Set	Overall	Unseen
MD-AMIRA	96.58%	77.60
Morph. Features	97.50%	84.36%
NE Features	97.31%	77.76%

Table 3: Performance with Additional Features

[2] We test statistical significance using an exact test for one sample binomial proportions, at the 0.05 significance level.

Adding morphological features results in a statistically significant improvement in accuracy and around 7% reduction in error rate for unseen words. Named-entity features, on the other hand, do not improve performance. Both gazetteer matches and capitalization are features that could be triggered by adjectives, nouns, and proper nouns as they have similar word forms in MSA. The neutral result suggests that these features add noise which offsets any improvement from proper noun identification.

7.4 Clustering

We performed Brown clustering as well as Google's word2vec K-means clustering using an automatically tokenized version of LDC's Arabic Gigaword dataset (Graff, 2003). The number of clusters, k, is empirically set to 500. Table 4 shows the effect of adding these cluster IDs as features on top of the basic model. Both clustering methods result in a statistically significant improvement in accuracy, especially for unseen words. Combining both clustering methods as features achieves additional gains in performance, suggesting that the two clustering methods provide complementary information.

Clustering Method	Accuracy	
	Overall	Unseen
MD-AMIRA	97.31%	77.60%
+Brown Clustering	97.49%	83.96%
+Word2Vec	97.44%	82.36%
+Brown & Word2Vec	97.52%	84.76%

Table 4: POS Tagging Accuracy with Clustering Features

7.5 Combining Features

We now evaluate the models with a combination of these features. Table 5 shows the performance of the different models as evaluated on the development set. Starting from the basic model, MD-AMIRA, with only lexical features, we add the feature sets one at a time and compare the accuracy.

Each set of features incrementally improves the performance, and the highest improvement is achieved by adding two tags from ALMOR. Adding more features can improve the performance, but the improvements are less evident when combined with the existing features. Adding morphological features in M_2, for example, does not help since the morphological features are implied in the POS tags already included in M_1, and in this case the accuracy drops slightly. In M_3, where we combine POS tags, morphological features, and cluster IDs, the accuracy improves for unseen words, and it performs better than M_3b where we exclude morphological features.

In M_4, we re-tune the penalty parameter ρ over M_3. Adding this penalty does not significantly improve the performance as it is outweighed by the improvements from the other features. Moreover, adding these soft constraints reduces the speed of the prediction model. Thus, we choose M_3 as our final model–note that the difference between M_3 and M_3b is not statistically significant and both have the same prediction speed. Using M_3, the accuracy of tagging words unseen in training is around 90%, a considerable gain over the baseline. We use M_3 as the POS tagging model in MD-AMIRA+EX.

Model	Accuracy	
	Overall	Unseen Words
MD-AMIRA	97.309%	77.60%
M_1	97.637%	88.96%
M_2	97.628%	88.72%
M_3	97.682%	90.64%
M_3b	97.677%	90.40%
M_4	97.686%	90.76%

Table 5: Performance of POS tagging models on ATB1-2-3 development set. **MD-AMIRA**: baseline model with surface features. **M_1**: basic features + top two tags from ALMOR. **M_2**:The features in M_1 + morphological features. **M_3**: The features in M_2 + clustering. **M_3b**: The features in M_1 + clustering. **M_4**: The features in M_3 + penalty $\rho = 0.45$.

8 Overall Performance

We evaluate the performance of the system as a whole process from tokenization to part-of-speech tagging. The performance of our final system MD-AMIRA+EX on ATB1-2-3 held out test set is compared against two systems: the baseline of basic lexical features, MD-AMIRA, and the state-of-the-art system, MD-MADA. In order to compare MD-MADA to our system, we reduce the MD-MADA tag set to the ERTS2 tag set.

Table 6 shows the overall accuracy of these systems in addition to the tagging speed in tokens per

Model	ERTS Accuracy		Broad Tags [3]	Speed
	Overall	Unseen	Accuracy	tokens\sec
MD-AMIRA	96.78%	73.38%	98.01%	~2415
MD-AMIRA+EX	97.15%	89.22%	98.24%	~1395
MD-MADA	96.91%	85.28%	98.19%	~1050

Table 6: Performance on ATB1-2-3 held out test set

second, which is evaluated on the same hardware.

The fastest system is MD-AMIRA, which can tag at least 70% more tokens per second than the other models, but results in lower accuracy. The performance on unseen words, which make up about 2.5% of tokens in this set, is particularly bad. MD-AMIRA+EX processes about 30% more tokens per second than MD-MADA while achieving a higher accuracy in this set, which is statistically significant. The large improvement on unseen tokens reflects the generalization power of this model compared to the baseline. Note that in each model, some errors are due to segmentation, but since MD-AMIRA, MD-AMIRA+EX, and MD-MADA systems achieved high segmentation accuracy on this set, the effect is minimal. As a demonstration of this effect, MD-AMIRA+EX achieved 97.64% accuracy on this set using gold tokenization; segmentation errors reduced the overall accuracy by about 0.5%. For unseen words, the accuracy using gold tokenization is 91.78%, more than 3% relative increase in accuracy compared to automatic segmentation. This indicates that we have a relatively robust and efficient POS tagging model.

Most of the errors in POS tagging are due to confusion between the main classes: nouns, adjectives, and verbs. Interestingly, MD-MADA have lower recall for proper nouns than MD-AMIRA+EX. Table 7 shows the number of proper noun misclassifications using both systems. We only show the count of proper nouns that are incorrectly classified as either adjective or verb, which account for the majority of errors related to proper nouns. The table illustrate one category in which MD-AMIRA+EX outperform MD-MADA in POS tagging.

Model	ADJ	VERB
MD-AMIRA+EX	69	50
MD-MADA	125	107

Table 7: Proper noun misclassifications

Table 8 shows the accuracy on cross-genre data. MD-AMIRA+EX achieves a significantly higher accuracy than MD-AMIRA with a large improvement in accuracy for unseen words, which make up about 5% of tokens in this set. Compared to MD-MADA, MD-AMIRA+EX performed worse on this set. This decline in performance is mostly attributed to the segmentation errors from MD-AMIRA+EX tokenization, which is worse than MD-MADA tokenization in this set as shown in Section 6.1. Using gold tokenization, MD-AMIRA+EX resulted in 95.4% POS tagging accuracy on this set; segmentation errors reduced the overall accuracy by more than 1%. For unseen words, the accuracy using gold tokenization is 80.16%, an increase of more than 5% over the accuracy using automatic segmentation. This is further evidence that MD-AMIRA+EX POS tagging model is robust as it achieves close to state-of-the-art accuracy in spite of having more segmentation errors.

Model	ERTS Accuracy	
	Overall	Unseen Words
MD-AMIRA	93.35%	55.92%
MD-AMIRA+EX	94.38%	75.53%
MD-MADA	94.71%	77.19%

Table 8: Accuracy on cross-genre data

9 Conclusions

We experimented with various feature sets to improve the performance and generalization power of linear part-of-speech tagging. Adding a couple of part-of-speech tags from a morphological analyzer as features greatly reduced the error rate and achieved the largest gain in performance in our final model. Adding morphological features from the same analyzer, while it achieved significant improvements when tested separately, did not achieve large gains in the final model's accuracy

[3]broad part-of-speech classes, such as noun, verb, etc.

since these features are mostly redundant given the POS tags. Similarly, using the POS tags as soft constraints on the SVM decision function did not achieve significant gains on the model that already incorporates these tags as features. Adding cluster IDs, on the other hand, reduced the error rate, particularly for unseen words and genres, even when combined with the other features.

The clustering methods we experimented with were implemented using a large dataset of newswire data: the same genre used for training. To achieve better generalization over different genre, clustering data from various genre would be an interesting experiment for future work. Furthermore, part-of-speech tagging performance depends on the accuracy of segmentation. Our final model achieved lower accuracy on cross-genre data due to segmentation errors. Improving the performance of tokenization can be another way to improve the final model. Overall, the model achieved close to state-of-the-art performance and good generalization over unseen words while being reasonably fast.

References

P. F. Brown, P. V. deSouza, R. L. Mercer, V. J. D. Pietra, and J. C. Lai. Class-based n-gram models of natural language. Computational Linguistics, 18(4):467-479, 1992.

M. Diab, K. Hacioglu, and D. Jurafsky. Automatic tagging of arabic text: From raw text to base phrase chunks. In Proceedings of HLT-NAACL 2004: Short Papers , pages 149152. Association for Computational Linguistics, 2004.

M. Diab. Improved Arabic base phrase chunking with a new enriched pos tag set. In Proceedings of the 2007 Workshop on Computational Approaches to Semitic Languages.

M. Diab. Second generation amira tools for arabic processing: Fast and robust tokenization, pos tagging, and base phrase chunking. In Proceedings of the Second International Conference on Arabic Language Resources and Tools , pages 285288, 2009.

Q.X. Do and D. Roth. Constraints based taxonomic relation classification. In Proceedings of EMNLP2010 , pages 10991109. Association for Computational Linguistics, 2010.

A. El Kholy and N. Habash. Techniques for Arabic morphological detokenization and orthographic denormalization. In LREC 2010 Workshop on Language Resources and Human Language Technology for Semitic Languages.

Rong-En Fan, Kai-Wei Chang, Cho-Jui Hsieh, Xiang-Rui Wang, and Chih-Jen Lin. LIBLINEAR: A Library for Large Linear Classification. Journal of Machine Learning Research, 9:18711874. 2008.

David Graff. Arabic Gigaword, LDC Catalog No.: LDC2003T12. Linguistic Data Consortium, University of Pennsylvania. 2003.

N. Habash and O. Rambow. Arabic tokenization, part-of-speech tagging and morphological disambiguation in one fell swoop. In Proceedings of the ACL-05 , pages 573580. Association for Computational Linguistics, 2005.

N. Habash, and F. Sadat. Arabic Preprocessing Schemes for Statistical Machine Translation. In Proceedings of the 7th Meeting of the North American Chapter of the Association for Computational Linguistics/Human Language Technologies Conference (HLT-NAACL06), p. 4952, New York, NY. 2006.

N, Habash, A. Soudi, and T. Buckwalter. On Arabic Transliteration. In A. van den Bosch and A. Soudi, editors, Arabic Computational Mor- phology: Knowledge-based and Empirical Methods. Springer (2007).

N. Habash. Arabic morphological representations for machine translation. In A. van den Bosch, A. Soudi (Eds.), Arabic Computational Morphology: Knowledge-based and Empirical Methods, Springer (2007).

M. Maamouri, A. Bies, and T. Buckwalter. The penn arabic treebank : Building a large- scale annotated arabic corpus. In NEMLAR Confer- ence on Arabic Language Resources and Tools, Cairo, Egypt. 2004.

T. Mikolov, K. Chen, G. Corrado, and J. Dean. Efficient Estimation of Word Representations in Vector Space. In Proceedings of Workshop at ICLR, 2013.

S. Kopru. An efficient part-of-speech tagger for arabic. In Computational Linguistics and Intelligent Text Processing , pages 202213, 2011.

A. Pasha, M. Al-Badrashiny, M. Diab, A. El Kholy, R. Eskander, N. Habash, M. Pooleery, O. Rambow, and R. Roth. MADAMIRA: A Fast, Comprehensive Tool for Morphological Analysis and Disambiguation of Arabic. Proceedings of the Ninth International Conference on Language Resources and Evaluation (LREC-2014).

V. Punyakanok, D. Roth, W. Yih, and D. Zimak. Learning and inference over constrained output. In IJCAI , pages 11241129, 2005.

R. Roth, O. Rambow, N. Habash, M. Diab, and C. Rudin. Arabic morphological tagging, diacritization, and lemmatization using lexeme models and feature ranking. In Proceedings of ACL-08: HLT, Short Papers , pages 117120, 2008.

Appendix: ERTS2 Tagset

- ABBREV
- ADJ
- ADJ+FEM_DU
- ADJ+FEM_PL
- ADJ+FEM_SG
- ADJ+MASC_DU
- ADJ+MASC_PL
- ADJ_COMP
- ADJ_COMP+FEM_SG
- ADJ_COMP+MASC_PL
- ADJ_NUM
- ADJ_NUM+FEM_DU
- ADJ_NUM+FEM_PL
- ADJ_NUM+FEM_SG
- ADJ_NUM+MASC_DU
- ADJ_NUM+MASC_PL
- ADJ_VN
- ADJ_VN+FEM_DU
- ADJ_VN+FEM_PL
- ADJ_VN+FEM_SG
- ADJ_VN+MASC_DU
- ADJ_VN+MASC_PL
- ADV
- ADV_INTERROG
- ADV_REL
- CONJ
- CV
- CV+2_FEM_SG
- CV+2_MASC_PL
- CV+2_MASC_SG
- DET
- INTERJ
- IV
- IV+1_PL
- IV+1_SG
- IV+2_DU
- IV+2_FEM_PL
- IV+2_FEM_SG
- IV+2_MASC_PL
- IV+2_MASC_SG
- IV+3_FEM_DU
- IV+3_FEM_PL
- IV+3_FEM_SG
- IV+3_MASC_DU
- IV+3_MASC_PL
- IV+3_MASC_SG
- IV_PASS
- IV_PASS+1_PL
- IV_PASS+1_SG
- IV_PASS+2_FEM_SG
- IV_PASS+2_MASC_SG
- IV_PASS+3_FEM_SG
- IV_PASS+3_MASC_DU
- IV_PASS+3_MASC_PL
- IV_PASS+3_MASC_SG
- NOUN
- NOUN+FEM_DU
- NOUN+FEM_PL
- NOUN+FEM_SG
- NOUN+MASC_DU
- NOUN+MASC_PL
- NOUN+PRN+1_SG
- NOUN+PRN+1_SG+FEM_DU
- NOUN+PRN+1_SG+MASC_DU
- NOUN+PRN+1_SG+MASC_PL
- NOUN_NUM
- NOUN_NUM+FEM_DU
- NOUN_NUM+FEM_PL
- NOUN_NUM+FEM_SG
- NOUN_NUM+MASC_DU
- NOUN_NUM+MASC_PL
- NOUN_PROP
- NOUN_PROP+FEM_DU
- NOUN_PROP+FEM_PL
- NOUN_PROP+FEM_SG
- NOUN_PROP+MASC_DU
- NOUN_PROP+MASC_PL
- NOUN_QUANT
- NOUN_QUANT+FEM_SG
- NOUN_QUANT+MASC_DU
- NOUN_VN
- NOUN_VN+FEM_DU
- NOUN_VN+FEM_PL
- NOUN_VN+FEM_SG
- NOUN_VN+MASC_DU
- NOUN_VN+MASC_PL
- OTH
- PART
- PART_FOC
- PART_FUT
- PART_INTERROG
- PART_NEG
- PART_VERB
- PART_VOC
- PREP
- PREP+NOUN
- PREP+PRN+1_SG
- PRN
- PRN+1_PL
- PRN+1_SG
- PRN+2_DU
- PRN+2_FEM_PL
- PRN+2_FEM_SG
- PRN+2_MASC_PL
- PRN+2_MASC_SG
- PRN+3_DU
- PRN+3_FEM_PL
- PRN+3_FEM_SG
- PRN+3_MASC_PL
- PRN+3_MASC_SG
- PRN_DEM
- PRN_DEM+FEM
- PRN_DEM+FEM_DU
- PRN_DEM+FEM_SG
- PRN_DEM+MASC_DU
- PRN_DEM+MASC_PL
- PRN_DEM+MASC_SG
- PRN_DEM+PL
- PRN_DO+1_PL
- PRN_DO+1_SG
- PRN_DO+2_FEM_SG
- PRN_DO+2_MASC_PL
- PRN_DO+2_MASC_SG
- PRN_DO+3_DU
- PRN_DO+3_FEM_SG
- PRN_DO+3_MASC_PL
- PRN_DO+3_MASC_SG
- PRN_INTERROG
- PRN_INTERROG+FEM_SG
- PRN_REL
- PRN_REL+FEM_SG
- PUNC
- PV
- PV+1_PL
- PV+1_SG
- PV+2_FEM_SG
- PV+2_MASC_PL
- PV+2_MASC_SG
- PV+3_FEM_DU
- PV+3_FEM_PL
- PV+3_FEM_SG
- PV+3_MASC_DU
- PV+3_MASC_PL
- PV+3_MASC_SG
- PV_PASS
- PV_PASS+1_PL
- PV_PASS+1_SG
- PV_PASS+3_FEM_DU
- PV_PASS+3_FEM_PL
- PV_PASS+3_FEM_SG
- PV_PASS+3_MASC_DU
- PV_PASS+3_MASC_PL
- PV_PASS+3_MASC_SG
- SUB_CONJ

Answer Selection in Arabic Community Question Answering: A Feature-Rich Approach

Yonatan Belinkov
MIT Computer Science and
Artificial Intelligence Laboratory,
Cambridge, MA 02139, USA
belinkov@csail.mit.edu

Alberto Barrón-Cedeño and **Hamdy Mubarak**
Qatar Computing Research Institute, HBKU
Doha, Qatar
{albarron, hmubarak}@qf.org.qa

Abstract

The task of answer selection in community question answering consists of identifying pertinent answers from a pool of user-generated comments related to a question. The recent SemEval-2015 introduced a shared task on community question answering, providing a corpus and evaluation scheme. In this paper we address the problem of answer selection in Arabic. Our proposed model includes a manifold of features including lexical and semantic similarities, vector representations, and rankings. We investigate the contribution of each set of features in a supervised setting. We show that employing a feature combination by means of a linear support vector machine achieves a better performance than that of the competition winner (F_1 of 79.25 compared to 78.55).

1 Introduction

Community Question Answering (cQA) platforms have become an important resource of punctual information for users on the Web. A person posts a question on a specific topic and other users post their answers with little, if not null, restrictions. The liberty to post questions and answers at will is one of the ingredients that make this kind of fora attractive and allows questions to be answered in a very short time. Nevertheless, this same anarchy could cause a question to receive as many answers as to make manual inspection difficult while a given comment might not even address the question (e.g., because the topic gets diverted, or the user aims to make fun of the topic).

Our task is defined as follows. Given a question q and its set of derived comments C, identify whether each $c \in C$ represents a `DIRECT`, `RELATED`, or `IRRELEVANT` answer to q. In order to do that, we take advantage of the framework provided by the SemEval-2015 Task 3 on "Answer Selection in Community Question Answering" (Nakov et al., 2015) and focus on the Arabic language. Our approach is treating each question–comment as an instance in a supervised learning scenario. We build a support vector machine (SVM) classifier that is using different kinds of features, including vector representations, similarity measures, and rankings. Our extensive feature set allows us to achieve better results than those of the winner of the competition: 79.25 F_1 compared to 78.55, obtained by Nicosia et al. (2015).

The rest of the paper is organized as follows. Section 2 describes the experimental framework —composed of the Fatwa corpus and the evaluation metrics— and overviews the different models proposed at competition time. Section 3 describes our model. Experiments and results are discussed in Section 4. Related work is discussed in Section 5. We summarize our contributions in Section 6, and include an error analysis in Appendix A.

2 Overview of SemEval-2015 Task 3

Task overview The SemEval-2015 Task 3 on "Answer Selection in Community Question Answering" (Nakov et al., 2015) proposed two tasks in which, given a user-generated question–answer pair, a system would identify the level of pertinence of the answer. The task was proposed in English and Arabic. In the case of English, the topic of the corpus was daily life in Qatar. In the case of Arabic, the topic was Islam. Whereas the English task attracted twelve participants, only four teams accepted the challenge of the Arabic one.

The evaluation framework is composed of a corpus and a set of evaluation measures.[1] The corpus for the Arabic task is called Fatwa, as this is the name of the community question answering platform from which the questions were extracted.[2] Questions (Fatwas) about Islam are posted by reg-

[1] Both resources are publicly available at http://alt.qcri.org/semeval2015/task3/.

[2] http://fatwa.islamweb.net

Proceedings of the Second Workshop on Arabic Natural Language Processing, pages 183–190,
Beijing, China, July 26-31, 2015.

q	أعمل محاسبا في شركة بالمملكة ـ تأخذ قروض **تورق** ـ وهى لا تتاجر في هذه المواد وتأخذ قيمة القرض تسدد بها مديوناتها الأخرى، وهي مستمرة على ذلك، وكذلك تعمل في مجال **الأسهم**، فما هو نصيبي من ذلك؟.	A person working for a company that has ***bonds*** and trades ***stocks*** is asking for an opinion.
c_1	فننبهك ـ أولا ـ إلى أن **التورق** إذا انضبط بالضوابط الشرعية، فلا حرج فيه [...] وكذلك المضاربة في **الأسهم** [...]	`DIRECT` answer addressing both ***bonds*** and ***stocks*** issues.
c_2	[...] فقد سبقت لنا عدة فتاوى في حكم المضاربة **بالأسهم**، وفيها بينا أنه يشترط لشرعية المضاربة في **الأسهم** تحقق أمرين [...]	`RELATED` answer addressing only the trading of ***stocks***.
c_3	[...] هذا النوع من البيع يسمى بيع **التورق** ولا يقصد منه صاحبه الانتفاع بالسلعة ولكن يقصد من ورائها المال، وقد انقسم العلماء في جوازه إلى فريقين [...]	`RELATED` answer addressing only the buying and selling of ***bonds***.
c_4	فليس للزوج أن يأخذ من مال زوجته إلا ما طابت نفسها به، ولا حق له في مالها [...]	`IRRELEVANT` answer discussing whether a husband is allowed to take money from his wife.
c_5	فلفظ العادة السرية لفظ أحدثه الناس ليطلقوه على ما يسمى عند العلماء بالاستمناء، والاستمناء لغة معناه: طلب خروج المني [...] وقد تقدم في أجوبة سابقة بيان حكم الاستمناء وأضراره	`IRRELEVANT` answer discussing masturbation habits.

Figure 1: Example of a question (`QID` 132600) and its answers from the Fatwa corpus. Key terms appear in bold italics. Note that the direct answer has a high overlap with the question's key terms, the related answers have a lower overlap, and the irrelevant answers have no such overlap.

	Train	Dev.	Test
Questions	1,300	200	200
Answers	6,500	1,000	1,001
`DIRECT`	1,300	200	215
`RELATED`	1,469	222	222
`IRRELEVANT`	3,731	578	564
Tokens	355,891	50,800	49,297
Word types	36,567	10,179	9,724
Stem types	15,824	6,689	6,529

Table 1: Statistics of the Fatwa corpus

ular users to Fatwa and answered by knowledgeable scholars. That is, a `DIRECT` answer exists for each question. In order to pose a challenging task, Nakov et al. (2015) linked more comments to each question. There are two other kinds of answers: `RELATED` are those associated to other questions in the forum which have been identified as related to the current question; `IRRELEVANT` comments were randomly picked from the rest of the collection. Each question in the final corpus has five answers. Figure 1 shows an example question and its answers, illustrating some of the challenges of this task. Table 1 includes some statistics on the Fatwa corpus.

The second part of the framework consists of the evaluation metrics. The official scores are macro-averaged F_1 and accuracy. Macro-averaging gives the same importance to the three classes even if there are two times more `IRRELEVANT` instances than instances in any other class. The intuition behind this metric is that showing `IRRELEVANT` instances to a user in a real scenario is not as important as showing her `DIRECT` ones.

Participating systems As aforementioned, four research teams approached this task at the competition. As the rules allowed to submit one primary and two contrastive submissions to encourage experimentation, a total of eleven approaches were submitted. In what follows, we describe all the approaches without distinguishing between primary and contrastive. Interestingly, all the approaches from each group appear grouped in the task ranking, so we review them in decreasing order of performance.

The best out of the three systems designed by Nicosia et al., (2015) used a variety of similarity features —including cosine, Jaccard coefficient, and containment— on word $[1, 2]$-grams. Additionally, the word [1,2]-grams themselves were considered as features. They applied a logistic regressor to rank the comments and label the top answer as DIRECT, the next one as RELATED and the remaining as IRRELEVANT. Their second system used the same lexical similarity, n-grams features, and learning model, but this time on a binary setting: DIRECT vs. NO-DIRECT. The prediction confidence produced by the classifier was used as a score to rank the comments and assign labels accordingly: DIRECT for the top ranked, RELATED for the second ranked, and IRRELEVANT for the rest. Their third approach is rule-based: a tailored similarity measure in which more weight is given to matching 2-grams than to 1-grams and a label assignment which depends on the relative similarity to the most similar comment in the thread. The output of this rule-based system was also used as a set of extra features in their top-performing approach.

Belinkov et al., (2015)'s best submission was very similar to the one of Nicosia et al., (2015): a ranking approach based on confidence values obtained by an SVM ranker (Joachims, 2006). Their second approach consisted of a multi-class linear SVM classifier relying on three feature families: (*i*) lexical similarities between q and c (similar to those applied by the previous team); (*ii*) word vector representations of q and c; and (*iii*) a ranking score for c produced by the SVM ranker.

The two best approaches of Hou et al., (2015) used features representing different similarities between q and c, lengths of words and sentences, and the number of named-entities in c, among others. In this case [1,2,3]-grams were also considered as features, but with two differences with respect to the other participants: only the most frequent n-grams were used and a translated version to English was also included. They explored two strategies using SVMs in their top performing submissions: (*i*) a hierarchical setting, first discriminating between IRRELEVANT and NON-IRRELEVANT and then between DIRECT and RELATED; and (*ii*) a multi-class classification setting. Their third approach was based on an ensemble of classifiers.

Finally, Mohamed et al., (2015) applied a decision tree whose output is composed of lexical and enriched representations of q and c: the terms in the texts are expanded on the basis of a set of Quranic ontologies. The authors do not report the differences among their three submissions.

	Gigaword	KSUCCA
Tokens	1.2B	50M
Word types	1M	400K
Lemma types	120K	40K

Table 2: Statistics of raw Arabic corpora used for creating word vectors.

We participated in the submissions of the top-performing models (Belinkov et al., 2015; Nicosia et al., 2015). As described below, here we explore effective combinations of the features applied in both approaches, as well as an improved feature design.

3 Model

We train a simple support vector machine (SVM) linear classifier (Joachims, 1999) on pairs of questions and comments. We opt for this alternative because it allowed us to get the best performance during the SemEval task (cf. Section 2); our previous experiments with more sophisticated kernels did not show any improvement. Each question q and comment c is assigned a feature vector. Some features are unique to either q or c, while others capture the relationship between the two. Our features can be broadly divided into fours groups: vector representations, similarity measures, statistical ranking, and rule-based ranking. We describe each kind in turn.

3.1 Vectors

Our motivation for using word vectors for this task is that they convey a soft representation of word meanings. In contrast to similarity measures that are based on words, using word vectors has the potential to bridge over lack of lexical overlap between questions and answers.

We start by creating word vectors from a large corpus of raw Arabic text. We use Word2Vec (Mikolov et al., 2013b; Mikolov et al., 2013a) with default settings for creating 100-dimensional vectors. We experimented with the Arabic Gigaword (Linguistic Data Consortium, 2011), containing newswire text, and with the King Saud University Corpus of Classical Arabic (KSUCCA), containing classical Arabic text (Alrabiah et al., 2013). Table 2 provides some statistics for these corpora. We were initially expecting KSUCCA to produce better results, because its language should be more similar to the religious texts in the Fatwa corpus. However, in practice we found vectors trained on the Arabic Gigaword to perform better, possibly thanks to its larger coverage, so we report only results with the Gigaword corpus below.

We noticed in preliminary experiments that many errors are due to lack of overlap in vocabulary between answers and questions (cf. Section 4.1). In some cases, this overlap stems from the rich morphology of Arabic forms, and can be avoided by lemmatizing. Therefore, we also lemmatize the Arabic corpus using MADAMIRA (Pasha et al., 2014) before creating word vectors. We notice that lemma vectors tend to give small improvements experimentally.

For each question and answer, we average all lemma vectors excluding stopwords. This simple bag-of-words approach ignores word order, but is quite effective at capturing question and answer content. We calculate an average vector for each answer, and concatenate the average question and answer vectors. The resulting concatenated vectors form the features for our classifier. Note that we do not calculate vector similarities (e.g. cosine similarity), letting the classifier have access to all vector dimensions instead.

3.2 Similarity

This set of features measures the similarity $sim(q, c)$ between a question and a comment, assuming that high similarity signals a DIRECT answer.

We compute the similarity between word n-gram representations ($n = [1, \ldots, 4]$) of q and c, using different lexical similarity measures: greedy string tiling (Wise, 1996), longest common subsequences (Allison and Dix, 1986), Jaccard coefficient (Jaccard, 1901), word containment (Lyon et al., 2001), and cosine similarity. The preprocessing in this case consists only of stopword removal. Additionally, we further compute cosine similarity on lemmas and part-of-speech tags, both including and excluding stopwords.

3.3 Statistical Ranking

The features described so far apply to each comment independently without considering other comments in the same thread. To include such global information, we take advantage of our previous work (Belinkov et al., 2015) and formulate the problem as a ranking scenario: comments are ordered such that better comments have a higher ranking. Concretely, DIRECT answers are ranked first, RELATED answers second, and IRRELEVANT answers third. We then train an SVM ranker (Joachims, 2002), and add its scores as additional features. We also scale ranking features to $[0, 1]$ and map scores into 10 bins in the $[0, 1]$ range, with each bin assigned a binary feature. If a score falls into a certain bin, its matching binary feature fires.

We found such ranking scores to be a valuable addition in our experiments. To understand why, we note that they are able to neatly separate the different labels, with the following average scores: DIRECT 14.5, RELATED 12.3, and IRRELEVANT 10.5.

3.4 Rule-based Ranking

In addition to the machine learning approaches, we adapted our rule-based model, which ranked 2nd in the competition (Nicosia et al., 2015). The basic idea is to rank the comments according to their similarity and label the top ones as DIRECT.

In this case our preprocessing consists of stemming, performed with QATARA (Darwish et al., 2014), and again stopword removal. In our implementation, the score of a comment is computed as

$$score(c) = \frac{1}{|q|} \sum_{t \in q \cap c} \alpha \cdot \omega(t) + pos(t)$$

where $\omega(t) = 1$ if t is a 1-gram, 4 if it is a 2-gram, and $pos(t)$ represents the relative position of t in the question and is estimated as the length of q minus the position of t in q. That is, we give significantly more relevance to 2-grams and to those matching n-grams at the beginning of the question. We compute this score twice: once considering the subject and once considering the body of the question, and sum them together to get the final score. In the first case, $\alpha = 1.1$; in the second case, $\alpha = 1$.

We map the scores of comments $c_1, \ldots, c_5 \in C$ into the range $[0, 1]$ such that the best ranked comment gets a score of 1.0, and assign a label to comment c as follows:

$$class(c) = \begin{cases} \text{DIRECT} & \text{if } 0.8 \leq score(c) \\ \text{RELATED} & \text{if } 0.2 \leq score(c) < 0.8 \\ \text{IRREL} & \text{otherwise} \end{cases}$$

All the parameters and thresholds in this rule-based approach were manually tuned on the training data.

	Development				Test			
	P	R	F_1	A	P	R	F_1	A
Vectors	80.44	78.13	78.67	83.60	71.22	70.92	70.99	76.32
Similarity	70.53	67.03	68.41	76.20	64.91	64.16	64.51	71.63
Ranking rules	87.88	85.99	86.73	90.10	77.88	77.44	77.61	82.42
Vecs + Sim	79.74	78.27	78.62	83.20	71.10	70.77	70.85	76.22
Vecs + Rank-rules	89.75	87.77	88.49	91.20	79.59	**78.94**	**79.25**	**83.42**
Sim + Rank-rules	88.05	86.16	86.89	90.20	78.37	77.89	78.10	82.72
Vecs + Sim + Rank-rules	89.58	87.62	88.32	91.10	79.40	78.88	79.13	83.32
#Vecs + Sim + Rank-rules	**90.06**	**88.45**	**89.17**	**91.50**	**80.17**	77.82	78.87	82.92
QCRI							78.55	83.02
VectorSLU							70.99	76.32
HITSZ-ICRC							67.70	74.53
al-bayan							67.65	74.53

Table 3: Results on the development and test sets. Top-performing (primary) submissions at competition time are included for comparison.

4 Experiments and Results

The aim of our experiments is to explore each set of features both isolated and combined. Thus we isolate rule-based features from similarity features and from vector-based features. In our experiments we combined vector-based and statistical ranking features, following our previous work (Belinkov et al., 2015). Note that the rule-based ranking system (Section 3.4) does not produce any features. Instead, we binarize its output to produce the features to be combined with the rest. We train and tune all the models on the training and development sets and perform a final evaluation on the test set. This experimental design mimics the competition setting, making the figures directly comparable.

Table 3 shows the results. It is worth noting that the performance of the different feature sets is already competitive with respect to the top models at competition time. On the development set, we found it useful to run an SVM ranker on the entire set of features and convert its ranking to predictions as follows: the top scoring comment is `DIRECT`, next best is `RELATED`, and all others are `IRRELEVANT`. This heuristic (marked with "#" in the table) produced the best results on the development set, but was not as successful on the test set. Instead, we observe that the best performing system is obtained by combining vectors and rule-based ranking, achieving 79.25 F_1 and outperforming the best result from the SemEval 2015 task.

4.1 Error Analysis

We analyzed a sample of errors made by a preliminary version of our system. We focused on the case of `RELATED` answers predicted as `IRRELEVANT`, as this was the largest source of errors. See Appendix A for examples of common errors. The analysis indicates the following trends:

- Under-specification: `RELATED` answers tend to have a smaller vocabulary overlap with the question, compared to `DIRECT` answers (c.f. Figure 1).
- Over-specification: `RELATED` answers sometimes contain multiple other terms that are not directly related to the question.
- Non-trivial overlap: occasionally, questions and answers may be related through synonyms or through lemmas rather than surface forms.

These observations shed some light on the contribution of our different features. In cases of under- or over-specification, text similarity features help the classifier determine the correct answer. Cases of non-trivial overlap require other solutions. We use lemmatization and stemming to collapse different surface forms. Finally, our vector-based features can capture synonyms between question and answer, thanks to their property of similar words having similar vectors.

5 Related Work

The SemEval 2015 Task 3 was the first to include an *answer selection in community* question answering task as far as we know. Previously, the importance of cQA to the Arab world has been recognized by Darwish and Magdy (2013), who mention two such forums: Google Ejabat, akin to Yahoo! Answers; and the Fatwa corpus. The authors identify several research problems for cQA, two of which resemble the answer selection task: their (3) ranking questions and answers; and (4) classifying answers.

Other efforts have been conducted on the analysis and exploitation of non-Arabic cQA data. Nam et al. (2009) analyzed a Korean cQA forum and identified interesting patterns of participation. For instance, users asking for questions do not answer to others' and vice versa, and they tend to "specialize" on a number of categories rather than participate all across the forum. The recognition of their peers (by means of a scoring schema) motivates the top users to more and better responses to questions. Whether these patterns remain in other fora represents an interesting problem for future research. Bian et al. (2008) aimed at ranking factoid answers to questions in Yahoo! Answers to identify the most appealing ones in terms of relevance to the topic and quality. In addition to text-based features (e.g., similarity between question and answer), they took advantage of user-interaction information including the number of answers previously posted by the user and the number of questions that they "resolved", determined by the question poster.

Non-community Arabic question answering has received a little more attention. The Question Answering for Machine Reading (QA4MRE) task included Arabic data sets in both its 2012 and 2013 editions (Peñas et al., 2012; Sutcliffe et al., 2013), although only the 2012 instantiation attracted participating teams for the Arabic task. This task focused on answering multiple choice questions by retrieving relevant passages. Participating systems used mostly information retrieval methods and question classification. For more details on this and other Arabic question answering efforts we refer to (Darwish and Magdy, 2013; Ezzeldin and Shaheen, 2012).

6 Summary

In this work we tackled the problem of answer selection in a community question answering Arabic forum, consisting of religious questions and answers. We explored a wide range of features in a supervised setting and achieved state-of-the-art performance on the SemEval 2015 Task 3. We demonstrated that using features of different kinds, along with raw Arabic corpora and existing preprocessing tools, is important for addressing the challenges of this task.

To conclude, we note some drawbacks of the Fatwa corpus: it was created by artificially retrieving answers that are not originally linked to the answer. This makes the detection of `IRRELEVANT` answers quite trivial, as observed by Nakov et al. (2015). In addition, there is little sense in using contextual information from different answers to the same question when some of them are retrieved randomly. We believe that future endeavors should focus on more natural community question answering forums in Arabic, for example Google Ejabat.

Acknowledgments

This research is developed by the Arabic Language Technologies (ALT) group at Qatar Computing Research Institute (QCRI), Hamad bin Khalifa University, within the Qatar Foundation in collaboration with MIT. It is part of the Interactive sYstems for Answer Search (Iyas) project.

References

Lloyd Allison and Trevor Dix. 1986. A bit-string longest-common-subsequence algorithm. *Inf. Process. Lett.*, 23(6):305–310, December.

Maha Alrabiah, AbdulMalik Al-Salman, and Eric Atwell. 2013. The design and construction of the 50 million words KSUCCA King Saud University Corpus of Classical Arabic. In *Proceedings of WACL-2*.

Yonatan Belinkov, Mitra Mohtarami, Scott Cyphers, and James Glass. 2015. VectorSLU: A continuous word vector approach to answer selection in community question answering systems. In *Proceedings of the 9th International Workshop on Semantic Evaluation*, SemEval '15, Denver, Colorado, USA.

Jiang Bian, Yandong Liu, Eugene Agichtein, and Hongyuan Zha. 2008. Finding the Right Facts in the Crowd: Factoid Question Answering over Social Media. In *Proceedings of the 17th International Conference on World Wide Web*, WWW '08, pages 467–476, New York, NY, USA. ACM.

Kareem Darwish and Walid Magdy. 2013. Arabic information retrieval. *Foundations and Trends® in Information Retrieval*, 7(4):239–342.

Kareem Darwish, Ahmed Abdelali, and Hamdy Mubarak. 2014. Using Stem-Templates to Improve Arabic POS and Gender/Number Tagging. In *Proceedings of the Ninth International Conference on Language Resources and Evaluation (LREC-2014)*. European Language Resources Association (ELRA).

Ahmed Ezzeldin and Mohamed Shaheen. 2012. A survey of Arabic question answering: Challenges, tasks, approaches, tools, and future trends. In *Proceedings of the International Arabic Conference on Information Technology (ACIT)*.

Yongshuai Hou, Cong Tan, Xiaolong Wang, Yaoyun Zhang, Jun Xu, and Qingcai Chen. 2015. HITSZ-ICRC: Exploiting classification approach for answer selection in community question answering. In *Proceedings of the 9th International Workshop on Semantic Evaluation*, SemEval '15, Denver, Colorado, USA.

Paul Jaccard. 1901. Étude comparative de la distribution florale dans une portion des Alpes et des Jura. *Bulletin del la Société Vaudoise des Sciences Naturelles*, 37:547–579.

Thorsten Joachims. 1999. Making Large-scale Support Vector Machine Learning Practical. In Bernhard Schölkopf, Christopher J. C. Burges, and Alexander J. Smola, editors, *Advances in Kernel Methods*, pages 169–184. MIT Press, Cambridge, MA, USA.

Thorsten Joachims. 2002. Optimizing search engines using clickthrough data. In *Proceedings of the Eighth ACM SIGKDD International Conference on Knowledge Discovery and Data Mining*, KDD '02, pages 133–142, New York, NY, USA. ACM.

Thorsten Joachims. 2006. Training linear svms in linear time. In *Proceedings of the 12th ACM SIGKDD International Conference on Knowledge Discovery and Data Mining*, KDD '06, pages 217–226, New York, NY, USA. ACM.

Linguistic Data Consortium. 2011. Arabic Gigaword Fifth Edition. `https://catalog.ldc.upenn.edu/LDC2011T11`.

Caroline Lyon, James Malcolm, and Bob Dickerson. 2001. Detecting short passages of similar text in large document collections. In *Proceedings of the 2001 Conference on Empirical Methods in Natural Language Processing*, EMNLP '01, pages 118–125, Pittsburgh, PA, USA.

Tomas Mikolov, Ilya Sutskever, Kai Chen, Greg S Corrado, and Jeff Dean. 2013a. Distributed Representations of Words and Phrases and their Compositionality. In C.J.C. Burges, L. Bottou, M. Welling, Z. Ghahramani, and K.Q. Weinberger, editors, *Advances in Neural Information Processing Systems 26*, pages 3111–3119. Curran Associates, Inc.

Tomas Mikolov, Wen-tau Yih, and Geoffrey Zweig. 2013b. Linguistic Regularities in Continuous Space Word Representations. In *Proceedings of the 2013 Conference of the North American Chapter of the Association for Computational Linguistics: Human Language Technologies*, NAACL-HLT '13, pages 746–751, Atlanta, GA, USA.

Reham Mohamed, Maha Ragab, Heba Abdelnasser, Nagwa M. El-Makky, and Marwan Torki. 2015. Al-Bayan: A knowledge-based system for Arabic answer selection. In *Proceedings of the 9th International Workshop on Semantic Evaluation*, SemEval '15, Denver, Colorado, USA.

Preslav Nakov, Lluís Màrquez, Walid Magdy, Alessandro Moschitti, Jim Glass, and Bilal Randeree. 2015. Semeval-2015 task 3: Answer selection in community question answering. In *Proceedings of the 9th International Workshop on Semantic Evaluation (SemEval 2015)*, pages 269–281, Denver, Colorado, June. Association for Computational Linguistics.

Kevin K. Nam, Ackerman Mark S. , and Lada A. Adamic. 2009. Questions in, Knowledge iN?: A study of Navers question answering community. In *Proceedings of the SIG CHI Conference on Human Factors in Computing Systems*, Boston, MA.

Massimo Nicosia, Simone Filice, Alberto Barrón-Cedeño, Iman Saleh, Hamdy Mubarak, Wei Gao, Preslav Nakov, Giovanni Da San Martino, Alessandro Moschitti, Kareem Darwish, Lluís Màrquez, Shafiq Joty, and Walid Magdy. 2015. QCRI: Answer selection for community question answering - experiments for Arabic and English. In *Proceedings of the 9th International Workshop on Semantic Evaluation*, SemEval '15, Denver, Colorado, USA.

Arfath Pasha, Mohamed Al-Badrashiny, Mona Diab, Ahmed El Kholy, Ramy Eskander, Nizar Habash, Manoj Pooleery, Owen Rambow, and Ryan Roth. 2014. MADAMIRA: A Fast, Comprehensive Tool for Morphological Analysis and Disambiguation of Arabic. In *Proceedings of the Ninth International Conference on Language Resources and Evaluation (LREC'14)*, pages 1094–1101, Reykjavik, Iceland.

Anselmo Peñas, Eduard Hovy, Pamela Forner, Álvaro Rodrigo, Richard Sutcliffe, Caroline Sporleder, Corina Forascu, Yassine Benajiba, and Petya Osenova. 2012. Overview of QA4MRE at CLEF 2012: Question Answering for Machine Reading Evaluation. *Working Notes, CLEF*.

Richard Sutcliffe, Anselmo Peñas, Eduard Hovy, Pamela Forner, Álvaro Rodrigo, Corina Forascu, Yassine Benajiba, and Petya Osenova. 2013. Overview of QA4MRE Main Task at CLEF 2013. *Working Notes, CLEF*.

Michael Wise. 1996. Yap3: Improved detection of similarities in computer program and other texts. In *Proceedings of the Twenty-seventh SIGCSE Technical Symposium on Computer Science Education*, SIGCSE '96, pages 130–134, New York, NY, USA.

Appendix A. Error Analysis

Errors typically occur when there are difficulties in finding a lexical overlap between question and answer. This may happen due to under-specification, where an answer is not specific enough to the question; over-specification, where an answer contains irrelevant material; or non-trivial overlap, for example when an answer contains synonyms of terms for the questions, or when lemmas overlap but surface forms do not. Following are examples where the `RELATED` answer was wrongly predicted due to vocabulary mismatches.

`QID` 123529:

هل العملية بالليزر تعتبر من الكي المحرم؟

`DIRECT`:

فلا يعتبر استعمال الليزر في أنواع العلاجات والجراحات الطبية من الكي المحرم، لاختلاف حقيقتهما. وقد سبق التنبيه على جواز التداوي بالليزر في أنواع من الأمراض كإزالة الشعر وإصلاحه، وحب الشباب، وقصر النظر، وغير ذلك، في الفتاوى التالية أرقامها: [...]

`RELATED`:

فإن التداوي مشروع، لقوله صلى الله عليه وسلم للأعراب الذين سألوه، فقالوا: يا رسول الله، أنتداوى، فقال: تداووا، فإن الله عز وجل لم يضع داء إلا وضع له دواء غير داء واحد الهرم [...] وبناء عليه، فلا مانع من هذه العملية، لأن مداواة التشويهات الخلقية لا تعتبر من تغيير خلق الله المحرم، لأن العلماء قد استثنوها نظراً للضرورة [...]

Discussion: The question asks if it is allowed to undergo laser treatments. The related answer says that treatments are allowed based on the authority of the Prophet, but does not mention laser, whereas the direct answer refers to laser explicitly.

`QID` 127396:

ما حكم المتاجرة في المحصول الزراعي وبيعه في بلد آخر، مع حظر الحكومة إخراجها من البلد وبيعها لبلد مجاور،لأسباب تعود لحاجة البلاد إليها؟ مع العلم أن الحكومة غيرمسلمة.

`DIRECT`:

فعلى المسلم إذا أقام في بلاد غير المسلمين أن يلتزم بقوانينهم ما لم تخالف هذه القوانين شريعة الإسلام [...] وعلى هذا فيلزمك التزام القانون المذكور وعدم المتاجرة بالمحصول خارج البلد المذكور- لا سيما - وقد ذكرت أنه موضوع لمصلحة البلد [...]

`RELATED`:

فمن دخل أرضهم بأمان وجب عليه أن يحترم قوانينهم ما لم تخالف هذه القوانين شريعة الإسلام، [...] وعلى هذا فلا يجوز أن تعملي عملاً غير قانوني [...]

Discussion: The question asks if it is allowed to trade farm products from a non-Muslim country out of that country, given that the law in that country forbids it. The related answer says that one has to follow a non-Muslim country's laws, as long as they do not contradict the Islamic law. This answer does not specifically address the matter of selling farm products, whereas the direct answer uses specific words that appear in the question.

`QID` 59300:

هل من الممكن أن أقترض من الدولة قرضا إنتاجيا بالفائدة أي بالربا وهذا بأن تأخذ لك الدولة مصنعا مثلا وتجهزه بمبلغ مثلا٨٠ ألفا وتقول لك ادفع لي ١٠٠ ألف هذا على سبيل المثال.

`DIRECT`:

[...] فالقروض الربوية من العقود المحرمة التي لا يجوز الإقدام عليها، ولكن راجع لزاماً الفتوى رقم: ، لمعرفة الفرق بين بيع البنك بالمرابحة والقرض الربوي. [...]

`RELATED`:

[...] فإن كان البنك يقوم بشراء الأدوات المطلوبة في مشروع العميل ويتملكها فتصبح في ضمانه ثم يبيعها للعميل بالمؤجل أو المقسط بثمن يزيد عن ثمن الشراء فهذا الذي يسمى بيع المرابحة للآمر بالشراء وهو جائز، وإن كان البنك لا يملك هذه الأدوات ولا تدخل في ضمانه فلا يجوز لأنه في حقيقة الأمر أقرضه ثمن هذه الأدوات ثم أرجع القرض بفائدة وهذا هو الربا، [...]

Discussion: The question asks whether it is allowed to borrow with interest from the state, for example when the state builds a factory for someone. Both the direct and related answers are very similar, pointing to a difference between interest loans and ownership of something by the bank. The related answer refers to equipment, which is different from the factory asked about in the question, while the direct answer does not refer to anything specifically.

EDRAK: Entity-Centric Data Resource for Arabic Knowledge

Mohamed H. Gad-Elrab **Mohamed Amir Yosef** **Gerhard Weikum**
Max-Planck-Institut für Informatik
Saarbrücken, Germany
`{gadelrab|mamir|weikum}@mpi-inf.mpg.de`

Abstract

Online Arabic content is growing very rapidly, with unmatched growth in Arabic structured resources. Systems that perform standard Natural Language Processing (NLP) tasks such as Named Entity Disambiguation (NED) struggle to deliver decent quality due to the lack of rich Arabic entity repositories. In this paper, we introduce EDRAK, an automatically generated comprehensive Arabic entity-centric resource. EDRAK contains more than two million entities together with their Arabic names and contextual keyphrases. Manual evaluation confirmed the quality of the generated data. We are making EDRAK publicly available as a valuable resource to help advance research in Arabic NLP and IR tasks such as dictionary-based Named-Entity Recognition, entity classification, and entity summarization.

1 Introduction

1.1 Motivation

Rich structured resources are crucial for several Information Retrieval (IR) and NLP tasks; furthermore, resources quality significantly influence the performance of those tasks. For example, building a dictionary-based Named Entity Recognition (NER) system, requires a comprehensive and accurate dictionary of names (Darwish, 2013; Shaalan, 2014). Problems like Word Sense Disambiguation (WSD) and Named Entity Disambiguation (NED) require name and context dictionaries to resolve the correct word sense or entity respectively (Weikum et al., 2012).

Arabic digital content is growing very rapidly; it is among the top growing languages on the Internet [1]. However, the amount of structured or semi-structured Arabic content is lagging behind. For example, Wikipedia is one of the main resources from where many modern Knowledge Bases (KB) are extracted. It is heavily used in the literature for IR and NLP tasks. However, the size of the Arabic Wikipedia is an order of magnitude smaller than the English one. Furthermore, the structured data in the Arabic Wikipedia, such as info boxes, are on average of less quality in terms of coverage and accuracy.

On the other hand, the amount and quality of the English structured resources on the Internet are unrivaled. The English Wikipedia is frequently updated, and contains the most recent events for example. It is important to leverage English resources in order to augment the currently poor Arabic ones. For example, both the English and Arabic Wikipedia have articles about `Christian Dior` and `Eric Schmidt` and hence the Arabic Wikipedia knows, at least, one potential Arabic name for both (the Arabic page title). However, Arabic Wikipedia knows nothing about `Christian Schmidt`[2], although, at least, his name can be learned automatically from only the English and Arabic Wikipedia's interwiki links.

To this end, it is compelling to automatically generate Arabic resources using cross-language evidences. This would help overcome the scarcity problem of Arabic resources and improve the performance of many Arabic NLP and IR tasks.

1.2 Contributions

Our contributions can be summarized into:

- Introducing EDRAK: an automatically generated Arabic entity-centric resource built on top of the English and Arabic Wikipedia's.
- Manual assessment of EDRAK, conducted by Arabic native speakers.

[1] `www.internetworldstats.com/stats7.htm`

[2] German Federal Minister of Food and Agriculture, 2015

Proceedings of the Second Workshop on Arabic Natural Language Processing, pages 191–200,
Beijing, China, July 26-31, 2015. ©2014 Association for Computational Linguistics

- Making EDRAK publicly available to the research community to help advance the field of Arabic NLP.

1.3 EDRAK Use-cases

EDRAK is an entity-centric Arabic resource that is a valuable asset for many NLP and IR tasks. For example, EDRAK contains a comprehensive dictionary for different potential Arabic names for entities gathered from both the English and Arabic Wikipedia's. Such dictionary can be used for building an Arabic **Dictionary-based NER** (Darwish, 2013).

In addition to the name dictionary, the resource contains a large catalog of entity Arabic textual context in the form of keyphrases. They can be used to estimate **Entity-Entity Semantic Relatedness** scores such as in Hoffart et al. (2012).

Furthermore, both the name dictionary and the entity contextual keyphrases are the corner-stone of state-of-the-art **Named Entity Disambiguation** (NED) systems (Hoffart et al., 2011).

Entities in EDRAK are classified under the type hierarchy of YAGO (Hoffart et al., 2013). Together with the keyphrases, EDRAK can be used to build an **Entity Summarization** system as in (Tylenda et al., 2011), or to build a **Fine-grained Semantic Type Classifier** for named entities as in (Yosef et al., 2012; Yosef et al., 2013).

2 Related Work

Different approaches to enrich Arabic resources have used cross-lingual evidences. Among the generated resources, some are entity-aware and useful for semantic analysis tasks. Others are purely textual dictionaries without any notion of canonical entities.

2.1 Entity-Aware Resources

Wikipedia, as the largest comprehensive online encyclopedia, is the most used corpus for creating entity-aware resources such as YAGO (Hoffart et al., 2013), DBpedia (Auer et al., 2007) and Freebase (Bollacker et al., 2008). Due to the limited size of Arabic Wikipedia, building strong semantic resources becomes a challenge. Several research efforts have been exerted to go beyond Arabic Wikipedia to construct a rich entity-aware resource.

AIDArabic (Yosef et al., 2014) is an NED system for Arabic text that uses an entity-name dictionary and an entity-context catalog extracted from Wikipedia. They leveraged Wikipedia titles, disambiguation pages, redirects, and incoming anchor texts to populate the *entity-name dictionary*. In addition, Wikipedia categories, incoming Wikipedia links page titles, and outgoing anchor texts were used in building the *entity-context catalog*. In order to overcome the small size of Arabic Wikipedia, they proposed building an *entity catalog* including entities from both the English and Arabic Wikipedia's. While their *catalog* was comprehensive, their *name dictionary* as well as *context catalog* suffered from the limited coverage in the Arabic Wikipedia. Hence, the recall of the NED task was heavily harmed.

Google-Word-to-Concept(GW2C) (Spitkovsky and Chang, 2012) is a multilingual resource mapping strings (i.e. names) to English Wikipedia concepts (including NEs). For *entity-names*, they harvested strings from Wikipedia titles, inter-Wikipedia links anchors, as well as manually created anchor texts from non-Wikipedia pages (i.e. web dump) with links to Wikipedia pages. The resource did not offer any *entity-context information*. The full resource contained 297M string-to-concept mapping. Nevertheless, the share of the Arabic records did not exceed 800K mapping. Finally, using **GW2C** in the entity linking task achieved above median coverage for English. In contrast, the results for the multilingual entity linking were less than the median.

BabelNet (Navigli and Ponzetto, 2012) is a multilingual resource built using Wikipedia entities and WordNet senses. They used the sense labels, Wikipedia titles from incoming links, outgoing anchor texts, redirects and categories as sources for disambiguation context. In addition, machine translation services were used to translate Wikipedia concepts to other languages. Nevertheless, translation was not applied on Named-Entities. They achieved good results using BabelNet as resource for cross-lingual Word Sense disambiguation (WSD).

2.2 Entity-free Resources

There exist several multilingual name dictionaries without any notion of canonical entities. Steinberger et al. (2011) introduced **JRC-Names**, a multilingual resource that includes names of organizations and persons. They extracted these names from multilingual news articles and Wikipedia. JRC-

Names contained 617K multilingual name variants with only 17K Arabic records.

Attia et al. (2010), built an Arabic lexicon Named-Entity resource using Arabic WordNet (Black et al., 2006) and Arabic Wikipedia. They extracted instantiable nouns from WordNet as Named-Entity candidates. Then, they used Wikipedia categories and inter-lingual Wikipedia pages to identify name candidates exploiting cross-lingual evidences. The resource contained 45K Arabic names along their correspondent lexical information.

Azab et al. (2013) compiled **CMUQ-Arabic-NET** Lexicon corpus, an English-Arabic names dictionary from Wikipedia as well as parallel English-Arabic news corpora. They used off-the-shelf NER system on the English side of the data. NER results were projected onto the Arabic side according to the word-alignment information. Additionally, they included Wikipedia inter-lingual links titles in their dictionary as well as coarse-grained type information (`PERSON` or `ORGANIZATION`).

3 High-level Methodology

Our objective is to produce a comprehensive Arabic entity repository together with rich entity *Arabic names dictionary* and entity *Arabic keyphrases catalog*. We augment an Arabic Wikipedia-based entity repository by translating English names and keyphrases. Off-the-shelf translation systems are not suitable for translating named entities (Al-Onaizan and Knight, 2002; Hálek et al., 2011; Azab et al., 2013). Therefore, we incorporate three translation techniques:

1. **External Name Dictionaries:** We harness the existing English-Arabic name dictionaries via semantic and syntactic equivalence, for example, if two strings from one or more dictionaries are linking to the same canonical entity, we consider them a potential translation of each other.

2. **Statistical Machine Translation:** We train an SMT system on English-Arabic parallel names corpora.

3. **Transliteration:** We build a transliteration system for persons names by training an SMT system on an English-Arabic parallel persons names corpora on the character level.

Data generated from all techniques are fused together to form a comprehensive Arabic resource obtained by translating an existing English one.

4 Creation of EDRAK

In this section, we start with describing EDRAK. Then, we explain the pre-processing steps applied on the data. The rest of the section explains in detail the creation process of EDRAK following the methodology explained in Section 3.

4.1 EDRAK in a Nutshell

EDRAK is an entity-centric resource that contains a catalog of entities together with their potential names. In addition, each entity has a contextual characteristic description in the form of keyphrases. Keyphrases and keywords are assigned scores based on their popularity and correlation with different entities.

EDRAK contains an entity catalog based on YAGO3 KB (Mahdisoltani et al., 2015), compiled from both English and Arabic Wikipedia's. We favored YAGO as our underlying KB over other available multilingual KBs because it is geared for precision instead of recall. Therefore, it is more salient for applying SMT techniques for example. We used the English Wikipedia dump of 12-January-2015 in conjunction with the Arabic dump of 18-December-2014 to build an Arabic YAGO3 KB.

EDRAK's *entity-name dictionary* is extracted from different pieces of Wikipedia that exist in YAGO3 KB. Namely, we harness Wikipedia page titles and redirects. In addition, we include YAGO3 *rdfs:labels* extracted from anchor texts and disambiguation pages in Wikipedia. *Entity context* is compiled from anchor texts, category names in the Wikipedia entity page. In addition, we include titles of Wikipedia pages linking to this entity.

The above data pieces extracted from the Arabic Wikipedia are included in EDRAK as it is, while those extracted from the English Wikipedia are translated/transliterated using one of the techniques introduced in the Section 3. We followed the same approach as in AIDA (Hoffart et al., 2011) to generate statistics about *entities importance* and *keyphrases weights*.

4.2 Data Pre-processing

Since Arabic is a morphologically-rich language, standard English text processing techniques are not directly suitable. Systems such as MADAMITA

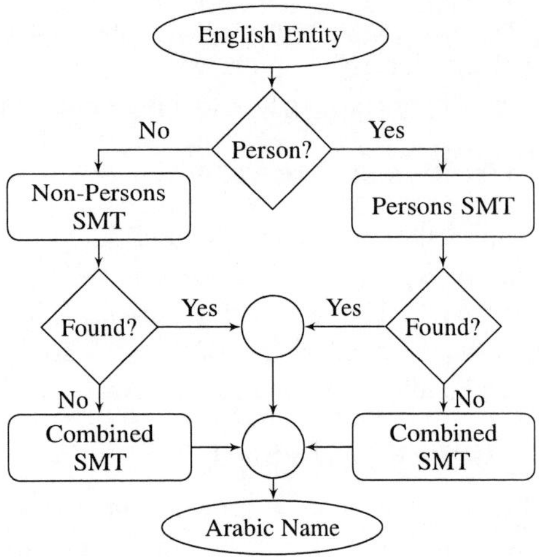

Figure 1: Architecture of Type-Aware Names Translation System

(Pasha et al., 2014) or Stanford Arabic Word Segmenter (Monroe et al., 2014) should be used to perform morphological-based pre-processing. Stanford Word Segmenter provides interpolatable handy Java API, hence has been used to pre-process the data. Text has been segmented by separating clitics, and normalized by *Removing Tatweel*, *Normalizing Digits*, *Normalizing Alif*, and *Removing Diacritics*. This helps achieving better coverage for our data, and computing more accurate statistics.

4.3 External Names Dictionaries

EDRAK harnesses *Google-Word-to-Concept (GW2C)* (Spitkovsky and Chang, 2012) multilingual resource in order to capture more names from the web. *GW2C* is created automatically without applying manual verification or post-processing. Therefore, it contains noise that should be filtered out. In order to include GW2C in EDRAK dictionary, we performed the following steps:

- **Language detection** We used off-the-shelf language detection tools developed by Shuyo (2010) to filter out non-Arabic records. Only 736K out of 297M were Arabic entries.
- **Filtering ambiguous names** We utilized the provided conditional probability scores to filter out generic anchor texts such as "Read more", "Wikipedia page" or "المزيد على ويكيبيديا". We ignore strings with conditional probability less than a threshold of 0.01.

	PER	NON-PER	ALL
CMUQ-Ar.	28,493	34,116	62,609
Wikipedia	33,962	79,699	128,790
Both	62,455	113,815	191,399

Table 1: Entity Names SMT Training Data Size

- **Name-level post-processing** We post-processed the data by applying normalization and data cleaning. (e.g. removing punctuation and URLs).
- **Mapping to EDRAK Entities** We used Wikipedia pages URLs to map extracted names from GW2C to EDRAK's Entity repository.

In addition to *GW2C*, we used lexical named-entities resources as look-up dictionary to translate English entity names. English names were matched strictly against those dictionaries to get the accurate Arabic names. We used the multilingual resource *JRC-Names* (Steinberger et al., 2011) that includes several name-variants along with partial language tags. After automatically extracting the Arabic records, English-Arabic pairs were included in our lookup dictionary. Similarly, we included*CMUQ-Arabic-NET* lexicon corpus (Azab et al., 2013) the lookup dictionary.

4.4 Translation

We trained cdec (Dyer et al., 2010), a full fledged SMT system, to translate English Names into Arabic ones. As training data, we fused a parallel corpus of English-Arabic names from multiple resources. We used a dictionary compiled from Wikipedia interwiki links together with *CMUQ-Arabic-NET* dictionary (Azab et al., 2013). While the latter contains name-type information, for the interwiki links, we leveraged YAGO KB to restrict our training data to only named-entities and to obtain semantic types information for each. 5% of the data have been used for tuning the parameters of SMT. The properties of the training data are summarized in Table 1.

We implemented two different translation paradigms. The first is depicted in Figure 1. We train three different system, on `PERSONS`, `NON-PERSONS` and a fallback system trained on `ALL`. In the first approach, depending on the entity semantic type, we try to translate its English

Table Name	Major Columns	Description
entity_ids	- id - entity	Lists all entities together with their numerical IDs.
dictionary	- mention - entity - source	Contains information about the candidate entities for a name. It keeps track of the source of the entry to allow application-specific filtering.
entity_keyphrases	- entity - keyphrase - source - weight	Holds the characteristic description of entities in the form of keyphrases. The source of each keyphrase is kept for application-specific filtering.
entity_types	- entity - types []	Stores YAGO semantic types to which this entity belongs.
entity_rank	- entity - rank	Ranks all entities based on the number of incoming links in both the English and Arabic Wikipedia. This can be used as a measure for entity prominence.

Table 2: Main SQL Tables in EDRAK

name using the corresponding system. If it fails, we switch to the fallback system. In the second COMBINED approach, we use the system trained on ALL dataset to translate all names regardless of the entity type.

In addition, we are translating Wikipedia Categories to be included in entities contextual keyphrases. To this end, we train the SMT system on English-Arabic parallel data of categories names harvested from Wikipedia interwiki links. The size of the training data is 43K name pairs, of which 5% have been used for tuning SMT parameters as well.

4.5 Transliteration

Recent research has focused on building Arabization systems that are geared towards transliteration general and informal text, without any special handling for entity names (Al-Badrashiny et al., 2014).

To this end, we had to build a transliteration system optimized for names. Transliteration is applicable on many NON-PERSON entities. However, applying it for such entities will create a lot of inaccurate entries that should be either fully or partially translated, or those that can only be learned from manually crafted dictionaries such as movie names. It is also worth noting that ORGANIZATION names that contain a person name such as *"Bill Gates Foundation"* will be correctly translated using the COMBINED system explained above.

Transliteration has been applied on PERSONS names only. We used the PERSONS part of the training data (Table 1) used for translation, and trained an SMT system on the character-level. 5% of the data have been used for parameter tuning of the SMT system. Each PERSON entity has English *FirstName* and *LastName*. Transliteration has been applied for each, and on a *FullName* composed by concatenating both.

5 Statistics and Technical Details

5.1 Technical Description

We are publicly releasing EDRAK for the research community. EDRAK is available in the form of an SQL dump, and can be downloaded from the *Downloads* section in AIDA project page http://www.mpi-inf.mpg.de/yago-naga/aida/. We followed the same schema used in the original AIDA framework (Hoffart et al., 2011) for data storage. Highlights of the SQL dump are shown in Table 2. EDRAK's comprehensive entity catalog is stored in SQL table entity_ids. Each entity has many potential Arabic names together stored in SQL table dictionary. In addition, each entity is assigned a set of Arabic contextual keyphrases stored in SQL table entity_keyphrases.

It is worth noting that sources of dictionary entries as well as entities keyphrases are kept in the schema (YAGO3_LABEL, REDIRECT, GIVEN_NAME, or FAMILY_NAME). Furthermore, generated data (by translation or transliteration) are differentiated from the original Arabic data extracted directly from the Arabic Wikipedia. Different generation techniques and data sources entail different data quality. Therefore, keeping data sources enables downstream applications to filter data for precision-recall trade-off.

Semantic Type	# entities
PERSON	1,220,032
EVENT	199,846
LOCATION	360,108
ORGANIZATION	196,305
ARTIFACT	359,071

Table 3: Number of Entities per Type in EDRAK

Technique	# of entries
Google W2C	241,104
CMUQ-Arabic-NET	23,338
JRC	4148
Translation	11,222,876
Transliteration	9,578,658

Table 4: Number of Entity-Name pairs per Generation Technique

5.2 Statistics

EDRAK is the largest publicly available Arabic entity-centric resource we are aware of. It contains around 2.4M entities classified under YAGO type hierarchy. The numbers of entities per high level semantic type are summarized in Table 3. The contributions of each generation technique are summarized in Table 4. Numbers show that automatic generation contributes way more entries than name dictionaries. In addition, translation delivers more entries than transliteration since it is applied on all types of entities (in contrast to only persons for transliteration).

The most similar resource to EDRAK is the one used in AIDArabic system to perform NED on Arabic text. However, AIDArabic resource is compiled solely from *manual* entries in both English and Arabic Wikipedia's such as Wikipedia categories, without incorporating any *automatic* data generation techniques. Therefore, the size of AIDArabic resource is constrained by the amount of Arabic names and contextual keyphrases available in the Arabic Wikipedia. In order to show the impact of our automatic data enrichment techniques, we compare the size of EDRAK to that of AIDArabic resource. Detailed statistics are shown in Table 5. Clearly, EDRAK is an order of magnitude larger than the resource used in AIDArabic.

	AIDArabic	EDRAK
Unique Names	333,017	9,354,875
Entities with Names	143,394	2,400,340
Entity-Name Pairs	495,245	21,669,568
Unique Keyphrases	885,970	7,918,219
Entity-Keyphrase Pairs	5,574,375	211,681,910

Table 5: AIDArabic vs EDRAK

5.3 Data Example

Many prominent entities do not exist in the Arabic Wikipedia, and hence do not appear in any Wikipedia-based resource. For example, `Christian_Schmidt`, the current German Federal Minister of Food and Agriculture, and `Edward_W._Morley`, a famous American scientist, are both missing in the Arabic Wikipedia[3]. EDRAK's data enrichment techniques managed to automatically generate reasonable potential names as well as contextual keyphrases for both. Table 6 lists a snippet of what EDRAK knows about those two entities.

6 Manual Assessment

6.1 Setup

We evaluated all aspects of data generation in EDRAK. Entity names belong to four different sources: *First Name*, *Last Name*, Wikipedia *redirects*, and *rdfs:label* relation which carries names extracted from Wikipedia page titles, disambiguation pages and anchor texts.

As explained in Section 4, we implemented two different name translation approaches, the first considers entity semantic type (which we refer to as **Type-Aware** system), and the second uses a universal system for translating all names (which is referred to as **Combined**).

Data assessment experiment covered all types of data against both translation approaches. Additionally, we conducted experiments to assess the quality of translating Wikipedia categories. Finally, we evaluated the performance of transliteration when applied on English person names. We randomly sampled the generated data and conducted an online experiment to manually assess the quality of the data.

[3]as of June 2015

Entity	Generated Arabic Names	Generated Keyphrases
Christian_Schmidt	جيسون	وزارة الدفاع الاتحادية الالمانية
	سشميد	سياسيون الاتحاد في بافاريا اجتماعية مسيحية
	شميت	مجتمع الاطلسي
	شميدت	وزارة الدفاع الالمانية الفيدرالية
	كرستيان	كريستيان شميدت مستقل
	كريستيان	وزراء المان الزراعة
	كريستيان تشميدت	هانز بيتر فريدرش
	كريستيان شميت	وزارة الدفاع الفيدرالية الالمانية
	كريستيان شميت مستقل	هانز بيتر فريدريك
	كريستيان شميدت	وزراء المان زراعة
	كريستيان شميدت مستقل	مجموعة الاطلسي
	كريستين	برلمانيون ألمان
		المجموعة الاطلسي
		سرطان الحكومة الثالثة
		هانز بيتر فريدريش
		سياسيون الاتحاد اجتماعية مسيحية في بافاريا
		كريستيان شميت مستقل
		سرطان الحكومة الثالث
		وزراء الزراعة المان
Edward_W._Morley	ادوار	كيميائيون فيزيائية امريكيون
	إدوارد	جائزة غيبس
	ادوارد	تجربة فيزو
	ادوارد دبليو مورلى	اكاديمية كيس و+ سترن
	ادوارد مورلي	فيزيائيون التجريبي
	ادوارد مورلى	جمعية فلكية الامريكية
	ادوارد وليامز مورلى	خريجو جامعة المحقق الفيدرالي الغربية
	ادوارد و+ مورلي	كاس جامعة كيس و+ سترن
	ادوارد و+ مورلى	فوهة مورلى
	ادوارد و+ يليامز مورلي	ف+ يزيائيون طيف
	ادوارد و+ يليامز مورلى	كيميائيون امريكيون فيزيائية الاميركى
	ادوار مورلى	الاكاديمية كيس و+ سترن
	ادورد	تاريخ الكيمياء البدنية
	اي و+ مورلى	الجمعية الامريكية فلكية
	دوارد	فائزون بوسام إليوت كريسون
	مرلي	التسلسل الزمني ل+ لكيمياء البدنية
	مورلي	مجلة شكوكية
	مورلى	غرب هارتفورد
	ميرلي	تجربة ميكلسون ومورلي
		اختبار فيزو

Table 6: Examples for Entities in EDRAK with their Generated Arabic Names and Keyphrases

	Approach	Source	Translations @ Top-K			Precision @ Top-K		
			1	2	3	1	2	3
Persons	Type-Aware	First Name	8	10	12	87.50	80.00	66.67
		Last Name	14	17	19	92.86	88.24	78.95
		rdfs:label	156	288	383	79.49	63.19	57.44
		redirects	113	210	285	69.91	57.62	50.18
	Combined	First Name	7	10	12	100.00	90.00	75.00
		Last Name	16	22	25	87.50	81.82	76.00
		rdfs:label	160	307	421	81.25	64.82	57.24
		redirects	108	210	288	67.59	60.00	54.51
	Transliteration	First Name	26	52	76	80.77	61.54	56.58
		Last Name	94	188	279	70.21	63.83	55.91
Non-Persons	Type-Aware	rdfs:label	269	519	742	53.16	43.16	36.66
		redirects	191	370	526	45.55	34.86	30.99
	Combined	rdfs:label	273	533	770	49.82	41.84	36.75
		redirects	195	378	539	46.67	39.42	34.69
Categories	Categories	Categories	118	234	340	67.80	52.99	46.18

Table 7: Assessment Results of Applying SMT for Translating Entities and Wikipedia Categories Names

6.2 Task Description

We asked a group of native Arabic speakers to manually judge the correctness of the generated data using a web-based tool. Each participant was presented around 150 English Names together with the top three potential Arabic translations or transliteration proposed by cdec (or less if cdec proposed less than three translations). Participants were asked to pick all possible correct Arabic names. Evaluators had the option to skip the name if they needed to. Each English Name was evaluated by three different persons.

6.3 Assessment Results

In total, we had 55 participants who evaluated 1646 English surface forms, that were assigned 4463 potential Arabic translations. Participants were native Arabic speakers that are based in USA, Canada, Europe, KSA, and Egypt. Their homelands span Egypt, Jordan, and Palestine. Translation assessment results are shown in Table 7. Evaluation results are given per entity type, translation approach and name origin. Since cdec did not return three potential translations for each name, we computed the total number of translations added when considering up to top one or two or three results. For each case, we computed the corresponding precision based on participants annotations.

6.4 Discussion

Data was randomly sampled from all generated data, and the size of each test set reflects the distribution of the sources included in the original data. For example, names originating from *rdfs:label* relation are an order of magnitude more than those coming from *FirstName*, and *LastName* relations.

The quality of the generated data varies according to the entity type, name source and generation technique. For example, the quality of translated Wikipedia *redirects* is consistently less than that of other sources. This is due to the nature of *redirects*. They are not necessarily another variation of the entity name. In addition, *redirects* tend to be longer strings, and hence are more error-prone than *rdfs:labels*. For example, "European Union common passport design" which redirects to the entity Passports_of_the_European_Union could not be correctly translated. Each token was translated correctly, but the final tokens order was wrong. Evaluators were asked to annotate such examples as wrong. However, such ordering problems are less critical for applications that incorporate partial matching techniques. Categories tend to be relatively longer than entity names, hence they exhibit the same problems as redirects.

Although the size of the evaluated *FirstName* and *LastName* data points is small, the assessment results are as expected. Translating one token name is relatively an easy task. In addition, cdec returned only one or two translations for the majority of the names as shown in Table 7.

Results also show that the type-aware translation system does not necessarily improve results, and using one universal system can deliver comparable results for most of the cases.

Person names transliteration unexpectedly achieved less quality than translation. Names are pronounced differently across countries. For example, a USA-based annotator is expecting "Friedrich" to be written "فريدريك", while a Germany-based one is expecting it to be written as "فريدريش".

Inter-annotator agreement was measured using Fleiss' kappa to be 0.484 indicating moderate agreement.

7 Conclusion

In this paper we introduced EDRAK: and entity-centric Arabic resource. EDRAK is an entity repository that contains around 2.4M entities, with their potential Arabic names. In addition, EDRAK associates each entity with a set of keyphrases. Data in EDRAK has been extracted from the Arabic Wikipedia and other available resources. In addition, we automatically translated parts of the English Wikipedia and used them to enrich EDRAK. Data have been manually assessed. Results showed that the quality is adequate for consumption by other NLP and IR systems. We are making the resource publicly available to help advance the research for the Arabic language.

Acknowledgments

We would like to thank the anonymous reviewers for their valuable feedback. We would also like to show our gratitude to the volunteers who participated in our manual assessment task. Finally, we are also immensely grateful to Waleed Ammar, Chris Dyer, and Hassan Sajjad for their valuable advice about translation and transliteration using cdec framework.

References

Mohamed Al-Badrashiny, Ramy Eskander, Nizar Habash, and Owen Rambow. 2014. Automatic Transliteration of Romanized Dialectal Arabic. In *Proceedings of the 18th Conference on Computational Natural Language Learning*, CoNLL 2014, Baltimore, Maryland, USA.

Yaser Al-Onaizan and Kevin Knight. 2002. Translating Named Entities Using Monolingual and Bilingual Resources. In *Proceedings of the 40th Annual Meeting on Association for Computational Linguistics*, ACL 2002, Stroudsburg, PA, USA.

Mohammed Attia, Antonio Toral, Lamia Tounsi, Monica Monachini, and Josef van Genabith. 2010. An Automatically Built Named Entity Lexicon for Arabic. In *Proceedings of the 7th International Conference on Language Resources and Evaluation*, LREC 2010, Valletta, Malta.

Sren Auer, Christian Bizer, Georgi Kobilarov, Jens Lehmann, and Zachary Ives. 2007. DBpedia: A Nucleus for a Web of Open Data. In *Proceedings of the 6th International Semantic Web Conference*, ISWC 2007, Busan, Korea.

Mahmoud Azab, Houda Bouamor, Behrang Mohit, and Kemal Oflazer. 2013. Dudley North visits North London: Learning When to Transliterate to Arabic. In *Proceedings of the 2013 Conference of the North American Chapter of the Association for Computational Linguistics: Human Language Technologies*, NAAC-HLT 2013, Atlanta, Georgia.

William Black, Sabri Elkateb, and Piek Vossen. 2006. Introducing the Arabic Wordnet Project. In *In Proceedings of the 3rd International WordNet Conference*, GWC 2006, Jeju Island. Korea.

Kurt Bollacker, Colin Evans, Praveen Paritosh, Tim Sturge, and Jamie Taylor. 2008. Freebase: A Collaboratively created Graph Database for Structuring Human Knowledge. In *Proceedings of the 2008 ACM SIGMOD International Conference on Management of Data*, SIGMOD 2008, New York, NY, USA.

Kareem Darwish. 2013. Named Entity Recognition Using Cross-lingual Resources: Arabic as an Example. In *Proceedings of the 51st Annual Meeting of the Association for Computational Linguistics*, ACL 2013, Sofia, Bulgaria.

Chris Dyer, Adam Lopez, Juri Ganitkevitch, Johnathan Weese, Ferhan Ture, Phil Blunsom, Hendra Setiawan, Vladimir Eidelman, and Philip Resnik. 2010. cdec: A Decoder, Alignment, and Learning Framework for Finite-state and Context-free Translation Models. In *Proceedings of the Association for Computational Linguistics*, ACL 2010, Uppsala, Sweden.

Ondrej Hálek, Rudolf Rosa, Ales Tamchyna, and Ondrej Bojar. 2011. Named Entities from Wikipedia for Machine Translation. In *Proceedings of the Conference on Theory and Practice of Information Technologies*, ITAT 2010, Velká Fatra, Slovak Republic.

Johannes Hoffart, Mohamed Amir Yosef, Ilaria Bordino, Hagen Fürstenau, Manfred Pinkal, Marc Spaniol, Bilyana Taneva, Stefan Thater, and Gerhard

Weikum. 2011. Robust Disambiguation of Named Entities in Text. In *Proceedings of the Conference on Empirical Methods in Natural Language Processing*, EMNLP 2011, Edinburgh, UK.

Johannes Hoffart, Stephan Seufert, Dat Ba Nguyen, Martin Theobald, and Gerhard Weikum. 2012. KORE: Keyphrase Overlap Relatedness for Entity Disambiguation. In *Proceedings of the 21st ACM International Conference on Information and Knowledge Management*, CIKM 2012, Hawaii, USA.

Johannes Hoffart, Fabian M. Suchanek, Klaus Berberich, and Gerhard Weikum. 2013. YAGO2: A Spatially and Temporally Enhanced Knowledge Base from Wikipedia. *Journal of Artificial Intelligence*.

Farzaneh Mahdisoltani, Joanna Biega, and Fabian M Suchanek. 2015. Yago3: A Knowledge Base from Multilingual Wikipedias.

Will Monroe, Spence Green, and Christopher D. Manning. 2014. Word Segmentation of Informal Arabic with Domain Adaptation. In *Proceedings of the 52nd Annual Meeting of the Association for Computational Linguistics*, ACL 2014, Baltimore, MD, USA.

Roberto Navigli and Simone Paolo Ponzetto. 2012. BabelNet: The Automatic Construction, Evaluation and Application of a Wide-coverage Multilingual Semantic Network. *Journal of Artificial Intelligence*.

Arfath Pasha, Mohamed Al-Badrashiny, Mona Diab, Ahmed El Kholy, Ramy Eskander, Nizar Habash, Manoj Pooleery, Owen Rambow, and Ryan M Roth. 2014. MADAMIRA: A Fast, Comprehensive Tool for Morphological Analysis and Disambiguation of Arabic. *Proceedings of the Language Resources and Evaluation Conference*, LREC 2014, Reykjavik, Iceland.

Khaled Shaalan. 2014. A Survey of Arabic Named Entity Recognition and Classification. *Computational Linguistics*.

Nakatani Shuyo. 2010. Language Detection Library for Java.

Valentin I. Spitkovsky and Angel X. Chang. 2012. A Cross-lingual Dictionary for English Wikipedia Concepts. In *Proceedings of the 8th International Conference on Language Resources and Evaluation*, LREC 2012, Istanbul, Turkey.

Ralf Steinberger, Bruno Pouliquen, Mijail Kabadjov, Jenya Belyaeva, and Erik van der Goot. 2011. JRC-NAMES: A Freely Available, Highly Multilingual Named Entity Resource. In *Proceedings of the International Conference Recent Advances in Natural Language Processing*, RANLP 2011, Hissar, Bulgaria.

Tomasz Tylenda, Mauro Sozio, and Gerhard Weikum. 2011. Einstein: Physicist or Vegetarian? Summarizing Semantic Type Graphs for Knowledge Discovery. In *Proceedings of the 20th International Conference on World Wide Web*, WWW 2011, Hyderabad, India.

Gerhard Weikum, Johannes Hoffart, Ndapandula Nakashole, Marc Spaniol, Fabian M Suchanek, and Mohamed Amir Yosef. 2012. Big Data Methods for Computational Linguistics. *IEEE Data Engineering Bulletin*.

Mohamed Amir Yosef, Sandro Bauer, Johannes Hoffart Marc Spaniol, and Gerhard Weikum. 2012. HYENA: Hierarchical Type Classification for Entity Names. In *Proc. of the 24th International Conference on Computational Linguistics*, COLING 2012, Mumbai, India.

Mohamed Amir Yosef, Sandro Bauer, Johannes Hoffart Marc Spaniol, and Gerhard Weikum. 2013. HYENA-live: Fine-Grained Online Entity Type Classification from Natural-language Text. In *Proceedings of the 51st Annual Meeting of the Association for Computational Linguistics*, ACL 2013, Sofia, Bulgaria.

Mohamed Amir Yosef, Marc Spaniol, and Gerhard Weikum. 2014. AIDArabic: A Named-Entity Disambiguation Framework for Arabic Text. In *The EMNLP 2014 Workshop on Arabic Natural Language Processing*, ANLP 2014, Dohar, Qatar.

Author Index